Networking Knowledge for Information Societies: Institutions & Intervention

Networking Knowledge for Information Societies: Institutions & Intervention

Edited by Robin Mansell, Rohan Samarajiva and Amy Mahan

DUP Science / 2002

DUP SCIENCE IS AN IMPRINT OF

Delft University Press
P.O. Box 98
2600 MG DELFT
The Netherlands

TELEPHONE: +31 15 2785678
TELEFAX: +31 15 2785706
E-mail: Info@Library.TUDelft.NL

ISBN 90-407-2300-1

COPYRIGHT 2002 – ROBIN MANSELL, ROHAN SAMARAJIVA AND AMY MAHAN FOR COMPILATION, AND INTRODUCTORY SECTIONS I, II.0, III.0, IV.0, V.0 AND VI.0. Authors retain copyright of their individual contributions.

All rights reserved. No part of the material protected by this copyright notice may be reproduced or utilized in any form or by any means, electronic or mechanical, including photocopying, recording or by any information storage and retrieval system, without written permission from the publisher: Delft University Press.

Printed in The Netherlands

Book and cover design by Elies van der Linden

There is nothing more difficult to plan, more uncertain of success, or more dangerous to manage than the establishment of a new order of government; for he who introduces it makes enemies of all those who derived advantage from the old order and finds but lukewarm defenders among those who stand to gain from the new one.

(*The Prince* by Nicolo Machiavelli, 1513, p. 27)

Table of Contents

List of tables, figures and boxes
xiii

Prologue...
Networking knowledge for information societies
Chris Freeman
xv

I About...
Robin Mansell, Rohan Samarajiva and Amy Mahan
3

II Inquiry...
Robin Mansell, Rohan Samarajiva and Amy Mahan
17

II.1 Universities, Research and the Public Interest
Nicholas Garnham
24

II.2 Universities in the Knowledge Economy
Peter Sheehan
28

II.3 The University, ICTs and Development in the Information Society
John B. Goddard and James Cornford
34

II.4 The Role of the Social Sciences in Policy Oriented Telecom Research
John Langdale
42

II.5 Integrating Social Sciences into Information Society Policy
Jean-Claude Burgelman
47

II.6 Virtual Solutions to Real Problems
Bella Mody
54

II.7 Challenging Orthodoxy
Liora Salter
60

III Change...
Rohan Samarajiva, Robin Mansell and Amy Mahan
71

III.1 Utility Deregulation in the United States: A Critical Evaluation
Harry M. Trebing
79

III.2 Telecom Policy for Information Economies: Unregulation is not Enough
Aileen Amarandos Pisciotta
86

III.3 The Toppling of the Natural Monopoly Doctrine
Edwin B. Parker
90

III.4 Never-ending International Telecommunication Union Reform
Tim Kelly
92

III.5 From Arctic Village to Alice Springs: Rural Telecom Myths and Realities
Heather E. Hudson
96

III.6 Setting the Reform Agenda: What Next, After Privatisation?
Márcio Wohlers de Almeida and Ricardo Tavares
103

III.7 Policy and Regulatory Challenges of Access and Affordability
Alison Gillwald
109

III.8 Technical Aspects of Rural Telecom
Rudi Westerveld and Carleen F. Maitland
115

III.9 Spectrum Management: Private Property Rights or Commons
Johannes M. Bauer
118

III.10 Spectrum Allocation Controversies
Martin Cave
123

III.11 3G Auctions: A Change of Course
John Ure
127

III.12 A Competitive Market Approach to Interconnection Payments
David Gabel
    132

III.13 Multi-Utility Regulation: Yet Another Convergence?
Jens C. Arnbak
    141

IV Next...
Robin Mansell, Rohan Samarajiva and Amy Mahan
    151

IV.1 Information Society Revisited: PICTuring the Information Society
Ian Miles
    160

IV.2 Falling Behind on ICT Adoption Indicators: Can We Afford This?
John W. Houghton
    166

IV.3 Information Societies: Towards a More Useful Concept
Knud Erik Skouby
    174

IV.4 Evolving the Information Society in the Caribbean: The Paradox of Orderliness
Roderick Sanatan
    179

IV.5 Revealing the Ties that Bind: Property and Propriety in the Information Age.
Oscar H. Gandy, Jr.
    184

IV.6 Critical Infrastructure Protection in the Information Age
Peter S. Anderson
    188

IV.7 Technology Determinism, the State and Telecom Surveillance
Peter Shields
    195

IV.8 Opportunities and Risks for India in the Knowledge Society
B. P. Sanjay
    202

IV.9 Infrastructure Development and the Digital Divide in Asia
Meheroo Jussawalla
    207

IV.10 Linking Information, Technologies and the Consumer Interest
Supriya Singh
    212

IV.11 Theses on Informatisation
Jörg Becker
216

V Bias...
Rohan Samarajiva, Robin Mansell and Amy Mahan
223

V.1 C is for Convergence (and Communication, Content, and Competition)
Sally Wyatt
228

V.2 Knowledge or 'Know-less' Societies?
Paschal Preston
232

V.3 When More is Less: Time, Space and Knowledge in Information Societies
Edward Comor
239

V.4 The Telecom-Economy Nexus: Innis and Du Boff Revisited
Cho, Sung Woon
245

V.5 Back to the Future of the Internet: The Printing Press
Ang, Peng Hwa and James A. Dewar
249

V.6 The 'Information Economy', Economics, and Ecology
Robert E. Babe
254

V.7 Bridging the Gap: Processes of Communication and Institutions of Political Economy
Vincent Mosco
260

V.8 Concrete Analyses Versus Abstract Deduction
Anders Henten
265

VI What...
Amy Mahan, Robin Mansell and Rohan Samarajiva
271

VI.1 Regulation and the Ethics of Distance: Distance and the Ethics of Regulation
Roger Silverstone
279

VI.2 In Search of the 'Shared Moment'
Anthony Smith
286

VI.3 Global Media and Cultural Diversity
Gaëtan Tremblay
    292

VI.4 Media Ownership – Does It Matter?
Werner A. Meier
    298

VI.5 Latin American Media: A Long View of Politics and Markets
Elizabeth Fox and Silvio Waisbord
    303

VI.6 Towards an Information Society: The Need for a Policy Perspective
Binod C. Agrawal
    311

VI.7 Media Policy and the Public Interest
Marc Raboy
    315

VI.8 Radical Media Projects and the Crisis of Public Media
John D. H. Downing
    320

VI.9 Towards a World System Perspective on Cross-National Web Research
Joseph Turow and Rivka Ribak
    328

Epilogue...
Economics of Infrastructures: The Ultimate Challenge?
Rolf W. Künneke
    335

Notes
    343
Bibliography
    345
Acronyms
    379
Contributors
    383
Author Index
    401

List of Tables, Figures and Boxes

Table IV.9.1
Broadband Penetration in Asia, 2000
209

Figure II.5.1
Telecommunications Prospects for 2000
49

Figure III.13.1
Policy and Competition Problems in Network Sectors
142

Figure IV.2.1
Composition and Balance of Trade in ICT Equipment,
Australia 1990-91 to 2000-01 (AU$ million)
168

Figure IV.2.2
Revealed Comparative Advantage in Communication Equipment, 1990 and 1999
170

Figure IV.2.3
Ratio of ICT Expenditure to Gross Domestic Product, 1999
171

Box III.11.1
A Model
131

Box IV.6.1
Critical Information Infrastructure Protection
193

Prologue...
Networking Knowledge for Information Societies

This is a magnificent *Festschrift* but no more than William Melody deserves. He has made an outstanding contribution to our understanding of the evolution of information and communication technology over the past half century, and to the problems of regulating and controlling it during a period of revolutionary change in the technology.

The Editors of the book have been more pro-active than is usually the case with this type of publication. They have insisted on short contributions and this has not only made them very readable, it has also made it possible to include a wide range of papers, reflecting the scope of William Melody's own activities and relationships. Furthermore, the Editors have so organised more than 50 contributions that they provide a lively and well-informed commentary on the various stages of his life and work. Finally, they have written an introduction to each of the sections highlighting the main features of his work and relating these to the evolution of ICT.

This does not leave much to say by way of a prologue, which means that it can at least have the virtue of brevity. I shall not try therefore to summarise or introduce the 50 chapters which follow. This would be both impossible and unnecessary. I shall rather make a few comments of my own on William Melody's life and work based on my own reading of this book and my own experiences of working with him.

As the Editors point out and as most of the chapters testify, William Melody made an excellent contribution to research, as conventionally measured by the quantity and quality of his publications. He published 150 or so papers in dozens of journals. However, to assess his work on this criterion would be vastly to underestimate what he has achieved. His publications were certainly not just bits of information; they were contributions to knowledge and in many cases to policy-making. Even when working in a university environment, his activity was certainly not confined to academic goals. His over-riding objectives have always been to influence policy and thereby to achieve social goals.

Policy research raises some special problems which William Melody encountered at each of the five stages of his career. To be realistic, policy research often has to be conducted in association with industrial or governmental organisations and in practical terms to be funded by them, at least to some extent. One does not have to subscribe to Marx's description of economists after Ricardo as 'hired prize fighters of reaction' to recognise that there are serious problems in this relationship. Indeed, the very first chapter in this book, by Nicholas Garnham, makes the point exceedingly well. The conduct of public interest research has become increasingly difficult in most universities in most countries for some time now and to establish a satisfactory two-way relationship between research sponsors and research performers is one of the most complex and difficult tasks for research management.

William Melody did not always succeed in this complex task, as the experience of CIRCIT in Australia demonstrates, but he succeeded more often than not. The researchers must be genuinely independent and the sponsors must be prepared to tolerate, even to welcome research results which may be critical of the sponsors themselves and of the assumptions, prejudices and interests which they represent. To recognise that this approach is in the long-term interest of the sponsors themselves requires great forbearance and sophistication, comparable to the tolerance of organised political 'opposition' in parliamentary democracies. It does not come easily to those who wield power in most industrial and government organisations. The researchers themselves may be tempted to opt for a quiet life and more ample rewards by currying favour with powerful interest groups, or more commonly and more reasonably, they may think that 'to speak truth to power' does not require them to speak the whole truth and nothing but the truth. As time goes by, they may gradually forget to do it at all.

Good policy research requires a special kind of civic courage, a quality which William Melody possesses in abundance. He has been determined to find truth, to debate it and to communicate it. Moreover, he did this whether he himself was in the role of researcher or sponsor, or both. As sponsor, he came close to the ideal of stimulus, tolerance, perseverance and challenge.

A remarkable feature of William Melody's career has been his ability to operate in a variety of different national environments. He actually led and coordinated research programmes (and not just short projects) in half a dozen different countries and as the following chapters amply testify, all of them ultimately produced fruitful results and a legacy of constructive achievements, despite all the difficulties. To succeed in so many different countries is not only a testimony to his ability to understand a variety of national cultures and institutions, but also to his spirit of internationalism. As the chapter by Bella Mody and the book edited by Mansell and Wehn demonstrate, he is deeply concerned with the disadvantaged position of poor countries and of poor 'excluded' people in rich countries during the ICT revolution.

Neither he, nor anyone else, has found solutions to all these problems of social and technical change. Although his work has done much to undermine the privileged position of public telecommunication utilities, he most certainly cannot be classified as a simple free marketeer or an advocate of solutions based on neo-classical economic dogmas. Nor can he be classified as an advocate of purely administrative or governmental solutions. Indeed, the editors comment that he cannot be classified as either 'right' or 'left'. He was searching for original solutions to new problems and he certainly accepted that such solutions might be very radical, even if they were achieved through a succession of incremental reforms and drastic 're-regulation' of the system.

Even though it is quoted by the Editors in one of their introductory notes, I cannot do better than to repeat Lindblom's (1988: 11) comment on incremental reform since it gives an excellent summary of the type of approach which Melody has advocated:

Do I believe that the political and social world is in such good shape that it needs only incremental improvement? ... Indeed not. ... Do we therefore need drastic change? Indeed, we do. Given, however, the existing political structures of the ostensible democracies, there is little hope of getting it except through long glacial sequences of incremental changes ... It looks as though anyone who wants drastic change will do best to promote rapid incremental change cumulating into drastic change.

Chris Freeman
April 2002

I

About...

SECTION 1

About...

Robin Mansell, Rohan Samarajiva and Amy Mahan

This book is a celebration of William H. Melody's achievements. At the time of his retirement in 2002, Melody was Professor of the Economics of Infrastructures in the Faculty of Technology, Policy and Management at the Delft University of Technology in The Netherlands, a post he held from 1997. He continues as Guest Professor in the Center for Tele-Information (CTI) at the Technical University of Denmark. He also continues as Managing Director of Learning Initiatives for Reforms in Network Economies (LIRNE.NET) which offers external training programmes, research support and dissemination in the areas of telecom reform and information infrastructure development. In this chapter we introduce the William H. Melody who we have come to know and we offer insights into what we understand to be the principal influences on his professional career. We acknowledge that there are others who might offer different interpretations based on their own interactions with him.

Melody, a Canadian by parentage and upbringing, born in Detroit, Michigan, obtained his Bachelors, Masters and Doctorate degrees in Economics at the University of Nebraska in the United States. After a brief period of teaching at Iowa State University, he joined the United States federal government. From 1966 to 1971 he was, respectively, Supervisory, Senior and Chief Economist at the Federal Communications Commission (FCC) in Washington DC. He directed a programme of research on current and long-term communication policy issues including those concerning satellites, cable television, computer/communications, radio frequency spectrum allocation, terminal equipment and system interconnection, the role of competition and monopoly, and pricing practices and subsidy policies. He participated in the development and implementation of major policy and regulatory changes in each of these areas.

He moved on to become Associate Professor of Communication Economics at the Annenberg School for Communications at the University of Pennsylvania (1971-1976). There he began building a programme of research encompassing telecom economics; the economic structure, behaviour and performance of communication industries; the effects of government regulation; the role of changing technologies; and the evaluation of public policy alternatives. He then returned to Canada.

About

From 1976 to 1979 he was Professor and Chair of the Department of Communication at Simon Fraser University on the west coast of Canada where he directed an interdisciplinary programme of undergraduate and graduate teaching and research in communication. This programme addressed the areas of the historical, theoretical and methodological foundations in the field of communication; interpersonal and organisational communication; communication media and telecom technology; the political economy of communication institutions and public policy; and communication, development and culture. From 1979 to 1985, as Professor of Communication his research and teaching focused on the study of the economic structure, behaviour and performance of the information and communication industries, and on regulation and public policy.

In 1985, Melody left Canada to become the founding Director of the United Kingdom's Programme on Information and Communication Technologies (PICT), which was established by the Economic and Social Research Council and continued until 1995. This was a major research programme examining the long-term economic and social implications of new information and communication technologies. Melody directed this programme until 1988, and from 1987 to 1989, he was a Senior Research Associate at St. Antony's College, Oxford University. His research during this period examined the economic and social characteristics of information; telecom reform in industrialised and developing countries; and the relations between information and communication technologies and services and economic development. He was then invited to Australia.

In Australia he founded the Centre for International Research on Communication and Information Technologies (CIRCIT) (1989-1994) which examined the economic and social implications of new communication and information technologies and was supported by four universities and several telecom firms, in addition to the Government of Victoria. He established a network of policy research and dissemination covering issues ranging from the local to the global and involving researchers, policy analysts, industrialists, trade-unionists, government agencies and community groups.

He returned to Europe in 1995 to help establish the Center for Tele-Information (CTI), an interdisciplinary research centre initiated in 1994 at the Technical University of Denmark. He served as Chair of CTI's International Advisory Board from 1995 to 2001 and continues a close relationship as Guest Professor. Here the focus was on telecom reform and the information society; the networked firm; internationalisation and regulation; and multimedia developments.

About

In 1997, he accepted an invitation from the Faculty of Technology, Policy and Management at the Delft University of Technology in The Netherlands, to establish a programme on the Economics of Infrastructures. The Delft programme addressed interactions among technologies, markets and policies in the traditional (energy, transport and telecom) and evolving new (information and knowledge) infrastructures.

The above paragraphs describe William H. Melody in terms of his formal professional appointments. But the description is incomplete without reference to his many achievements. Melody participated in the earliest stages of telecom reform and computer-communication convergence while he was at the FCC in the late 1960s, and this is described in more detail under *Change*. In 1970, he advised the Organisation for Economic Cooperation and Development (OECD) on regulation and competition in data communication markets. In 1972, he participated in OECD deliberations on the potential applications of convergent computer and telecom systems. He was adviser and expert witness on economic and regulatory issues for the US Department of Justice in *US v. AT&T*, the court case that ultimately led to the AT&T divestiture in 1984. He provided expert testimony in innumerable regulatory and legal proceedings in the United States and Canada and as far a field as Sri Lanka.

He has contributed to the research and policy literature for more than 30 years and has authored more than 150 books, reports and professional journal articles. A selected list of the academic journals in which he has published or in which his works have been cited gives an indication of the disciplinary coverage of his work – *American Behavioral Science, American Economic Review, Cambridge Journal of Economics, Canadian Journal of Communications, Chasqui, Computer Communication, Economic Geography, Futures, Info, International Journal of Technology Management, Journal of the American Society for Information Science, Journal of Economic Issues, Journal of Law and Economics, Media Culture and Society, Media Development, New Media and Society, Policy Studies, Prometheus, Regional Studies, Research Policy, Revue Tiers Monde, Telecommunications Policy, Telecommunications and Space Journal, Telos, The Economic and Social Review, Third World Quarterly*, and *Urban Studies*.

Melody has been directly involved in planning and implementing training programmes on telecom and infrastructure reform for senior staff of public utility and telecom regulatory agencies and stakeholders, initially in the United States and Canada, and then in other countries. He has acted as a consultant and advisor to universities and research centres around the world, to United Nations agencies and other international organisations, as well as to governments and corporate organisations in many countries (again, described in detail in *Change*). He has held and holds a variety of positions in professional associations and on editorial boards of journals and advisory boards of research centres and university programmes.

We can only speculate about his formative influences. But we can offer some insight into where Melody found his most important intellectual home and how he was galvanised into pursuing a lifetime commitment to inquiry and public policy intervention. To do so, we need to look into the history of ideas and the particular 'habits of thought' which have guided his work. We might begin with Professor Martin G. Glaeser who examined public utilities as 'going concerns' and provided many lasting insights into the relation between public regulation and market dynamics. In the preface to *Public Utilities in American Capitalism*, Glaeser (1957: i) wrote that:

The author is more than ever satisfied with the general orientation in the study of social problems afforded him by his teachers, the late Professor John R. Commons of the University of Wisconsin, and Roscoe Pound, former Dean of the Harvard Law School. The former, an institutionalist in economics, and the latter, an institutionalist in the law, have provided him with a technique of investigation and of intellectual coordination which make theory and practice truly complementary.

John R. Commons served on the faculty at the University of Wisconsin, providing the intellectual muscle for the populist reforms of the Progressive Movement headed by Governor Robert (Fighting Bob) LaFollette. Pound, a polymath who served as the Director of the State Botanical Survey while practising and teaching law in Nebraska, made his name as a reformer while heading the Harvard Law School, a post he held for twenty years. Glaeser began his studies at the University of Wisconsin, but completed them at Harvard as a result of his opposition to the United States' participation in the First World War. He returned to Wisconsin to join the faculty.

We might then turn to Glaeser's student at the University of Wisconsin, Professor Harry M. Trebing, founding Director of the Institute of Public Utilities at Michigan State University, and now Professor Emeritus. It was Trebing who influenced Melody to pursue his doctorate at the University of Nebraska where he was at the time and who served as Melody's mentor. Trebing left the University of Nebraska to work for the US federal government and Professor Ray Dein served as Melody's formal advisor. It was also Trebing who brought Melody to the FCC and involved him in the programmes of the Institute of Public Utilities at Michigan State University. And so the concepts and values of institutional economics were passed down through generations of scholars. When Robin Mansell and Rohan Samarajiva (two of the editors of this book) met Melody at Simon Fraser University their required readings included Berle and Means, Commons, Glaeser, Hamilton, Pound, Trebing, Veblen and of course Melody, as well as many other contributors to the rich vein of theory and practical research that constitutes Institutional Economics.

In this book, we have elected to refer formally to the honouree as William Melody as a mark of respect. As editors, we have imposed this form of salutation in all the chapters. But we want readers to know something of the warmth of the (sometimes contested) relationships between Melody and his colleagues and students. This was evident in many of the first drafts of the essays. Some of those whom we contacted were unable to provide us with an essay in accordance with our deadline. Their messages to us conveyed insights into Melody's personality. The e-mail message from Professor Manley Irwin, Professor Emeritus at the Whittemore School of Business and Economics, University of New Hampshire, who worked with Melody at the FCC is illustrative. He told us that Melody 'was one of the few staff members who possessed the courage to take the witness stand and endure cross examination; that took grit and stamina. In my [Irwin's] own investigation of Western Electric and Bell Labs in the '70s, not one of my thirteen member staff was willing to endure cross examination, and they were the experts!'

Irwin also commented that, 'given the information revolution that, despite the dot.com implosion, is now global, I suspect America's latest export, the philosophy of Glaeser and Commons, is an exercise in quaint nostalgia; fascinating, but hardly relevant in a world driven by Moore's Law …'. As editors of this book, we want respectfully to claim otherwise. We do not argue that the foundations of Institutional Economics that inform much of Melody's research and teaching are the only, or even a sufficient, lens through which to develop a critical analysis of the dynamics of technological and institutional change. But we do argue that this tradition of theory and practice continues to offer one – still very valuable – means of achieving a strong and rewarding interaction between inquiry and intervention.

Another institutionalist, Professor Dallas W. Smythe, a pioneer in the field of the political economy of communication, played an important role in Melody's life, especially after they found themselves working in the same department at Simon Fraser University from 1976. Smythe, a Canadian, had been Chief Economist at the FCC in the 1940s. He had written extensively on the way corporate interests were shaping the broadcasting and telecom industries in both Canada and the United States. Melody was inspired by Smythe's thirst for critical inquiry and by his early efforts to develop a comprehensive and systematic approach to the study of communication and of political economy. Smythe's work took a Marxist turn in his later life which meant that the foundation assumptions of his work diverged from Melody's. Melody and Smythe treated their students at Simon Fraser University to numerous displays of the best of scholarly debates as they sought to persuade each other of the priority that should be given to a class-based analysis of capitalism and its consequences for industry and for public policy intervention and activism.

This book is structured around five themes. These are facets, not necessarily mutually exclusive, of the rich and varied contributions that Melody has made, and continues to make, to academic research, to policy reform and to institution building. We asked contributors to restrict their essays to 2,000 words and did our best to abbreviate their contributions when they did not. We invited each author to be guided only by his or her preference as to how to honour Melody. Some have told us that they felt constrained by this stricture on length and that they would have liked more guidance. We believe that our resistance to shaping the style or the content of contributions beyond our initial brief designation of themes is consistent with Melody's emphasis on networking knowledge. Some contributors chose to emphasise the process of learning and working with Melody; others, the process of making and changing policy. Others emphasise theoretical insights; yet others, the pragmatics of contesting ideas in the world outside the university. The resulting interplay of perspectives, approaches and styles is something we relish and that we believe is reflective of the complexity and depth of Melody's yet incomplete career.

The five themes of this book are – *Inquiry*, *Change*, *Next*, *Bias* and *What*. These terms require explanation. They are chosen to encapsulate central ideas in Melody's contributions to the creation, networking and application of knowledge about interactions between changing technologies and societies. The themes are not organised chronologically. Melody's life and work are far too complex for a simple linear ordering. At the beginning of each section, we introduce the theme as we understand it to be represented in Melody's work, highlight issues that are addressed by contributors, and point the reader to supplementary sources of information. Believing that the sum of these contributions is greater than the individual parts, we have sought to emphasise the connections between them as well as the connections to Melody's work.

We begin with *Inquiry*, a theme that captures Melody's unflagging commitment to the idea that the academy must inform the public policy process through its research and teaching activities. This is a common theme in every university programme that he has been involved with. The path-breaking Programme on Information and Communication Technologies (PICT) and the Centre for International Research on Communication and Information Technologies (CIRCIT) are perhaps the best known of these efforts. In each endeavour, Melody has argued in favour of interdisciplinarity, in support of academic independence, and for an emphasis on critical and informed theoretical and empirical research that has a good chance of contributing to problem-solving.

In Melody's view, inquiry should lead to change. *Change* is the second theme of this book. The analysis of the social and economic dynamics of the institutions through which people are mobilised into action is central in Melody's work. A workable definition of the term 'institution' would read as the (old) Institutional Economist Walton H. Hamilton (1932: 84, 89) put it.

Institution is a verbal symbol which for want of better describes a cluster of social usages. It connotes a way of thought or action of some prevalence and permanence, which is embedded in the habits of a group or the customs of a people. In ordinary speech it is another word for procedure, convention, or arrangement; in the language of books it is the singular of which the mores or the folkways are the plural. Institutions fix the confines of and impose form upon the activities of human beings. The world of use and wont, to which imperfectly we accommodate our lives, is a tangled and unbroken web of institutions. ... Institutions and human actions, complements and antitheses, are forever remaking each other in the endless drama of the social process.

Change occurs through institutionalised action – action that is social, highly political, and subject to economic pressures and accommodations. This *Change* theme is present in all the sections of the book, but we elected to focus on Melody's contribution to institutional change principally in the context of telecom reform. Melody is perhaps most closely identified with work in this area. His academic research and policy interventions are always directed to helping regulators, policy makers and other stakeholders to make the ongoing process of world-wide telecom reform a success. He has consulted, taught, and undertaken research with professionals involved with telecom reform in countless countries around the world. The key to reform for Melody lies in analysis and informed action and, most importantly, it lies in effectively networking ideas and sharing insights in specific institutional contexts.

About

Melody understands that the telecom industries he has been seeking to reform are involved in something much larger than the development of the networks themselves. Even if the word – telecom – is interpreted very loosely to encompass the convergent components of the information and communication technology and service industries, this still does not provide sufficient insight into Melody's motivation for reform. His motivation is strong because of his realisation that changes in network technologies are closely bound up with social transformations that may allow for greater participation in the processing of information, the production of knowledge and the sharing of meaning. Melody has always recognised that all societies – historical and modern, western and eastern, wealthy and poor – are information societies. The difference today is in the modes of processing information. The third theme of this book is, therefore, *Next*. The emergence of information societies in a period characterised by the rapid spread of a cluster of digital technologies is, for Melody, the next problem for social and economic analysis. Melody has argued throughout his career that the dismantling of the public and private monopolies in the telecom sector and the curtailing of their monopolisation strategies would trigger a wave of technological and social innovations.

Melody has never expected utopias. Societies in which people become intensive producers and users of information conveyed and processed by complex global networks, have been seen as destabilising all institutions. Distortions of wealth within the global economy and within countries would give rise to an uneven distribution of the benefits and risks of changes in the role of information and communication. Melody seeks to position recent developments in information and communication technologies in their historical context, inspired partly by the seminal contributions of Harold Adams Innis, the Canadian political economist and historian. Intrigued by the process of technological innovation, Melody has attempted to maximise the potential advantages of technological change. In an effort to persuade the publisher Elsevier to allow greater ease of access to the content of the academic journal *Telecommunications Policy*, for example, he established a website of his own, <www.tpeditor.com>. This became a site for experimentation that led subsequently to a portal devoted to providing information and hosting discussion about regulatory issues in the field, the provision of a resource library, and an inchoate online journal.

Melody has been even more concerned with the ways in which scholars and others have sought to accommodate, resist and interpret the meanings and implications of the new technologies. The fourth theme of the book is *Bias*. Bias is the term used by Innis to describe distortions in economies and societies that give varying emphases to space and time and to different modes of information exchange and communication. Invariably, the interplay of these biases leads to institutional change and to the rise and fall of empires and of monopolies of knowledge. The analysis of systemic biases in power relationships that become embedded in technologies and institutions in the industrialised and the developing countries is an ever-present element in Melody's work. So too is attention to the possibilities of altering the determinants and consequences of biases that produce inequalities in people's capacities to access and use the new technologies.

Melody has argued that rapid innovation in information and communication technologies has the potential to destabilise monopolies. For Melody, the goal is not competition *per se*, but rather, workable competition as a process that enables socially valued change. The task of social scientists and of other stakeholders is to generate the knowledge needed to help shape existing and new institutions so that they may encourage new ways of networking socially and economically valued knowledge. This viewpoint is present in Melody's work on the 'plumbing' or the infrastructure of information societies and it is also reflected in his attention to information and the content of the media that are produced for, and carried through, that infrastructure. The final section of the book focuses on the *What*; on the information and content of the media and communication industries and on the institutions and reforms that might ensure that commercial programme production is in the public interest, that may sustain public service broadcasting, and that will create opportunities for alternative media using older and newer technologies.

The contributors to this book write in honour of William H. Melody. They contribute from all points of the social science compass and all inhabited continents. They draw upon their experiences as labourers within institutions of higher education around the world and as mobilisers of change in the formal and informal corridors of policy institutions and in many other public, private and civil society organisations. They have been invited to make these contributions by the editors. Each of us has, at one time or another, worked with, and learned from, Melody. As a result of these privileges, we have come to know those whom we invited. Each contributing author similarly has been either a colleague or student of Melody's within or outside the university. As editors, we consulted only amongst ourselves in compiling this book. Responsibility for any omissions or errors rests entirely with the editors.

We want to thank all those who supported us in our endeavour to prepare this volume. First, we wish to express our gratitude to the contributions made by the

56 authors based in 18 countries, but representing, like Melody, more countries and cultures than simply those of the countries of their residence. Their adherence to a very tight schedule and their flexibility regarding editorial intervention ensured the success of this endeavour. We are particularly appreciative of their willingness to join in the conspiracy to produce a multinational *festschrift* unbeknownst to the honouree. We are most grateful to Professor Chris Freeman for contributing the prologue.

At the London School of Economics and Political Science, Robin Mansell was supported by her assistant, Kathy Moir, whose contributions include the preparation of the bibliography and biographical details of contributors. Professor Roger Silverstone, Director of Media@lse (Interdepartmental Programme in Media and Communications) made suggestions regarding publication. He also must be thanked for choosing, along with Robin's other colleagues and students, to ignore her occasional lapses in support of Media@lse during the final phases of manuscript preparation. At SPRU (Science and Technology Policy Research), University of Sussex, Cynthia Little, Robin's former assistant, helped produce a penultimate hard copy of the manuscript for Chris Freeman and offered assistance in the final stages of proof-reading the manuscript.

At the Delft University of Technology, Rohan Samarajiva and Amy Mahan were assisted and encouraged in many ways by Dr Rolf Künneke, Universitair Hoofddocent of the Economics of Infrastructure Section, who also contributed the epilogue. The assistance of Karin van Duyn-Dewort and Françoise Dunant, the secretaries of the Section, is appreciated. At the Ohio State University, Divakar Goswami, Lilia Perez Chavolla and Sanghyun Moon provided invaluable long-distance research assistance. Professor Harry M. Trebing answered questions from afar and provided wise counsel. Dr Walter Bolter, an associate of Melody's since Melody and Trebing produced a major report for the US President's Task Force on Communications Policy, was another source of encouragement, providing us with recent and early photographs of Melody. They, along with the many personal statements embedded in the first drafts of the contributions to this book were presented to Melody on the ceremonial occasion in May 2002 when the Delft University of Technology set him free to launch, with no less vigour than in the past, yet another enterprise.

We acknowledge the invaluable assistance of Professor Dr Henk G. Sol, Dean of the Faculty of Technology, Policy and Management at the Delft University of Technology, which made possible the expeditious publication of this volume. Heleen Gierveld and her colleagues at the Delft University of Technology Press enabled this book to be published in what must amount to a record time in academic publishing and contributed greatly to make it a book worthy of its subject.

Finally, and on behalf of all our co-conspirators, we offer this book to William H. Melody as a token of our appreciation of what he has taught us. Our hope is that it will keep alive the tradition of committed intellectualism he has so powerfully embodied.

II

Inquiry...

Nicholas Garnham

Peter Sheehan

John B. Goddard
and James Cornford

John Langdale

Jean-Claude Burgelman

Bella Mody

Liora Salter

II

Inquiry...

Robin Mansell, Rohan Samarajiva and Amy Mahan

Charles Lindblom's (1990) book, *Inquiry and Change: The Troubled Attempt to Understand & Shape Society*, provides the key to the theme of this section. Lindblom juxtaposes the ideal and the reality of scientific inquiry and problem-solving, concluding that the process of inquiry, itself, is inevitably impaired. He argues that 'impairments' can be ameliorated to a degree through processes that provide for the contestation of knowledge and its wide circulation. *Networking Knowledge*, the first part of the title of this book, similarly emphasises the importance of the circulation of knowledge through networks of mediating institutions involved in the process of social inquiry. William Melody's commitment to social inquiry invariably means a resistance to the notion of the social scientist as the Platonic 'philosopher-king'. Like Lindblom (1990: 7), he regards problem-solving as 'a broad, diffuse, open-ended, mistake-making social or interactive process, both cognitive and political'. In Lindblom's (1990: 10) analysis, the whole notion of scientific expertise is called into question because, as he argues, 'inquiring citizens and functionaries must choose, with the help of experts willing to probe rather than to hold tightly to conventional scientific inquiry'.

The contributors to this section examine considerations that spring from a commitment to scholarly excellence as defined by universities *and* to social change resulting from improved understanding and action in the world beyond the universities. From different perspectives, they address how it may be feasible to foster institutional arrangements to facilitate high quality research and teaching that is interwoven with the concerns of non-university based actors. Melody (1986b: 3) once argued that 'the purpose of research is to generate information that will increase understanding'. He never treats information as a neutral concept and he is always acutely aware that 'the historic assumption that more information will lead to increased understanding is less and less defensible' (Melody 1986b: 3). In pursuit of the creation and the circulation of new knowledge, Melody champions, not more research output *per se*, but the creation of institutional settings that favour achieving research outputs of the highest quality and with the greatest potential for circulation and appropriation by others.

This, arguably, is what drives Melody's unflagging effort to create institutional arrangements within and outside the university that will provide useful policy research and that will contribute to the training of new cadres of professional researchers (Melody 1985a). In 1976 he took up the Chair of the Communication Department at Simon Fraser University in Canada. As Liora Salter suggests, this interdisciplinary programme generated many contests within the university over the definition of its subject and the standards of excellence. In 1985, in the United Kingdom, Melody designed a new institutional environment for research. This time it was a long-term programme of social science research located within a network of research centres, all operating within university settings. Assessments of the results of this initiative vary. Jean-Claude Burgelman argues that the Programme on Information and Communication Technologies (PICT) in the United Kingdom gave its researchers a lead in European policy research in the field. Nicholas Garnham is sceptical, however. He argues that the force of politically-defined research agendas, and the increasingly pragmatic and 'vocational' remits of universities, are eroding the institutional foundations for critical, public interest policy research. In 1989, Melody forged yet another institutional model for the kind of research he has worked to encourage. In Australia, as Peter Sheehan reports, the Centre for International Research on Communication and Information Technologies (CIRCIT) was located outside the university but with a mission to forge strong academic links. This centre was buffeted by politics and its research output was met with criticism when it directly addressed the concerns of companies and policy makers.

The strengths and pitfalls of various institutional arrangements as sites for critical reflection and learning, and for policy-relevant social science research, are examined from several different perspectives in this section. Melody's position on issues of the structure and conduct of the social sciences, the appropriate standards for determining excellence, and the way to foster research that is both policy-relevant and independent or critical is a complicated one. He wants social science research to be accountable. In the case of the economics discipline, for instance, he said early in his career that,

... if economic theory is to approach that dangerous area where it would be really useful in the formulation of public policy, it must go beyond the task of providing terminology that is supposed to help decision makers select what they think is best from a predetermined number of alternatives. It must provide a basis for the improved assessment of the efficiency of decisions in light of the market reality that develops (Melody 1974: 299-300).

This emphasis on a continuous interaction and interrogation of theory and practice resonates throughout his research and teaching. There could be many explanations for his commitment to a dialectic within the very conduct of social science. The one that we favour is to be found in Melody's exposure to the writings of the Canadian political economist and historian, Harold Adams Innis.

Innis (1951: 190) suggested that:

... mechanization has emphasized complexity and confusion; it has been responsible for monopolies in the field of knowledge; and it becomes extremely important to any civilization if it is not to succumb to the influence of this monopoly of knowledge to make some critical survey and report. The conditions of freedom of thought are in danger of being destroyed by science, technology and the mechanization of knowledge ... .

He argued that the application of technologies for communication and the circulation of information influence the types of knowledge that are disseminated. Within the university, he saw the great danger that the institutional boundaries of disciplines, 'reinforced by the mechanization of knowledge' would conspire to weaken the university's capacity to encourage '... the release of mental energy'. There would be an 'overwhelming tendency ... to build up and accept dogma...' (Innis 1951: 209-10). For Melody, the unchallenged acceptance of dogma is simply not to be countenanced; it is antithetical to the whole agenda of social problem-solving. Melody has retained a commitment to the university as a place that still may provide spaces for the conduct of critical inquiry. But this commitment jostles with his equally strong commitment to 'research in the wild' (Callon 2002 forthcoming), that is, outside the academic world.

Gibbons et al. (1994) and Nowotny et al. (2001) draw attention to the shifting balance between Mode 1 knowledge production (the traditional conception of the scientific enterprise conducted within the university); and Mode 2 knowledge production (the production of knowledge in the context of its application). They argue that knowledge production and learning are social processes. These work best when they involve the close interaction of multiple stakeholders. Universities must find ways of adapting to a shift in the sites of socially relevant knowledge production. This viewpoint is contested by those who admit to the social character of research, but who are committed to pursuing self-determination and the institutions of open science (David, Foray and Steinmueller 1999).

The discussion about how best to organise, fund and evaluate social science research rages on (see Etzkowitz and Leydesdorff 1997; Geuna 1999). Melody persists in the task of experimenting with new institutional formations, more effective ways of networking knowledge, and innovative ways of combining insights from across the disciplines of the social sciences (and often the physical sciences and engineering). He sees it as his responsibility to encourage researchers to become deeply involved with the stakeholders in their research through networks that span the world. He experiments with the application of the new means of communication and information exchange using the Internet and the Web, but he examines the opportunities and dangers of their space and time-binding limitations in true Innisian style.

Nicholas Garnham argues that it is quixotic to regard universities as places (or even electronic virtual spaces) where disinterested public interest research is conducted. For him, Melody's ambitions for the conduct of independent research (at least in the United Kingdom) are an unattainable holy grail in the modern university setting. He suggests that the linkages between public funding and politically-defined research agendas are so binding that they stifle critical research, especially in the field of information and communication policy. Garnham also takes seriously the pressures on the academic labourer that stem from the application of the new technologies. Their implementation, he argues, comes at a cost; a cost that threatens to stamp out the critical perspectives that are essential for social problem-solving. The bias of new media technologies like the Web serves to lock the universities' faculty and students into a supporting chorus for the momentum of the information society, whatever its consequences might be. Melody would most likely admit to these dangers. He would no doubt then set off on another venture to gain the commitment of research funders to his conception of independent research.

Like Garnham, *Peter Sheehan* contrasts the ideal and the reality of the modern university. His contribution contains echoes of Innis' concerns about tendencies toward the monopolisation of knowledge that take hold wherever institutions gain the power to possess and control knowledge. He acknowledges the pressures towards the corporatisation of knowledge and the coincident reduction in funding for independent long-term research. In this case, Melody's initiative to establish a greenfield research institution in Australia was met with jealousy and rigidity within the universities. Those in government and the private sector distanced themselves from the consequences of the social scientists' critiques of their policies and actions. The former were threatened because they believed their funding base would be eroded. The latter were unable to countenance the political or economic implications of what Melody insisted was independent research.

The role of the latest information and communication technologies in support of the global circulation of knowledge via the virtual university is taken up by *John Goddard* and *James Cornford*. They dismiss the rhetoric about the benefits of virtuality and look instead to the experience of the take-up of the new technologies by universities. Like Garnham, they find evidence of unexpected costs and of the need for attention to the coordination of initiatives that set out to create universities 'without walls'. The unbundling of the traditional pedagogic role of the university appears to turn these institutions into intermediaries on a global stage. But Goddard's (1994) and his colleague's commitment to understanding the relationships between space, place and technological change, means that they seek empirical evidence of the consequences of these initiatives. The evidence shows that universities remain rooted in their locations and that, in contrast to the ideal of an elite institution that disseminates knowledge, they are poorly organised to plot a course for change. The tension between pedagogical ideals and interactions of researchers with those in their communities, is one, they argue, that can be worked through. However, success requires strategic action to encourage local experimentation within universities and improved linkages with industrial and social agencies. In line with Melody's ambition of networking knowledge, Goddard and Cornford call for a re-institutionalisation of universities in a way that is sensitive to social and economic transformation and its consequences.

John Langdale is pessimistic about the present capacity of social scientists to generate useful insights into the ways that advanced information and communication technologies are implicated in the economy and in society. Writing from a vantage point of close involvement with changes in the telecom industry as operators have sought to adjust to global competition and to incursions into their domestic markets, Langdale is disappointed by social scientists' contributions to the analysis of the causes and consequences of these changes. He suggests that if the results of some social science research had been networked more effectively within policy and corporate communities, the failure of the telecom operators' mega-carrier strategies and of efforts to capitalise on the earlier dot.com boom would have been less damaging for investors. Langdale calls for more funding and interdisciplinary work as the antidote to the limited ability of researchers to adequately forecast developments in the telecom arena.

The structural features of institutional settings in which social science research is conducted are central to improvements in the contributions of researchers to understanding the implications of the new technologies. In *Jean-Claude Burgelman*'s contribution, pessimism is tempered with optimism insofar as he argues that the technology push agenda for the information society is gradually giving way to an agenda that sees interactions between social and technical processes of innovation as central. Yet, he asks, where are the social scientists who are ready to participate in the process of social problem-solving? Burgelman's (2000) own commitment to networking knowledge is evident in his work on issues of access to, and exclusion from, the information society. He argues that research networks in the social sciences need to be scaled up with commensurate funding so that social scientists can learn how to engage with technical and non-technical issues. Melody's work takes the past and the present as a prelude to the future. He does not favour forecasting as an exercise in 'crystal ball gazing'. Like Innis (1951: 61) who argued that 'knowledge of the past may be neglected to the point that it ceases to serve the present and the future', Melody is always exploring the relationships between older and newer technologies and forms of social organisation. Burgelman argues that social scientists can contribute to technological forecasting if the techniques are used to evaluate counterfactual developments, based on careful analyses of history.

Bella Mody has long been an advocate of the potential benefits of information and communication technologies for development (Mody and Dahlman 1992). Mody points out that the study of communication has provided little insight into how the privately supported media industries might be complemented by initiatives that use the new technologies for the empowerment of people. She argues that far too much emphasis is being given to 'ICT for growth' strategies rather than to 'ICT for distributional equity' strategies. Mody challenges us to examine the way structures of power in the pre-digital age are being replicated in the digital age. She suggests as well that critical communication researchers are disadvantaged in the poorest regions of the developing world by their limited resources to develop teaching materials that distinguish their position in the global economy from that of the wealthier countries.

Liora Salter develops a detailed analysis of what interdisciplinarity means for researchers within universities. She shows that, not only must they rise to the challenge of forging alliances with those outside the academy, but they must fight for recognition within the university. In theory, interdisciplinary research and teaching are meant to produce venturesome advocates of the generation of new knowledge. In practice, the monopolists of knowledge (and funding) within universities raise institutional barriers to change at any sign that their comforts might be disturbed. Salter emphasises that challenging institutional inertia entails more than the penetration of new intellectual spaces. It means careful mapping of the intellectual territory and its boundaries and clear thinking about where core contributions can be made. In the case of Simon Fraser University's Communication Department, this was at the boundary between changing communication processes and technology and policy. Salter argues that it is not simply the scope or the complexity of the subject matter of communication that the university found unsettling. It was Melody's advocacy of a critical approach – part philosophy and part ideology – that worried the establishment of the university. Melody advocated a link between the natural and technical sciences and the social sciences and humanities because he recognised that this coupling could offer a foundation for challenging orthodoxy inside and outside the university.

Innis argued that different media for the circulation of knowledge imply biases in the organisation of space and time with very real consequences. He argued that the introduction of any new medium would be influential (not determining) in setting the conditions for the monopolisation or the de-monopolisation of knowledge (Innis 1950). Networking knowledge clearly requires the latter. The social scientist's challenge is to analyse the specific conjunctures of institutional organisation, technology and knowledge with a view to revealing the biases so that they might be altered. Lindblom, similarly, was committed to the idea that knowledge must be contested.

Universities, Research and the Public Interest

Nicholas Garnham

The major unifying thrust of William Melody's work has been the application of the tools of regulatory economics across a range of communication industries – particularly broadcasting and telecom. In contrast to the dominant trend in regulatory economics with its often simple-minded faith in the market, and associated narrow conception of market failure, Melody's work has been inspired by the school of institutional economics. True to the spirit of that school, and of its populist socio-political roots in North America, central to this work has been the search for and defence of the public interest and of the institutional forms and practices – in particular regulatory policies and agencies – that might deliver that public interest.

Any body of work that centrally mobilises the concept of public interest faces the problem of how and by whom the public interest is to be defined. This is particularly problematic for institutional economists like Melody because they reject the easy equation of the public interest with the maximisation of consumer welfare, defined as the aggregation of consumer demands through an undistorted market, and are at the same time fully aware of the extent to which both policy debate and regulatory practice can be manipulated by special interest groups. Moreover, if, like Melody's, the aim of regulatory analysis is broadly democratic and activist rather than merely critical, one faces the dilemma, long ago debated by Dewey and Lippman, about the necessary role of experts in what are technically complex policy fields. This dilemma must be faced in the full awareness that one of the key ways in which special interest groups exert power over policy and regulation is through their ability to mobilise, using the incentives of money or power, expert opinion.

It is this search for a locus of expert opinion that can be mobilised in the construction, propagation and defence of public interest policies in the field of communication that has led Melody to place a central emphasis on the role of university research. This has been evident both in his own move out of regulatory agencies and into academia and in his key role in the creation and direction of publicly funded, university-based research programmes and centres on information and communication policy in the United Kingdom, Australia, Denmark and The

Netherlands. In his own consultancy work from an academic base for such agencies as the International Telecommunication Union and the World Bank and in the design and running of these research programmes and centres the aim has been, on the one hand, to escape the taint of special interest pleading, while, on the other, avoiding the lure of academic ivory-towerism by ensuring that publicly-funded research takes on a public responsibility.

I want here to suggest that, while the dilemma is real and the aim laudatory, one has to ask whether university research can, if it ever could, any longer be seen as a source of disinterested public interest expertise, especially in the field of information and communication policy and regulation. Leaving to one side the general sociological question as to whether university-based researchers always represent a special, elite interest, I suggest that the current evolution of universities, and of the national policy frameworks within which they work, make it more and more quixotic to see university research as a way out of the public interest dilemma, especially with regard to information and communication policy. In writing from my experience in the United Kingdom, the trends seem to be general. While policy makers continue to pay lip service to the disinterested, critical and blue-sky nature of university research, in reality, such research is increasingly driven, in a competitive search for funds, either to seek corporate support with its associated research agenda, or public funds which are increasingly distributed, in the name of relevance and the supposed rights of tax payers, according to a politically-defined research agendas. This linkage between public funding and a politically-defined research agenda is, of course, particularly problematic where policy research is at issue. With particular relevance to information and communication policy, universities are now seen by governments, and to an extent by their management, as major corporate players in the so-called information or knowledge economy.

The incorporation of the university sector into the information economy agenda has two major effects. First, universities are seen as key producers of the human capital – the so-called knowledge workers – upon which national economic competitiveness and future economic growth are seen to depend. This is also often linked to a skills gap interpretation of inadequate rates of productivity growth and higher than necessary levels of unemployment. This view of the universities' role is having two major effects. It tends to make both the curriculum and the research agenda more narrowly pragmatic and 'vocational'. The properly critical element of university education and research gives way in the face of a corporate and government agenda and students are encouraged to see themselves primarily as clients whose investment pays off in terms of the job market. At the same time, the laudable aim of extending access to higher education beyond a narrow social elite is justified, not in terms of widening choice and freedom and extending general capabilities, but in terms of avoiding training that would involve any wasting of economically valuable human capital.

Unfortunately, this extension of access comes up against two constraints. It misreads the labour market and thus tends to produce greater competition for supposedly graduate level jobs – which do not require the specialised technical skills claimed by the skills gap school, but rather the social skills which the older more elitist system was designed to filter. This then produces a hierarchy within the university system between elite and non-elite universities, since employers still want universities to bear the cost of doing their employment filtering for them. At the same time, it lowers the general economic returns to the personal investment in higher education, thus both threatening to create a disappointed body of graduates, and discouraging the more socially disadvantaged from pursuing a university education.

Second, it faces the unwillingness of governments to fund the expansion of access through taxation. This results in a general lowering of the quality of provision and in the creation of a hierarchy, not now between those with access to higher education and those excluded, but between students and between institutions within the overall system. It also results in a drive for productivity growth. This directly affects both teaching and research. As anyone who has either conducted or managed research will know, the most valuable resource is time. The less time there is, the more likely it is that the risks involved in the very uncertain outcomes of critical inquiry will be eschewed, in favour of incremental developments of the tried and tested. As anyone who has taught will know, the teaching which develops and expands critical intelligence is an intensive user of the time for both teacher and student.

But, of particular relevance to the field of information and communication policy, in the search for increased productivity, universities have turned, encouraged by government, to information and communication technologies – and, in particular, to the World Wide Web. The provision of higher education is, like all knowledge-based service businesses, labour intensive. Major productivity gains can only be achieved by extending reach. The highly trained and relatively scarce labour inputs required to design a syllabus and conduct lectures and seminars cannot be reduced. Put crudely the only way to increase productivity is to increase the audience, that is, the number of students in receipt of this scarce input. For over 50 years, a succession of technologies has been seen as the magic solution to this dilemma of educational productivity, and therefore cost – radio, then television, then computers, and now the Web. Each, in its turn, failed to deliver the goods. Indeed, while in each case these technologies may have had the potential to enhance learning, they could only do so at extra cost – a cost that funders were unable or unwilling to sustain. This leads not just to disappointment, but to the cruel disappointment of wasted effort and hopes dashed.

There seems to be no good reason why the virtual university will not go through the same experience. Indeed, the first wave of initiatives has disenchanted with unusual swiftness. Moreover, this pursuit of virtuality is combined with a global vision linked to the much-vaunted supposed distance destroying capabilities of the Web. From this policy perspective, national universities are seen, not as institutions designed to widen and deepen the intellectual and cultural capabilities, and thus autonomy, of citizens in the general public interest, but as potentially global knowledge businesses competing for a share of a global education market. Universities are expected to compete both with the universities of other developed nations and with corporate providers of higher level training. Such developments threaten reduced intellectual and cultural diversity on a global scale. They are already shifting the power structure within universities from the collegial, based on free debate and intellectual openness, to the managerial, based on a corporate model of labour relations and, crucially, intellectual property ownership.

In general, these developments undermine universities as a base for critical, public interest policy research. But more specifically, to the extent that universities become locked into the logic of such a development and become major players in the information society policy game, they will hardly be neutral on either macro matters of information society policy, for instance, and perhaps most urgently, criticising its very logic – or matters of infrastructure planning, pricing and access.

II.2

Universities in the Knowledge Economy

Peter Sheehan

Introduction

The continuing tension between ideal and reality lies at the heart of the human condition. The struggle to embody a high ideal in the harsh reality of the actual world has provided some of humanity's greatest achievements, as well as some of its most depressing failures. Finding ways to realise an ideal in a changing world has been central to many great reform movements.

This tension between ideal and contemporary reality is acutely evident in the modern university. Heir to a great ideal of the disinterested community of scholars seeking truth for its own sake, the university has become a central institution of the modern era. Operating as they do in a world in which wealth and power have become increasingly tied to knowledge, universities are now massive, prestigious and powerful. They are also the focus of the ambitions of individuals, companies and governments.

In the communities of scholars that did so much to shape the modern world, knowledge may have been pursued for its own sake. But the knowledge acquired proved to have enormous social and economic implications. Possessing and controlling existing knowledge and being in position to generate valuable new knowledge, confers power and economic advantage, and attracts the attention of those whose interests are far from scholarly. In some ways the success of communities based on the ideal created conditions that make it harder to pursue the ideal.

The issues which emerge from this tension – the position of the university as an independent, scholarly institution, the ways in which relevant economic and social knowledge can be generated and disseminated, and the maintenance of an independent critique of strategies and values – have been central to William Melody's life and work. In this contribution, I discuss some elements of this tension as they appear at the beginning of the 21st century in the light of what we have learned from him on these matters. My empirical focus is implicitly on universities in Australia; readers may recognise similarities in many other countries.

Inquiry

The Timeless Ideal and the Contemporary Reality
Many cultures possess the ideal of the committed community of scholars seeking truth in a disinterested way, and sharing both the way of life and the results of the search with young members being initiated into the community. While having substantial resonance in many other cultures, this ideal has been particularly influential in the West. After the rediscovery of the civilisation of the ancient Greeks in the 10th and 11th centuries, this ideal became embodied in the new universities of Europe, which grew to maturity by the 13th century.

The role that these universities, and many others established subsequently, played in the intellectual, cultural and economic history of the world need not be recited here. Suffice to say that they have, for several centuries, played a pivotal role in shaping economic and social trends. Thus, they have contributed greatly to the emergence of a knowledge-based society. That is, to a society in which knowledge is central to both economic and social developments, and in which access to knowledge is rightly seen as critical to employment, income and power.

The following are some of the key features of the situation in which universities now find themselves, partly as a result of their own success. In terms of the role of knowledge, and of the nature of knowledge generation and of education, four features stand out.

The Economic Importance of Knowledge
In the community of scholars, knowledge was to be sought for its own sake. This did not mean that knowledge had no value – indeed, knowledge was seen as supremely valuable, and 'the truth shall make you free' – but that it was not sought for such extrinsic benefits as it might provide. Thus knowledge was a public good, both in a value sense and in the more technical sense of being non-rival and non-excludable. It should be both generated and distributed in a free and open environment.

But when knowledge is recognised as a primary economic good, the dynamics change a good deal. What knowledge is generated, who controls it and who is trained to use it, become matters of central importance throughout the broader community.

Technical Specialisation
In recent decades, the academic enterprise has become much more specialised, with these specialisations often being linked to the application of particular techniques or bodies of theory. Particular narrow areas generate their own

intellectual communities, journals, career paths and so on, and the number of specialised areas of study seems to have proliferated greatly. This also seems to have led to a high proportion of academic work being driven by the technical demands of various disciplines, rather than by the requirements of real world problems. In economics, for example, the bulk of published work still relates to theory development or testing using econometric techniques, rather than to problem-driven empirical studies.

The Globalisation of Research and of Knowledge Flows

Modern information and communications technologies have led to greatly increased globalisation of research and of knowledge flows over the past decade or so. This is evident not only in the 24-hour corporate R&D effort, operating sequentially in eight hour shifts in various parts of the world, but in many more mundane effects. These include the instantaneous flow of articles and working papers across the Internet, so that researchers, students and clients can all share the latest information.

Knowledge and Education as Corporate Goals

Reflecting the economic importance of knowledge, R&D and education have become central corporate goals. This is true in two senses: large firms have established major R&D and education facilities to achieve their own corporate objectives, and many smaller firms have been set up to undertake R&D or to provide education on a commercial, profit maximising basis.

In terms of the operation of the universities themselves, and of their place in the broader community, four further features stand out.

Mass Participation in Higher Education

Given both the high prestige of university life and the economic rewards associated with knowledge, it was inevitable that there would be a demand for mass participation in higher education. Thus, most industrialised countries, at least, have seen massive expansion in higher education in recent decades. In Australia, for example, the number of persons enrolled in higher education increased twenty-fold over the four decades to 1995, rising from 30,800 in 1955 to 604,200 in 1995. For the OECD as a whole, by 1999 four in every ten school-leavers attended a tertiary institution to study for a bachelor or higher tertiary degree (OECD 2001a).

Diverse Education and Training Functions

If four in every ten school leavers attends a higher education institution, then the educational and training functions of these institutions must be enlarged and greatly diversified. While the dispute about the inclusion of professional faculties in universities was settled in the first half of the 20th century, the last two decades of that century saw a massive expansion of these functions.

Corporatisation, Self-funding and Competition

In many countries, governments funded this massive expansion of university education, initially. But by the 1980s there were widespread attempts to shift the costs of continued growth, both by direct and indirect fees for students and by forcing the universities into a corporatist, self-funding model. In many cases, this has led to universities being driven by the values of the marketplace – managers and marketers are in the ascendancy, there are heavy pressures of a non-academic kind on staff, competition is rife between universities for funding and students, teaching and admission standards are in decline, there is increased use of sessional and casual staff, and so on. Thus, a significant part of the costs of expansion have been borne by the universities themselves, in terms of increased pressures, declining conditions and standards, and fundamental value shifts (for the case of Australia, see Coady 2000).

Policy Research and Social Critique

Finally, one effect of these various changes and pressures has been a drying up of independent, long-term policy research, and the social critique to which it can give rise. When it is publish or perish, limited technical publications are the way to go. If research is funded externally, the agenda of the funding body determines the research undertaken. Even if funds are available through the competitive processes of government funding bodies, these very processes often impose their own constraints, requirements and fashions. The end result of these and other factors has been less fundamental policy research and social critique. To take economics again, the major shifts in policy which have swept the world in the past 10 to 15 years have been driven mainly from the market and market-related institutions, and have still not been the subject of much sustained academic research.

REALISING THE IDEAL

We have barely begun to address the place of the university in the knowledge-based society, where knowledge is at the heart of economic and social affairs and, hence, also the focus of the ambitions of individuals, companies and governments. While trading on the cherished ideal, most universities have developed into quite different institutions, where the pressures of teaching, fund-raising, administration, publication and competition make a mockery of the disinterested search for truth.

To a distant observer, the most obvious exceptions to this generalisation seem to be many of the great universities of the United States. Backed by history and prestige, by massive endowments, by high levels of government funding, by links to successful knowledge-based businesses and by inflows of many of the best staff and student talent from around the world, many of these universities still seem to be able to create a viable university experience. But, even if this is so, it simply highlights the situation of those who are not so fortunate.

As I have said, these issues have been, in one way or another, at the heart of Melody's life and work. Not only has he written about them on many occasions (Melody 1997c) but he has tried to do something about them. This is true both of his long involvement in many universities, but also of his work in setting up several research institutions at the interface between universities and public policy. In these activities, he has experienced many of the tensions, conflicts and contradictions inherent in seeking to realise the ideal within the contemporary reality.

The Experience of CIRCIT

The Centre for International Research on Communication and Information Technologies (CIRCIT) is a case in point. This centre was set up in 1988 by the Victoria Government, to be an independent centre for high quality research on the economic and social implications of the emerging information technologies. It was relatively well-funded, at least by Australian standards, and was encouraged to build a respected international position in the area. It was expected to cooperate with, but not to fund, activities in the universities, on the basis that a new organisation with critical mass needed to be created. Melody, fresh from his experiences with the British Programme on Information and Communication Technologies (PICT) endeavour, was involved in its initial specification and was engaged as founding director in 1988.

The early years of the new centre were exciting. A strong team was quickly assembled, some very good work was done and CIRCIT soon became well-known in the international community. The centre was achieving much of what its founders had intended. But within Australia, the position was rather different. Many research groups in the universities and elsewhere saw the centre as a competitor, rather than as a source of funds, and were at best reluctant to cooperate, and at worst hostile. Many bureaucrats within the Australian Government saw the centre as a threat to their power, and to their control over the policy-making process. In many companies, CIRCIT was seen as too independent and uncertain, and as not necessarily generating results consistent with company interests. Thus, in a period in which Australia was blundering through the early stages of telecom reform, the centre was seen more as a threat to vested interests than as an opportunity to throw new light on issues of great national importance.

Such signs of rejection of a new irritant into the body corporate are not uncommon, and can often be temporary. But in different circumstances they can be fatal. By the early 1990s, the Government of Victoria had changed, and those who had promoted CIRCIT were no longer in a position of influence. The Government was short of money, and the voices of vested interests could still be heard. In 1993 the Government ceased funding the centre and Melody resigned as Director. Reflecting the heroic efforts of a number of individuals, the centre has continued, and has done some important work since then. But this has involved the hand-to-mouth existence of much Australian research, and incorporation within a university. The opportunity to create a major new star on the international firmament, with a strong funding base and critical mass, had been lost.

Conclusion

Many of us, at least outside the United States, are struggling within university institutions that have lost their way in the welter of conflicting demands, expectations and vested interests. To sort through these problems, and to preserve some space for the historic ideal, will require both clear thinking and committed action. Melody has given plenty of both in a long career, and will surely give much more in a vigorous retirement.

The University, ICTs and Development in the Information Society

John B. Goddard and James Cornford

Introduction

A distinctive feature of William Melody's contribution has been his concern with the role of established institutions as agents promoting or inhibiting social, economic and technological change. He has been particularly concerned with the contribution of university-based critical research in shaping policy in relation to the information society, including issues of uneven economic and social development. This essay takes these concerns forward by focusing on the university as an institution and how it responds, primarily to the challenges posed by information and communication technology (ICT) in managing its internal affairs, and, secondarily, to external requirements for greater engagement with processes of regional economic and social development. We draw upon new empirical work which challenges the hyperbole surrounding the so-called virtual university that has no campus and a growing body of policy research, on the way in which universities engage with their local communities. In summary, we seek to show that, notwithstanding the space-transcending capabilities of ICTs, geography still matters for the university as an institution.

The Vision of a Virtual University

The virtual university has emerged as a potent vision for the future of higher education, utilising new ICTs to radically restructure higher educational provision. What is envisaged in this scenario is a 'university without walls'. Freed from the confines of the campus and its region, the university becomes a virtual institution. In terms of teaching and learning, it consists of little more than global connections of potential students (recruitment), learners and teachers (students and staff), employers (the careers function) and alumni; in terms of the institution's research mission it joins a complex web of researchers, research funders and research users, all held together by sophisticated ICT applications. The vision is one of flexible ever-changing organisations for knowledge creation and distribution. The university, as an institution, appears to dissolve.

This agenda has implications for the whole university. With regard to the university's pedagogic role, it envisages the separation or unbundling of the development of course materials (packaging), the assembly of students (recruitment), the provision of learning and the assessment of competencies. With this unbundling, the university ceases to be an end-to-end supplier of the higher education process and may undertake one or more of these roles, with other organisations undertaking complementary functions. The university, then, becomes far more externally oriented, an intermediary on the global stage, acting as collaborator, client, contractor and broker of higher education services. Of course, the extent of unbundling varies for different sub-markets, being greater in postgraduate, vocational and life-long learning markets than in the undergraduate 'rite of passage' market.

In terms of research, the vision is one in which research teams cross disciplinary, institutional, and national boundaries. In part, this arises from the growth of big science with its huge research teams and massive resource requirements, but it also builds on disciplinary traditions in all subject areas. More significantly, research increasingly involves working much more closely with users in what has been called 'the new production of knowledge'.

The administration of the university, too, is transformed in the visions of the virtual university. At the heart of this change is the provision of comprehensive information systems to support teaching and research networks. Significantly, there is a shift from an administrative culture to a culture of professionally-supported academic self-management.

The Traditional University and the Virtual University

The most celebrated (or perhaps feared) examples of progress towards the vision of the virtual university are new, for profit institutions, mainly in the United States. The University of Phoenix or Jones International University are often held up as exemplars. The significance of these 'new' institutions, however, lies not in their direct impact: they actually provide a tiny, although growing, proportion of higher education in the United States. Rather, their implication is primarily indirect, operating through the perceived threat to established Higher Education Institutions (HEIs) in terms of their markets for students, and in terms of their demonstration effect. They have added a new impetus and urgency to the body of experimentation and innovation with the use of ICTs within existing institutions. For example, a recent survey found that 41% of universities in the United Kingdom saw ICT as critical for future development, and a further 38% had ICT 'high on the agenda'. It is in this traditional higher education sector, where we would argue that the most quantitatively significant moves towards the virtual university are to be found; what we might call brownfield, rather than greenfield, sites.

The significant point here is that it is not ICT-based new institutions that are the locus of change, but a host of structural forces within higher education which are forcing traditional institutions to adopt ICTs. The key driving force has been the shift from elite to mass systems of higher education linked to declining financial resources per student. This has led universities to seek to use ICTs to achieve efficiency gains in teaching, research and administration. A more diverse student population has also required more ICT-mediated student support. Increased competition for students has encouraged the use of ICTs in targeted recruitment, and in utilising alumni as a resource. Students, as ICT-literate and discerning customers, and governments, as funders, have required more emphasis on quality assurance and accountability through ICT-based reporting systems.

If the locus for change is within the traditional campus university, this raises the key empirical question of how its customs and practices of teaching, research and administration interact with the requirements of virtuality. What is the 'traditional' university? It is conventionally, if mythically, thought of as a band of scholars coming together to create, maintain and disseminate knowledge, governed by a more or less collegiate model of organisation, based around a complex structure of committees and with a high degree of individual and departmental autonomy. In this sense, 'the university' as an institution tends to lack a clear identity, primarily existing in the heads of people who constitute it and a myriad of locally negotiated practices and interactions. The central social role of the traditional university has been to provide a place-based 'rite of passage' for entry into middle class professions through its undergraduate, vocational and extramural provision, together with the provision of ideas-driven 'academic' research. In institutional terms, it has been described as an exemplar of a 'loosely coupled system' characterised by a lack of clearly articulated policy and weak control over the implementation of policy. The traditional university, as an institution, often appears to be only virtually present. Nevertheless, it has proven to be both highly flexible and responsive, in particular, to financial incentives from government, *and* highly rigid and resistant to changes which threaten its autonomy.

Realising the Virtual University

In our research on how universities respond to ICTs, we focused on the strategies, initiatives and programmes within three campus universities in the North East of England (see Cornford 2000; Cornford and Pollock 2002). We found no sign of the break-up of the traditional university. Rather, the traditional university and the virtual university exist in a tense relationship. We found that, in each case, the implementation of the new ICTs appeared to require a *re*-institutionalisation of the university, often as a more corporate body with more explicit goals, roles, identities, rules and operating procedures. In practice, the moves towards the virtual university seemed to be associated with demands for a far more 'concrete' organisation than the traditional university.

It appears, on the basis of our research, that as computer systems are rolled-out through universities, there is a need for more than a mere standardisation of working practices and a clarification of roles. Policy must be tightened up and applied across the university, in effect, calling the university into being as a far more corporate institution. A stronger centre to the university is required, one capable not just of making policy, but of ensuring that it is implemented.

The progress of the virtual university may seem assured, but this is by no means a straightforward process. Electronically supported processes in the teaching and administrative spheres do not seem to be displacing traditional ways of doing things (even where this is what was intended at the start of the process). Rather, the outcomes are often a matter of the new 'virtual' and the old 'traditional' notions of the university co-existing in a tense relationship. Critical to this hybrid of old and new ways of doing things is the intermediation role undertaken by key members of staff at the 'interface' between the old and the new ways. Often these members of staff have to face in two directions. They are obliged to translate between, we might even say perform, the traditional university to the virtual institution, and they have to perform the virtual university to the traditional university.

For example, in our case studies, administrative staff in departments who were operating with the management information system had to interpret or translate their department (with its local specificity) into the standardised framework of the new information system (and the system designers), *and* to translate the outputs of the system back to the academic staff in their departments (and their established and time honoured practices).

This almost benign state is by no means typical, but it represents one mode of co-existence between the old and the new. Many of the initiatives and projects that we studied *presupposed* structures, roles, responsibilities and processes in the university that simply were not there, or were not capable of supporting the functions which the new virtual university projects expected of them. For example, in one of the sites, there were no procedures for the validation of online courses.

Much of the work undertaken by those building the virtual university appears to be a rather desperate attempt to construct the institutional settings (roles and responsibilities, structures and agencies, categories and classifications) necessary for the technology to operate in. In almost all cases, this work constituted a far greater proportion of the workload than was expected at the outset of the project or initiative. As one senior manager put it to us: 'Actually, the thing that trips it up isn't that the technology doesn't work, it's trying to recreate the organisation so we can usefully apply the technology rather than just crippling it to do things the way we did them before'. In short the (re)building of the institution and the roll-out of technological systems necessarily proceed together.

What happens where such institution-building is not undertaken or is not successful? A number of the projects that were unsuccessful in re-engineering the institution around them, stalled. Without strong institutional bonds to maintain the commitment of all the necessary actors (students, teachers, assessors, validation agencies, librarians, partner institutions, etc.), projects seemed to fall apart. It might be concluded that bottom-up initiatives tend to fade away when they are not mainstreamed and systemised, that is, when the whole change process is not managed.

Our research offers insight into the changing attitudes and relationships between ICT projects and the campus location of institutions. In much of the rhetoric and, indeed, in the plans and proposals which secured funding for projects, the university campus figured as a barrier that ICTs could enable the institution to overcome or transcend. Indeed, this capacity to 'escape' the confines of place and enter a (potentially) global space is, of course, a recurrent theme within the technological discourse. Yet, when attempts are made to operationalise this transcendence, for example, through the provision of completely remote Internet-based courses, there is often a rapid re-evaluation of this position.

When courses are abstracted from the campus setting, there is a considerable volume of 'work' which the campus discretely undertakes for the institution. For example, the campus constitutes a large and very concrete symbol of the university, its durability and reliability. When courses are abstracted from this (in most cases literally) concrete setting, the issue of how these qualities might be symbolised comes to the fore. Rather than meet the costs of seeking to compensate for the lack of a campus, projects and initiatives are increasingly seeking to develop hybrid forms of provision which combine on- and off-campus elements.

THE REGIONALLY-ENGAGED UNIVERSITY

If the vision of the virtual or 'un-packed' university with which we opened this essay was to be realised, it would pose a real threat to the many agencies seeking to mobilise universities as key institutions for economic development by further enhancing university disengagement with place (Goddard and Chatteron 1998; Charles and Benneworth 2001). While they are located in regions, universities are being asked by a new set of regional actors and agencies to make an active contribution to the development of these regions. These demands are driven by new processes of globalisation and localisation in economic development, whereby the local environment is as relevant as the national macro-economic situation in determining the ability of enterprises to compete in the global economy. Within this environment, the local availability of knowledge and skills is as important as physical infrastructure and, as a result, regionally engaged universities can become a key locational asset and powerhouse for development, especially in less prosperous regions.

The requirement for regional engagement embraces many facets of the 'responsive university' which are being generated by evolving priorities within the higher education system. These priorities include: meeting the needs of a more diverse client population – for lifelong learning created by changing skill demands; for more locally based education as public maintenance support for students declines; for greater links between research and teaching and for more engagement with the end-users of this research. Regional engagement, as well as ICT, are becoming key drivers shaping the way in which many universities are responding to overall trends within higher education.

Responding to the new demands requires more active management that enables universities as institutions to make a dynamic contribution to the development process in the round. Within the university, the challenge is to link the teaching, research and community service roles by internal mechanisms (for example, funding, staff development, incentives and rewards, communications) and, within the region to engage the university with all facets of the development process (for example, skills enhancement, technological development and innovation, cultural awareness) in a region/university 'value added management' process within a 'learning region'. There can be no doubt that effective use of ICTs is critical to this process.

Conclusion

Both the virtual university and regional engagement agendas require the university to become a more corporately-managed institution. As traditional universities seek to respond to the threat of an electronic commerce-based vertical marketplace for students, learning materials and knowledge products, managed by non-university 'infomediaries', they are being forced to make more explicit both their policies and procedures. This process extends well beyond the technology systems (the standardisation of data types and communication protocols) and into the core of the university as an institution, bringing established categories, identities, roles and responsibilities into doubt. The virtual university requires the active re-institutionalisation of the university and we suggest that the myriad of short-term initiatives supporting *ad hoc* projects is not the way to build virtual universities. Such a fragmented and piecemeal approach, although going with the grain of much university tradition, is prone to failure. Rather, higher education policy needs to pay much more attention to policy formation and implementation and to capacity building, internally, across institutions and in terms of stronger engagement externally with technology vendors and other partners.

Internal capacity building implies a key role for *strategic* action-orientated research at the university centre to support local initiatives and to counter forces for fragmentation. The lessons of local (individual, departmental) experimentation need to be learned and absorbed by the institutions and incorporated into policy. Externally, capacity building implies a key role for national bodies to create common service platforms for all HEIs (an infrastructure of wires, content and people). Improved linkage to the knowledge economy constituencies of R&D, industry, international trade, employment, social inclusion agencies will also be required. Collective action by HEIs can help them to achieve the sheer scale required to manage the relationship with technology and information suppliers. In this context, the single- or multi-site campus should not be seen (only) as a barrier to be overcome, but should (also) be seen as a significant resource, a platform upon which to build hybrid provision. Indeed, collaboration between institutions within a region could be a more realistic way to realise the virtual university than the global partnerships that have been promulgated without much success.

Finally, in relation to their contribution to regional development, there are clear implications for national, regional and local governments in terms of the need to establish policies and practices that enhance the capability of universities to engage with a range of development processes that cross institutional boundaries. In the context of pleas for more joined-up government, it is becoming increasingly obvious that there are few public policy concerns to which universities are not contributing. For example, their research outputs are raising industrial competitiveness through support for innovation and technology transfer; enhancing skills levels in the labour market through graduate placement and continuing professional development; addressing social exclusion through widening participation in higher education; enhancing health and social well-being through the work of medical schools and social policy departments;

cultural development through arts and humanities faculties; and contributions to the public sphere through debate and community leadership. While the functional stovepipes of central government may inhibit cross-cutting initiatives at this level, within the local scene the potential of a university as the key diversified institution is becoming widely appreciated. But to realise that potential, universities must become more integrated internally. In order to achieve this, effective exploitation of ICTs is a key challenge.

II.4

The Role of the Social Sciences in Policy Oriented Telecom Research

John Langdale

INTRODUCTION

William Melody and I in the early 1990s served on a Committee of the Telecom Fund for Social and Policy Research which at that time funded social and policy research in the telecom field in Australia. Committee members extensively discussed what constituted good quality telecom research and Melody and I continued this discussion over several years. A key question that arose was how might the social sciences make a contribution to policy-oriented telecom research? Most academic telecom research was not read by policy makers. This contribution represents a renewed attempt to come to grips with these issues. I argue here that academic, business and policy-oriented telecom research has had limited success in analysing the social, economic and political forces shaping the telecom industry. At the risk of oversimplification, telecom researchers have a somewhat superficial understanding of these forces. As a result, analyses of telecom demand tend to be characterised by black-box approaches.

My argument is a general one, but I illustrate it here by examining two telecom-related issues: the globalisation of telecom operators (telcos) and the Internet and dot.com boom of the late 1990s. In both cases, the enthusiasm for simplistic strategies, which were based on an inadequate understanding of supply and demand as well as of the impact of broader social and political factors, led to disastrous losses for the companies and for society.

These two cases illustrate different but interrelated issues. The first examines the argument that globalisation is the future for the telecom industry and that telcos have no choice but to become mega-carriers and to expand globally. The second illustrates the naïve belief of the dot.com entrepreneurs in the role of technology to satisfy demand and, more fundamentally, their lack of understanding of social, economic and political factors that are shaping demand. In both cases, the extent to which academic research based on an understanding of social, economic and political processes could have tempered the enthusiasm of business and policy makers for the latest management fads or 'new economy' theories is considered.

Globalisation of Telecom Operators

The emerging globalisation of society is one of the most significant changes taking place in the past 20 years and it has had a major impact on the telecom industry. Academics, industrialists and policy makers have struggled to understand the implications of globalisation for the telecom industry. The problem of responding to the pressures of globalisation is common across a range of industries. For example, it is argued that the telecom, airline and media industries will be dominated by five or six global mega-carriers in the future. While trends towards global mega-carriers exist in these industries, their profitability has been poor over the decade of the 1990s. British Telecom, in particular, has been one of the most prominent proponents of the need to go global, but has been forced to reinvent its global strategy regularly in the light of its declining profitability. The global mega-carrier thesis, nevertheless, has survived over the past decade, despite scant evidence of its success.

A fundamental problem in the globalisation of the telecom industry has been a lack of understanding of the complexity of global-local interrelationships. Firstly, a global telco must satisfy the local, national, macro-regional (for example, European) and global communication needs of firms and individuals, as well as provide better quality and cheaper services than nationally-oriented telcos. Global telcos have found that the profitability of serving major transnational corporations (TNCs) is less than they had envisaged.

Secondly, TNCs must be able to respond to the multiple regulatory environments in which they operate. This is a particular problem in the telecom industry, given the continuing role of the state. The global mega-carrier thesis argues that privatisation, deregulation and competition throughout the world will open up the market. While the role of the state has changed significantly in the past 20 years, global telcos are still severely restricted in their ownership structure and operations in many countries. Global operators have learned to their cost that privatisation, competition and deregulation have different meanings in different countries. Much of the research on global telecom regulatory changes has failed to understand the importance of differences in institutional structures in different countries.

Thirdly, and perhaps most importantly, global telcos need a profitable home base from which to cross-subsidise their loss-making global operations. If profitability in the home base collapses, then the global strategies tend to collapse as well. For example, the financial problems of European telcos in their home markets in the early 2000s has severely restricted their global ambitions. This issue, however, is not confined to the telecom industry.

The global mega-carrier thesis fails to come to grips with the complex economic and political issues shaping the demand for telecom services. While there is a strong demand for seamless global telecom services, the extent of demand for sophisticated telecom services is less than has been asserted. Do we need global telcos to satisfy the demand for global telecom services (*Economist* 1997)?

The Internet and dot.com Boom

The Internet and dot.com boom of the late 1990s and its subsequent crash in 2000 also illustrate the power of wishful thinking and the lack of attention to fundamental supply and demand issues. The boom and crash are considered here from the perspective of the concentration on supply-side factors, mainly technology, and the optimistic views of the demand for e-commerce. While many early e-commerce applications in the business-to-consumer (B2C) and the business-to-business (B2B) areas have been poorly designed, it seems clear that B2B e-commerce has a significant long-term role in the economy.

The business-to-consumer e-commerce boom illustrated a number of problems. Pre-eminently, it demonstrated a woeful lack of understanding of people's purchasing decisions. Traditionally, consumer purchasing behaviour was analysed using socio-economic variables such as age, sex, stage in family lifecycle, ethnicity and income. In addition, shopping satisfies important psychological needs of people. Many people like to touch and try on items of clothing. These issues were ignored in the technology-led enthusiasm for the e-commerce revolution in the 'new economy'. The subsequent debacle for the B2C e-commerce companies came as no surprise. A broadly-based social sciences perspective should have been able to indicate which areas of shopping and which consumer groups might be most amenable to the adoption of electronic shopping. In particular, it should have been recognised that the provision of telecom services is just *one* component of a more complex set of factors shaping purchasing decisions.

The B2B e-commerce boom also exhibited a lack of understanding of the nature of supply and demand factors. Its adoption is more likely to be evolutionary than revolutionary, an argument illustrated by the results of research on the role of foreign TNCs in Australia (see Thorburn, Langdale and Houghton 2002). The respondents in this study varied considerably in the importance they attached to e-commerce. However, a common theme was that the role of e-commerce needed to be seen in the context of industry developments to encourage common industry e-commerce systems, as well as in terms of the competitive rivalry between firms. E-commerce was expected to become more important in their businesses over time, but, in general, it was regarded only as *one* of many factors shaping corporate profitability. Far too often, telecom researchers who examine information and communication technology issues, fail to understand the broader industry and corporate contexts in which this technology is adopted.

Conclusion

My experience on the Telecom Fund in the early 1990s led me to strongly question the policy-relevance of contributions of academic telecom researchers. In discussions at the time, Melody and I agreed that there was a lack of good social scientists in Australia applying to the Fund. The situation has not changed since that time and will not in the future unless there is a greater commitment from the government to long-term funding in this area. The research agendas of social scientists from disciplines such as anthropology, economics, politics, sociology and geography need to be reoriented towards policy-oriented issues in the telecom field and in the information society.

More fundamentally, a substantial shift in the focus of telecom research is needed. We need to see electronic communication in the context of broader social, economic and political forces shaping human behaviour. Good social science telecom research may have been able to warn business and policy makers during the e-commerce boom about the poor business models being advocated at the time. This would not necessarily have stopped the speculators, but it would have been a welcome relief from the chorus of 'new economy' gurus that emerged in the late 1990s. Similarly, good social science research should have been able to warn telcos that their understanding of globalisation was flawed and that other models of corporate strategy were needed.

The social science contributions to research have been poor at technology forecasting in the telecom field. For example, the mobile communication boom of the 1990s clearly tapped into a market, with various groups in society wanting mobile communication for social and business purposes. In particular, the youth market grew rapidly to become a significant component of the overall mobile market. However, few social science telecom researchers predicted or understood its growth.

Similarly, major social changes are transforming the nature of Western society. While telcos may undertake market research on how households use telecom services, to what extent have they understood the long-term communication implications of changing family size and structure? Where is the academic research linking changes in the social fabric of society with developments in the telecom field? For example, households are generally smaller and more mobile. The nuclear family is less common today than in the past. To what extent do these social changes have long-term communication implications?

Clearly, many more telecom researchers need to move beyond the black-box approach to understanding demand towards a more sophisticated understanding of social, economic and political trends shaping the society. Melody's research and editorial contributions over many years have assisted these trends, but much more is needed.

Integrating Social Sciences into Information Society Policy

Jean-Claude Burgelman

INTRODUCTION[1]

My central thesis is that, although there are clear limits, the knowledge produced by the social sciences about social dynamics should be an integral and legitimate part of innovation strategies and Information Society policy. To a large degree social scientists seem to avoid this topic. This contribution offers some propositions aimed at optimising the relation between Information Society policy, innovation and the role of the social sciences (see Burgelman 2001a,b for an earlier version). I have had the pleasure of discussing this topic with William Melody whose articles on it were particularly influential in shaping my own thinking and research perspective (Melody and Mansell 1983; Melody 1987b; 1990a).

INNOVATION REQUIRES MORE THAN TECHNICAL KNOW-HOW

Technology policy, in general, and information society technology (IST) related innovation policy, in particular, is characterised to a great extent by extreme technological determinism or by a technological 'bluff' (Ellul 1990). It is taken for granted that what is technologically feasible simply will occur. Innovation policy should then merely concentrate on the technological performance of systems. Further, as the conventional wisdom goes, the technological impetus for the development of these technologies is unrelated to social forces. This view generates a tendency to accept technical innovative capacities as sufficient and/or necessary conditions for social change. A typical example of this technologically deterministic reasoning is as follows – innovation in IST research should concentrate on technologies that can deliver more bandwidth, because that inevitably leads to more communication and hence to a better life. Put simply, if one wants to realise an Information Society, which it is assumed will embrace a 'higher' level of civilisation than the industrial era, as many technologies as possible must be provided.

This type of technological determinism helps to explain why there is so much IST hype. This hype suggests that each technology that transmits a kind of communication, for example, graphics, sound, text, or data, in a better way than existing technologies must be regarded as being highly successful. The burst of the

Internet bubble, for example, can be explained as nothing more than the deflation of the belief that new technologies automatically equate with new social practices.

There have been many of these bubbles, although none with the intensity of the dot.com one. Many examples can be given of 'superior' technologies that have failed. The CD-i was assumed to be in great demand in the late 1980s and to be the killer application for the multimedia revolution. But at the end of 1997, after years of fierce marketing and heavy investment, Philips decided to terminate this product line and to close its multimedia division.

The videodisc was forecast to become a very successful technology that would push its competitor, the Video Cassette Recorder, out of the market. The videodisc disappeared together with RCA, which had developed it at an extremely high cost. Similarly, cable television, launched in the 1950s and 1960s, was regarded in the same way as the Internet is today, that is, as a technical channel which could lead to a social (r)evolution. The social revolution has not occurred. But something has changed. The number of television channels has multiplied by a very significant factor. In short, technological know-how and technological superiority are not the sole determinants of the success or failure of an IST. These are only two of the factors that influence whether a certain innovation breaks through.

An example from European Union (EU) policy offers another illustration of this point. At the end of the 1980s in Europe an often-discussed book within EU policy circles was *Telecommunications in Europe* (Ungerer and Costello 1988). Ungerer, an EU official, was regarded as one of the most important 'brains' in matters of telecom policy and was influential in Directorate General XIII's (now the Information Society directorate) liberalisation policy decisions. In this book it was predicted, on basis of forecasts for the development of microelectronics, that the number of available ISTs would multiply exponentially by the beginning of the millennium. A comparison with the development of automobile technology was used to illustrate the breathtaking technological advances in the personal computing world. The book predicted numerous intelligent applications of the new technologies (see Figure II.5.1).

Figure II.5.1 Telecommunications Prospects for 2000

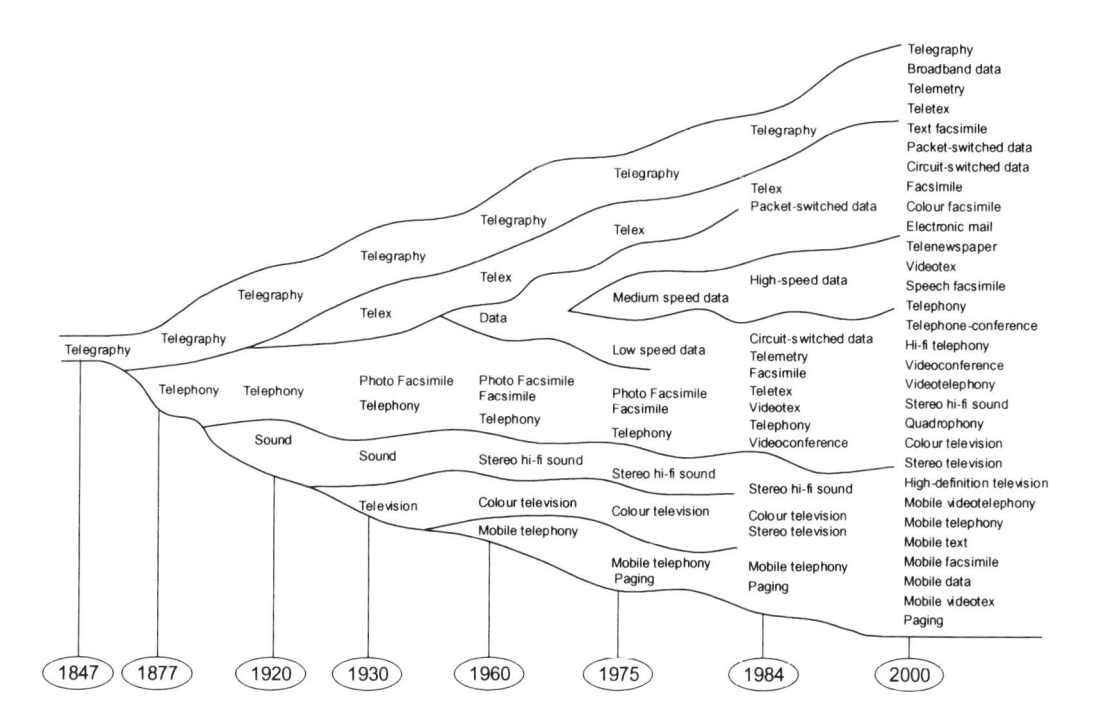

1847	1877	1920	1930	1960	1975	1984	2000
Telegraphy	Telegraphy	Telegraphy	Telegraphy	Telegraphy	Telegraphy	Telegraphy	Telegraphy
	Telephony	Telephony	Telex	Telex	Telex	Telex	Broadband data
			Data	Low speed data	Medium speed data	Packet-switched data	Telemetry
		Photo Facsimile	Photo Facsimile	Photo Facsimile	Photo Facsimile	High-speed data	Teletex
		Telephony	Facsimile	Facsimile	Telephony	Circuit-switched data	Text facsimile
		Sound	Telephony	Telephony	Videoconference	Telemetry	Packet-switched data
			Sound	Stereo hi-fi sound	Stereo hi-fi sound	Facsimile	Circuit-switched data
			Television	Colour television	Colour television	Teletex	Facsimile
				Mobile telephony		Videotex	Colour facsimile
					Mobile telephony	Telephony	Electronic mail
					Paging	Videoconference	Telenewspaper
						Stereo hi-fi sound	Videotex
						Colour television	Speech facsimile
						Stereo television	Telephony
						Mobile telephony	Telephone-conference
						Paging	Hi-fi telephony
							Videoconference
							Videotelephony
							Stereo hi-fi sound
							Quadrophony
							Colour television
							Stereo television
							High-definition television
							Mobile videotelephony
							Mobile telephony
							Mobile text
							Mobile facsimile
							Mobile data
							Mobile videotex
							Paging

Source: Ungerer and Costello 1988

Considering this forecast in retrospect teaches us that most of what was predicted for the market by 2000 either still does not exist, already existed at the time of the prediction, or that the technology in question simply failed. Most strikingly, the one technology that was not foreseen was the Internet and its percolating capabilities that are transforming most of the ways in which we live, do business and work. This omission of what may be one of the most important IST-related innovations ever, shows that extrapolation on the basis of a limited technological paradigm, oversimplifies the whole business of innovation. Indeed, the Internet appears as a technology that became an overnight success by sheer accident. But a closer look reveals that it was not accidental or sudden at all. In fact, the Internet's history dates from its conception as a military technology in the 1960s. The breakthrough for the Internet's growth was the introduction of the World Wide Web interface which triggered the important social factor of improved user-friendliness of computer communication systems. Equally important were the reduced telecom prices induced by state-led liberalisation policies. The Internet's success was preceded by 20 years of (military) government subsidies, academic R&D, and a considerable policy initiative.

Social and economic 'engineering' surrounded the breakthrough, growth and success of the Internet. Contrary to the dominant view that the government should not play a vital role in the innovation process, in the Internet case, government policy was essential in encouraging technical innovations which allowed this platform to develop. All major breakthroughs involving IST innovations are characterised by a long-term view or vision. Much time and money are devoted to allowing experiments to learn from mistakes and to strong enabling policy, without knowing the direction that innovative activity should follow.

If the aim is to assess future technology developments as accurately as possible, it does not suffice to keep an eye only on the technological capacities of certain innovations. ISTs are only the carriers of communication processes. The latter are exclusively human affairs and are influenced by people's social, economic and political incentives. Innovations in IST do not occur in a vacuum. They are closely embedded in human action and they are very strongly influenced by social and economic contextual forces.

FULL SUBSTITUTION OR SUDDEN EXPLOSIONS
Older information and communication technologies are rarely fully substituted by newer ones. The television industry has not ousted the film industry in contrast to what had been predicted initially. In fact, the film industry is one of the most important actors in the multimedia business. Likewise, e-mail and other forms of electronic communication do not appear to be supplanting the postal service. On the contrary, a complementary co-evolution between these two channels is taking shape. In the same manner, the massive introduction of the personal computer has not led to the disappearance of printed-paper or the arrival of the paperless office.

This general rule of complementary co-evolution (or creative destruction in Schumpeterian terms) (Schumpeter 1943) is an exception as far as innovations in processes or procedures are concerned. In this type of process or procedure innovation, the innovation cycles tend to be rather short (10 to 15 years) before full substitution occurs and markets support the innovative activity. In contrast, complementary co-evolution occurs in the case of a radical innovation – in the neo-Schumpeterian sense. The innovation introduces new modes of operating, it generates new social relationships and it takes place in technological clusters as in the case of the combustion engine or the Internet. The innovation process is often more laborious; often taking 20 to 30 years requiring a supportive policy environment.

Strikingly, policy-discussions about IST-related innovations often mix both these types of innovation. For instance, a new stage in the evolutionary process leading to the IS by means of innovations in information networks suggests a classical neo-Schumpeterian perspective, but the policy framework to realise this often proposes to let market forces play. This is counterproductive because it is unlikely to enable a flourishing innovation process. The way the Universal Mobile Telecommunication Service (UMTS) licences were granted is a good example of this. This new technology which enables mobile Internet services is a radical innovation which needs time to achieve widespread take up. Most west European countries auctioned these licences at very high prices. With no time to experiment because the licensees must recover the costs of the licences, the companies are incurring debts substantial enough to cause the Bank of England and the Bank of France to issue debt warnings. Japan chose not to follow the auction path, deciding instead to grant licences to the most competent bidders or the winners of the 'beauty contest'. The Japanese UMTS operators can now concentrate on deploying the (expensive) network and the services over a longer period of experimentation and with the support of government policy.

Breakthroughs and Emergent Qualities

There are limitations to the foregoing argument, however. If one studies the greatest or most radical breakthroughs in the field of ISTs (such as the telephone, radio, or the Internet), it is clear that they are all marked by certain emergent characteristics. Borrowing from evolutionary biology, this concept suggests that an innovation is often unexpectedly and unintentionally more than the sum of its parts (Calvin 1992: 109):

Things can have certain qualities in combination, qualities which they do not have taken separately. The additional features are derived from the osmosis of the separate parts. We call them 'emergent qualities'. ... The flying of birds was probably the result of the simple invention of applying feathers for insulation. We cannot always predict what will happen. Most new acquisitions in evolution are probably the result of these emergent qualities.

Breakthroughs in ISTs can be seen as emergent qualities. This means that, depending on the socio-economic context and with variations through time and space, completely unexpected applications of technologies may pop up. For instance, the invention of the telegraph was an accidental spin-off during the search for a more efficient means of railroad management. Radio was discovered when researchers were side-tracked in their search for a better telegraph system. The Internet was a spin-off of the search for an efficient and less vulnerable military communication system. These spin-offs were unintentional and could not have been planned. But they can be explained in terms of a technical emergence within the context of their socio-economic dynamic. The emergent qualities principle is very important because it implies that radical changes are unpredictable.

The emergent qualities principle also implies that social knowledge has limits and that we should avoid a socially deterministic approach as well. Fine-tuning research in line with existing demand cannot be effective. The engineer's argument that social scientists failed to foresee the success of the personal computer and that it would have been wrong to stop research in this area is correct. But that does not mean that forecasting is pointless. Forecasting can be used to consider counterfactual developments and to ask, on the basis of past experience, what developments are least likely to achieve a breakthrough.

WHERE ARE THE SOCIAL SCIENTISTS?
The IST industry has worked within a strong 'technology push' paradigm and policy orientation. Non-technical scientists have been asked mainly to write business plans or to provide regulatory advice. But the policy spectrum is changing. The demand for social science is rising in policy circles and within firms. Unfortunately, the social sciences are not well-prepared for this, at least not in Europe. The reason seems to be that a lot of social science research on ISTs simply misses the boat. Many European Union studies on the impact of ISTs on employment, on the competitiveness of the consumer electronics industry in Europe, and on the relevance of these technologies for the accession countries joining the EU are important for social and economical policy. But it is extremely difficult to find good, comparative data and analysis. It is particularly amazing

that good social research is missing on the development and prospects of the content industries in Europe because the communication studies field is one of the most popular and fastest growing areas in academic research. But the more technologically complex the topic is, the less attention it seems to receive.

This tendency towards a lack of theory on technology or towards non-empirically based theory is certainly a reflection of the fact that ISTs are emerging in a complex world. Therefore, social science analysis of ISTs requires the addition of:

- Motivation: It is easier and more productive in terms of academic publications to study the impact of 'Baywatch' than to study broadband communication;

- Scale and multi-disciplinarity: Studying ISTs involves at least economic, social, legal, linguistics and ergonomic perspectives;

- Considerable resources: Teams and networks are needed and research is costly. Other costs include those for data gathering for reports and attending industrial conferences in the IST area. These costs must be incurred as this is the only way to keep abreast of this fast changing field.

The reasons that the social sciences are not delivering enough of what IST policy makers need can be attributed mainly to disciplinary lock in, on the one hand, and to the costs of research, on the other.

CONCLUSION: SHORTENING THE LONG WAY AHEAD

In order to become more relevant for IST policy, social scientists should, in the first place, produce good research. To facilitate this there is a need for specific structural conditions. Much more money should be made available for the social sciences in order to research the sector and to build interdisciplinary teams. The speed of change of the sector and its intrinsic complexity create the need for large research groups. Successful places where social science research in support of IST policy is produced has these characteristics as did the Programme on Information and Communication Technologies (PICT) in the United Kingdom, directed at the outset by Melody. It showed that significant results could be achieved quickly and that the spin off effects for the wider academic community could be large. Indeed, thanks to PICT, the United Kingdom has now a lead in social science IST research.

II.6

Virtual Solutions to Real Problems

Bella Mody

INTRODUCTION

Corporate and government decision makers in the world's only superpower have not been influenced by media coverage of starving populations in developing countries, United Nations resolutions, academic publications, or homilies from pulpits, and fundraisers to feed starving children for a few pennies a day. The bombing of the World Trade Center in New York in 2001 does not seem to have directed their attention to the root causes of poverty, inequality and disparity, in spite of threats to national security and corporate economic expansion. The response of the United States and its allies has focused chiefly on destroying symptoms (the 'enemy' in Afghanistan, the Philippines, Iraq, Iran or Somalia; and anti-globalisation protests), rather than attending to possible causes such as the present acceleration of international investments by industrial and financial capital without democratic regulation to benefit citizens, workers and consumers.

The globalisation of US-owned news and entertainment television media has enabled the world's population (approximately half of whom live on less than two US dollars a day) to see life with running water, homes with heat, clinics with antibiotics and schools with teachers. The expectation that humans have a right to food, clothing, shelter and communication has been globalised; constrained by purchasing power, economic demand has not followed. The expectation that all humans should enjoy the benefits offered by democracy has also been globalised; royal families and military dictatorships continue, with government support in some cases. Clearly, globalisation has not gone far enough beyond a specific form of economic expansion proposed by investors and bankers.

William Melody has questioned the recommendations of major international institutions on telecom policy recommendations for developing countries. This contribution focuses on what communication researchers who follow can do in the light of the material needs of people in developing countries. The essay presents some of the human development problems, reviews what communication researchers focusing on developing countries have done, and raises questions about future possibilities.

The Realities of Life and Death in Developing Countries

The 2001 UNDP Human Development Report describes significant gains in education, health and income over the last 30 years alongside continuing (and in some cases, worsening) levels of deprivation. The Arab states have made the most progress in education, health and income, while South Asia and Sub-Saharan Africa lag behind other regions. Gender inequality continues in every region, although the extent varies considerably between countries. Most countries have far to go to extend economic and political opportunities for women. Absolute gaps in income have increased between the richest 29 countries of the world (members of the OECD) and the rest of the world. Inequality between the rich and poor is very high: the richest 25 million in the United States had a combined income greater than the 2 billion poorest people in the world.

Of the 4.6 billion people in developing countries, 1.8 million live in extreme poverty on less than a dollar a day. More than 850 million are illiterate. Nearly a billion lack access to improved water resources. Some 826 million people are hungry and undernourished. Another 113 million primary school age children do not attend school. Girls account for less than two-thirds of boys' enrolment in secondary school in many countries. Poor people in low income countries have been the initial victims of HIV/AIDS, the virus spreads from them to all education and income groups.

Goals for poverty eradication set for 2015 by the United Nations General Assembly address these areas. Can research on expediting information access or on particular formats and interfaces for information provision play some part in addressing these basic problems? Under what conditions? Have they done so before?

The Contributions of Communication Researchers

The study of Communication as a formal discipline with its own university departments started in the United States in the 1950s. An early focus on media production skills (broadcasting and print journalism) training was supplemented by teaching and research on the psychology of persuasion and attitude change. Journalism, political propaganda and social psychology combined to staff Cold War initiatives to win friends for the United States from among developing country nationals, who were also being wooed by the Soviets. This was followed by UNESCO and USAID initiatives to use media to promote national modernisation attempts and sectoral improvements in education for agriculture, health, nutrition and family planning. Prominent players included American universities and their grantees supported by USAID money: Stanford University, Michigan State University, Wisconsin (Madison) and Iowa.

Everett M. Rogers and Wilbur Schramm evaluated a decade of their own work on the use of media for modernisation and development support to particular sectors and found it wanting. Since the constant drip of media programmes into homes in the United States continues to be financed by advertisers, the programmes must be succeeding in attracting audiences for their advertising. As part of a larger well thought out marketing plan, advertising works well. Is there a well thought-out development plan that communication interventions support?

Whether there are any lessons from the overall planning of consumption promotion and the role assigned to advertising-supported entertainment for the administration and design of distinct consciousness-raising empowerment initiatives has not been investigated. With the decline in funds for international development in the Reagan era, graduate programmes in Communication and Development closed down in the United States. Some opened in the United Kingdom and in other parts of Western Europe. Promotional research on particular formats and approaches, for example, entertainment, education and soap operas, continues with foundation support for Rogers and his former students. The World Bank and specialised agencies of the United Nations (for example, WHO, UNICEF, UNESCO) use like-minded consultants on an ad-hoc basis. Without the prescriptive focus of high-level funders, scholars with a disinterested critical agenda have begun to ask societal questions about the role of the state, the power of transnational corporations, development-support versus public participation, post-development goals, empowerment and, most recently, liberation theology and spirituality.

In the mid-1970s, USAID funded demonstrations of the power of telecommunication technology to bring about pro-social outcomes in developing countries as satellites were being introduced. These projects focused on how to use satellite technology and when. The US National Aeronautics and Space Agency also involved American universities in designing and evaluating national and regional pilot projects on satellite use for development. Policy-related telecom research came into its own with the deregulatory turn in the United States and the United Kingdom in the early 1980s. Research on the telecom industry in developing countries has included institutional analyses of funding agencies, analyses of who benefits and who loses from privatisation and deregulation, and studies of access expansion attempts through new technologies, tussles over regulatory models and the connectivity impacts of the Internet, for example, networking in virtual communities of low-income activists.

A new area of content research on manipulating information to teach, entertain and persuade focuses on virtual reality tools. Basic and applied research is taking place on immersion, interactivity and information intensity through wearable computers and networked simulators (of educational experiences such as surgery, aircraft flying and gaming among others). With foundation support, the MIT Media Lab has been working in Costa Rica to create an economically sustainable Internet connectivity solution. Computer networks are forging global communities, for example non-governmental organisations at the World Social Forum in Brazil protesting the present intensification of world trade and investment rules. The MIT Media Lab has also received initial funding from the Government of India to explore cutting-edge applications for developing country contexts and underserved populations in sectors such as commerce, agriculture, health care and education. The Indianisation of Linux is a possible agenda item. A thousand neighbouring villages are being connected to investigate whether viable markets exist for information services in rural areas. Stanford University and the Reuters Foundation are hosting research sabbaticals for digital entrepreneurs from developing countries.

Departments of Communication (frequently focused on journalism or mass communication, and, more recently, on information studies) have followed the United States curricula in Africa and in parts of Asia, based on where the faculty member did her scholarly preparation in the communication field. US-produced texts of the 1950s' vintage reprinted in low-cost Third World editions for developing country markets have been found in some countries. The most innovative work in indigenising conceptualisations of communication for the region has taken place in Latin America.

Is This the Best that We Can Offer?
In the 1960s, educational and entertainment media were seen as tools for development. Their impacts were not significant, for a variety of reasons, only some of which have been identified, for example, the lack of pre-production formative research for programme development to parallel similar research used in the successful design of advertising, and the lack of a financing mechanism for programme development in an era of advertising-free broadcasting. In the 1970s, it was satellites: their present day applications for telephony, data communication and remote sensing are substantial. In 2002, access to stand-alone unconverged media continues to be woeful in low-income countries that are home to the majority of the world's population.

Whether virtual tools will find financing and applications of significance in resource-strapped developing countries and whether virtual design will be preceded by task analysis and formative research that were lacking in the design of broadcast programmes remains to be seen. The focus on cutting-edge research on virtual reality in academic departments brings to mind the economic growth versus redistribution conflict in development economics. Could it be that what this world of inequitably distributed food, clothing, shelter and communication resources needs is down-to-earth organisation of interactive media access policies and content carriage models to balance the emphasis on economic growth-oriented content design?

Communication research that focuses on economic growth *alongside* communication research on public access and public distribution is essential. We need both growth research *and* distribution research. It is the slow distribution of antibiotics through an inadequate public health infrastructure that contributes to vulnerability to AIDS (through lack of treatment of genital ulcers) among the poorest regions of the world. Public access to the Internet is crucial through appropriate hardware. Appropriate software applications are also essential: stories are rife about villagers who come to tele-centres and ask operators to conduct searches to identify what jobs are available for unskilled illiterate agricultural labourers. Surely, this identifies a prior deficit in national job creation policy rather than only a deficit in database development with graphic user interfaces and touch screens for the illiterate.

Conclusion

Mansell and Wehn (1998) have written extensively about the challenges of moving developing countries into the information age. Developing indigenous solutions (for example, the low-cost Simputer designed in India) and then finding venture capital and production capital to get them to market is a major hurdle. The needs of the other half of the world's population do not constitute market demand: they have limited purchasing power. There is no incentive for private sector research and development to focus on how to meet their food, clothing, shelter and communication needs. Depictions of how ideas, goods and services diffuse when there is a middle-class marketplace (as in Everett Rogers' diffusion of innovation model) show that to those that have education, income and youth, more is given. How much research in international organisations, industrialised country universities and in developing countries is focused on developing models of distribution for those who live on less than $2 a day?

As historical hurt and contemporary grievances about the inequitable distribution of food, clothing, health and communication resources are harnessed by different global or local supporters of marginalised nations (for instance, Palestinians), workers, outcaste groups (for instance, the Dalits in India), religious splinter groups (such as fundamentalist Hindu, Christian and Islam), or women's and gay rights groups, where will high-income populations of the West find safety from hungry, angry mobs armed with weapons supplied by manufacturers of Cold War vintage? In 'gated compounds', fortresses with dungeons and dragons, and nuclear-safe bomb shelters the size of a sub-continent? The basic question for researchers who work on information and communication technologies in the public interest will be: what did we do to clearly identify and address the pre-digital social, economic and communication divides that will continue to ground digitally converged text, data, voice and video?

II.7

Challenging Orthodoxy

Liora Salter

INTRODUCTION

When William Melody came to Simon Fraser University in Canada, he faced a fractious department with an uneven record of teaching and research. By the time he was ready to turn his attention elsewhere, he had laid the foundations for a department with the profile and content of single field of study. Melody's challenge was far greater than, and quite different from, what any new Chair of a dysfunctional department might face. The job to be done was complicated by the fact that Communication was not a discipline, but an interdiscipline. The stresses and strains faced by established departments are multiplied many fold when interdisciplinarity is involved. The new field must be cut from fresh cloth, even while its faculty members define their work mainly in opposition to whatever discipline they have escaped from. Melody had to confront not only the entrenched interests of faculty members and students long accustomed to having their own way, but also the significant challenge of identifying a common bond and securing allegiance to it. That he succeeded in laying the foundations for a genuinely interdisciplinary department is without doubt, given that the Department of Communication grew, over time, to have an international reputation. This contribution explores what it is about interdisciplinarity that makes his accomplishment so noteworthy.

ALL DISCIPLINES BEGIN AS INTERDISCIPLINES

Some things look obvious but are not. The value of interdisciplinarity is one of those things. Any student of the history of disciplines knows that nothing is inherent in the collection of themes and approaches that today characterises disciplines (see Salter and Hearn 1996; Chubin et al. 1986; Klein 1990; Messer-Davidow et al. 1993; and Whitley 1984). Boxer (1998: 387) describes Women's Studies thus:

Women's studies is both a discipline and an interdisciplinary field. This seemingly oxymoronic statement can be seen on closer examination to reflect the pervasive confusion within higher education between departments and disciplines, the evolutionary process through which subjects (such as economics, political science and psychology) come to be considered disciplines, and the multiplicity of subject matters and research methods now housed in fields (such as anthropology, biology and classics) that are commonly called disciplines.

All disciplines began as interdisciplines. Even today, disciplinary fields are characterised by internal variety, by individual faculty members straining against the prevailing assumptions of their discipline to define new sub-fields and approaches. Battle lines are drawn to support the appearance of coherence.

The history student would also know that interdisciplinary scholars are only following in the footsteps of the great social theorists when they carve out new territory and bring up new topics for study. The story of interdisciplinarity is simply this: some academics want to break free from the labels and conventions of disciplines, and think they should be given licence to do so given that the academy is committed to supporting a restless and boundary-less search for knowledge. Seen in this light, interdisciplinarity should be less of a bold venture than the natural process of evolution in academic life, an example of academics fully engaged with ideas and social problems.

Theory and practice often diverge, especially when institutional constraints intervene. Universities in Canada fall over themselves to endorse the concept of interdisciplinarity, but jealously guard their resources in support of established disciplines.[2] They typically, but foolishly, cross-list courses without any regard for the different cultures associated with each field of study, or the operational problems posed for cross-appointed faculty members and students alike. They cast young faculty members into the role of institutional pioneers, asking them to challenge the entrenched interests of the established disciplines at the very moment when these young scholars must build a record of teaching and publishing to achieve tenure. They import senior faculty members from a variety of departments into the new interdisciplinary field, usually those on the margins of their existing department for one reason or other. Then they make no provision in terms of workload for the time needed to create intellectual credibility. They create so-called new units for no other reasons than administrative convenience, and wrap their actions in the cloak of virtue by reference to interdisciplinarity. When the result is a mish-mash of courses in a department without departmental status, or legitimacy and resources, the weakest students enrol. Interdisciplinary offerings are widely perceived to be 'bird courses', further lessening the possibility that something strong, in an intellectual and institutional sense, could ever be built. Simon Fraser University went against the grain in establishing several interdisciplinary fields of study as full departments with dedicated faculty members. Its foresight has been rewarded today with Schools and Departments of international repute. The path taken at Simon Fraser has not been followed in most other universities.

The difficulties of establishing interdisciplinary fields of study are intellectual as well as institutional, so much so that, even if universities were to change their priorities, serious obstacles would remain. Interdisciplinarity is tempting for poor scholars. Unfortunately, it is all too easy to turn one's attention to the intellectually fashionable, social problems of the day or to play with brilliant twists of logic in high theory (see Salter and Hearn 1996). Interdisciplinarity also gives licence to the hurried and careless, to scholars who dip, with impunity, into various literatures unaware of the historical meaning of their concepts and the long-standing debates among their practitioners. Vivid metaphors, an important component of scientific reasoning at its best, become excuses for not working through the implications of what is being said. The importance of the issues and the panache of theory become rationales for poor scholarship. Misrepresentation and distortion result. As Friedman (2001: 505) suggests, 'The dangers of epistemological and cross disciplinary travel are great, just as they are for spatial travelling – the tendency to misunderstand the other, appropriate the other, misuse the other or decontextualise the other'.

Method is Crucial

Method is crucial and in this, an interdisciplinary field of study is no different from a topic area within a discipline. In both cases, broad scope of inquiry and breadth of knowledge are important, but only if they can be achieved without sacrificing depth. Interestingly, Melody promoted interdisciplinarity, but his own work fits neatly within a single paradigm and a long-established tradition of scholarship, institutional economics. His is not the only method for achieving intellectual rigor in interdisciplinarity, but it is one of the more credible ones.

Unlike many interdisciplinary scholars, Melody did not think of interdisciplinarity as intrinsically connected to particular subject areas, such as Gender Studies, nor to metadisciplines, say Cultural Studies, nor even to new approaches to theory, for instance, postmodernism. He understood the content of interdisciplinarity much more loosely to mean the intellectual churn and challenge to the authority of established hierarchies within the disciplines. It was his contention that interdisciplinarity lent vibrancy to the academic enterprise. At its best, it forced serious scholars to reach beyond the confines of their narrow worlds, to use knowledge as well as collecting it. But Melody also understood that challenging orthodoxy would not be enough to establish the coherence of a field of study, nor the scope of its intellectual endeavours. Melody's phrase for what was needed, beyond a contrary and rebellious turn of mind, was 'a common bond'. He argued vociferously that those of us in Communication who wished to see it gain intellectual legitimacy needed to do some boundary work of our own (Gieryn 1983). A field of study that encompasses everything without focus or distinction has, by its very nature, no centre, he said. Nothing other than personal friendships would sustain a network of scholars beyond the point where going to conferences was still an exciting thing to do.

The process of constituting the subject matter for a field of study is not an easy one, of course. While it need not require exclusion (even the most well established disciplines have people on the margins continually challenging orthodoxy), serious work needs be done to identify the particular purchase of the field of study within the academic enterprise. Communication competes with Cultural Studies and Media Studies and Journalism. While the insiders to the competition appreciate the subtle differences amongst these three fields of study, the inside view is not good enough. The common bond of any field of study must be intelligible not only to the institutions that provide support (universities, granting councils, etc.) but also to colleagues and prospective undergraduate and graduate students. It must have intellectual weight.

In Communication, these difficulties were complicated yet again because several of the established disciplines claim some or all of the same intellectual resources. For example, Sociology has widened its span of interests to include such topic areas as media, interpersonal communication, cultural theory and the like. It is easy to envisage a situation where fully two-thirds of the curricula of Sociology and Communication might overlap, and where the same books and articles are represented on the two sets of course outlines. No one field of study should be able to claim property rights over the kinds of ideas that are the stock and trade of universities. Within the universities, however, intellectual resources often are treated as intellectual property. What Sociology or Economics have, Political Science and Communication must ignore, and so on.

At Simon Fraser, these problems were resolved, more or less. The common bond of Communication was eventually deemed to be technology and policy. Media Studies were included in the Department's offerings, as anyone would expect they should be, but the defining characteristic of Communication as a subject of study (at Simon Fraser) lay in the connection between media studies, on the one hand, and policy and technology, on the other. From this core focus, it was then possible for the Communication Department to expand its intellectual horizons outward, encompassing Cultural Studies and Publishing as integral but not defining components of the field. The lessons for others from the Simon Fraser experience are these: defining and agreeing upon a common bond for any field of study, whether interdisciplinary or not, is very time consuming, contentious and intellectually demanding. It matters little whether the same reference material is used in different fields of study if there are different angles of study, different focal points for each one. Finally, gathering a variety of loosely related research topics under a single umbrella, without identifying the common bond among them, is an excuse for poor scholarship, whatever the value of interdisciplinarity. Established disciplines face the same problems as interdisciplines, but they have an advantage in the struggle. Their institutional histories and privileges mask their lack of coherence. Interdisciplinary fields of study have to create and re-create themselves continually, and justify their efforts time and time again.

Interdisciplinarity

The emergence of interdisciplinarity is not helped by the fact that the word 'interdisciplinarity' can be an ideograph. The notion of an ideograph is McGee's (1980), and it requires some explanation before it is applied here. McGee's goal was to take account of ideological predisposition, specifically how predisposition is established in the face of a vast array of competing ideas and images in society. McGee argued that the crucial variable in ideological formation is language, or rather, individual words. Some words become more akin to pictographs than words (hence the term ideograph). That is, a single word can be used to stand in for whole philosophical or ideological approaches. Ideographs are used as handy linguistic shortcuts to convey a host of ideas; they represent a paradigm wrapped up in a single word. Adopt and use these words, thoughtlessly, and the result is that the paradigm, philosophy or ideology is adopted too, McGee argued. Ideology can thus be written into conversation carelessly, and without a single reference being made to the speakers' underlying assumptions and political messages. Words can be used as strategic resources in ideological battles never made explicit.

McGee had a much larger intellectual agenda than appreciating the fate of interdisciplinarity, but it is useful to think of interdisciplinarity as sometimes being an ideograph. Doing so allows us to appreciate that there can be more at stake in the fights about interdisciplinarity (and the institutional battles about the status of interdisciplinary fields) than is first apparent. Truth be told, new fields are created all the time, without much fuss. No-one sees the need to mount a campaign about the value of cognitive psychology or management of technology, yet Communication and Gender Studies would never have gained recognition without battles having been won. Something is happening when battles break out over interdisciplinarity, and McGee's notion is helpful in locating it.

One sees evidence of the ideograph when the label 'interdisciplinary' is claimed by those who see themselves dealing primarily with social issues (the environment, black or gender studies, etc.) or as intimately connected to politics (including the politics of knowledge) and policy making. What is on offer with this use of interdisciplinarity is not so much a new field as it is a serious challenge to the philosophy of the university as currently practised. In these instances, interdisciplinarity is not associated with new subject matter, nor with a common bond for a new field of study, nor even with new methodologies, so much as it is with a challenge to the intellectual priorities of the university. The challenge is this: while no-one seriously doubts that curiosity-driven research has social and political (and practical) implications, interdisciplinarity means reversing intellectual priorities. Politics and the pragmatic objectives of interdisciplinarity should be the driving force, and curiosity-driven research should be the instrument of their realisation. The long-standing self-image of the university as a seeker of untainted knowledge should be cast aside in favour of what William Melody, Dallas Smythe and others called a critical approach.

The second example of interdisciplinarity being used as an ideograph requires a little background information about events at Simon Fraser long after Melody had left. Faced with the dissolution of the catch-all faculty unit that had previously housed all of the evolving interdisciplinary departments, the Communication Department elected to join the Faculty of Applied Sciences, not the Faculty of Arts. A monumental battle culminated at Senate. In retrospect, it could not have mattered less where the Department of Communication was located within the University. The argument put forward by the Department (about working with colleagues who truly understood communication technology) had merit, but it was neither strong nor weak enough to carry the day. The real issue was that Communication had chosen a common bond that put it outside the social sciences/humanities nexus, where everyone expected it to be. Indeed, Communication had elected to perch itself on the cultural divide between the natural and technical sciences, on the one hand, and the social sciences/humanities, on the other.

The conventional wisdom at Simon Fraser, as elsewhere, is that the 'two cultures' mentality is a bad thing. The battle about the location of Communication at Simon Fraser tells another story. University bureaucrats argued that it was 'unnatural' for Communication to be located in the Faculty of Applied Sciences. In doing so, they drew attention to distinctions in the intellectual landscape that they regarded as unproblematic. This was no merger of natural and social sciences, as happens in cognitive psychology, for example. Rather, Communication was demanding that the traditional distinction between science and social science be put aside in favour of a new organisation of knowledge, one based upon 'interest groupings'. Communication researchers were saying that 'we have more in common with engineers studying communication technology than with sociologists studying the family'.

Simon Fraser is not a special case. The dividing line between the two cultures remains firm everywhere, despite protestations about the importance of interdisciplinarity. Each new interdisciplinary field of study is placed in its 'natural' home within the university, and no-one thinks anything of it. Social studies of science and technology are located within Faculties of Arts, for example, ensuring that science students are not really exposed to them. Science students take a token course in the humanities, but otherwise confine themselves to subjects within the sciences. University administrators create special faculties units to house everything that does not fit. Thus Urban Studies is grouped with Mass Communication and Gender Studies as if they had something in common. All are distinguished from disciplines like Political Science and Geography. This has the effect of ensuring that the new does not contaminate the old. Of course there are exceptions, but they are rarer than one might expect, given the almost universal support accorded to interdisciplinarity even by those who sequester it within the universities.

Conclusion

The Communication Department at Simon Fraser has now become the School of Communication, garnering strong institutional support despite its unusual faculty placement and its pride in being interdisciplinary. In the last 25 years, universities everywhere have rushed to embrace interdisciplinarity. But the reality is not very encouraging. What seems to be a smooth transition from discipline-based knowledge to interdisciplinarity is anything but. Environmental Studies is under siege in at least one Canadian university, and its enrolments are falling. By and large, Women's Studies has done well, institutionally speaking, but in almost every case, Women's Studies lacks departmental status (even though it often has graduate programmes) and dedicated faculty resources. Many other 'Studies' programmes have fared poorly, fading out after the initial burst of enthusiasm that gave them birth. Meanwhile, the granting agencies everywhere seem to believe that interdisciplinarity is a simple matter, something accomplished by team research, huge and unwieldy research centres, and partnerships with industry or by conveying research results to the public.

When he called for interdisciplinarity, Melody expected trouble. He relished a fight about important intellectual issues, then and now. He did not mind that interdisciplinarity represented something more than invigorating challenges to orthodoxy, that it was an ideograph as well as an idea. He liked the fact that the conceptual map informing university planning could be challenged even as new fields of study were created. He was quite prepared to use interdisciplinarity as a strategic resource to promote worthy intellectual and institutional purposes. Melody appreciated the fact that interdisciplinarity was (and is still) carelessly flung about in university Senate meetings, in their public relations and grant proposals, even though it bespeaks ideological conflicts of some magnitude. In this context, he equated the ideograph with opportunities to do more than the granting councils ever believed possible. The results of his efforts speak for themselves.

III

Change...

Harry M. Trebing

Aileen Amarandos Pisciotta

Edwin B. Parker

Tim Kelly

Heather E. Hudson

Márcio Wohlers de Almeida
and Ricardo Tavares

Alison Gillwald

Rudi Westerveld
and Carleen F. Maitland

Johannes M. Bauer

Martin Cave

John Ure

David Gabel

Jens C. Arnbak

Change...

Rohan Samarajiva, Robin Mansell and Amy Mahan

William Melody joined the US Federal Communications Commission (FCC) in 1966 as a member of its then very small economics staff. In the six years that he spent at the Commission, regulatory decisions that led to massive changes in the United States telecom sector, such as the Carterfone decision and the licensing of MCI, were taken. It can be argued that the proactive role played by the FCC in this period contributed to the efflorescence of the computer industry and the Internet, first in the United States and then world-wide. The reshaping of the telecom sector that began with the Carterfone decision that led to terminal devices including privately purchased telephones and computers being allowed to be attached to the network – continued through the Consent Decree breaking up what was at that time the world's largest company, AT&T. Melody, back in the university by this time, served as an expert witness in the Department of Justice case and in related private court cases that resulted in the Consent Decree.

In 1984, the year that AT&T divested itself into eight companies, significant sector reforms occurred in the United Kingdom and in Japan. In the United Kingdom, a new kind of regulatory agency, the Office of Telecommunications (OFTEL), was created. The processes of sector reform that have swept the world since then may be traced to these seminal events. From a world dominated by national Post, Telephone and Telegraph authorities (usually functioning as government departments) and private monopolies such as AT&T and Bell Canada, there emerged a blooming, buzzing confusion of multiple and varied operators. They were not fully unshackled from the bonds of incumbent domination, but were still relatively free to innovate, experiment, provide services, make money and, sometimes, fail. Users, first businesses and then others, have been given greater opportunities to gain access to a range of telecom and information services and, to some degree, to shape those services to their requirements. The heavy black telephone with the rotary dial gave way to, among innumerable others, the Mickey Mouse telephone. The world of telecom that Melody entered in the 1960s has changed beyond recognition.

There is evidence to suggest that Melody made a significant contribution to these changes. Edwin Parker, in this collection, argues that Melody's work on the economic theory of competition was a major contributor to economic growth throughout the world. It is, of course, not easy to establish definitively the individual causal links that underlie Parker's claim. Nor is it necessary, given the multiplicity of forces that transformed the monochromatic world of integrated-monopoly provision of telephony to the complex, many-hued reality of today. But it may be of interest to read some testimony from contemporaneous witnesses in addition to Parker. The then chief of the Common Carrier Bureau of the FCC, Bernard Strassburg, recounts the process leading to the decision in 1967 to issue the initial licence to Jack Goeken, the founder of MCI, then known as Microwave Communications Inc.:

There was a lot else going on, and what I had heard of the [MCI] hearings was mostly negative. Moreover, based on very few personal encounters with Goeken, I could not help but question his credentials to construct, own, and operate a common carrier system to compete with the likes of AT&T or Western Union. ... A week before the proposed findings were due, I initiated getting together with two of the staff economists who had worked on the case, Manley Irwin and Bill Melody. ... So I issued instructions to rewrite the bureau's position, which had been drafted as a denial, to recommend a grant (Henck and Strassburg 1988: 102-103).

Parker's contribution also refers to an AT&T executive being assigned to monitor Melody's activities. An erudite and passionate participant, perhaps made more so by his assignment, this executive wrote a book on the divestiture, in which he stated:

Differ as they might on particulars ... what is the relevant cost standard for competitive ratemaking, for example ... AT&T's economists and those of its opposition shared a common philosophy ... what here has been characterized as the economist's view of the way the world ought to work. Indeed, the layman is at a loss to discern any fundamental difference in the philosophies of, on the one hand, William Baumol, Alfred Kahn and Otto Eckstein, AT&T's original "board of economic advisors," and, on the other, the philosophies of William Melody, Bruce Owens or Manley Irwin, the company's *bêtes noirs*. ...

Others may have preceded Dr William F. Melody (sic) in forwarding the market prescription. None, however, have been more persistent in its articulation, not only in representations to the FCC but in testimony on behalf of plaintiffs against AT&T in antitrust suits, public and private. Indeed, Dr Melody's staying power has given rise to a ritualistic observation in regulatory circles that is so obvious that, if he must, the reader may supply for himself (von Auw 1983: 125, 132).

Melody's efforts at change did not stop at the United States border. Even if his contributions to sector reforms in the United States were to be considered in isolation, it may be argued that those reforms created the conditions for the changes in the United Kingdom and Japan in 1984. Those changes, in turn, affected the habits of thought (or institutions, according to Veblen 1899/1994: 131) that shackled the telecom sectors in the rest of the world. Contributors to other sections of this book describe his activities in establishing policy-relevant research centres and programmes in Australia, Canada, Denmark, The Netherlands and now, in cyberspace, in the form of LIRNE.NET (Learning Initiatives on Reforms for Network Economies, see <www.lirne.net>) and the World Dialogue on Regulation for Network Economies, at <www.regulateonline.org>. In addition, he has sought to assist regional or national organisations in Bhutan, India, Mexico, Morocco, Peru, South Africa and in numerous other countries.

The two international government organisations that affect telecom sector reform most are the International Telecommunication Union (ITU) and the World Bank. Melody has assisted both organisations in specific reform activities. He has also sought to contribute to institutional change within these organisations, most recently by conducting an assessment of the telecom and related initiatives of the World Bank Group in 2000. This evaluation prepared the ground for a new Sector Strategy Paper that will shape the Bank's activities in the information and communication technologies area. It is too early to reach conclusions on the efficacy of Melody's efforts at the Bank, but *Tim Kelly* provides an appreciative assessment of his earlier contributions to institutional reform at the ITU, the other multilateral body with a role in telecom sector reforms. The fact that these contributions are appreciated more than a decade later is testimony both to the historical sensibility of the writer and to the impact made by Melody.

The contributions made by Melody's colleagues in this section deal with many aspects of the processes of institutional change that he participated in and was affected by. Some address the global thrust of reform, looking at sectors across the world and situating specific reforms in an historical context. Others examine the telecom sector and the information infrastructure that the sector is in the process of becoming in relation to other network industries such as electricity and transport. In this section, one feels the excitement generated by the interplay of ideas that is characteristic of the academy, and also the import of those ideas in the policy arena.

Melody and others who belong to the same knowledge network or epistemic community (Haas 1990), continue to grapple with ideas on how to devise solutions to the many problems that remain and the new problems that have been created, with regard to delivering basic necessities for society through capital intensive systems or infrastructures. There cannot be a consensus or a party line on these matters. The questions are complex enough, as Heather Hudson points out in her contribution, that the process of arriving at answers must involve many voices.

Melody has, for most of his career, been associated with the institution of the university, but he has at no time been confined to it. The theories, the research, the findings, the questions have always been taken out to where they matter: 'Examination of research theories, methods, results, and policy proposals by contending interests in a real-world policy context can provide a more rigorous critical assessment of views than any provided in the more antiseptic atmosphere of professional journals and meetings' (Melody and Mansell 1983: 113).

The contributions in this section include an illustration of the interplay of ideas and policy in the real world – the case of the recent European third-generation mobile spectrum auctions. Not only are the basic concepts worked and reworked over many years, they are worked over by many people, some represented in this volume. The ideas are not taken to the policy process in some linear fashion, but in the ways so well described by Lindblom (1990). The conference, the workshop, the research report, the 'opening of the minds' by one for the ideas of another that John Ure describes in this section are the elements of the process that Melody continues to be engaged in. There were successes, one recent one being described by Ure; there also were failures. But there has been one constant: the 'staying power' denoted by Melody's shadow. It is certain that formal retirement from one university will not result in any change to that.

In his contribution, Melody's mentor, **Harry M. Trebing**, assesses the reform process in the United States, with emphasis on the growth of concentration and the resultant implications for the pricing and investment strategies of the 'deregulated' firms. He points out that after decades of reform in the United States, most, if not all, public utility industries still exhibit the well-established qualities of tight oligopolies: 'four leading firms, combined have 60 to 100% of the market and significant barriers to entry exist'. The problems in the areas of pricing and investment merit, in Trebing's view 'new inquiries into both industry performance and public policy reform'.

Aileen Pisciotta considers the problems facing regulation in the United States, bound as it is to a massive legacy of regulatory practices and a litigious culture, and proposes solutions that she argues will allow the realisation of the objective of hastening the transition to an information economy. While her subject matter is American, the problem of institutions or habits of thought serving as a drag on the achievement of social objectives, is certainly universal.

The final contribution in this group by *Edwin Parker* develops the argument that the theoretical and application-oriented work of Melody and his colleagues at the time of the beginnings of sector reform in the United States contributed to increased investment in the underlying infrastructure for information and communication technology services and thereby contributed to productivity gains and economic growth in the United States and elsewhere. Parker, a kindred spirit who also experienced the pain and joy of speaking truth to power, leavens his contribution with an account of the monitoring of dissenting experts by monopoly firms.

Increasing connectivity, a subject that has for long been, and continues to be, a priority in Melody's work, is addressed by Hudson, Wohlers and Tavares, Gillwald, and Westerveld and Maitland. *Heather Hudson* debunks a series of myths that she considers to be bedevilling reform processes, especially with regard to rural and under-served areas. She draws on her comprehensive experience in studying and advising governments and organisations throughout the world and presents lessons for policy. Wohlers and Tavares, and Gillwald, located in Brazil and South Africa, two of the most prominent countries of the developing world, address the urgent questions of post-privatisation reforms. Privatisation, the single decisive action so beloved by the multilateral agencies, has been completed. But the problems it sought to solve are not all solved; in fact, some new problems have arisen. Citizens, awakened from the torpor of government-owned integrated monopoly provision, have high expectations. The exigencies of surviving, if not prospering, in an interdependent, globalised economy require that businesses and citizens of developing countries have access to, and use, the information and communication services provided over telecom infrastructures. Privatisation, Wohlers and Tavares, and Gillwald argue, cannot be the end-all of reform.

Márcio Wohlers de Almeida and *Ricardo Tavares* situate the current phase of sector reform in the broader context of the Schumpeterian waves, so well described, and critiqued, by Freeman and his colleagues (Freeman and Soete 1997; Freeman and Louçã 2001). Their contribution identifies three key elements of the post-privatisation reform agenda, drawing from the rich experience of Brazil. The elements are the creation of a level playing field in service provision, the solution of the problem of increasing trade deficits in telecom equipment (also discussed in John Houghton's contribution in the *Next* section), and the cluster of issues around the theme of digital exclusion. While not every developing country has telecom and information technology R&D and manufacturing sectors that require repositioning in the new open-economy environments, the three items are of significance throughout the developing world. It may be argued, as would be by Melody (1999c; 2000; 2001c), that they should be on the reform agendas of industrialised countries as well.

Effective governance as a key, and under-appreciated, factor in the success of reform contributing to increased access to telecom and Internet services is the focus of *Alison Gillwald*'s discussion of access and affordability. Her contribution must be read in the context of the South African sector reform process that was accompanied by high expectations and has resulted in correspondingly deep disappointment (Horwitz 2001; International Telecommunication Union 2001). It is also instructive to read the Hudson, Wohlers and Tavares, and Gillwald contributions together. They are of one mind on the overall objective of providing access to telecom and Internet services to those who were hitherto excluded by monopoly providers. However, there are significant differences on issues such as cross-subsidies and assumptions regarding the ability to pay, especially between Hudson and Gillwald.

A former regulator and now an active participant in South African policy and regulatory processes, Gillwald reflects on the experience of post-Apartheid South Africa's telecom reforms and locates the solution in effective and workably independent regulation that allows informed and inclusive participation. It is interesting that Hudson, and Wohlers and Tavares also end their contributions with this same conclusion. This is an issue that has absorbed much of Melody's energies in recent years, as manifest by the mission and activities of his current organisational vehicle, LIRNE.NET.

Rudi Westerveld and *Carleen Maitland* outline the broader technological menu that is now available to policy makers and entrepreneurs wishing to provide rural connectivity. Reflecting the rapidly moving and decentralised nature of technological innovation in this area, their contribution describes an Indian variation of digital European cordless telecommunications (DECT) technology, that potentially could address Hudson's concerns about the limited capacity of the European standard.

The contributions by Bauer, Cave and Ure constitute a fascinating vignette on the interplay of inquiry and change that characterises Melody's career. Informed by the recent dramatic developments in the application of economic theory to regulatory practice in the form of third generation mobile spectrum (3G) auctions, *Johannes Bauer* urges the careful comparative assessment of the efficacy of different regimes, ranging from private property rights to rule-governed commons approaches, for managing the scarce resource of spectrum.

Martin Cave, a participant in the recent spectrum policy debates, examines Melody's early and recent contributions on the efficient management of this resource. Melody who criticised the limitations of administrative procedures and advocated a limited use of market mechanisms in his early interventions also strongly criticises the recent introduction of market mechanisms in the form of auctions. Cave suggests that Melody's critiques are valid but that he should go further, to adopt a full-fledged private property rights solution, of the type outlined in Bauer's contribution.

John Ure speaks from the trenches of policy debate. He describes the pernicious effects and fallacious premises of the European 3G auctions in 2000. He also illustrates the interplay of inquiry and change with Melody's speech to policy makers in Hong Kong, the first indications of a change in legislative thinking, his own policy interventions, and academic debate with Martin Cave. That Hong Kong, along with Denmark, another country where regulators listened to Melody, adopted a novel, royalty-based solution to the problem of assigning 3G spectrum is indicative of the efficacy of informed engagement with the policy process.

The contribution by *David Gabel* on debates in United States policy circles about telecom interconnection regimes covers both the history of the different forms of interconnection schemes and considerations about how this 'cornerstone of competition' (Melody 1997a: 53) is affected by the new patterns of traffic and cost causation resulting from the increased presence of data communication operators in the market and the spread of packet switched networks.

Readers familiar with interconnection debates in developing countries may be somewhat bemused to find that serious recommendations are being made from within what is claimed to be the 'oldest telecommunication regulatory agency in the world' to abandon the reciprocal compensation model for 'bill-and-keep' or 'sender keeps all'. In most developing countries, bill-and-keep is a stop-gap solution implemented while the prices for reciprocal compensation are calculated or negotiated. Its primary attraction is ease of implementation because it does not require the measurement of traffic nor the settlement of payments. It is therefore considered ideal for situations where the regulatory agency is not well-established and the 'high degree of cooperation' between the interconnecting networks that Gabel refers to is non-existent. It is widely recognised that bill-and-keep type schemes are inimical to the extension of service to rural areas. It would be ironic if, for the sake of addressing a small problem of termination payments to new entrants that host Internet Service Providers, the United States were to deviate from the principle of cost-oriented rates enunciated in the Regulatory Reference Paper of the World Trade Organization (1997: Art. 2.2(b)).

Jens Arnbak is the founding Chairman of the Dutch regulatory authority, Onafhankelijke Post en Telecommunicatie Autoriteit (OPTA). Arnbak's contribution addresses multi-sector regulation, an issue of contemporary interest that is discussed in depth in Samarajiva, Mahan and Barendse (2002) and in Samarajiva and Henten (2002) within the World Dialogue on Regulation for Network Economies, directed by Melody. Wohlers and Tavares also touch on this issue in their contribution in this section. Arnbak closes the circle, taking as his starting point the work by Trebing on network industries that was an element in Melody's intellectual formation. Arnbak systematically analyses aspects of contemporary network industries, including questions of market power and incentives to interconnect on the part of Internet Service Providers, an issue that is discussed in the United States context by Gabel. He draws his conclusions from technical and economic analyses and also from the pragmatics of policy making and regulation.

Utility Deregulation in the United States: A Critical Evaluation

Harry M. Trebing

INTRODUCTION

William Melody has devoted much of his professional career to the critical evaluation of the institutions and methods by which society meets its needs. He has studied a wide range of topics from telecom policy to economic growth in developing economies. Melody has always recognised that academic research must be complemented by an active involvement in education programmes to reach the widest public audience. Throughout his work, he has never hesitated to examine the shortcomings and abuses inherent in the application of neo-classical economics to the problems facing society. His well-known criticisms of marginal cost pricing and the natural monopoly concept as applied by AT&T have been major contributions to the literature, as has his work directed toward rehabilitating costing as a tool for proper pricing.

This contribution examines a number of the results of deregulation of public utility industries in the United States. It endeavours to show how institutional economics, as practised by Melody and others, sheds new light on the nature of the problems and the shortcomings of potential solutions. The deregulation movement grew after 1970 because of a lack of confidence in regulatory institutions as a source of protection, the poor performance of many incumbent public utility managers, the desire of large buyers for price concessions and a belief that pluralistic supply would promote innovation and efficiency. It was widely accepted that emerging competition would put the most efficient infrastructure in place, that market power would not be sustainable in the long run because of new entry, and that any network economies could be easily realised through full interconnection.

Experience in the real world turned out to be quite different. The decline in economic regulation has been matched by a parallel growth in market concentration at national and global levels. Concentration, in turn, has created new opportunities for manipulative pricing and investment strategies that will adversely affect both industry performance and society as a whole. These interrelationships between concentration, pricing, and investment are examined, together with options for reform.

Factors Promoting Concentration

Public utility industries have long been recognised as capital intensive systems of supply providing basic necessities in differentiated markets. There are two forms of economic advantage inherent in these systems that will benefit players able to take advantage of them. Network economies arise because public utility production and distribution systems are capable of achieving substantial joint production economies, economies of scale and scope, and gains in the form of improved network functionality. Coordination economies arise from matching diverse usage and demand patterns with a capital-intensive supply system. Both gains require a minimum size and a minimum market share.

Once realised, these economies will permit peak demand to be met with minimum capital investment, new services to be added at successively lower incremental costs and improvements in reliability and flexibility. The prospect of such gains will appeal to both facility-based utilities and to deregulated marketers, brokers and resellers. If a marketer or reseller wants to offer one-stop shopping or rebundled service at the retail level, it must contract for the input as a commodity but must also lease capacity and network components and services. In effect, the marketer or reseller is acting as a network manager who must achieve all inherent network and coordination economies.

Successfully exploiting these features creates an opportunity to exercise market power that will give the firm discretionary control over prices and investment. This market power will further reinforce concentration. It is not unexpected, therefore, that tight oligopoly is becoming a distinctive feature of deregulation. Tight oligopoly exists when the four leading firms, combined, have 60 to 100% of the market and significant barriers to entry exist. A review of recent pricing and investment strategies under tight oligopoly follows.

Pricing Strategies

Pricing can be employed to foreclose entry, retain existing customers, enter new markets, employ new technologies, recover stranded costs, and mitigate price wars. Recent electricity pricing initiatives demonstrate entry foreclosure and customer retention tactics. Residential and small business customers are given standard offers that consist of a low initial price for a given time period. At some future date this price will switch to market-based prices. If the residential customer selects an alternative supplier and is dropped by that supplier (especially at a peak period), the customer can return to the utility but only at a high default price. Under this arrangement there is no incentive for rivals to enter the market at the standard-offer price. Large buyers of electricity will be offered special contracts that tie them to the incumbent utility for six to ten years in return for a promise to match lower prices offered to other large buyers or the lower prices offered by new entrants.

Pricing to enter new markets, employ new technology, or recover capital and stranded investment requires the skilful application of customer differentiation, price discrimination and cross-subsidisation. The goal will be to shift costs to the basic service customer whenever possible. At the same time, the oligopolist will vigorously resist any regulatory attempt to impose new costing standards on the grounds that these markets are competitive and the information is proprietary. Stranded costs in electricity, for example, can be recovered by the simple expedient of imposing a surcharge on anyone using the grid, whether buying from the incumbent or from a new entrant.

Price leadership or conscious parallelism will be driven by the need to maintain or enhance profits. It will be reinforced by the need to cover the heavy debt burden associated with carrier and utility merger and acquisition programmes. On the other hand, excess capacity and large buyers with oligopsony power will erode such pricing. There are a number of empirical examples of price leadership or conscious parallelism in telecom, primarily among the long-distance carriers (interexchange carriers, or IXCs) where prices were raised in lock-step even though the access fees they paid to the local phone companies fell significantly.

Conscious parallelism can translate into collusive behaviour when constrained supply exists. Constrained supply can be achieved through limitations on access to the network or, in the case of electricity, by taking generators out of service. For example, in California, five times as many power plants were out of service in August 2000 as in August 1999. This aggravated the wholesale price fly-up while facilitating manipulation of bid prices paid to deregulated generators and marketers. These tactics under constrained supply prompted California to claim that it had been overcharged by US$ 8.9 billion during the period May 2000-July 2001 (Schmitt 2001).

Investment Strategies

Tight oligopoly facilitates the employment of investment to maintain or expand dominance through mergers, acquisitions, and a variety of alliances and joint ventures. There have been horizontal, vertical and conglomerate mergers in electricity, telecom and natural gas. In electricity, the number of pending and completed mergers increased from US$ 8.9 billion in 1994 to US$ 312.5 billion in 2000. In telecom, IXCs have merged vertically, seeking to reach their final customers directly. Concurrently, the seven original Regional Bell Holding Companies (RBHCs) were reduced to four by merger, with each retaining over 95% of the local exchange market. In natural gas, El Paso Energy acquired Coastal Corporation and other properties to become the largest American pipeline and the world's largest and most broadly based pipeline and natural gas producer. Concurrently, a number of aggressive electricity utilities have created deregulated trading affiliates and acquired generating plants in other service territories as well as outside the United States. The financial markets enthusiastically supported all of these investment programmes, viewing them as part of the utility industries' adaptation to the 'new economy'.

By late 2000, however, it was evident that major segments of the telecom industry were being severely impacted by an economic downturn and the emergence of excess fibre optic capacity. New broadband entrants, competitive local exchange carriers (CLECs) and IXCs were particularly hard hit. The incumbent local exchange carriers (ILECs), consisting primarily of the RBHCs, were less adversely affected. These differential effects are shown in the relative fall in stock prices for each group. Between 4 April 2000, and 4 April 2001, share prices for the 28 CLECs and new broadband carriers fell 94%; share prices for five IXCs (including AT&T Wireless) fell 70%; and share prices for the four RBHCs fell 39%. These declines also had broad ramifications for the entire economy. The *Wall Street Journal* estimated that 'The telecom bust ... has wiped out almost $2 trillion in stock market wealth, losses which are dampening household spending. Billions more stand to be lost on defaulted telecom debt. ...' (Blumenstein et al. 2001).

Additional conclusions can be drawn from this experience. First, financial markets will accelerate a boom and undoubtedly worsen recovery. Second, entry has proven to be an ineffectual constraint on market power at the local exchange level. CLECs, cable companies, and IXCs have had a negligible impact on the market shares of ILECs. Third, the RBHCs – especially as they enter into long-distance and broadband markets – have emerged as the new source of market power in the United States telecom industry, possibly placing them in the best position to enjoy network and coordination economies. Fourth, it is far from clear that rivalry between cable and Digital Subscriber Line (DSL) for broadband customers will approximate to a competitive outcome. Fifth, alliances and joint ventures appear to have fallen into disfavour as the major American and European telecom carriers proceed with financial and organisational restructuring.

Electricity investment has not suffered from excess capacity or a decline in demand. However, there are danger signals for the future. First, new entry into residential retail markets has been insignificant. This will minimise consumer choice and reinforce incumbent utility market power. Second, greater wholesale price volatility will increase risk and the cost of capital, thereby raising retail prices. Third, the rapid growth of holding companies will strengthen the position of affiliated generators and marketers by giving them access to lower capital costs. Fourth, the organisation of the grid as a common carrier remains to be satisfactorily addressed. Under these conditions, it is highly probable that any threat of excess capacity will be resolved through mergers leading to further concentration.

Impact on the Poor

Deregulation has attempted to handle the impact of rising prices for electricity and natural gas by introducing federal and state welfare or energy assistance programmes for the poor. During the winter of 2000, there was a 30% increase in the number of people requesting such aid. It is clear that this problem will worsen over time as residential rates rise while industrial rates for electricity decline. In telecom, the problem not only involves the consequences of rising rates for local basic phone service, but also the need to assure adequate service in rural markets and the need to bridge the digital divide between low-income families and the rest of the economy. The universal service fund appears to be the principal effort to maintain service in rural, high-cost telecom markets.

The Challenges for Institutionalist Reformers

This overview of the outcomes of deregulation points to the need for new inquiries into both industry performance and public policy reform. It is no longer sufficient to rely on tailoring reality to fit the axioms of neo-classical economics. The Melody legacy will be a rich source of knowledge for everyone carrying on this task. Of particular value will be William Melody's efforts to create meaningful cost-of-service standards for controlling cross-subsidisation as part of public policy reform (see Melody 1971; 1976a; 1976b).

United States utility policy is currently at an impasse. The popular response to the US electricity crisis is to call for price caps, but price ceilings are only an interim stopgap that does not mitigate oligopolistic pricing practices. In telecom, the principal constraint appears to be reliance on excess capacity and intermodal rivalry between cable and DSL to control market power. Proposals have been made to protect consumers through the introduction of countervailing power, municipal ownership and structural reform. Countervailing power has been employed on a very limited basis through buyer aggregation to purchase electricity and natural gas. The difficulty is that when aggregation is applied only to residential customers, the poor load factors of these customers greatly diminishes their bargaining power and their ability to participate in joint production economies. California introduced a form of countervailing power when it purchased electricity directly from deregulated suppliers. The problem, of course, is that overpayment may occur under conditions of constrained supply. Municipal ownership is staging a modest recovery as at least 12 cities (ranging from Seattle, Washington, to Glasgow, Kentucky) have created new, high-speed fibre networks to serve their citizens. This has prompted cable and local telephone companies to convince nine state legislatures to prohibit municipal provision of telecom services. California also entered public ownership by creating a California Power Authority in 2001 with US$ 5 billion in bonding authority to finance power generation projects. This could serve as a yardstick to measure the performance of deregulated merchant generators.

Structural separation of networks has received significant attention. The proposals vary from functional separation with nominal changes in actual ownership to full structural separation with complete independence in ownership, management and financing. Anything less than full structural separation, especially for power grids and pipelines, creates a potential for manipulative strategies. In telecom, voluntary separation and divestiture are taking place among IXCs because of financial difficulties. At the same time, the Pennsylvania Public Service Commission has mandated full structural separation of the local phone network from the marketing of services on that network. A final decision is still pending. In New York, structural separation was successfully applied to the Rochester Telephone Company in 1995, with the local network and basic service remaining under regulation while the parent holding company was free to provide a host of deregulated services.

The Enron scandal has shown that market failure and remedial public intervention must be considered in a holistic context. Enron moved on a number of fronts to rapidly establish itself as the largest American trader in electricity, natural gas, broadband communication, and ancillary services. Through aggressive political lobbying it was able to exempt its lucrative derivative trading activities from federal oversight. At the same time, it was able to manipulate profits, disguise corporate losses, persuade the independent auditor to destroy records, and possibly fix the prices for trading contracts and hedging derivatives at artificially high levels. Regrettably, a badly fragmented system of residual regulation was incapable of constraining Enron's aggressive strategies. Enron collapsed completely in 2001 creating the largest bankruptcy in American history. Many sectors were adversely affected and there have been demands for reform. Unfortunately, salvage efforts appear to focus only on selected parts of the Enron problem, such as accounting reform and improved auditing. What is absent is a recognition of the full panoply of steps needed to prohibit Enron-type behaviour in the future.

On balance, all of these partial solutions leave the door open for the followers of William Melody and institutional economics to make a major contribution. The problems created by deregulation have hardly begun to be resolved.

III.2

Telecom Policy for Information Economies: Unregulation is not Enough

Aileen Amarandos Pisciotta

THE CHALLENGE

The past two decades have witnessed major reforms of telecom markets and regulatory structures around the world through privatisation and liberalisation (Pisciotta 1997). These reforms have been focused primarily on changes in ownership models and market entry opportunities. They have not yet substantially addressed an essential challenge facing modern telecom policy, namely, how to reconcile sector-specific policies with the emerging exigencies of a digital information-based economy.

There is a sea-change underway in the way networks and services are configured, operated and used: the expansion of 'dumb' networks carrying smart information packets, the continuous innovation of multimedia terminals at the edges of networks, the evolution of business niches across both vertical and horizontal layers of networks, and the emergence of voice applications as secondary features of data services. Telecom services, combined with information technology, provide the infrastructure for data applications that drive all facets of industrial economies, including utility services, financial services, manufacturing, media, retail and even government services. More than revolutionising the telecom industry, these changes are transforming it into an integral element of the economy as a whole.

Information service innovations, however, strain against the reins of traditional regulatory concepts. Clear distinctions between types of services are proving elusive. Established regulators yearn for a multimedia future, but find themselves caught in the bonds of the voice telephony paradigms of the past. New regulators struggling to master the tools to referee competition in conventional telecom industries must leapfrog into the information age. This requires that decision makers around the globe grapple with a familiar, but suddenly confounding question: what is being regulated and why?

TRADITIONAL IDEAS

Established regulatory and policy traditions obscure the answer to the question. One tradition is that public voice telephony is a protected service to be specially licensed and regulated for the public good, either as a service 'affected with the public interest' as recognised in common-law countries, or as a 'public service', in civil-law countries (Melody 1997b). Another traditional concept equates 'universal service' to the widespread availability of voice service over traditional technologies funded through service-specific subsidies.

Regulatory systems that accord a special status to public voice telephony tend to perceive the Voice over Internet Protocol (VoIP) as threatening the viability of traditional telephony. To the extent that the Internet is used for voice applications that might otherwise be sent over the public network, regulators may view it as a form of bypass that avoids universal service contributions. Such a view supports policies that impose on the new service the inherited constraints of the old. Such 'technological neutrality', however, places the public interest in legacy handcuffs. The debate should not be about how VoIP can be made to be more like circuit-switched telephony, but about how to best utilise the full range of multimedia applications, including voice. The problem posed by VoIP is not how to avoid bypass of a subsidy, but rather how to restructure the subsidy so that it does not impede acceptance of the valuable new service. Many regulators have yet to address this issue.

A new approach will become necessary as voice becomes increasingly indistinguishable from other data traffic. Traditional features of telephony regulation (for example, the licensing of 'facilities', control of per-minute rates, ensuring non-discriminatory offerings) cannot meaningfully be applied to voice provided over multimedia platforms. Such platforms are characterised by integrated feature-rich services provided over internetworked facilities and layered applications involving multiple interdependent niche players. In such a context, it becomes very difficult to identify or license individual providers of discrete 'facilities', or to price basic voice separately from other value added features. The more public policy tries to segregate and safeguard the provision of pure voice telephony over a particular technology, the more it denies the future.

Similarly, in light of the ubiquity of packet-based multimedia applications throughout the economy, efforts to ensure universal service solely through voice-telephony subsidies ultimately will be unsustainable.

THE UNITED STATES EXPERIENCE
In the United States, the Federal Communications Commission (FCC) sought to preserve an unregulated environment for new information services in the hope that it would reveal alternative regulatory concepts (Oxman 1999). Instead of

clarifying regulation appropriate for Internet services, this approach has created uncertainties and required a stretch of logic.

For example, enhanced-service providers in the United States have long been classified as 'end users', exempt from access charges and permitted to use interstate access services under local tariffs (Federal Communications Commission 1983). To ensure the same benefit to Internet Service Providers (ISPs), the FCC has had to creatively assert jurisdiction over the compensation regime for local ISP-bound traffic on the basis of a 'one-call' theory, that is, the end-to-end transmission between the end user and the Internet is not actually local, but is inherently interstate (Federal Communications Commission 2001a). Similarly, the FCC is currently trying to reconcile a series of decisions containing widely divergent views on the regulatory classifications of 'information', 'telecommunication', or 'cable' service applicable to interactive broadband offerings on cable television systems (Federal Communications Commission 2001c). In another example, both phone-to-phone telephony over IP networks and facilities-based Internet transport services have been characterised by the FCC as 'telecommunication services' subject to Universal Service Fund obligations (Federal Communications Commission 2001b). Nonetheless, these offerings have never been regulated as telecom services and remain exempt from universal service contributions.

Zero-based Policy

To avoid the difficulties experienced in the United States, information and telecom policies ideally should be 'zero-based'. Beginning as if there were no public voice telephony legacy, an understanding should be developed about how information networks operate, who the players are, and how they function, including in secondary markets. Careful consideration should be given to what aspects of information networks, if any, raise public interest concerns, exactly what those concerns are and which regulatory tools can address them effectively.

In reality, there are strong incentives to work within current statute and case law, to retain familiar regulatory classifications and standards, to avoid significant disruption of industry relationships, and to avoid major changes to existing subsidies. Incumbent power, fear of local rate increases and reluctance to regulate the Internet are likely to preclude the zero-based policy approach.

The Practical Alternative

An alternative to 'unregulation' and zero-based policies is a deliberate evolution towards the future. This requires proactive regulatory intervention to realign industry relationships that may hinder the transition to the information economy. It also requires regulatory forbearance on innovations leading to the information age. At least three essential legs of a transitional regulatory platform may be discerned.

First, regulation should promote an information-based economy. Universal service should be redefined in terms of such an economy, and with different facets requiring different approaches. To the extent that universal service objectives include advanced information systems, subsidies might best come from general tax revenues. On the other hand, to the extent that universal service objectives are focused on voice telephony, alternatives to market-distorting service surcharges might be explored. For example, voice may be provided as a secondary application over many types of platforms. A variety of voice activated and interactive information services, including those developed for transportation systems, utilities, home security and on-line retail applications, may provide serviceable substitutes for voice telephony, particularly if they interconnect with the public network. New subsidy mechanisms that will promote such alternatives should be devised.

Second, regulation must be incentive-based. Specifically, incumbent companies must be given appropriate incentives to open their networks to competitive suppliers and to refrain from abusing their market power. To benefit from an open and interoperable network of networks, regulation should ensure that infrastructure is not designed and managed solely in the interest of incumbents, but that, at least on a wholesale basis, non-discriminatory interconnection is ensured for all technologies supporting a full spectrum of innovative business plans. This will require that non-discriminatory interconnection of all types of networks and technologies be made financially attractive. It will also require an intensive regulatory focus on standards of interconnection as well as on the swift resolution of disputes.

Third, to the greatest extent possible, market distortions, including asymmetries in the treatment of different technologies and selectively applied subsidies, must be removed. For example, transport systems should be treated consistently, whether they are provisioned over fibre, cable television, terrestrial wireless systems or satellite. The treatment of content should be harmonised across different delivery systems. In doing so, however, public policy should not burden new delivery systems with legacy obligations, but instead should reduce such obligations from traditional services.

All three legs must be implemented as, in the case of a three-legged stool, the absence of one leg will make the stool become completely unstable.

III.3

The Toppling of the Natural Monopoly Doctrine

Edwin B. Parker

William Melody's early work on the economic theory of telecom competition was a major contributor to economic growth throughout the world in the latter part of the 20th century. In the 1950s and 1960s, the prevailing economic theory was that telecom was a 'natural monopoly' and therefore should be a government-regulated or government-owned monopoly.

In the United States the AT&T monopoly, familiarly known as Ma Bell, dominated all aspects of telecom. Other telephone companies did operate in geographic locations not served by AT&T, but they interconnected with AT&T for long distance services and did not compete with AT&T. Most economists who researched or wrote on telecom issues were supported financially by AT&T or accepted the prevailing natural monopoly theory.

Melody was foremost among the very few qualified and respected economists whose research, writing and public testimony challenged the prevailing dogma. What was new in the decades following World War Two was the emergence of a new telecom technology, microwave radio communication. Melody's then novel argument (later proven correct) was that when technology is changing, the assumption of natural monopoly is not correct. Melody's economic arguments were a key factor in persuading the US Federal Communications Commission to grant to a start-up entrepreneurial company called Microwave Communications Inc. (MCI) licences for microwave radio frequencies on the route between Chicago and St Louis and a licence to sell private line long distance services on that route.

AT&T understood the risks to its monopoly and vigorously opposed Melody's arguments at every opportunity. An AT&T executive was assigned to work full time on monitoring all of Melody's writings and oral public statements. (Since AT&T's regulated monopoly status permitted telephone charges to users that recovered all costs plus an allowed profit, AT&T users paid all of the salary and other costs associated with that executive's work.) The executive had the task of monitoring all statements by Melody and coordinating AT&T's public response to his novel arguments.

One of Melody's arguments was that if the provision of long distance telecom service by any and all technologies was a natural monopoly, then AT&T had nothing to fear from a risk-taking entrepreneurial company. If AT&T's natural monopoly assumption was correct, then the MCI experiment was doomed to failure. If the natural monopoly assumption was correct, there was no need to protect that monopoly with regulations barring competitive entry. If, as Melody believed, the assumption was false, there was no need for government regulations designed to protect a contrary-to-fact economic theory.

That early work by Melody was a major factor that led to the regulatory precedents that opened the United States telecom market to competition. The total investment in telecom infrastructure following those precedents increased because competitors made investments that the incumbent monopolist would not have made. The pressure of competition also forced the incumbent to invest in new technologies at a faster pace than would otherwise have been the case. The resulting increased investment in the telecom sector in the United States was a major contributor to the productivity gains and the growth of the United States economy in the last third of the 20th century. A number of econometric studies have confirmed that telecom investment leads to economic growth (Parker et al. 1995; Hardy 1980; Cronin et al. 1991; 1992; 1993a,b).

The demonstrable success of telecom competition as an engine of economic growth in the United States led to competitive policy being emulated by other countries that were serious about growing their economies. Melody deserves credit as a major contributor to the resulting global economic growth.

III.4

Never-ending International Telecommunication Union Reform

Tim Kelly

Introduction[3]

Throughout his long and distinguished career, William Melody had a number of dealings with inter-governmental organisations, like the International Telecommunication Union (ITU). Melody worked for the ITU on a number of occasions, especially in seminars and workshops in developing countries and in providing training to students from those countries. One particular contribution, for which the membership of the ITU is eternally grateful, came in the work of the high-level committee on ITU Reform that sat in the late 1980s and early 1990s. For the high-level committee, which was headed by another Canadian, Gaby Warren, Poul Hansen and Melody (1989) contributed an analysis of 'The changing telecommunication environment'. The report was influential in shaping the future of the ITU. Indeed, the phrase 'changing telecommunication environment' entered the lexicon of the ITU. Even to this day, its use is *de rigueur* when drafting an ITU report or resolution.

The history of the ITU stretches back to 17 May 1865 and it would not be inaccurate to say that the process of reform began the very next day. Getting agreement on a direction and a programme for reform is hard, especially in an inter-governmental organisation with a diverse membership of different countries. It is harder for one like the ITU where, uniquely, the private sector works in partnership with member governments. There have been a number of key moments in reform, notably in times of international crisis, such as in the early 1930s, when different component parts were brought together, and just after World War Two, when the ITU joined the United Nations system. In the absence of such external stimuli, it is hard to get the membership to agree upon much at all beyond bland statements, and even harder to get them to implement change.

Significance of the 1989 Reforms

It is all the more remarkable therefore that the 1989 reform (which was partially enacted at the Plenipotentiary Conference in Nice that year, and completed at an additional Plenipotentiary Conference in Geneva in 1992) achieved so much. Certainly, the subsequent attempts, in 1994, 1998 and in the build-up to the Marrakesh Plenipotentiary in 2002, have been nowhere near as radical or successful.

The main achievement of 1989, to which Melody contributed greatly, was to create a three-sector structure of the ITU: the ITU-T (Telecommunication Standardisation) sector took over from the former CCITT; the ITU-R (Radiocommunication) sector combining the CCIR and the International Frequency Regulation Board (IFRB); and a new ITU-D (Development) sector was created, giving the policy work on telecom development and, latterly, regulatory reform, the same status as the technical work of the other sectors.

The 1989 reform also tidied up some of the internal management of the ITU, which had become dominated by the five permanent members of the IFRB. With the new structure, each of the Directors of the Bureaux of the Sectors had one voice alongside the Secretary-General and the Deputy Secretary-General on the Coordination Committee of the ITU. The IFRB was converted into the Radio Regulations Board and separated from the management of the Union. Eventually, the full-time members became part-time members, though their number continues to be debated at every subsequent plenipotentiary conference.

To an outsider, these changes may appear cosmetic, but they marked the end of an era. Like much of the United Nations system during the Cold War, the ITU had become paralysed by the superpowers. Control of the radio frequency spectrum and of satellite orbital slots had many implications for defence, as well as for broadcasting and telecom. The superpowers used the IFRB to play out the different battles they were carrying out by proxy in their satellite states around the world. Views became polarised and the ITU itself was reduced to the status of a dumb secretariat, translating and photocopying the various bargaining positions. The international treaty that governs the use of the international frequency resource, the Radio Regulations, had become so full of footnotes and caveats that only a handful of people around the world could interpret it. They used this power to block anything they did not like.

One would expect that control of the ITU by the radio mafia would have been good for the radiocommunication industry. In fact, this was not really the case. New developments, such as the spread of privately owned satellite operators or the use of auctions to allocate spectrum, were fiercely contested. When the Europeans wanted to develop a common standard for digital mobile communication, they did not come to the ITU to draft the standards that make up GSM. It was during this period that the ITU lost much of its power on radio issues for the simple reason that the interesting, commercial developments were too threatening to the dominant state interests.

An Outsider's Role in Institutional Change

What was Melody's role in the reform? Having worked with regulatory agencies around the world, from both the inside and the outside, Melody was familiar with the concept of regulatory capture. Although it usually takes place for commercial reasons, the techniques of regulatory capture for strategic and political reasons are just as easy to spot for someone with a trained eye. Melody was able to expose the true nature of the ITU at that time. He also had the persistence to press on where mere mortals would have become discouraged. He pushed the ITU to take an interest in policy, regulatory and market issues rather than in the purely technical work it had traditionally done and which remained one of the few areas where it could still make progress.

Melody's encyclopaedic knowledge of the industry, and his unique gift for interpreting and predicting trends, enabled him to alert ITU Members to the imminent changes facing the sector, notably in the form of privatisation and market liberalisation. Although, with the benefit of hindsight, such changes seem obvious and necessary, this was far from being the case in 1989. By drawing upon his experience in Canada and the United States, Melody was able to demonstrate the inevitability of change. Moreover, he was able to link the two aspects of market change and institutional change together.

Results of the Reforms

How do things stand, more than a decade later? The ITU's policy work is now on a firm footing, especially in the areas of sector reform and the collection and analysis of telecom indicators. The Standardisation Sector is now free to develop new ways of working in which the private sector plays the leading role; something which would have been impossible before 1989. Even the Radio Sector, under the energetic leadership of another Canadian, Robert Jones, has rediscovered its vitality in areas like 3G mobile communication and mobile satellite services. The ITU-R is now leading the way in terms of introducing cost recovery and rational operational planning – again something which would not have been possible before 1989 when the secretariat was held in such mistrust.

Progress is being made, but it is mainly in the corporate culture of the ITU, rather than in structural reform. Arguably, cultural change is itself part of the liberating experience of the 1989 reforms. But new challenges are on the horizon, notably the need to fully separate out regulatory and operational functions. This has been successfully achieved in most ITU Member States but not yet in the ITU itself, where the operators debate and decide upon regulatory issues like numbering policy, while Member States debate the minutiae of technical interface standards.

Perhaps Melody's biggest strength is that, when he speaks, people listen. Compelling arguments backed up by anecdotes and, where necessary, biting satire, reinforce the point. Of course, it would be inaccurate to give the impression that Melody was some kind of superman, single-handedly achieving change. Reform was a process that involved many gifted individuals. But Melody's leadership characteristics and his ability to say what needs saying were pivotal. It is a shame that there is no one with his stature among those assisting the ITU in its current reform process.

III.5

From Arctic Village to Alice Springs: Rural Telecom Myths and Realities

Heather E. Hudson

> We went from house to house taking care of the sick ...
> We had no phones ... but used the school's radio to report
> [on] our patients.
> There was no nonsense about confidentiality.
> (Alaskan health aide quoted in Hudson and Pittman 1999)

INTRODUCTION

I was privileged to work with William Melody in northern Canada, Alaska, and Australia, and to collaborate with him on research and advocacy concerning communication needs of other rural and disadvantaged populations.[4] I learned in working with him that if affordable access is to be available to all, telecom policies need to be based on realistic premises – not wishful thinking or simplistic generalisations. What follows is a summary of some of the myths that I believe must be challenged and the lessons that must be applied to extend affordable access to information and communication technologies and services in rural and developing regions.

DEBUNKING MYTHS

Myth: Rural Demand is Limited

Planners often assume that there will be little demand for telecom in rural areas. Such forecasts are typically based solely on the lower population densities, coupled with an assumption that all rural residents are likely to have lower incomes and, therefore, lower demand for telecom than urban dwellers. Rural population density, however, varies dramatically from one country to another and often within the borders of larger nations. Rural population densities in India, Indonesia and China enormously exceed those in Mongolia and Kazakhstan.

Of course, income is a useful predictor, but there may be many other factors that generate demand. Villagers in Rwanda and Burundi may be very poor, but the coffee and tea plantations they work need to communicate to order parts and supplies and arrange transport to foreign markets. Tuna fishermen in poor coastal communities in the Philippines use mobile phones to arrange cargo space on aircraft to transport their catch to Tokyo. The service sector is also a major component of rural economies. Thus, in addition to commercial activities, there may be significant demand from government agencies and non-governmental organisations operating health care services, schools, other social services and development projects.

As rural and isolated peoples gain greater control of natural resources and demand more political autonomy, their needs for communication also increase. Organising by indigenous peoples to lodge land claims in Alaska, northern Canada, and Outback Australia, required extensive communication within these regions and with major urban power centres over many years. It is hard to imagine that land claims would have been settled without reliable communication to discuss strategy, lobby political and business leaders and build public awareness and support.

Myth: One Size Fits All
Another common assumption is that voice telephone service is all that rural and developing regions will ever need. While there may never be demand for a modem in every hut, demand for Internet access is likely to grow among government offices, small businesses, cooperatives, schools and health centres. Some providers preclude that option by installing wireless local loop technologies with very limited capacity such as digital European cordless telecommunications (DECT), which is used in some rural areas of South Africa. In more developed rural regions, telecommuters work from home and farmers want Internet access from their homes. Yet even in industrialised countries, 'basic rural service' is typically considered to be only voice telephone service, often with lower reliability – as well as at higher prices – than would be found in urban areas.

Myth: Rural Benchmarks Must be Lower
A persistent assumption is that 'something is better than nothing' for rural areas. However, a corollary of the above analysis is that it is no longer technically or economically justifiable to set rural benchmarks lower than urban benchmarks for access – both to basic telecom and to the Internet.

For example, the US Telecommunications Act of 1996 requires that rural services and prices are to be *reasonably comparable* to those in urban areas. While the United States and other industrialised countries must upgrade outdated wireline networks and analogue exchanges in rural areas, developing countries can leapfrog old technologies and install fully digital wireless networks. Thus, developing country regulators can adopt rural comparability standards to minimise service quality and pricing differences.

Myth: An Operator of Last Resort is the Best Means to Ensure Rural Access
Some countries require the dominant operator to act as an 'operator of last resort', with a Universal Service Obligation (USO) to provide rural service. Typically, the operator with the USO is entitled to a subsidy to provide the service based on its cost estimates. However, this policy can be flawed if there is no incentive for the operator with the USO to use the most appropriate technology and to operate it efficiently. It can also serve as a justification for protection from competition because the dominant operator has additional costs and obligations not required of new entrants. If subsidies are provided to serve high-cost areas, they should be made available to any operator willing to provide the service. Rather than designating a single operator of last resort, Chile established a development fund and implemented a competitive tender for subsidies for unserved areas. Surprisingly, 16 projects were awarded to bids of zero subsidy. As a result of preparing for the bidding process, operators were able to document demand and a willingness to pay in many communities.

Myth: Build It and Jobs Will Come
Justification for rural telecom policies and investments is often based on the assumption that investment in telecom alone will result in economic development. However, numerous studies have shown that telecom is necessary, but not sufficient, for development (Hudson 1997a). The reality is that many other factors contribute to rural economic development, including other infrastructure (particularly electrification and transportation), a skilled workforce and the cost of operations including facilities and labour.

Rural regions with all of these advantages may well be able to attract new jobs by encouraging investment in modern and competitively priced telecom networks. Western Ireland has become the 'back office' for many companies, building on its assets of a well-educated and comparatively low-cost labour and high-quality infrastructure, including telecom. In North America, Nebraska and New Brunswick have attracted thriving call centre businesses. Software engineers in India and Russia write computer code for high tech firms in North America; lawyers in Senegal transmit legal summaries to Paris over the Internet.

Lessons for Planning and Policy

Universal Access Must be a Moving Target
The definition of universality varies across developing regions. India has set targets of public telephones within a radius of a few kilometres in rural areas. The state of Alaska mandated telephone service in every village of 25 or more

residents. Universal service must be considered a dynamic concept with a set of moving targets that can be revised to take into consideration changes in technology and user needs. Goals should not be stated in terms of a specific technology or service provider (such as wireline or wireless service provided by the local telephone company), but in terms of functions and capabilities, such as the ability to transmit voice and data. And because information access is important for socio-economic development, universality should be assessed not only in terms of the number of individuals that have access, but also in terms of whether schools, clinics, libraries and community tele-centres have access (Hudson 1997b).

In developing regions, the demand for services besides basic voice telephony is now spreading beyond businesses and organisations, to small entrepreneurs, non-governmental organisations and students, driven by demand for access to e-mail and the Internet. Such services can be valuable even for those who are illiterate. Like the scribes who helped earlier generations, 'infomediaries' ranging from librarians to tele-centre staff can help people with limited education to send and receive electronic information.

If Subsidies are Needed, They Must be Targeted

The traditional means of ensuring provision of service to unprofitable areas or customers has been through cross-subsidies, such as from international or long-distance services to local telephone services. However, in a competitive environment, new entrants cannot survive if their competitors are subsidised. If subsidies are required, they must be made explicit and directed to specific classes of customers or locations. Subsidies may target economically disadvantaged areas or groups that could not afford prices typical for installation and usage. Operators may be subsidised to serve locations that are isolated and/or have a very low population density that makes them significantly more expensive to serve than other locations.

Old Distinctions are No Longer Relevant

Classifications and distinctions that once were useful may no longer be relevant. Regulators typically issue separate licences and approve separate tariff structures for fixed and mobile services, yet these distinctions have become blurred. In many developing countries, wireless has become the first and only service for many customers. Eliminating these licensing distinctions may accelerate access.

The distinction between voice and data no longer makes sense; bits are bits, and can be used to transmit any type of content from voice to video. Yet in many developing countries, voice communication is still considered a monopoly service, precluding the use of Internet Protocol (IP) telephony, which can reduce the cost of voice dramatically. In contrast, China has encouraged its operators to build parallel IP networks.

Separate the Goals from the Means

Policy makers and regulators have a tendency to confuse the goals with the means. The role of the government should be to set goals and not to determine how they are to be achieved. For example, in the United States, the Federal Communications Commission initially tried to dictate the technology to be used in two-way very small aperture terminals (VSATs), in order to minimise interference. Innovative engineers were able to convince the regulatory agency to set the technical specifications and to let the industry determine how to meet them. The result was smaller and cheaper terminals. A developing country example is the mandate in India to upgrade all village payphones for data communication. Perhaps the goal should be stated as providing access to e-mail and the Internet in every village, with the means (payphone, kiosk, Internet teashop, etc.) left to the community.

Long Periods of Exclusivity Do Not Serve the Public Interest

In a liberalised environment, the length and terms of operator licences can influence the pace of growth of networks and services. Regulators typically face choices concerning how long to protect incumbents to enable them to prepare for competition, and how long to grant periods of exclusivity or other concessions to new operators to minimise investment risk. Yet exclusivity may be the wrong variable to focus on if the goal is to increase the availability of telecom services. Instead, investors cite a transparent regulatory environment with a 'level playing field' for all competitors as key to their assessment of risk.

A few countries have granted licences with as much as 25 years of exclusivity, although ten years or less seems more common. Even five to ten years may seem excessive, now that Internet time is measured in 'dog years'. Some jurisdictions such as Hong Kong and India have negotiated terminations of exclusivity periods with monopoly operators in order to enable their economies to benefit from competition in the telecom sector.

Users Will Find a Way...

Protecting dominant carriers not only penalises users, but drives the more agile to find alternatives. The users' response to unaffordable prices is increasingly to bypass the network, for example, by using callback services or Voice over Internet Protocol (VoIP). Many operators claim that callback and VoIP siphon off revenues that they need to expand their networks, which would also probably create more jobs. However, the relationship is not so simple. Affordable Internet access can create new jobs in value-added services and an information resource for economic development.

If the Government is Slow to Act, Regulation Becomes Policy
A distinction is often made between policy making, typically carried out through a government ministry or department with responsibilities for telecom, and regulation, carried out by an independent body, that is, not related to the operator nor directly responsible to a minister. However, the distinction between regulation and policy quickly becomes blurred because of the pace of technological change and market pressures. One strategy to avoid this problem is to set firm enforceable deadlines for decisions on licence applications and other time-sensitive matters.

Effective Regulation Requires Participation
It is often thought that the issues in telecom policy and regulation are so arcane that most citizens could have nothing useful to contribute to the decision making process. However, all regulatory agencies are overworked and understaffed. The staff cannot find or analyse all of the data that would be useful to guide decision making. Major users are likely to have well thought out views on the impact of proposed regulations or on the need for reforms. The ability of small users and consumers to contribute may seem less likely. It may take some time for their representatives to get up to speed on telecom technology and the economics of the industry. However, the contributions of such groups can also provide perspectives that may otherwise be overlooked. A problem for consumer groups is the cost of tracking the issues and preparing testimony or other interventions. In order to ensure that such consumer perspectives are represented, in some countries the regulator pays the costs of participation in hearings by consumer organisations that contribute evidence, which would not otherwise be available. Melody has assisted numerous consumer groups and indigenous organisations in regulatory hearings and policy filings throughout his career.

CONCLUSION: OVERSIGHT WITH ENFORCEMENT WILL BE NEEDED
The marketplace is generally the best mechanism for bringing innovative and affordable services to most users, including those who live in rural and developing regions. However, there will be an ongoing need for oversight to monitor progress toward meeting targets, to enforce compliance with performance standards and to review and revise benchmarks. Otherwise, operators may not meet targets that are conditions of their licences in areas that they think will not be profitable. Or they may install facilities but not maintain

them adequately if they assume the revenue generating potential is low. Operators must also be held to their licence conditions if licensing is to be an effective means of extending access.

Setting the Reform Agenda: What Next, After Privatisation?

Márcio Wohlers de Almeida and Ricardo Tavares

INTRODUCTION

In most countries, the post-privatisation telecom agenda is now centred on policy implementation and not any more on policy development for institutional reforms, as presciently set out in Melody (1999e). In Latin America the progress of reform has been very impressive. Some critical problems of the old telecom regime have been successfully addressed: the negative political influence on state-owned operators' business decisions; the government budget constraint on telecom investments; and the bundling of operations, regulation and monitoring in a single entity. As a result, remarkable changes have been introduced. The new private operators are free to make their investment decisions. These same operators have tackled the pent-up demand, generating rapid growth in the sector. New regulatory frameworks have emerged, giving birth to independent and flexible regulatory agencies.

SECTOR REFORM IN THE SCHUMPETERIAN CONTEXT

Some significant events have taken place, however, since Melody's paper was published: the telecom industry recession and the bursting of the dot.com bubble. Both events are linked to a deeper phenomenon, associated with what may be called the maturity phase of a Schumpeterian wave of innovation. This fifth Schumpeterian wave of industrial innovation started during the 1980s when vast arrays of semiconductors, fibre optic networks and software began to be diffused in the market. Successful firms such as Cisco Systems, Intel and Microsoft enjoyed healthy margins, set standards, and killed off weaker rivals in order to became the leaders of this fifth Schumpeterian wave of innovation (*Economist* 2001).

Broadly speaking, each wave of innovation has three main periods: energetic eruption, maturity and decline. The third period takes place when a new block of innovation is just beginning. We do not see a collapse of the current wave of innovation. It is experiencing a period of maturity, more precisely an initial phase of maturity. The innovation wave unleashed by abundant bandwidth and Internet based-solutions appears to have a long way to go. Nonetheless, the maturity of this wave of innovation has had significant implications for telecom reform in developing countries. Most telecom reforms in Latin America, for instance, were implemented in the 1990s, when the international economy was growing fast and Foreign Direct Investment (FDI) was abundant. At the start of the new century, however, there has been a reversal of the previous trend: a telecom recession, the shrinking of the main operators and vendors, high levels of debt among the main players and an investment slump are very much in evidence.

The Post-Privatisation Reform Agenda

This new environment makes policy implementation a harder task. This second phase of policy implementation encompasses tougher competition enforcement, regulatory adjustments related to other fundamental social and economic policies, and the challenge of creating incentives for the spread of telecom innovations throughout all sectors of the economy (the digitalisation of the economy itself). This phase requires high investments in broadband and information and communication infrastructure. The recession will generate important constraints for reforms to enable the attraction of new investments.

Especially in Brazil during this second phase, three critical issues have emerged on the telecom agenda: how to create a *level playing field* in fixed-line telephony; how to address the trade deficit in electronics and telecom equipment by increasing domestic production; and how to address the issue of digital exclusion effectively, develop e-commerce as part of the market economy and bring more efficiency and transparency to government with e-government approaches.

The first critical issue is how to create a level playing field in basic telecom. This issue goes back to the privatisation phase in Brazil (1995-1998), when the government gave priority to selling state-owned assets in its effort to create a competitive environment. Privatisation in most countries did not address the issue of the fixed-line monopoly. In Spanish-speaking Latin American countries, monopolies of four to ten years were awarded to the new private owners, while in Brazil the regulator established a fictitious duopoly or quasi-monopoly.

The reason for the survival of monopolies or quasi-monopolies lies in the assumption that such market structures create incentives for network expansion. Under conditions of pent-up demand, monopolistic or quasi-monopolistic market structures can indeed attract significant private investment. This gives operators a solid cash flow and return on investment. In exchange for quasi-monopoly market conditions, regulators can impose tough universal service and quality goals.

Cellular telephony, however, experienced more competition – with a real duopoly taking root in Brazil. The new entrant in cellular telephony also could benefit from pent-up demand and quasi-monopoly conditions in a market segment in which network deployment can take place quickly. In many countries, there was also competition in the supply of corporate services. In Brazil, there was some intra-regional competition in domestic long-distance services and a duopoly at the national level.

The problems with monopolistic concessions become manifest when their term ends. One problem is the *timing* of the sunset of monopoly rights. In Brazil, the timing was clear since 1998, as part of the rules of privatisation: either the end of 2001 or the end of 2003, depending upon the success of fixed-line operators in achieving the universal service goals imposed on them. The other problem is the *conditions* through which the new competitive environment will emerge. The Brazilian regulator, ANATEL, delayed the announcement of the new rules of competition as long as possible.

The requirements for new players to obtain new operating licences – international long-distance, national long-distance and local services – were announced by the Brazilian regulator only at the end of 2001. The requirements are of two types: some licences are tied to each other, that is, the acquisition of a long-distance licence is tied to acquisition of a local services licence; the local licence is required to cover 1% of all major cities in four years.

ANATEL argued that the local users needed protection, given the fact that the intended duopoly never took root. The so-called mirror licensees, or new entrants in fixed-telephony, have not challenged incumbent operators. The incumbent fixed-line operators continue to be dominant; therefore, the regulator reasoned that new coverage requirements were necessary. Incumbents, new players and trade associations opposed the new rules. They especially criticised the 1% coverage requirement in all major cities. They argued that given the international crisis in telecom financing, the coverage requirements would discourage investment. ANATEL has agreed to modify, but not eliminate the rules.

Local competition cannot be equated only with more or less requirements for local penetration, however. Analysis by CELAET (Center of Latin American Studies of Economics of Telecommunications <www.celaet.com.br>) demonstrated that local competition is a global issue with roots in economies of scale and scope that originate in economies of density and first-comer advantages. In industrialised countries, there has been intensive research into local competition. In France and Italy, energy and railway utilities have formed consortia, leveraging their rights of way in alliance with equipment manufacturers who know the telecom business well. These alliances have rights of way that connect the facilities to end-users. The Brazilian model of telecom reform fragmented the different segments of the industry excessively. As in Europe, the new utility/telecom alliances must be encouraged in Brazil. The United Kingdom example, where cable operators challenged British Telecom, does not apply well in Brazil, where cable television has not been able to widen its network reach or market share.

The second critical issue in Brazil is the manufacturing sector's links to industrial policy. Brazil's trade balance and current accounts have suffered from rapid increases in imports related to the telecom sector's energetic expansion. Incentives for telecom vendors to locate production in Brazil are key to the debate on telecom policies in Brazil.

The old telecom regime was relatively successful in terms of industrial policy. There were three poles: 1) the CPqD, the national institute of telecom technology, producing local technology; 2) local manufacturers, who licensed the CPqD technology and manufactured products; and 3) the state-owned Telebras operators, who bought the products. The Tropico digital switching centre is the greatest success among these groups. Promon, a Brazilian technology company, took control of Tropico's business and later allied with Cisco Systems to further develop products. Two other successes are the telephone card for pay phones and the local production of fibre optic cables. The old industrial policy model, however, is dead. The causes are multiple: the growing complexity of digital systems, the new openness linked to trade liberalisation and globalisation and the privatisation of operators.

How can Brazil create incentives for telecom vendors to locate production in Brazil and keep the country competitive within the new logic of global manufacturing? A truly new model to encourage local production is still in the making. In the first phase of policy reform, the government assigned the Brazilian National Development Bank the task of financing operators' purchases of equipment, as long as the products were produced in Brazil. That worked well for finished products, but not for high-technology parts, which affected the trade balance in any case.

The struggle to establish Brazil as a centre of technology creation continues. In addition, FUNTTEL is a new technology research fund that receives resources from taxes on telecom services as well as from the government. FUNTTEL nurtures research at the CPqD and universities. The CPqD – transformed into a Foundation – has also succeeded in maintaining its relationships with operators.

In addition, next-generation IP-based networks' intense use of several kinds of parts and software provides opportunities for local companies to occupy niches that their international competitors have not found. Government incentives seem necessary, but they must be well-conceived to have an impact in a new environment of open trade and globalisation.

Finally, the third issue is digital exclusion. Digital exclusion can have a great destructive impact in developing countries because it undermines efforts to improve income distribution. In Brazil, an interesting paradox emerges from the recent increase in fixed-telephony penetration. As the fixed-network reached the neighbourhoods of the poor, these citizens gained access to basic telephone services, but are defaulting on their bills for lack of income. How can these citizens be provided with information technology tools and Internet access? There is only so much that the democratisation of access to telephony can do to reduce income inequalities.

Digital exclusion has become a serious debate in Brazil. Organisations that support small enterprises are devising ways to assist them to become Internet-smart. Training in e-commerce is also taking place. All levels of government are creating computer-training programmes. In addition, the Telecom Universal Service Fund, which collects a tax from telecom operators, will soon begin to invest in Internet access for public schools, libraries and health centres. The government is pursuing a broad e-government initiative to facilitate access of citizens to the government.

Nonetheless, for a country with these complex social problems and a labyrinthine bureaucracy, policies to reduce digital exclusion cannot be isolated from broader social policies. Sub-utilisation and inefficiencies could plague well-intentioned digital access promotion policies. For instance, computers could stay locked in schools far from the hands of teachers and students, because of lack of security. Teachers with access to computers may not use them for lack of computer training. Communities receiving expensive equipment to connect to the Internet might actually have more pressing priorities such as food, clean water and sewage treatment. The key for success here is coordination of policies among different levels of government and the targeted communities.

Conclusion

The scope of the new policy agenda is broad and the new Schumpeterian wave generates policy uncertainties. The new agenda is not as powerful as privatisation in attracting mass media attention, but it is no less important. A powerful public sphere that openly debates the issues, nurtures policy makers with a wide range of alternatives, and maintains pressure for solutions is as important as ever. We are in the midst of an information revolution – our region and our countries will be shaped by how we deal with the key issues of access to the new information-based economy. Most countries that privatised state-owned monopolies, especially in Latin America, have also become democracies. Nurturing a more inclusive policy discourse is without doubt a key part of the solution to these critical issues.

Policy and Regulatory Challenges of Access and Affordability

Alison Gillwald

INTRODUCTION

Affordable access and the skills to utilise increasingly advanced but essential services remain the central public interest issues for regulators in the area of information and communication technologies (ICTs). This is true for all countries, but particularly for developing countries. The contemporary policy dilemma is that as the urban centres are connected to global networks, illuminating critical paths of planetary contact and influence, the gap between those that are connected and those that are not is widened. At a time when information is power, the inequities of access to and dissemination of information extend to citizens' differential ability to be politically or economically effective.

The major policy and regulatory challenge for the ICT sector is identified as the harmonisation of domestic policy and regulation with international best practices as identified in multilateral agreements and organisations and centred on the concept of efficiency. This includes a deregulated and competitive market structure; private ownership with strong foreign investment; a reduced role for government; cost-reflective prices; and universal service policies to deal with market failure.

The Bretton Woods institutions have argued that privatisation of the incumbent monopoly and liberalisation of the market will remedy the ills of inefficient monopoly provision. The introduction of competition serves the public interest by inducing suppliers to become more efficient and to offer greater choice of products and services at lower prices. However, the imposition of free-market conditions onto the inequitable conditions in most developing countries without programmes of redress, would simply reinforce the iniquitous status quo. A more focused competition programme, enabling market entry by new kinds of players able to offer innovative and sometimes more affordable services, is likely to extend services and enable better integration of marginal markets into the global economy.

COMPETITION: PANACEA OR REGULATORY TOOL?

What is known is that monopoly provision did not roll out telecom services in most countries. Despite claims that cross-subsidies from international calls and high revenue settlement rates were needed to extend services to the under-served, they were not, by and large, used for this purpose. After decades of monopoly provision by the mid-1990s in Africa, the average teledensity was below 1%.

In the course of the limited reform since the mid-1990s, insufficient emphasis has been placed on institutional arrangements to deal with the inevitable market failures. Effective regulation has been a cornerstone of competitive markets in the countries calling for open access to developing country markets, but it has not been implemented alongside competition policies, often expediently adopted by developing countries to offset debt or secure aid. The introduction of competition, without the regulatory capacity or political will to manage a competitive framework, can be entirely counterproductive to the achievement of the very goals of liberalisation.

In a study of the eastern European Internet market, the Global Internet Liberty Campaign (GILC) reached a conclusion of broader relevance:

Open and competitive markets make a necessary but not always sufficient contribution to securing the public interest objectives of universal access, affordable prices, pluralism and diversity. Indeed, in the absence of countervailing regulation, liberalization could worsen the situation. Tariff rebalancing in favor of high volume and long distance users could benefit business and urban customers, while resulting in increases to residential and rural customers (GILC 2000: 9).

PRIVATISATION: SOLUTION TO INFRASTRUCTURE DEVELOPMENT OR STIFLER OF SECTOR DEVELOPMENT

Due to the lack of success of incumbent telecom operators to build out the infrastructure adequately after decades of monopoly, the solution of privatisation proffered by multilateral agencies has been widely adopted. In many developing countries, privatisation has been implemented through the introduction of a strategic equity partner with the promise of a period of extended monopoly. The rationale for this is a strong one. Often indebted monopolies need injections of capital, skills and technology transfer in order to roll out service to the vast majority in many developing countries, to modernise their outmoded networks and to prepare for competition.

There are now over 120 signatories to the General Agreement on Trade in Services (GATS) – of which over 100 are developing countries. Of these, over 70 have signed the Basic Telecommunications Agreement, and a significant number of them have adopted the Regulatory Reference Paper, which includes a commitment to establish independent regulators. In practice, however, when regulators are established they are usually incapacitated by a lack of resources and the weak political will of their governments. The absence of the necessary regulatory arrangements, together with the experience that privatisation is often adopted without a commitment to general liberalisation of the market, result frequently in market distortions, rather than in an opportunity to reap the potential benefits of reform.

What then are some of the early outcomes of these privatisation strategies? There is some evidence to suggest that countries that have gone this route, especially those that did so at the advent of large-scale public usage of the Internet, may have met their formal rollout targets but possibly at considerable cost to the broader development of their information and communication technology (ICT) sectors. The decline of South Africa's world ranking from fourteenth in 1997 to twenty-eighth in 2000 in terms of Internet hosts may be partly attributed to the inability of the highly competitive Internet Service Provider (ISP) sector to obtain sufficient bandwidth from the incumbent or to utilise alternative means. Where stringent monopoly rules apply or where regulation fails to enable the liberalised components of the sector to compete effectively, innovation and customer service are unlikely to flourish.

The impact on the industry, and on the economy more generally, of operators being prevented by law from using cheaper and more effective telecom solutions than those offered by the monopoly must be weighed carefully against the contribution of the monopoly to the sector. This is so not only at the value-added end of the market where innovation tends to occur, but also in terms of universal access provision. Where alternative access networks have been permitted and the provision of services to under-served areas has been opened up to other players besides the incumbent, service rollout has often been quicker and more widespread (Melody 2001a). For example, South Africa (with a teledensity of 11.4% in 2001) has exhibited much slower growth in fixed-line connectivity than other economies such as Turkey (28% teledensity), Poland (28%), Argentina (21%) and Chile (22%).

Why is it that privatisation has been more readily adopted by many developing countries than other aspects of liberalisation? Although often couched in more acceptable public policy rationales, the uneven commitment to the process of liberalisation can best be understood in terms of the immediate benefits to often-indebted exchequers. The main driver of the granting of exclusivity periods has been the price that can be extracted from investors. This is not bad thing in and of itself. Countries all over the world have long used revenues from the telecom sector to cross-subsidise other areas of social delivery, to offset debt and for other legitimate ends. The danger lies in the conflation of short-term revenue gains with the promotion of the national interest. Extracting a few extra million in revenues for a period of exclusivity or Initial Public Offering needs to be carefully weighed against its negative impact on the growth, diversity and quality of services. The resulting privatised monopoly, driven by shareholder demands and the imperative to stifle competition, requires even more rigorous regulation than the public monopoly, which, despite the inefficiencies associated with it, at least is bound by a public service ethos.

Such potentially negative impacts of short-term political decisions on the attainment of broader national goals can be mitigated by institutional arrangements such as the establishment of workably independent regulators.

Access: Infrastructure or Affordability

Privatisation is likely to be accompanied by the rebalancing of tariffs, to bring prices in line with costs, resulting generally in higher local prices, which were hitherto cross-subsidised by international calls. The result has been the exclusion on the grounds of affordability of precisely those intended to be the beneficiaries of the exclusivity. A study conducted for the South African telecom regulator found that 44% of households could not afford a service at R30 (about US$ 6 at the time) a month and that 60% of all households would not even be able to afford the monthly line rental then of R50 (US$ 8), if it was assumed that only 2% of household income could be allocated for telephony (Stavrou and Mkize 1998). The South African incumbent Telkom SA's Annual Report (2001) indicates that while it had met its annual target of installing 675,000 lines, 'a complete review of non-paying customers and crackdown on commercial fraud resulted in a disproportionate number of fixed lines being disconnected'. This resulted in a decline in customer lines from nearly 5.5 million in 2000 to less than five million in 2001. Over half a million households were disconnected.

While a portion of these can be assumed to have 'churned' or switched to mobile services, as the report indicates, many of these customers either terminated their service or were cut off due to their inability to pay. While cross-subsidies have become a dirty word in discourse of this kind, it is clear that for many years to come access to the home for a vast numbers of citizens in developing countries will only be possible through some form of subsidy or life-line tariff. Rather than jettisoning cross-subsidies as a legitimate social strategy, regulators should set up systems that will ensure that they are transparent and not used anti-competitively, that they are serving their objectives, and that they are targeted and form part of broader collective access strategies such as tele-centres and payphones. Accounting mechanisms and strict reporting requirements would also be needed to facilitate this outcome.

THE CONUNDRUM OF WIRELESS

The juxtaposition of the above discussed affordability issues and the massive growth of wireless mobile services in developing countries poses an interesting conundrum. All over Africa mobile telephones have overtaken fixed telephones. The dramatic growth of mobile is attributable to the introduction of pre-paid services which are now used by around 70% of subscribers, but which yield less than 30% of subscriber revenue in South Africa. Unlike in the rest of sub-Saharan Africa, these figures cannot be explained solely by the lack of access to the lower-priced fixed phones in South Africa. Pre-paid mobile tariffs are considerably higher even than the relatively cheaper contract tariffs.

Besides the convenience of mobility, and indeed the status, something about the ability of the consumer to control costs make the pre-paid option attractive for people, despite that fact that the up-front cost of purchasing the handset may be as high as half of their monthly income. If, on the other hand, the duopoly mobile providers are exploiting an opportunity created by the fixed monopoly's inability to supply, then this is a glaring case of market failure that needs regulation, rather than being a wireless success story.

GOOD GOVERNANCE: KEY TO TRANSFORMATION

All policy and regulatory responses in the ICT sector are dependent on good governance, including greater transparency, accountability and increased participation by interest groups and individuals in decision making processes. In some parts of the world civil society has shifted the power that traditionally resided in formal government to more democratic and participatory forms of governance:

It hinges on equal partnerships, collective wisdom, co-operation and responsible action on the part of all actors in governance (the public sector, the private sector, academia and the media). It relates to the rule of law, accountable administration, legitimate power, responsive relation and is defined as effective, participatory, transparent and equitable (Global Knowledge 2 2000).

The majority of the world's people do not experience these participatory systems of governance, reflecting and determining their very underdevelopment. All initiatives to redress this unevenness should be premised on developing organic, transparent and participatory forms of decision making.

The application of the general principles to the local conditions rather than the mimicking of the complex forms of governance in other jurisdictions is what must be achieved in the regulatory arena. To require costly and skill-intensive systems of regulation is to set developing countries up for failure. The urgent need is to devise and implement appropriate systems of governance that conform to the central principles of transparency, public accountability, public participation and equity.

Conclusion

Throughout the developing world, monopolies have failed to meet the mandates of universal and affordable service, quality service provision to users and product innovation. But the first round of privatisation and liberalisation in many developing countries does not demonstrate significant gains either.

The reasons for this are multiple and specific to the political economies of different countries. What is common to many of them is the absence of the necessary capacity and resources to enforce restructuring policies. It is increasingly evident in developing countries that, while privatisation and competition may be necessary conditions to expand access to basic and advanced communication services, they are far from sufficient. Competition is an effective tool in regulating the efficiency of the market, but its ability to contribute to public interest outcomes of access, affordability, quality and choice of service is dependent on the existence of capacities and resources to implement, monitor and enforce the relevant policies. If these conditions do not exist, as they do not in many developing countries, the adoption of privatisation and liberalisation strategies could be counterproductive.

The challenge, therefore, is to create conditions that are sufficiently certain and predictable to secure the investment necessary for infrastructure development. At the same time they must engage in the sometimes contradictory task of creating an enabling environment for the introduction of innovative services and products that are necessary to engage effectively in the new economy and to ensure affordable access.

Technical Aspects of Rural Telecom

Rudi Westerveld and Carleen F. Maitland

Evaluations of rural telephone systems assume that technology plays an important role. Indeed, the long distances to the nearest connection point of the urban telecom networks create special requirements for appropriate technology that can be operated profitably. Despite the significance of technology for the development of rural networks, it must be seen as just one of many links, following the chain metaphor popularised by the Maitland Report (Independent Commission for World-Wide Telecommunication Development 1984), contributing to the success of a complex system. This point was illustrated at the ITU Telecom Africa 2001 Policy Development Forum, where in response to the question: 'what is the most important barrier to the provision of access to all Africans?' participants ranked lack of funding (47%), regulation (23%), lack of public and private sector cooperation (18%) and inadequate technology (12%) as the barriers. In spite of being one of the least important links in rural telephony, it is useful to understand the development of technology and, in particular, recent significant innovations.

In any particular rural application the choice of technology depends on the local conditions. Subscriber density, clustering possibilities, distances to the nearest national network connection points and terrain characteristics have to be considered, in addition to local technical expertise and adoption capacity.

WIRELINE SYSTEMS

The oldest telecom technology, copper wire, has evolved over the past few decades. When rural systems were first developed, service over long distances was provided with open wire connections, suspended on poles or trees. In some areas single line open wires were used to save on copper. Here, the earth served as the return conductor. When the number of users increased, copper pairs were shared as party lines. Then, carrier systems were introduced. Through frequency multiplexing and the use of coaxial cables, calls of many users were transported on the same line. With the introduction of digital technology this was augmented by time division multiplexing (digital loop carrier). With properly conditioned feeder cables, multiplexing allows a more economic extension of the network.

Radio Systems

Although multiplexing enabled network extension it did not resolve the issue of providing low-cost service over large distances. Radio systems have the advantages of scalability and easy deployment in serving distant rural areas, particularly sparsely populated ones. While radio systems solve the problems of poles and copper wire theft, they require an external source of power, which is not an issue for fixed lines. Solar power may be a solution, although it is not deployable in all locations and may also be subject to theft.

Radio systems have evolved from analogue to digital technology. So-called point-to-multipoint systems are widely deployed in rural areas. Unfortunately standardisation of these systems has been limited and many manufacturers have ceased production.

Fixed Access Cellular Networks

With the arrival of cellular mobile telephone systems new options for rural areas have emerged. Early on, it became clear that investments made in mobile networks to serve urban users could also benefit rural subscribers (Westerveld 1994). At first, these systems were deployed using a variety of analogue standards. Digital systems are now in use in many developing countries. Apart from telephone booths with one line, another implementation uses large metal shipping containers connected to the mobile network through multiple lines to provide local access through a managed telephone service (a phone shop). This system has proved to be a good solution in areas with cellular coverage.

Wireless Local Loop

A third category of radio-based service is Wireless Local Loop (WLL). Although standard implementations have not evolved, vendor specific solutions, both analogue and digital, have been used for some time. They continue to suffer from a relatively high cost per line. The Indian design and deployment of corDECT, a system based on the original digital cordless system, DECT, offers a potential solution. The corDECT system provides extended coverage of about 10 km for about half the price of standard WLL. The corDECT system also provides some mobility, which the WLL systems do not. This, however, gives rise to disputes between corDECT operators and mobile operators who have paid high licence fees. Another advantage of corDECT is its ability to provide data connections with speeds up to 70 kbps.

Satellite Services

When Global Mobile Personal Communications by Satellite (GMPCS) systems were announced there were high expectations of use in rural areas. Various consortia offered developing countries free use of access channels in return for the necessary authorisations. By 2002, Iridium and Globalstar, the only two firms in operation, were struggling to attain profitability. Consequently, their deployment for general access in rural areas has been limited. The only other alternative is Very Small Aperture Terminal (VSAT) systems that are being deployed in many countries. These systems are a good solution for isolated areas, particularly where terrestrial connections would be costly.

Maintenance in a Rural Context

Providing a technological solution to the rural telecom problem is one thing; providing a working and sustainable solution is another. An obvious negative consequence of a newly installed system breaking down is loss of revenue. However, little is said about the demotivating effects of breakdowns, particularly when the time to restoration is measured in months. In such conditions it is difficult to persuade people to use a system, let alone pay for that use. The rural environment puts a lot of stress on equipment. Beyond climatic conditions, there are failures of power systems and problems created by unforeseen human interventions. The level of reliability of rural systems has to be higher than normal, because the higher costs of reliability can be recovered through lower maintenance costs and higher revenues. An effective maintenance strategy must be adopted from the beginning of the design of a rural network. This includes use of remote monitoring and maintenance centres, the reservation of sufficient funds for spare parts, and the logistics for getting these parts at the right time to the technician who needs them.

# III.9

Spectrum Management: Private Property Rights or Commons

Johannes M. Bauer

INTRODUCTION

The growing demand for mobile services has led to a world-wide reconsideration of established methods of spectrum management. The potential flaws of the dominant administrative licensing process are known and include rigidity, long delays and patterns of over- and under-allocation of spectrum to uses. Following the general trend towards a more market-based organisation of the information and communication industries, an increasing number of countries has replaced administrative licensing procedures with spectrum auctions. However, a much broader range of alternative approaches, including more radical proposals to privatise spectrum but also strong voices in favour of creating a true spectrum commons, is being discussed. The specification of the rules governing the use of spectrum has implications for the evolution of the wireless industry. Sound spectrum policy will have to understand this nexus and the advantages and disadvantages of alternative regimes. This contribution offers a preliminary exploration of these issues.

A PROPERTY RIGHTS PERSPECTIVE

Efficient spectrum management has to address three interrelated problems: 1) the allocation of the correct amount of spectrum to certain uses or classes of uses; 2) the assignment of frequencies to certain users or groups of users; and 3) the adjustment of these allocations and assignments as technologies and markets evolve over time. Inefficiencies can be introduced at any one of these levels. Inappropriate attention to the allocation of spectrum will distort otherwise efficient assignment methods (Melody 2001b). Even if an efficient allocation is established at a particular point in time, it will have to be continually adjusted to reflect technological advances and changing market conditions. In general, new applications in hitherto unused frequency bands pose fewer problems than modifications in occupied spectrum bands, as existing users will have to migrate to other frequency bands (or be shifted off the air entirely) and possibly compensated for stranded investment.

Property rights are complex bundles of rights and obligations. Spectrum management regimes also define different bundles of property rights. Three principal spectrum management regimes are possible: 1) full privatisation;

2) common property; and 3) open access. These approaches differ in how they define rules for spectrum access and use; management of a certain band; exclusion of others from that band; and alienation, that is the right to sell or lease spectrum to others. In a private property regime the owners of spectrum can execute all these rights. In an open access setting, everybody would have access to the spectrum resource but no user would enjoy any of the other rights. Although these models recently have attracted an increasing number of supporters, they are the exception rather than the rule. The most widespread approach is the treatment of spectrum as a common property resource.

While spectrum differs in important respects from other forms of common property resources, such as fisheries or forests, important insights can be gained from the vast literature on common resources. Various specifications of property rights are possible within a common property framework (Stevenson 1991; Ostrom 1990). Schlager and Ostrom (1993) identify four different roles based on the assignment of rights: authorised users, claimants, proprietors and owners. Authorised users only have the limited right of access to and use of the resource. Claimants have management in addition to usage rights. Proprietors also have the right to participate in decisions excluding others from the use of the resource. Owners have all these rights plus the right to sell or lease their use. The only difference to pure private property is that common resources usually restrict ownership rights in the interest of the common good. Thus, the governance options for spectrum management within a common property framework span a range that touches on private property at one end, and on open access at the other. A key question for spectrum management is how efficient these alternative are and how they influence industry performance.

Private Property and Open Access
After early proposals to establish private property rights for spectrum in the 1950s (Herzel 1951; Coase 1959) were largely ignored, this model is receiving renewed attention in more or less radical versions. Privatisation requires the initial assignment of private property rights, typically using a market-based mechanism such as spectrum auctions. For existing licensees, Spiller and Cardilli (1999) have suggested the auctioning of warrants to convert existing usage privileges into ownership rights. In principle, the private property model can solve the three problems of spectrum management simultaneously as market forces drive allocation, assignment and dynamic adjustment.

So far, there is only limited experience with privatisation of spectrum in New Zealand and Guatemala. However, serious conceptual objections were raised, including the pervasiveness of externalities, the non-competitive nature of wireless markets and the fact that large portions of spectrum are used by non-profit organisations or for purposes that defy market pricing (Melody 1980). Moreover, where international frequency coordination is necessary and spectrum is allotted to regions, a private market mechanism may raise serious equity issues. Whereas some of these issues probably could be overcome by appropriate institutional design, privatisation does not offer a panacea.

The introduction of spectrum ownership could also alleviate some of the potential problems of auctions, namely that the licence fee affects the emerging market. It is true that under ideal conditions, such as the existence of perfect capital markets, bids at spectrum auctions would reflect the present value of spectrum to a potential licensee. Licence fees therefore are only transfers of rent from the private to the public sector and do not affect subsequent prices or investment (Cave and Valletti 2000). However, both theoretical and empirical objections were raised against this stance. Building on work by Sutton (1991), Gruber (2001) showed that under real world conditions of imperfect information and imperfect capital markets bids may systematically deviate from their competitive level and, consequently, increase concentration in the post-auction market. In an empirical study of the GSM and Personal Communication Service (PCS) market, Bauer (2001) showed that licence fees increase the cost of supply and thus increase the market price. These potential disadvantages must be netted against the advantages of auctions in assessing their overall efficiency.

Another avenue to utilise market forces is advocated by Noam (1998). He endorses opening access to spectrum but proposes the introduction of market-based fees to reflect the opportunity costs of spectrum. This model would allow the establishment of futures and derivative markets in spectrum and hence would allow users to sign long-term contracts. As it would convert sunk licence fees determined in an auction into variable payments determined in spot and future spectrum markets, the proposal would avoid some of the potential distortions of auctions. A key problem in this approach is that so far no workable mechanism has been devised for the collection of the spectrum fees.

Spectrum as a Commons
Throughout most of the history of radio communication, spectrum was treated as a common property resource. Licences typically give temporary, exclusive usage privileges to an individual or an organisation as long as certain eligibility criteria are met. Most licences also can be transferred to third parties as long as these meet the same eligibility test. This transferability is not equivalent to the right of

alienation granted by full ownership rights. However, licensees typically do not have direct rights to participate in the management of the spectrum resource nor do they have a direct voice in determining who should be excluded from spectrum use. In terms of the common property research, the role of spectrum licensees resembles the role of the authorised user. Surprisingly, empirical studies of common property arrangements have found that authorised user models are less efficient than proprietor or owner models, as the latter have higher incentives to invest in the development of the resource.

It is therefore a legitimate question whether a modification of property rights within the common property framework would improve the efficiency of frequency management. One particularly interesting suggestion is the reliance on more community-based arrangements for spectrum management. Two rationales can be associated with these proposals. It is first pointed out that recent advances in spread spectrum technology eliminate the necessity of assigning a specific channel to a user. Rather, the technology of ultra-low power code division multiplexing allows the orderly use of broad spectrum bands by competing uses and users. As the efficiency of spread spectrum technology increases, ever more applications may be able to use the same spectrum band. This would allow a radical reorganisation of spectrum management. Exclusive use privileges would not be required for an orderly use of spectrum; they would even become unconstitutional (Benkler 1998). Spectrum could be shared and managed by the user community based on rules developed in a decentralised fashion (Buck 2002 forthcoming).

Second, the proponents of this position point to the specific nature of innovation and the new organisation of the production process in advanced information and communication industries. Innovation in the information industries is often cumulative, with developers of information goods and services highly dependent on access to previously created knowledge. Likewise, there is anecdotal evidence and a swelling conceptual debate linking the speed of innovation on the Internet to the availability of an open access platform (Bar et al. 2000; Lemley and Lessig 2001). The next generations of mobile communication will resemble the value chain in the fixed Internet and a large innovation impetus is expected from open access to the wireless network platform. Unfortunately, the use of auctions will likely increase the incentive of network providers to close access to their own affiliates, potentially reducing the overall dynamics of the entire sector. Therefore, the development of spectrum as a commons is seen as crucial in supporting innovation processes and maximising the benefits from advanced mobile communication.

The US Federal Communications Commission has designated more than 300 MHz of spectrum in the 2 GHz and 5 GHz bands as unlicensed. Critics point out that the experiments with unlicensed spectrum have resulted in low investment and local overuse. These observations would seem to indicate the weaknesses of the commons model of spectrum management. However, it seems that the major flaw of unlicensed spectrum is the lack of rules that would allow its systematic utilisation. Buck (2002 forthcoming) discusses eight meta-rules for a spectrum commons, including a clear definition of boundaries, congruence between appropriation conditions and local conditions, collective choice arrangements and appropriate monitoring procedures. Based on general insights from the commons literature, these rules could create a structured environment for spectrum use without creating exclusive rights based on financial strength.

Defined spectrum commons are a promising alternative institutional arrangement for addressing the three issues of spectrum management. Like privatisation, in principle, they could address allocation, assignment and dynamic adjustment simultaneously without the disadvantages associated with financially-driven spectrum markets. Moreover, they would allow modification of broad principles of spectrum management based on the needs of the local user community. However, this approach is afflicted with potentially significant transaction costs. These will, in part, depend on the state of technology and application in question. If an application requires national or even international allocation of a specific band, a commons-based approach may be too cumbersome and not be very different from the status quo of International Telecommunication Union spectrum management. If local mobility and interconnectivity are the main objectives, however, the model will likely be superior to the existing administrative process and the market-based alternatives.

Towards a Comparative Analysis

Despite the strong push towards privatisation, spectrum policy has a choice of a range of options. As this discussion illustrates, these approaches define systematically different sets of property rights. In turn, they will influence pricing, investment and innovation processes in the wireless industry. Given the vast range of uses of spectrum, it is unlikely that one model will suit all situations. Both the market-oriented models as well as commons-based proposals have their own advantages and disadvantages. It will be necessary to carefully monitor the experience with these approaches. The coexistence of multiple institutional arrangements for spectrum management should facilitate a better understanding of their impacts for the evolution of wireless markets.

Spectrum Allocation Controversies

Martin Cave

INTRODUCTION
Ever since Leo Herzel proposed in 1951 that the radio spectrum is an input which can be traded like other scarce inputs, there has been an ongoing debate between proponents of a market-based procedure for allocating spectrum and proponents of the traditional administrative procedures.

The current impetus behind the market approach has been slow in building. Ronald Coase's 1959 article on the Federal Communications Commission gave Herzel's ideas greater prominence and they were developed in somewhat more detail in the 1970s. But it was only in the 1990s that the idea really caught fire. In particular, a wave of auction fever affected governments in many continents. New Zealand was among the first, followed by Australia and the United States, where the design of simultaneous ascending order auctions engrossed many of the word's best micro-economists, while finance ministries relished the revenues. The opportunity to assign frequencies for 3G mobile services was used by many European governments as a test bed for auction techniques. The results were highly dramatic, with the United Kingdom and German governments emerging with €35 billion and €50 billion, respectively. Subsequent auctions, some of them following the telecom slump, left other European governments less well-rewarded.

However, despite the prominence given to these experiences, spectrum throughout the world is still allocated predominately by administrative methods. Indeed, trading in secondary (post-auction) spectrum markets remains unlawful in the European Union, and will remain so at least until mid-2003.

LIMITS OF ADMINISTRATIVE ASSIGNMENT
William Melody has made two important contributions to the spectrum debates, over a period of two decades. Melody (1980) reflected the sentiment of the times. That is to say, he noted the inefficiencies in the present arrangements, but also identified the practical difficulties in implementing market solutions. These were, among other things, because interdependence among users makes cooperation necessary, and because its use cannot be objectively specified due to the probabilistic nature of spectrum use. He also cast out the possibility of legally

enforcing rights to use. In his view, it was likely that 'transaction and enforcement costs as well as loss of spectrum use would far exceed any claimed allocative efficiency benefits [from the use of a market type system]' (Melody 1980: 395).

Melody also noted that spectrum served social as well as economic purposes, and that it was important to devise a spectrum management régime which enabled those objectives to be realised as well. Accordingly, what he proposed was an administrative pricing system to be introduced in high value areas of the spectrum, the prices being derived from observations for commercial transactions, such as the prices at which broadcast licences were exchanged in the marketplace. This would make it possible for the State to derive some of the rents involved in the process, and encourage the relevant spectrum users to explore economies at the Ricardian intensive and extensive margins – the former referring to the incentive to compress signals and use less spectrum; the latter to the incentive to explore new frequencies. He forecast (with commendable accuracy) that the spectrum will continue to be allocated and designed by means of an administrative process.

Twenty years later, Melody (2001b) returned to the topic, to deliver a highly unfavourable verdict on the 3G (Third Generation mobile) auctions in Europe. In essence, he accuses the European governments of first restricting the amount of spectrum available for 3G mobile telephony, and then profiting from the resulting artificial scarcity to extract the maximum revenue from the auctions. In fact, governments were to some extent caught in the dilemma over the timing of the auctions. On the one hand, the amount of spectrum readily available for 3G mobile was limited; on the other hand, European governments wanted to get the process of 3G rollout going as quickly a possible. The result was a scramble for limited frequencies.

It is not wholly convincing that the auction processes were designed to extract the maximum from bidders; if this were true, then why would the United Kingdom Government have insisted upon reserving one licence for new entrants into mobile telephony? Moreover, if that were the intention, then it demonstrably failed in the case of the later auctions, where the number of applicants converged to the number of licences available, with predictable consequences for the revenue raised.

Nonetheless, it is certainly true that where competition for licences was intense, governments were able to extract from the industry not only a substantial portion of firms' estimates of their profits from 3G services (moreover, in the case of Germany and the United Kingdom, estimates made at a time of considerable optimism), but also excess returns from 2G activities (given the belief that operators could only credibly maintain themselves as 2G suppliers if they also had the means to allow their customers to migrate to 3G).

Melody's remedy for this was the correct one of seeking to eliminate the monopoly rents associated with scarce spectrum by allowing more entry into the market. He proposes that:

- bidders should be told that more spectrum would be made available at the time of the auction;
- existing mobile licensees should be authorised to use their spectrum for 3G services;
- all the spectrum designated by the World Radiocommunication Conference (WRC) should be allocated to 3G networks;
- there should be no limit on 3G licensees, but a target of at least eight;
- entry by virtual mobile network operators should be encouraged; and
- public service requirements traditionally associated with administrative assignment should be maintained as priority obligations under all 3G licences.

Melody's diagnosis and proposed cure is on the right lines, but it may not go far enough. He proposes loosening the allocation system, so that the same spectrum can be used for either 2G or 3G mobile telephony. But why stop there? Why not have a system in which the starting point is that, in the absence of compelling reasons to the contrary, spectrum can be employed for whatever purpose the licensee chooses? This would imply the development of a régime in which not only would auctions be used to assign new spectrum, but there would also be secondary trading in spectrum, without (necessarily) restrictions on its use (see Cave 2001; Valletti 2001).

Spectrum Marketplace

A system of this kind for spectrum used for commercial purposes could happily co-exist with the reservation by governments of spectrum required for public services. At the limit, one could imagine, for example, a system in which the Ministry of Defence competed directly with Vodafone in a spectrum marketplace, just as the two organisations compete with one another, to a limited extent at least, in the labour market. However, this is probably too radical a step to contemplate at the moment, and reservation of spectrum seems sensible. Public service users could, of course, be obliged to pay an administrative price for the spectrum that they use, in order to encourage efficiency in spectrum use.

A system of trading in spectrum used for commercial purposes would clearly have to deal with problems arising from interference, but this problem can be resolved by the proper specification of licensees' rights. In Australia, for example, spectrum is auctioned subject to restrictions relating to frequency and when and where it can be used. The last objective is achievable by placing restrictions on the power of any signal that can be transmitted outside a given geographical area. This does not prevent owners of adjacent frequencies making mutually acceptable agreements among themselves to vary these conditions.

There is, however, a further argument in favour of restrictions on use – that it forces equipment manufacturers and operators to harmonise spectrum use globally, with consequent benefits in the form of economies of scale in equipment manufacture. However, there is no reason why this harmonisation cannot be achieved by agreement among firms. It would clearly be foolish of them each to choose a different frequency if that increased their cost of service. Yet there may be genuine disagreements among firms as to where the best technical and market solutions lie. These disagreements are more satisfactorily resolved through competition in the marketplace than through an administrative solution. Under this more radical approach, harmonisation decisions would be taken out of the hands of regulators and given to operators and equipment manufacturers.

Finally, there is the question of social obligation. The introduction of the market system will clearly make it more difficult to impose social obligations on operators, than an administrative system in which the assumption of the social responsibility is the sole or principal price paid for the licence. However, rollout restrictions, social pricing requirements and other obligations can be put into effect via a competitive licence process. The obligations simply reduce the value of the licence and the costs of enforcement rise. Moreover competition for the right to implement social obligations can yield better results than the simple use of regulatory fiat.

Conclusion

In summary, it seems to me that Melody's work on spectrum has identified the fundamental nature of the problem – the inefficiency associated with the administrative methods of assigning frequencies. He has also identified the weapons available to promote efficiency – administrative pricing and a combination of markets with increased flexibility for spectrum use. But in my opinion he could have gone further, without sacrificing those social objectives to which he has throughout his life attached so much importance.

3G Auctions: A Change of Course

John Ure

Introduction

From the viewpoint of the telecom industry, debacle is probably not too strong a word to use to describe the outcome of the European auctions for third generation (3G) mobile telephone licences during the summer of 2000. The United Kingdom and German governments raised close to US$ 80 billion between them, a feat hailed as a great success at the time. Martin Wolf (2001: 23) of the *Financial Times* of London responded passionately to criticisms that high auction prices would cripple the industry and burden consumers with high costs:

> When critics complain ... , they have to be saying one (or more) of four things: that the government should have made a present of the excess profits – or, more exactly, of the scarcity value of the spectrum – to the likes of Vodafone AirTouch and British Telecommunications; that the managers and owners of these companies are incapable of working out what a licence is worth to them; that taxpayers should protect shareholders against their own irrational exuberance; or that the interests of taxpayers should be sacrificed to those relatively well-off consumers. These propositions are ridiculous, outrageous, or both. ... It is perfectly possible that the victors have been over-optimistic and will suffer from the "winner's curse". But this should be of little concern, since the licences are "sunk costs" and are unlikely to have any long-term effect on pricing.

As a critic of the auctions, I believe that the managers and owners of these companies were incapable of working out the worth of a licence. The level of uncertainty that surrounds the business case for 3G is quite different from that of 1G or 2G or even 2.5G. Even in 2002, the technology is not fully known and nor are alternative technologies that can serve as broadband wireless substitutes, for example, the 802.11 standard. Still, no one knows what services will be available, which of them will sell, who will buy them or how the revenue will be collected along the value chain.

The 3G value chain is different from earlier mobile phone markets. 3G provides mobile access to the Internet. The demand for that access is derived from demand for services delivered over the Internet. These services may not even be delivered to the same device used to make the request. Unlike in the case of voice-focused 1G and 2G, the range of services likely to be in demand is not intrinsic to the network.

It appears that the managers who paid such high auction prices had not stopped to think through the implications. What did they think they were buying when they bought licences? The right to provide access, yes, but what else? No licence is required to provide content. In the Internet world, the idea of locking customers into a 'walled garden' restricting access to the content and applications provided by a single 3G service operator is a non-starter, not to say illegal in France and unacceptable to the regulator in the United Kingdom.

Ken Binmore (2001), advisor to the British and Hong Kong governments on spectrum auctions, stated that 'nobody but a fool bids more in an auction than he thinks the licence is worth'. Had he not read the admission by Sir Peter Bonfield, British Telecom's CEO, that 'We spent £10 billion too much?' (*Sunday Times* 2001). Sir Christopher Gent, CEO of Vodafone, concurred: 'We wish we hadn't paid so much'. Paul Klemperer (2001), an architect of the United Kingdom auction process, commented that 'At £1 billion or £10 billion the psychology is the same'. After all, designers of auctions think their job is to raise as much money as possible for their client. Less convincing was *The Economist*'s hindsight in May 2001. 'The real cause of the companies' troubles is that the market has changed. They did their sums before they made their bids. They knew the risks. Who else knows what the market is worth?' This nicely misses the point, as well as the irony of its own rhetorical question. If no one could know the sensible value to place on a 3G licence, then an up-front money auction was totally inappropriate.

The debate moved from the financial press to academic journals with Cave and Valletti (2000) arguing the orthodox position regarding sunk costs, responding in particular to Nicholas Negroponte's assertion that the United Kingdom auction fee imposed an 'economically unsustainable' tax on mobile Internet services. Already deeply engaged in the public debate in Hong Kong, I responded (Ure 2001).

Hong Kong's 3G Debate
The popular view in Hong Kong throughout the summer of 2000 was that the government should follow the United Kingdom and Germany. A turning point in the debate was William Melody's keynote lecture to the Telecom InfoTechnology Forum (TIF), a quarterly industrial roundtable in 2000. Representatives of the

Hong Kong regulatory authority and policy makers regularly participate in the TIF. At the 2000 forum, a member of the Legislative Council who had been leading the demand for a British-style auction admitted that the issue was more complex than it first appeared to be. To turn the Legislature from the idea that the primary purpose of a 3G auction was to raise as much money as possible was a precondition for clear thinking on the issue.

In his lecture, Melody reviewed the history of thinking about spectrum allocation and assignment, drawing on his experience at the US Federal Communications Commission. The purely administrative or beauty contest approach was inadequate and was usually determined by lobbying skills. As the supply of spectrum is not market determined and its public good aspects require the adoption of standards, market mechanisms were unlikely to solve all the problems. These arguments subsequently appeared in *info* (Melody 2001b) and they undoubtedly opened minds to my own contribution, first submitted in May 2000 in response to a regulatory Consultation Paper, with a follow-up in October which was published subsequently (Ure 2001)[5].

First, the sunk cost problem. On the one hand, it is not true that sunk cost will have no impact in a competitive market. If there is a common denominator sunk cost, namely the lowest winning bid, then it makes good sense for operators to aim to recover at least that. They will build it into their annual forward-looking costs. If one firm breaks ranks and cleans up, then its resulting market power will give it the opportunity and, therefore, the incentive, to recoup at least this amount, even at the cost of slowing growth under certain circumstances. On the other hand, a large overhang of debt raises the risk premium on lines of credit and the cost of capital, and acts as a disincentive to build out the network to areas of marginal profitability.

The enormous 3G debt overhang in Europe entirely overshadows the arguments of economists. The outstanding corporate debt of British Telecom, Deutsche Telekom, France Telecom and KPN was a staggering €185 billion as of June 2001. As their credit ratings declined, their interest payments rose. 'This is the year 1929 for the telecom industry' was how one telecom executive put it to the *Asian Wall Street Journal*. It gives a very different meaning to telecom reform than is associated with Melody's work. Even lending banks have faced warnings from financial regulators in Europe. It is also true that this debacle coincided with recessionary trends in the United States and Europe. But the fact remains that consumer confidence has not been the principal problem facing would-be 3G operators, and their 2.5G progenitors. Consumer indifference is more the case, compounded by technological glitches that disappoint those who have tried the new mobile phones, such as WAP handsets (*Asian Wall Street Journal* 2001).

My royalty auction proposal sought to achieve two objectives: to provide a guaranteed return on the use of spectrum to the community, and to avoid the large up-front costs of a 3G licence, the value of which was impossible to determine. The latter proposition is perhaps best underlined by reference to real options valuations (Alleman and Noam 1999). In my model, using a straightforward net present valuation of a hypothetical Hong Kong 2G operator with a 20% market share, and quite generous assumptions about future customer demand and average revenue per user (ARPU), the estimated value of a 3G licence turned out to be US$ 72 million. This rose to US$ 88 million if the capture of a 25% market share by 2010 was assumed. In reality there were only four bidders for four licences and they each went for an estimated net present value (NPV) reserve price of US$ 50-60 million, depending upon the discount rate. The real option value, using the Black Scholes model that requires *inter alia* data on past share price variations, was six times this value. The collapse of share prices reduces the value of the real option exercise. Yet the real option underlines the possibility of valuing future business, in this case, on the basis of the options a 3G licence offers. Few in the industry doubt that over the long term 3G will become a successful business, but none can place a value on it.

Conclusion

If the regulatory authorities view 3G as a business that will bring wider benefits to the community and economy, for example, by stimulating the sectors capable of producing content and applications, it makes sense not to second-guess the future. It makes better sense to synchronise the need to pay a fee for spectrum with the ability to pay. A royalty auction does exactly that. An alternative approach is to replace the guaranteed minimum payment to the public purse with an incentive to reduce prices to consumers. This would be justified if the public externalities were considered very important.

Box III.11.1 – A Model

A tax rate or royalty payment on revenue, call it X, shall be bid such that $X = x^*$ when $B \leq L$, where x^* is the auction reserve price, B is the number of bidders and L is the number of licences on offer; and $X = X^*$ when $B > L$, where X^* is the auction bid price. An alternative is to set $X = 0$ if income $Y \leq Y^*$, and $X = X^*$ when $Y \geq Y^*$, where $Y^* = P^* \bullet Q^*$, where P^* is the ceiling price offered by the licensee, and Q^* the number of subscribers at the ceiling price that triggers Y^*, and where X^* is some positive tax rate or royalty payment on revenue.

NOTE: $X = X^*$ if $Y \geq Y^* = P^* \bullet Q^* \leq P^\wedge \bullet Q^\wedge$,
where $P^\wedge = P^* \bullet [(P^* - P)/P^*]$ where $[(P^* - P)/P^*] \leq 1$,
and $Q^\wedge = Q^* \bullet [(Q - Q^*)/Q^*]$ where $[(Q - Q^*)/Q^*] \geq 1$
so that $P^* \geq P^\wedge$, and $Q^* \leq Q^\wedge$

This model says that as the licensee reduces P below the ceiling price P^* the number of subscribers required to trigger Y^* rises above Q^*. In cases where the price elasticity of demand is > 1, revenues and therefore royalty payments will increase as prices fall. In cases where the price elasticity of demand < 1, the benefits of price reductions fall exclusively to consumers.

A Competitive Market Approach to Interconnection Payments

David Gabel

Introduction

Telecom networks are unique because they require a high degree of cooperation from all parties involved and because of the interdependency of network components. Technical standards, service definitions, and pricing arrangements all must be well understood by the various users of the network in order to ensure efficient provision of the network's services (Melody 1997a). Therefore, in order to allocate properly the joint costs and benefits of the telecom network, a sound interconnection pricing policy is of paramount importance.

Establishing the price for interconnection, however, is a challenging undertaking, and there has been pressure on regulatory commissions to adopt interconnection arrangements that set termination charges at zero. This is due to the perception that regulators cannot measure costs correctly and historically have chosen interconnection prices that are too high (DeGraba 2000: paras 69, 91). In addition, proponents of zero termination charges argue that the market distortions from high interconnection prices have induced new entrants in telecommunication services since 1996 to target firms, such as Internet Service Providers (ISPs), that terminate large volumes of traffic.

In this contribution, the concept of 'bill-and-keep' whereby the calling party's network does not have to pay the receiving party's network to terminate the call is discussed. Whether this outcome is efficient and consistent with competitive markets is examined. An explanation of why the flow of traffic has been unbalanced between incumbent long-distance operators and competitive local-access operators is offered. This outcome is the natural outcome of the barriers to entry created by incumbents in their refusal to provide collocation to ISPs.

Setting the Correct Price

Interconnection arrangements in the telecom industry have a long history. Beginning in 1894, when the initial patents expired, the Bell System had to enter into interconnection contracts with independent telephone companies, and the Independents similarly signed contracts with each other. Bill-and-keep contracts were negotiated where traffic was balanced. In other cases, the company that originated more calls made a settlement payment. However, the most prevalent form of interconnection was revenue sharing. For example, a typical interconnection contract for a long-distance call required that 15-25% of the originating revenue be paid to the network (Gabel 1987: 171-2). The contracts were established before the advent of federal or state regulation, but the terms varied little after regulation was established. For local traffic, Bill-and-Keep was adopted where traffic was balanced. Otherwise, reciprocal compensation or access charges to recover the cost of interconnection were used.

The originating party paid for the cost of interconnection under calling-party-pays arrangements, and where traffic was balanced under bill-and-keep. Furthermore, the retail prices generally were designed so that the customers who initiated the calls paid for the calls, rather than having the cost of interconnection distributed evenly among the customers. This has been standard practice in the telecom industry on the basis that the decision made by an originating party to place a call is the decision that imposes costs on the network.

The history of interconnection of telephone companies illustrates that: the costs of interconnection traditionally have been recovered from the calling party on the basis that the calling party is the cost-causer; the practice of calling party pays predates the establishment of state or federal regulation; and; bill-and-keep has been adopted in situations where traffic is balanced – where traffic is not balanced, the carrier on which the majority of traffic originated has made payments to the terminating carrier.

Practical Constraints on Interconnection Pricing Arrangements

In a world with no externalities (positive or negative) and perfect information, interconnection pricing would be straightforward for regulators. In such a world, telephone service would represent a service for which two parties benefit and a call would be placed so long as the sum of the benefits exceeds the costs. At the margin, costs would be shared based on the benefits obtained by each party. In the real world, however, it is impossible to allocate the benefits to the calling and called parties. Thus, it is problematic to ascertain how costs should be shared, that is, we cannot allocate costs on the basis of benefits because we do not know how to measure the benefits. Lacking information on valuation, the appropriate policy fallback is a second-best solution, using cost-based prices.

Moreover, with the growth of competition in the telephone industry, it is even more important that prices be established that govern the connection from one network to another. Regulators should be concerned that incumbent local access companies will try to establish barriers to entry, and to block entry by establishing too high an interconnection price. To avoid too high a price, regulators could impose a zero price on interconnection (that is, bill-and-keep). But would this be reasonable?

Most other industries do not rely on bill-and-keep, for example, financial services, credit and ATM cards, package delivery services and airports (Shy 2001). In the telephone industry we are beginning to observe the operations of competitive markets and policy makers should not be enticed by simplistic and non-competitive zero-price solutions like bill-and-keep.

THE DISTRIBUTION OF BENEFITS FROM PHONE CALLS

The strongest argument for bill-and-keep would be if the receiving party equally benefits from a call. This has been argued by DeGraba (2000: para 4), but the benefits of a telephone call are not shared evenly by the caller and the receiver.

Telephone calls are characterised by joint demand since there are at least two parties involved in any call. Similarly, the call is jointly provided by both the caller's and the call receiver's network. Consequently, the issue arises as to how to allocate joint costs.

Since there are at least two parties to any telephone call, presumably both benefit from the call. DeGraba (2000) argues that this is a justification for reversing the historical use of calling-party-pays, by shifting termination charges to the receiving party. However, even though call receivers benefit from some calls, it is impossible to say how the benefits of the call are shared. Therefore, it is inappropriate to assume that both parties benefit equally, and to base policy changes thereon. For example, calls from telemarketers surely benefit the caller more than the receiver. Many would argue that these calls have negative value for the receiver since he/she is unlikely to be interested or is interrupted in the middle of another activity.

Proponents of mandatory bill-and-keep interconnection arrangements argue that callers make fewer calls since they must bear the entire costs of the call rather than sharing them with the receiver as would be the case under bill-and-keep arrangements (Allegiance Telecom 2001: 21). However, the fact that call receivers have the option of having toll-free numbers (for example, many businesses choose to do this to encourage more calls) suggests that call receivers have the option of purchasing a specific service which encourages them to receive more phone calls, and that the network is not under-utilised as suggested by proponents of mandatory bill-and-keep interconnection arrangements.

There is no empirical evidence that callers would place more calls under Bill-and-Keep arrangements. Under 'toll-free' services, the call receiver pays because he/she has decided that the benefits justify the additional costs incurred, whereas customers who choose not to have toll free numbers are saying implicitly that they benefit more by making phone calls than receiving them. Moreover, the proliferation of products to screen unwanted calls (for example, Caller ID or Call Waiting) clearly contradicts the assumption under bill-and-keep that calling and called parties benefit equally from phone calls (Allegiance Telecom 2001: 21). Without these devices, only the calling party has complete information regarding the purpose of a telephone call, and thus he or she should bear the costs of termination. Since not all consumers can afford or desire call-screening devices, policy changes that unnecessarily encourage their purchase would be a costly technology distortion.

INTERCONNECTION AND NETWORK EXTERNALITIES

Using a calling-party-pays system as opposed to bill-and-keep is more likely to internalise positive network externalities between calling and called parties and is one of the main justifications for interconnection charges. [6] Suppose that as a result of the called party being able and willing to accept a call, the calling party receives a direct benefit. This is an externality flowing from the called party to the calling party. Assuming that this externality is larger compared to the externality going in the other direction (which would seem logical since the call was initiated by the caller who presumably has a higher willingness to pay), then there may be efficiency grounds for having the calling party subsidise the called party.

The incentive required to capture positive network externalities can be introduced using a termination charge since it encourages the receiving party to accept phone calls, whereas termination charges assessed on the receiving party will discourage the use of telephone services. A termination charge received by the terminating network will, through competition, be passed back to the called party by way of cheaper retail prices for services provided. If the calling party funds this termination charge, then this could be an efficient transfer between the two types of callers. An example where such network externalities are likely to be very important is the case of interconnection between fixed line and mobile networks. However, by imposing mandatory bill-and-keep such transfers will be eliminated. This will lead to serious inefficiencies where there are significant network externalities.

ECONOMIC EFFICIENCY PRINCIPLES

Under bill-and-keep, switching cost recovery would be folded into all the other costs that must be recovered. The final price would be either traffic-sensitive or a fixed per customer charge. However, if regulators cannot set traffic-sensitive prices correctly, as argued by the proponents of bill-and-keep, how can these costs be recovered efficiently?

Having the user pay a per minute price would discourage the use of telecom services since there would be an incentive for parties not to answer calls to reduce termination charges assessed on them, that is, bill-and-keep would not capture the positive network externalities associated with the Calling Party Network Pays (CPNP) principle.

Per minute charges also are not desirable for covering termination costs under bill-and-keep arrangements because they would tip the market towards monopoly since consumers would have an incentive to subscribe to larger networks in order to avoid these charges.

Any proposal to replace usage sensitive terminating access fees with a fixed customer charge contradicts the view that economic efficiency dictates that traffic sensitive costs be recovered through traffic sensitive prices. Aside from the argument that the cost-causer is not the cost-payer, there are a number of reasons that bill-and-keep arrangements violate the principles of economic efficiency.

- Reforming the existing CPNP regimes with bill-and-keep will require a reduction in per-minute charges to the caller and an increase in flat end-user charges to recover the lost revenue since the called parties' providers would have no other way to recover termination costs except through flat-fees to its customers.
- A fixed monthly per-line subscriber charge ignores the capacity costs associated with termination of phone calls – all customers would pay the same fee for termination of calls regardless of the number of calls received.
- In unregulated markets bill-and-keep interconnection arrangements exist only under the restrictive condition of balanced traffic – however, in dynamic and partially regulated markets like telecom there is no guarantee that the traffic between any two operators will remain balanced over time and thus a bill-and-keep arrangement does not afford adequate flexibility.
- Under bill-and-keep and a fixed monthly subscriber line charge, the terminating company has less incentive to provide good service since it is not getting paid for the termination service on each call on a per call basis – there will be under-investment in termination services and over-investment in other services since recovering costs from a fixed monthly line subscriber charge does not send the proper signals about the cost of individual calls.

Bill-and-keep amounts to setting termination charges at zero, which is clearly below cost since termination costs are non-zero.

Setting the Price of Interconnection

Interconnection pricing has been based traditionally on reciprocal compensation agreements reached between various local access companies. But, what is the impact of traditional interconnection pricing arrangements on Internet service? Specifically, ISPs receive calls, but do not make calls. Consequently, some argue that this one-way traffic has led to a significant amount of money flowing away from incumbent local access companies as the ISPs do not pay termination charges and collocate facilities with competitive local access companies.

Regulators have begun to rethink how to price interconnection and to consider bill-and-keep interconnection pricing arrangements in order to force ISPs to cover termination costs (Federal Communications Commission 2001a). However, imposing mandatory bill-and-keep to correct for the ISP collocation problem is arguably misguided and unsound.

The incumbent local access companies claim that the competitive local access companies have targeted ISPs in order to take advantage of high reciprocal compensation rates. However, it is not a problem that the new entrants have targeted ISPs as customers. There is a reason why ISPs should collocate with the new entrants which has nothing to do with reciprocal compensation. Incumbents have said that ISPs cannot collocate in their central switching offices. ISPs can save a tremendous amount of money by collocating with the competitors.

It should also come as no surprise that new entrants have targeted ISPs as customers. Since before the passage of the US Telecommunications Act of 1996 it has been understood that fledgling local access companies would, at least in the early stages of competition, primarily target businesses and other high margin telecom customers. Empirical evidence suggests that the Internet expanded rapidly around the same time the Telecommunications Act opened the door for competitors to provide local telecom services.

The marketplace for ISPs expanded significantly at the same time as newly formed competitive local access companies began searching for customers. There is a fundamental difference between ISPs and other businesses which makes it easier for the new entrants to attract ISP business. There were no longstanding relationships with incumbents to overcome and local number portability was not a concern. The competitors attracted business by offering state-of-the-art local fibre networks and by offering to collocate ISP equipment (Focal Communications Corporation et al. 2001: 19-22).

The beneficial relationship between the competitive local access companies and ISPs is not a one-way street. They have become natural business associates because the new entrants provide certain synergies that are not present in an incumbent-ISP relationship. In order to avoid unnecessary switching and transport costs (Gillett 1995), ISPs require the ability to aggregate Internet-bound traffic in a facility that is collocated in order to avoid the cost of buying local loops that carry dial-in traffic and additional loops to carry the aggregated traffic back to the central switching office. The traffic is returned to the central switching office in order to be shipped onto the Internet.

Collocation is normally not offered to ISPs by incumbents because the FCC (Federal Communications Commission 1996) declined to require that incumbent local access companies make collocation space available to Enhanced Service Providers. The incumbents would only be willing to create such barriers if they believe that the regulators will rescue them if a clever entrant finds a way around the barrier. Regulators can improve the process of interconnection by holding parties to the terms of trade that they initially proposed. In the US, the FCC has been too willing to accept the ISP traffic imbalance as a problem, rather than as an appropriate penalty imposed on an incumbent that has created a barrier to entry and is unwilling to allow the efficient collocation of ISPs.

Pricing Based on Capacity Charges

One problem with the current pricing of interconnection is that termination in the switch is based on a per minute charge with an equal charge on- and off-peak. It would be more efficient to set charges based on the manner in which costs are incurred. On digital switching machines, incremental interconnection costs are incurred when the interoffice trunk is terminated. This capacity cost should be the basis for setting prices.

In the case of termination costs that are traffic sensitive, capacity charges are the best mechanism for recovering termination costs since the cost of terminating a call is determined by peak usage. Provided that the capacity charges are based on forward-looking economic costs, they are an efficient means of recovering termination costs.

Capacity charges are an effective and efficient way for one carrier to pay another for using its network. Yet, it would be virtually impossible to levy such charges directly on end users. Hence, it is reasonable – and pro-competitive – for each carrier to determine on its own how to recover the capacity charges from its customers.

It is also important to point out that technological advances argue in favour of more carrier-paid capacity-based charges rather than direct end-user charges. Packet switching is replacing circuit switching, and carriers are interconnecting with high-capacity links. Consequently, increased reliance on per minute prices instead of capacity charges is nonsensical because the former will impose unnecessary operational constraints and costs on carriers and equipment manufacturers.

Packet switching is offered on a capacity basis (Qwest 2001: s. 11), and cost analysts are able to determine the cost of providing capacity on a packet switched system. There is no evidence that firms that interconnect packet switching networks rely on bill-and-keep. The imposition of bill-and-keep would be contrary to the manner in which telecom pricing has evolved to reflect the cost structure of new technologies.

Conclusion
It is impossible to measure the value or benefits of a telephone call – especially for the party receiving the call. Value-laden policy decisions that have no empirical or theoretical basis are bad policy. The cost-causer-pays approach is relatively more efficient as it avoids value-laden judgements about the benefits of telephone calls and the issue of to whom the benefits accrue.

Interconnection payment schemes should be based on market forces and they should reflect the fact that the benefits of phone calls are not evenly distributed between callers and receivers. These schemes should capture the positive network externalities associated with the CPNP principle so as not to encourage the under-utilisation of telecom services; and capacity charges that reflect traffic sensitive costs should be employed instead of fixed end-user charges to recover termination costs.

A one-size-fits-all interconnection pricing regime should not be used to cover the costs of interconnection of network traffic. This is not efficient in a market comprised of a variety of types of services that is very dynamic and innovative. Adopting such schemes to cover the costs of interconnection of network traffic is not sound policy. Telecom networks are unique. They require a high degree of cooperation from all parties involved because of the interdependency of network components. Cooperation is only economically efficient and conducive to competition when it is voluntary and contractual. This would not be the case under bill-and-keep interconnection pricing arrangements. Receiving no payment for handling traffic of rival firms would undermine competition in the telecom industry.

# III.13

Multi-Utility Regulation: Yet Another Convergence?

Jens C. Arnbak

INTRODUCTION: *Et in Arcadia Ego*
Midsummer 1988 at Cumberland Lodge, Windsor Great Park, was an Arcadian setting under royal oaks for a conference about the new challenges for communication policy research posed by deregulation and privatisation. Telecom reform had been put on the academic agenda in the United Kingdom and given the moral support of the Director General of the Office of Telecommunications (OFTEL), the new telecom regulator. The national Economic and Social Research Council planned a multidisciplinary programme dedicated to this field called the Programme on Information and Communication Technologies (PICT). And the impressive, border-crossing North American academic to whom this *Festschrift* is dedicated became the programme director.

William Melody did not present papers at the Communication Policy Research (CPR) conferences in Windsor that I attended in the late 1980s, but his impact and experience became clear in the vivid discussions. With hindsight, some *ex ante* influence might also be inferred: The opening paper at CPR '88 analysed common problems of deregulation of different network industries in the United States; its author was Professor Harry Trebing (1988), the founder of the Institute of Public Utilities at the Michigan State University – and Melody's academic mentor.

In this contribution, I first revisit Trebing's classical network industries – railways, airlines, telephony and power utilities – and also consider modern specimens such as mobile communications and Internet backbones and their special regulatory problems. I then offer a discussion of the institutional convergence of the associated regulators. Should multi-utility regulation be given more weight than, say, the familiar technological convergence between information technology, computers and communications or the use of general antitrust principles for market analysis in the new sector-specific European Union (EU) legislation on electronic communications (European Commission 2000)?

KEY REGULATORY ISSUES IN DIFFERENT NETWORK SECTORS
Figure 3.13.1 summarises characteristic policy and competition problems inherent in the key network sectors frequently described as public utilities. The different

history and economic or physical characteristics of each sector have resulted in various regulatory regimes. These *ex-ante* regimes have been designed to repair specific market failures or address generic public policy concerns, for example, safety, network integrity, universal service, user billing and terminal addressing, plurality of content, etc.

Figure III.13.1 Policy and Competition Problems in Network Sectors

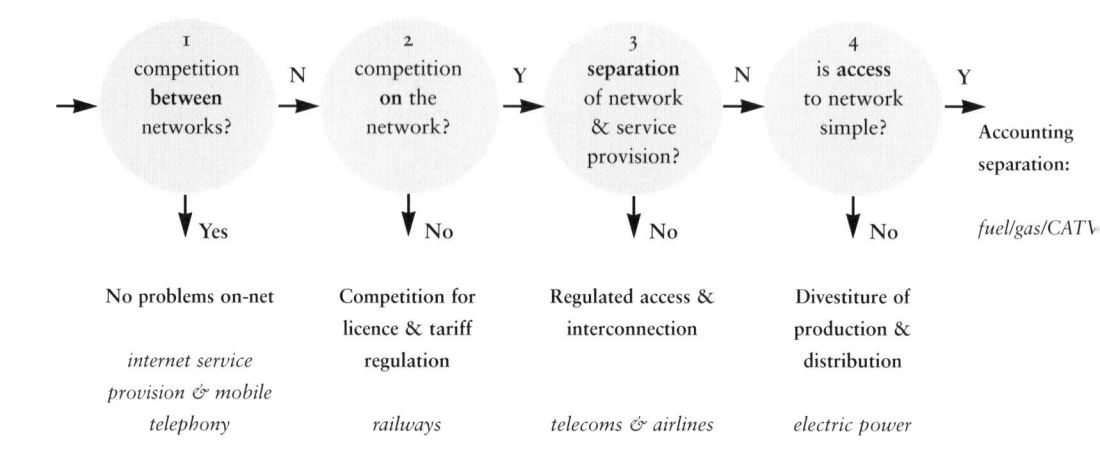

```
→  1                    N   2                 Y   3                  N   4                  Y
   competition     →       competition   →      separation      →      is access       →   Accounting
   between                 on the               of network             to network           separation:
   networks?               network?             & service              simple?
                                                provision?
        ↓ Yes                   ↓ No                 ↓ No                   ↓ No              fuel/gas/CATV
   
   No problems on-net      Competition for      Regulated access &     Divestiture of
                           licence & tariff     interconnection        production &
   internet service        regulation                                  distribution
   provision & mobile
   telephony               railways             telecoms & airlines    electric power
```

Source: Derived from a White Paper on Network Industries, The Netherlands Ministry of Economic Affairs (2000), in Dutch.

General competition law applies to all network sectors in Figure 3.13.1. However, antitrust authorities have seldom seen fit to deal, in a timely manner, with public issues emerging in network markets. Arguably the most successful cases of invoking the doctrine of misuse of power in the communications sector resulted in abolition of network operators' traditional prohibition of competitive provision of terminals – such as the Carterfone decision (Federal Communications Commission 1968) and the BT Telex case (European Court of Justice 1985) – more famous as crowbars opening monopoly markets than for instant economic or social impact. The flexibility of competition case law enables definition of all relevant markets for potential regulatory action. Still, the actual repertoire of interventions by antitrust authorities is a binary choice between complete *laissez-faire* and a heavy penalty. The duration of such *ex post* proceedings is illustrated by the long running case against Microsoft for its alleged tying of a new Internet browser (Explorer) to its dominant Windows '95 operating system.

Where targeted prescriptions with significant economic or social impact need to be designed and invoked *ex ante* to ensure, for instance, appropriate network (co)operation or service pricing, the specific features of technology and access methods in the network sector need consideration. These features explain the different possibilities for competition in the various sectors in Figure 3.13.1.

The different analytical branches (hereafter roundabouts) in this flow diagram outline key criteria for determining the feasible degree of liberalisation of network sectors, and the associated regulatory tools. The initial – and most fundamental – question (Roundabout 1) addresses the possibility of choice for customers. Can they freely choose between different network operators, or does customer capture prevail? In many OECD countries, the national mobile telephony market has become competitive, particularly where number portability lowers consumers' barriers for switching to another operator. The same applies to access to the Internet via international backbones, which now often have a capacity glut. Note that freedom of network choice does not ensure *off*-net users reasonable prices, as evidenced by the retail prices for calls from fixed to mobile phones in Europe (more generally, this applies in markets where the calling party pays for calls to mobile terminals) and for international mobile roaming. Such protracted problems arise from unregulated issues in Roundabout 3.

In the absence of an effective choice *between* competing networks, Roundabout 2 is entered. If service competition *on* the net is also absent, as is generally the case for railways and (local) bus lines, price regulation is appropriate. Other regulatory tools to be considered are terms for re-licensing the service periodically or in the event of an unacceptable degradation of service levels.

Roundabout 3 provides, in principle, for competition *on* the network(s). Examples are carrier selection in liberalised transport industries and telephone markets. However, the incumbent operators here are often vertically integrated, that is, with no clear-cut business – let alone legal – separation between their upstream carrier facilities and their downstream service provision. Hence regulatory intervention may be required to ensure non-discriminatory interconnection of competing networks and equal access to key facilities, such as terminal gates or luggage-handling facilities in airports. Whereas retail price regulation should be rolled back as effective competition develops, wholesale prices for handling traffic between competing networks continue to need monitoring and, in the event that commercial negotiations between parties fail or are not in the public interest, determining by the regulator.

The threshold for economic market power in a wholesale market cannot be set notionally at a fictitious level of 50% of all customers or of the on-net retail revenues of the dominant operator(s) concerned. Rather, it is related to the actual percentage(s) of total traffic passed *off*-net to the interconnecting operator(s). Therefore, the relative bargaining power of a network operator when negotiating an interconnection agreement for *two-way* traffic is roughly proportional to the *square* of its number of retail customers. This non-linear relationship explains the ongoing erosion of peer-to-peer agreements between Internet Service Providers (ISPs). The increasing imbalance in their sizes caused by rapid horizontal market consolidation raises unresolved interconnection concerns. Vertical integration with content provision may add the additional public policy issue of discriminatory access to information.

Such regulatory concerns may seem less important in the linear situation encountered in classical one-way (that is, purely distributive) networks for cable television and power delivery. So far, legal or accounting separation of upstream production from downstream distribution has been sufficient (Roundabout 4). However, recent events in the United States (increasing vertical concentration of media production and distribution and the risk of failure of major integrated power companies) have raised concerns about the adequacy of regulatory oversight of activities in converging sectors. Two examples suffice to illustrate the issues:

- the use of power lines for public electronic communication, for example, Internet broadband access; and
- upgrading the smart (SIM) card used in GSM mobile terminals to serve as a credit card for financial services that is underway.

Both, as yet fictitious, will raise the question of the appropriate authority to oversee the problems from overlapping, but differently regulated, domains. In the former example, a US-style utility commission could well have both the jurisdiction and the expertise. The latter example suggests a more far-fetched integration of the communication regulator and the financial regulator(s) setting conditions for consumer loans and unpaid sales. So what are reasonable criteria for deciding on the institutional convergence of regulators?

Convergence of Regulatory Institutions?

Justification for joint regulation of different network industries may be found in the substitutability of their output products on the relevant market, in economies of scale and scope of regulatory expertise and, above all, in constitutional and political tradition. The United States has a long history of independent regulatory agencies at both federal and state levels. Elsewhere, government departments were made responsible for setting and enforcing the desired national standards in most network markets of strong public interest. Traditionally, government authority was often reinforced by state ownership of such network industries, and by international regulatory organisations established by treaties between states, such as the International Telecommunication Union (ITU). With the rapid globalisation of trade in the last decades of the 20th century, the traditional arrangements are under review or being reversed in many countries.

The more fundamental changes occur in the geographic regions and economic sectors relying mostly on high-speed international connections with high transaction volumes, for example, in financial markets, electronic communication and civil aviation. The European Central Bank has replaced national banks or government treasuries in setting the key interest rates to ensure monetary stability in member states. Since 1998, the EU telecom directives on Open Network Provision (ONP) require Member States to make their National Regulatory Authorities (NRAs) independent, not merely of the incumbent operators, but also of shareholding governments. The new EU directives, entering into force in 2003, will make the next step towards supranational regulation of electronic communication, by giving the European Commission the right to veto NRA definitions of relevant markets and the designation of dominant players in these markets. Why did this become necessary so soon?

Digital information and communication technologies offer a unique combination of features and options with substantial economic significance (Arnbak 1998; 2000). These include:

- transport with the speed of light (unlike pipelines, rails, roads, etc.);
- transport without loss of quality and value (unlike dissipation in electric power transmission);
- copying/broadcasting, bundling and re-routing/refiling of information (unlike the post, printing and publishing sectors);
- complementary customer access options – choice between wired access and wireless networks (with different economic and operational advantages); and
- lightweight, portable and tradable terminal devices (unlike sea, air and rail networks).

These dynamic features explain why the World Trade Organization (WTO) has been able to reach trade agreements in telecom earlier than in most other networked service areas. New types of switching (such as the Internet protocols) and bulk transmission (on optical backbones) change network economies radically from the inside. Where sufficient economies of scale can be achieved with optical cables, the marginal cost of long-distance transmission tends toward zero. This 'death of distance' reveals, in turn, the increasingly dominant cost of the local networks providing access to individual customers and the economic impetus that broadband access might provide if appropriately introduced.

When traditional benefits and costs can shift to different user communities, or to other parts of communication networks, modifications to the regulatory framework for public control of tariffs and access obligations are required. In the terminology of competition law, the relevant product and/or geographical markets will have to be ascertained much more frequently, due to ICT dynamics. The ONP rules prescribe a limited number of relevant product markets (leased lines, fixed telephony and mobile telephony), rather than a procedure for (re-) defining them. Hence, the insistence of the European Commission on the right to veto erratic NRA decisions in this critical area.

On re-examining Figure 3.13.1, it becomes clear why other network sectors are likely to present quite different regulatory issues. Even within one roundabout, a different network technology often raises other access and management problems. In Roundabout 4, for example, synchronous combination on a single alternating current power grid of electricity from several competing high-power plants calls for independent network management to control the technical difficulties and risks. Slow, non-oscillating pipeline flows from different suppliers of natural gas are far easier to combine and control.

Conclusion

On the basis of these observations and comparisons of regulatory priorities in different network sectors, I conclude with several tentative theses on the scope for convergence and harmonisation of different regulatory tasks.

There is considerable scope for harmonising the concept of an (independent) national regulatory authority in the EU in 2003 when the new ONP directives for electronic communication enter into force. In at least three Member States (France, Italy and the United Kingdom), the NRAs will then also deal with all aspects of broadcast regulation not related to programming of public channels. In three Member States (Austria, Spain and The Netherlands), the government will continue to reserve frequency spectrum regulation to itself.

From 2003, the European Commission will monitor the *ex ante* definition by NRAs of relevant markets and economic market power, consistent with general competition law. This may reduce the need for a parallel scrutiny by the competent national authority. It also renders concurrent powers for the NRA to apply the doctrine of misuse of market power as a more appropriate and effective complement to ONP rules.

Melody's lemma (attributed):
A multi-utility regulator's ability to deploy some staff (accountants, hearing officers, legal counsel, support personnel, etc.) in several sectors is a practical advantage which, however, cannot outweigh the political risk of collateral damage in the likely event of strong criticism of the regulator in any single sector.

IV

Next...

Ian Miles

John W. Houghton

Knud Erik Skouby

Roderick Sanatan

Oscar H. Gandy, Jr

Peter S. Anderson

Peter Shields

B. P. Sanjay

Meheroo Jussawalla

Supriya Singh

Jörg Becker

IV

Next...

Robin Mansell, Rohan Samarajiva and Amy Mahan

In the early period of telecom reform from the 1960s to 1980s, William Melody's commitment to change was clear. Some might speculate that his motivation for change was simply to destroy the monopolistic power of the incumbent firm, AT&T. But others would argue that Melody's principal preoccupation in mobilising forces for change is to achieve improved responsiveness of industry to what he takes to be the public interest in communication and information. The public interest in an efficient and affordable telecom infrastructure extends far beyond the interests of firms. For Melody, it always includes the interests of consumers, citizens and small businesses. In fact, Melody's commitment to change is motivated by his fundamental interest in, and commitment to, what happens *next*, after reform. What society-wide developments are likely to spring from renewed innovations in the voice and data services markets? Where will new concentrations of power congeal as we become increasingly dependent on digital technologies and information services?

Even during the hectic days of preparation for testimony before regulatory agencies and the courts in the most contested periods of telecom reform, not just in North America, but in many other regions, Melody has found time to write and lecture about the significance of information society developments. He has argued, for instance, that:

the functioning of society depends upon information and its effective communication among society's members. Information, and the means for its communication, have a fundamental and pervasive influence upon all institutions. The economic characteristics of information and communication systems affect the nature of the information that is generated and the conditions under which it is used and interpreted (Melody 1987b: 1313).

For Melody, investigation of the economic characteristics of information requires attention to both the supply and the demand sides of the market. The term economic has to be considered carefully here. Melody's definition of the 'economic' is drawn from Institutional Economics, a field of inquiry that embraces features of many other disciplines. For this reason, the distinctive uses and cultural and social variations in the interpretations of information are always of concern in his analysis.

There is no necessary law of progression from one stage of economic or social development to another. Melody's consideration of questions about what next is always measured and open to the potential of alternative pathways. Since societies have always been information-based, the problem is to understand how new means of creating and distributing information might lead to new risks, uncertainties, and, potentially greater opportunities especially for the disadvantaged. These issues cannot be examined without understanding the underlying fissures and conflicts in the long-run accumulation of capital in society and in the application of new technologies. Except for resolving very specific and narrowly-defined economic problems within a market context, Melody gives short shrift to the neo-classical preoccupation with the concept of information conveyed by short-run price signals. In fact, he observes that,

In this market environment neoclassical price theory is somewhat akin to a set of decision rules for optimising the arrangement of the deck chairs on the *Titanic* ... The price signals tell us nothing about the speed and direction in which the economic ship is headed. Short-run prices are likely to be very misleading as guides to resource allocation (Melody 1985c: 534).

It is always much more important to consider the determinants of social change from the vantage point of the long-run. It is this perspective that informs Melody's analysis of information society or knowledge economy developments. Thus:

The most significant application of the concept of information is with respect to the long-run accumulation and diffusion of knowledge in society. Its direct connection to the economic problem of the long-run accumulation of capital is through the concept of technology. If capital accumulation is stimulated by the application of new technologies, then the accumulation of information is at the heart of the capital accumulation process (Melody 1987b: 1318).

The analytical frameworks for answering questions about information society developments are most appropriately devised by constructing bridges between branches of economics and science and technology studies (and other fields of research). The intellectual heritage for the former comes from Commons (1959), Hamilton (1919) and Veblen (1904) who studied institutional formations and their stabilities and instabilities. For the latter, it comes from Schumpeter (1943; 1961), Freeman (1982), Freeman and Soete (1997) and Nelson and Winter (1982) who laid the foundations for examining the importance of innovations in technologies and their implications for the economy. Melody states that, 'although this line of research is not often associated with institutional economics, it is operating within the same theoretical framework' (Melody 1987b: 1320-1).

Since digital technologies have become commonplace, discussions about the information society often centre on whether this new generation of technology is the main driver of change. The 'technology push' proponents have been challenged by the proponents of social shaping, but Melody has followed neither of these groups. Instead, he argues that 'the assumption that technology is autonomous has characterised both the utopian and the critical literature on communications technology' (Melody 1983: 2). He has been consistent in claiming that,

... if history has taught us anything, it is that new machines will not solve old economic and social problems. They may significantly change power relations in society in favour of those who control, and benefit from, the new machines. But there is no magic embodied in new technologies that will suddenly transform the nature of social and institutional relations in beneficial ways (Melody 1986b: 2).

Because of his commitment to institutional reform, he engages mainly in promoting collective action as a means of shaping technology rather than in the analysis of the reflexivity and the power of individuals.

Melody offers insights into the trends and possibilities of information societies based on his analysis of the predominant trajectories of technological innovation and the likely stabilising and destabilising factors in society. For Melody, institutions matter; therefore, the outcomes of developments in information societies are certain to be differentiated and varied. This is because 'the characteristics of information define the state of knowledge that underlies all economic processes and decision-making structures' (Melody 1986a: 3). The contributors to this section are all concerned with how information societies around the world are unfolding. They are intent on demonstrating how technological innovation, institutions and a variety of social, cultural and political practices are intertwined through time, giving rise to societies in which the power of information – often highly unequally distributed – brings new risks and benefits to human endeavour.

Ian Miles follows Christopher Freeman's lead in developing a socio-technical approach for examining the implications of new information and communication technologies. Miles asks: in what sense should we think of the information society as a radical break from previous ways of organising society and the economy? He suggests that there are discernible phases of learning and organisational change that accompany rapid diffusion of advanced microelectronics-based technologies. He argues that there are signs that, as a result of organisational change, in the industrialised economies at least, firms are beginning to benefit from the new socio-technical paradigm. But Miles warns against generalisations. He argues that 'the' information society simply does not exist. Regions, countries, cultures and social groups are defining new and distinctive patterns of organisation. This view resonates with the networking knowledge theme that is central to Melody's work. Miles emphasises the role of learning in shaping information societies and highlights the uncertainties that accompany a world of interpenetrated global and local networks. He has advocated the need to monitor developments in technologies and society using combinations of formal and informal statistics. The next contribution by John Houghton illustrates how such empirical research can yield insights for policy makers.

Progress can be made in mapping and measuring information society developments by using national official statistics and data provided by organisations such as the OECD. Despite their limitations in accounting for the intangible value of information services, these data can support research that may signal the need for policy interventions at the national or regional levels. In his contribution, *John Houghton* takes up a hotly debated issue. All countries are facing difficult questions about whether they should be primarily 'users' of information and communication technology systems. Abramovitz (1986), and Perez and Soete (1988) suggest, for instance, that developing countries can leapfrog the experiences of the industrialised countries by applying the latest technologies. Questions about whether it is necessary to invest in producing and using new technologies in order to remain a player on the global stage occupy policy makers in the industrialised countries as well. Houghton demonstrates how liberalisation of the Australian telecom industry has been accompanied by increased trade deficits in information and communication technology products. Houghton wants Australia to become a leading user and producer of the new technologies. This is a difficult area for policy. Investment allocated to encouraging research and technology development in the hardware and software (as well as content) industries may jeopardise investment in other important areas. Efforts to demonstrate causal links between investment in digital technologies and economic growth are controversial. Houghton shows how difficult it is to persuade policy makers of the need for action that may alter the pattern of information society developments at the national level.

In his contribution, *Knud Erik Skouby* comments on the way many policy makers have turned to information and communication technologies as a means of galvanising social and economic development in exactly the manner that Melody so often advises against. Rather than attempting to understand the distinctiveness of a new generation of technologies, policy makers often treat the new technologies as just another component of industrial policy. Skouby observes that all social communication depends upon and is shaped by technology, always within socially-and historically-specific contexts. Like Melody, Skouby insists on the use of empirical evidence within an interdisciplinary framework to interpret social, economic and technical trends. He gives highest priority to scrutinising interactions between supply and demand in order to assess the benefits and risks of industrial restructuring that accompanies the diffusion of new systems and services. Skouby's emphasis on the social context is informed by another strand of social science research on the changes associated with ICTs. For instance, Slack and Williams (2000) and MacKenzie and Wajcman (1999) are sensitive to the social processes that shape and embed advanced technologies within society.

Roderick Sanatan worked at the heart of the telecom reform process in the Caribbean region. He is closely involved in the development of training programmes that aim to build up the skills base to take advantage of the potential of ICTs (Sanatan and Melody 1997). He shows why it is important to develop sectoral policies for telecom and broadcasting reform if the aim is to ensure that new technologies support economic and social development goals. The distinctive characteristics of information societies are partly a result of how technologies are absorbed. This depends on the way institutions influence the absorption of the new by the old. Sanatan also suggests that de-linking labour policy issues from telecom market reform is not viable in small, low income states. Like Melody, Sanatan wants equitable reform that will sustain the growth of economies in the region. Systems of innovation (Lundvall 1992; Nelson 1993) are comprised of institutions – norms and practices – that can be destabilised by technological and other socio-economic developments. Sanatan shows how difficult capacity building can be for smaller, low-income countries where financial and human resources in the education sector are scarce. Overall, he calls for better coordination of the whole system of innovation.

Institutions are in the spotlight in *Oscar Gandy*'s contribution. Institutions establish the system of property rights necessary to create markets for information. Melody has always argued that it is essential to distinguish between information as a resource and as a product (Melody 1981a; 1987b). Like another Canadian institutionalist, C. B. MacPherson (1978), Melody distinguishes between the role of information as part of the information commons and its role in the marketplace. Gandy takes up this distinction to shows how institutions of property ownership can reproduce structural inequalities within the social system (see also Agre and Rotenberg 1997; Mansell and Steinmueller 2000). When facing market incentives to more precisely target products to consumers, firms seek to capture and process information about individuals in greater depth (Samarajiva 1996). Melody (1986a: 7) argued that 'significant changes in information and communication networks require a reinterpretation of traditional notions of public and private information and the terms and conditions for access to it'. Gandy shows that marketing techniques can be used to pinpoint particular types of consumers in order to exclude them on the basis of race, gender and/or age. The consequences of market exclusion may be an 'enhanced sense of difference' that polarises people along class or ideological lines. The dominant trends in the organisation of markets for information also have the potential to negatively affect citizens' capacities for participating in the democratic processes.

Gandy's emphasis on the implications of the commodification of information is complemented by *Peter Anderson*'s contribution which turns to the problem of managing critical information resources for safety and security. Technical change and the convergence of networks are leading to increased risk, new vulnerabilities to physical hazards, and cybercrimes. Anderson emphasises that these are not simply technical issues. Instead, the greatest hurdles are organisational. They include the need for world-wide coordination among large numbers of actors. The hurdles are also political in that there are strong national sensitivities about sharing various types of information. In addition, efforts to reduce the risks entailed in managing the critical information infrastructure have an economic dimension. Protection comes at a cost that must be borne by someone. Anderson's approach to these issues is informed by his detailed understanding of the technical capabilities of networking. He argues that these capabilities increase the complexity of networks, making policy formulation and implementation much more difficult.

In his contribution, *Peter Shields* addresses the problem of unintended consequences of institutionalised action. He demonstrates the dangers of policies informed by technology deterministic approaches. In the United States (and elsewhere), law enforcement agencies often take the position that the Internet and encryption technologies are eroding their abilities to intercept and monitor electronic communication. They argue that they are losing control. This is a theme that recurs in many studies of technological change (see Beniger 1986; 1996) and it resonates with Melody's (1973b) concern that a technology-determined understanding of policy issues only narrows the scope for action. Shields shows that measures to cope with the perceived risks and problems of surveillance lead to further technological measures. These, in turn, produce further escalation. The resultant process can stifle the concerns of civil rights groups about individuals' rights to privacy.

Risk is a central issue for Gandy, Anderson and Shields. **B. P. Sanjay** considers the risks to developing economies of an 'ICT fetish'. This occurs when policy makers come to see investment in the new technologies as a panacea for development problems. His assessment of the opportunities and risks of joining the global knowledge society through major investment reflects Melody's (1985c: 526, 536) observation that,

... taken collectively, these changes introduce new elements of risk ... they
also provide new opportunities to shift these risks away from TNC
investors and managers to the particular localities where production
occurs, and the institutions that reside there, that is, local government,
labor, and consumers ... It would appear that Third World nations will
bear the brunt of the risk and instability associated with the exploitation
of information industry technologies and markets.

Some may want to argue that times have changed. After all, the Internet enables many more people – in India and other developing countries – to access global stocks of knowledge and to produce and export information services, including software. But Sanjay shows that little consideration is being given to tailoring the new applications to the needs of the majority of citizens in India. Even when access to global networks is established, the property rights regime threatens to weaken access to scientific and technical information in key fields and even to erode the perceived value of local knowledge. Like Rappert and Webster (1997), Sanjay highlights the problems that can arise as a result of the commercialisation of scientific data. In this case, investment in the telecom infrastructure cannot serve, in a straightforward way, as a catalyst for development (Melody 1993a). Many other measures are needed.

The World Trade Organization plays a significant role in governing international trade in information and communication technologies. As a global institutional actor, it significantly influences investment in the Asian region. **Meheroo Jussawalla** contrasts the potential of the new technologies to enhance global information flows with the risk of expanding digital divides. Taking China as an exemplar, she shows that national institutions still are able to influence investment strategies. Just as Melody (1999a) argues that diversity in social and economic conditions means that there will be diversity in the institutions of regulation and market liberalisation, Jussawalla shows that China – and other countries in the region – are seeking to manage their participation in the 'new economy' in distinctive ways. Advances in the information infrastructure in these countries tend to aggravate political concerns about threats to sovereign decision-making. Despite a growing view that nations can no longer enforce distinctive policies in the face of globalisation, Jussawalla identifies an emergent and distinctive policy regime in China.

Gandy's emphasis on the implications of the design and implementation of technologies for citizens and consumers is complemented by **Supriya Singh**'s contribution. She emphasises the importance of demand – not just supply – for the future of information societies. Melody's work is motivated by a conviction that advocacy is necessary to create spaces for ordinary people to experiment with the potential of new technologies. Informed demand is the key and people are not informed if all they can do is respond to the diktats of the marketers. As long ago as 1972, Melody was stressing that policy makers should focus on the way applications of new computer and telecom systems might become more responsive to people's needs (Melody 1972). Singh argues that if policy neglects citizen and consumer needs, there is a risk of a mismatch between the design of technologies and the social processes that underpin society. Attention to all aspects of technology development processes and use is essential for strategic information policy advocacy. Like Dervin and Shields (1990) and Silverstone (1995) in the media and communication field, and von Hippel (1978) and Rothwell (1994) in the science and technology policy field, she suggests that technology users both accommodate and, at times, resist innovations spawned in laboratories.

Jörg Becker's summary theses on the informatisation process set out the contradictory implications of these technologies when they become embedded in the social order (see also Becker 1983; 1984; 1994). His concern, like Melody's, is to detect and expose changes in the balance of economic power and dominance on a global scale. Those who have been marginalised in the past, stand to lose to an even greater extent from the current round of informatisation. This is because the resources available to producers and consumers in poorer, peripheral countries and regions do not match those in the wealthier countries. Becker insists on the need for open debate and critical discussion. Social scientists, he suggests, have failed in this regard. He looks to others to identify winners and losers in the emerging information society, and to propose what can be done to balance the scale.

The contributions in this section offer insights into the effects of attempts to monopolise knowledge. Whether these efforts stem from the desire to profit from information, to control critical information flows, to seek protection from crime and to protect sovereignty or scientific and technical expertise, or from assuming that the 'user' cannot comprehend technical design, there are consequences for citizens and other stakeholders. This critical assessment of consequences is the essence of Melody's (1973b) conception of the public interest in the information societies of the future. It provides the foundation for his advocacy of greater equity in the distribution of the potential benefits of the new technologies. These contributions are illustrative of social science inquiry that contributes to social problem-solving.

Information Society Revisited: PICTuring the Information Society

Ian Miles

INTRODUCTION

In the mid-1980s, William Melody directed the Programme on Information and Communication Technologies (PICT) (see Dutton 1996; 1999), funded by the United Kingdom's Economic and Social Research Council. Six research centres brought together social scientists with diverse backgrounds to grapple with the challenges of understanding technological change. Lively debate concerned the 'Information Society' – a term then gaining considerable currency, which has since been institutionalised in European Union and United Kingdom policy.

One view expressed within PICT was that the term was anodyne. Information is constitutive of all societies. A more theorised term (for example, post-Fordism) is required to identify new social epochs. Another approach noted that flows of information, and especially the production, ownership and trade in information products and communication media, are of growing economic significance. Thus, Information Economy should mean Economy of Information. A third stream sought to appropriate the terminology of information society/economy (IS), to refer to epochal changes related to the emergence of new information technology. This *socio-technical* approach drew on the work of Christopher Freeman and his associates (see Freeman and Louçã 2001), who, in studying major technological revolutions, had pointed to new information technology as being at the core of an ongoing technological revolution.

The IS involves transformations in social and economic affairs associated with the ongoing development and application of the underlying knowledge that underpins new information technology. Widespread social recognition is generated of the scope for using knowledge of new ways of storing, communicating and processing data. The technological innovations involve new trajectories of change based on knowledge of microelectronics, optronics, new generations of software and so on; and social and economic developments go beyond an incremental continuation of established social trends. These actions and counteractions of social actors, wielding (among other resources) differential access to the new knowledge about information processing, produce changes in:

- products and processes (consider industrial automation, in-car electronics);
- working practices and interfirm relationships (consider distance working, interfirm networks);
- the relative influence of firms and sectors (consider Microsoft, the telecom industry);
- the leisure activities and strategies for structuring everyday life (video games, the daily use of mobile phones);
- the understandings and expectations about the costs and opportunities associated with effecting the sorts of transformation permitted by the new technology and associated markets (consider storing and manipulation information about customers as exemplified by data mining);
- expectations about technological improvements, and market responses, leading to focusing of efforts, creating design platforms (for example, the stabilisation of the personal computer and Internet platforms) and technological trajectories (for example, Moore's Law as a description or prediction of decades of improvements in microprocessor power).

In a PICT study, *Mapping and Measuring the Information Economy*, Miles and contributors (1990) explored this approach to the IS through available statistical instruments and in the collection edited by Robins (1992) a variety of qualitative and quantitative indicators were employed. A wide variety of data were brought to bear on the topic, demonstrating extremely rapid development and diffusion of the new technologies in some areas and much more limited uptake in others. A number of questions were raised, and answers suggested.

Questioning Information Society

Does the IS constitute a radical break from the industrial society, just as industrialism displaced agricultural society? Much of what we now see represents an intensification of industrialism – for example, many service industries have adopted Fordist principles of organisation, increasing the spatial and social division of labour of processes, and the standardisation of products. Some developments are better labelled post-Fordism, reshaping of industrialism in manufacturing and service industries alike – with flexible customisation of products, more responsibility and variety in (many, not all!) occupations, and flatter organisational forms. These latter developments have co-evolved with, rather than been caused by, new information technology. Many commentators relate post-Fordism to a crisis in Fordism (which itself co-evolved with earlier generations of information technology, such as the telephone). Management information systems, mobile communication, and data warehousing and mining have rendered new organisational forms more viable. But little can be identified as an overturning of industrialism – even such widely-touted uses of new information technology as teleworking have taken off much more slowly than proponents expected. Established social, economic and political systems are making use of the new knowledge and technologies. The IS as so far experienced more resembles deep changes within industrial society than revolutionary breaks away from it. Perhaps there will be major discontinuity in the future – but probably by then we will not be calling it the IS.

Can we mark a point at which a society becomes an IS? Some commentators seem to believe that a valid concept identifying an historical period has to be sharply demarcated from other periods. But historical processes may be better described in terms of quantitative change along a series of parameters sharing underlying novelty (such as the new technological knowledge involved in the development and application of new information technology). For some purposes it might make sense to develop a set of indicators of features that characterise the IS, and to seek to compare and contrast societies, sectors, etc. in such terms – just as researchers measure degrees of industrialisation for historical and international development studies. But this is a far cry from identifying the IS with a single parameter, let alone with a threshold point on such a parameter – for example when 50% of firms are using personal computers or when 50% of households are using the Internet.

*Does talk of **the** Information Society, imply that all societies move toward a common model?* Consider the analogy with industrialisation. Industrialisation has been a long process, involving distinct phases of development and taking very different forms in different countries and regions. Countries that have industrialised later than others feature very different socio-economic structures than early industrialisers. The growing pains of industrialisation led to the new political ideologies, and schisms that preoccupied the 20th century – and distinctive modes of capitalist and (state) socialist industrialism. The high levels of international trade and communication may make such schisms (or their informational variants) less likely in the 21st century, though cleavages may occur along lines other than those of nationhood. But informatisation still takes different forms in different societies, where attitudes to freedom of information and privacy, civil liberties and social exclusion, entrepreneurship and regulation, and a host of other relevant elements are very different. Newly industrialising countries are also becoming information societies in forms that are often dramatically different from those seen in the advanced industrial societies. Information societies are liable to vary considerably, and future international conflicts – whether trade or military ones – will often contain divergent views of what an IS should be.

Are distinctive forms of IS evolving over time? Just as there have been earlier periods of industrialism (sometimes defined in terms of technology, such as the steam age, sometimes in terms of social organisation, such as Fordism or the welfare state), can the IS similarly be characterised as undergoing its own evolutionary phases? In *Mapping and Measuring*, the problem of dealing with different generations of new information technology was taken up only briefly, discussing the problems from freezing indicators around extremely fluid technologies, and noting the generations of equipment identified by industry experts. Subsequent work (Miles 2001; 2002 forthcoming) has gone on to identify several phases in the development of the IS over the last few decades: *island*, *archipelago*, and *continental* phases. They are distinctive in many ways (though not as dramatically different as the great phases of earlier industrialism). The steps reflect the social and organisational learning processes that have informed the application of continually accumulating new technological knowledge. Here, I can only give a brief flavour of this approach.

PHASES OF INFORMATION SOCIETY

In the *island* phase, up to, say, the late 1970s, the computer, telecom, and broadcasting systems were highly distinctive. Information technology facilities during this early phase of the IS were few, physically large and cumbersome, but very low in terms of power compared to modern systems. Mainframe and minicomputers were used mainly in very large enterprises and government. Each computer served a large number of users, but only experts were doing more than data entry. High levels of expertise were required to operate computers, and the visual displays and keyboard interfaces were very basic. Public attitudes to the new technology were very mixed. Fears about the dehumanising effect of large databases coexisted with awe of computers. Government policies typically supported national champions (with their own designs and standards). Organisations concentrated information technology facilities in data processing centres, centralising information processing.

In the 1980s, the *archipelago* is characterised by a proliferation of devices of many sizes, usually with limited (two-way) communications. Telecom deregulation and support for strategic research programmes on satellite television were introduced in many countries. At the same time, many new industrial and consumer products using microelectronics were widely diffused. The personal computer found large markets in offices and homes, though early online information systems were (with a few exceptions) disappointing. Public fears about the impact of information technology use on employment were joined by the concern about deskilling. In fact, in the workplace the trend was more one of upgrading of work; isolated components of the existing division of labour were frequently automated, but there was much less systematic reorganisation of work structures and integration of different functions. The decentralised use of personal computers (mainly as stand-alone devices) caused problems for corporate data processing managers. Equally, economists were puzzled by the lack of reflection of information technology investment in productivity statistics.

In the 1990s the *continent* was criss-crossed by information superhighways, networks bridging islands of automation. The Internet became a near-universal medium for computer linkages, and mobile systems of many sorts became prominent for voice and data communication. This is not to say that networking was universally diffused – many computer systems remained stand-alone. And the Internet was not particularly easy to use – many organisations required new skills in the form of network administrators and managers, website authors and editors, etc. – and *effective use* required considerable change in organisational practices. But as access to the Internet became widespread, and the Web provided a design paradigm for information exchange, the online transfer of data mushroomed. Existing services migrated to these media *en masse* – reaching out to broader and less specialised user bases, exploiting the lessened learning costs of a common interface. Electronic commerce applied new information technology to the transactional elements of economic activities; and, despite the stock market boom-bust frenzy, it does represent significant network integration across the islands of automation of factory floor production, warehouses, offices, etc. It offers scope for new modes of doing business, for integration of internal and external processes and restructuring of supply chains. This requires considerable organisational learning and re-engineering. By the turn of the millennium, there was evidence of performance improvements in information technology-using firms and of new trends in the United States economy, suggesting that increasing networking and/or organisational learning were beginning to overcome the productivity paradox.

What Next?
PICT made progress along several different approaches to understanding the IS. The socio-technical view of the IS, and the mapping and measuring project, could valuably be revisited – for example, to examine what indicators we might use to illuminate the different phases of the IS. The utility of distinguishing such phases for examining evolving policy challenges and policy learning that are posed by distinctive configurations of the IS is substantial. And, if the approach is even approximately valid, it suggests that there would be much mileage in a new PICT programme.

It is very difficult to generalise about *the* Information Society, despite shared novel features (the use of certain new knowledge). Even during the distinctive phases of the IS, very different patterns emerge in different regions, countries, cultures and social groups. Generalisations based on one phase may not apply to others – they vary in the ways in which organisations use new information technology to transform their relations with staff, clients, etc. Much of the theoretical apparatus developed in PICT to understand the social shaping of technology remains valid; but evolving empirical circumstances mean new relationships and practices – new complexities. Thus, productivity or employment trends, challenges to civil liberties or media quality – these may have very different manifestations over social times and spaces.

The immediate implication is that simple extrapolation is insufficient. We cannot assume that the new technologies have the same meaning today that they had yesterday. We are in the business of generating better ways of understanding what these meanings are and why they take the forms they do. There remains a need for more sustained analysis of underlying relations and processes, and how these are mediated by the continued application of human creativity in generating social and technical innovations, in applying strategies and counterstrategies in the pursuit of their (emergent, and only partly consciously articulated) objectives.

These complexities, and the elaboration of strategies and innovations generated by numerous parties (possessed of imperfect knowledge), create considerable uncertainty in the systems; but leave much to play for. Controlling the future is not possible. Even if others did not seek alternative futures, our knowledge is very limited, and practically the only certainty we can have about our choices is that unintended consequences are inevitable. An active and better-informed role in shaping the future is an option, however. It requires an experimental attitude, open to more intensive and extensive processes of learning. Organisational strategies (and structures to facilitate learning) remain crucial in the shaping of future phases of the IS, as they have been in the past. Information technology can enable the more rapid exchange of intelligence about good and bad practice, winners and losers, emerging problems and challenges, unexpected consequences and opportunities. Thus awareness of the potential significance of information and information technology strategies will grow, implying increasingly wide participation in the shaping of the IS at local levels. It is easier to predict this than it is to anticipate the approaches that will be adopted, and the winners and losers. Future phases of the IS (the *ecosystem* phase, perhaps) will continue to be worthy of close attention – and to require analyses from social scientists, such as the PICT Programme developed under Melody's stewardship.

Falling Behind on ICT Adoption Indicators: Can We Afford This?

John W. Houghton

INTRODUCTION

Like many countries, Australia faces a dilemma in developing a leading-edge information infrastructure. On the one hand, we cannot afford to do it; and, on the other, we cannot afford not to. The analysis in this contribution illustrates the changes over a decade in the trade position of Australia in information and communication technology (ICT) equipment and the consequences in terms of the costs that must be incurred to build up a sophisticated national information infrastructure that includes telecom, computing and software applications. From a relatively strong base in domestic production capability in the early 1990s, rather than forging ahead, the country shows every sign of falling behind world-leaders on both production and usage indicators. This essay examines contributing factors to this development and suggests why a continuation of current trends may be problematic for Australia.

STRUCTURAL CHANGE IN THE COMMUNICATION INDUSTRY

High network infrastructure costs present a significant barrier to entry and have ensured that telecom supply remains a game for large players. There are compelling forces towards further global integration – held back more by regulatory demands to see competition at the national level than by the underlying market dynamics. 'The telecommunications sector is the best example of how rapid technological development, in combination with regulatory reform, both enable and force companies to seek new partners across national and technical borders'. Between 1995 and 2000, there were 1,055 cross-border mergers and acquisitions (M&As) in telecom, more than five times the number in the first half of the decade; and at US$ 244.3 billion, the deal value was more than seven times that of the first half (OECD 2001b: 74-75). One consequence of this rapid globalisation is that in most smaller countries, including Australia, the major influences and larger players are from overseas.

Deregulation in the telecom sector not only introduced market forces into telecom services, but also into the entire communication value chain; from equipment, software and systems suppliers through to carriers and their major clients. Traditionally, suppliers to the major carriers faced monopsony purchasing, with many national carriers pursuing strong local purchasing agendas. This led the major equipment suppliers to adopt a multi-domestic structure with production in many, if not most, industrialised countries. Deregulation brought with it the breakdown of monopsony purchasing, increasing trade in communication equipment and software and global rationalisation of production amongst the major equipment suppliers.

Between 1990 and 1999, OECD trade in ICT equipment increased from US$ 161 to US$ 475 billion, while communication equipment trade increased from US$ 20 to US$ 90 billion. Over the same period, Australia's ICT equipment trade increased from US$ 1.9 to US$ 4.3 billion, while communication equipment trade increased from US$ 308 million to US$ 1.4 billion. Growing demand accounts for some of this increased trade in communication equipment, but not all. For example, between 1992 and 1999, OECD country spending on ICT equipment increased by 78%, but ICT equipment trade increased by 156%. So a significant proportion of the recent increase in communication equipment trade is due to globalisation – the global rationalisation of production and the shift of the communication equipment industry from a multi-domestic to a transnational structure.

Policy Research and Practice

By the early 1990s, researchers at the Centre for International Research on Communication and Information Technologies (CIRCIT) in Australia were identifying major opportunities for this country in the production of communication equipment and software. In the 1980s, Australia's communication equipment trade performance showed promise, with exports increasing from AU$ 31 million in 1980-81 to AU$ 216 million in 1990-91, or by 600% over the decade. Imports greatly exceeded exports, at AU$ 111 million in 1980-81 rising to more than AU$ 600 million in 1989-90, but the communication equipment deficit had plateaued in the mid 1980s and began to decline in 1989-90. CIRCIT researchers also warned that, in the absence of policy intervention, the end of local monopsony purchasing and underlying structural transformation in the industry would lead to a decline in Australian communication equipment manufacturing.

In the early days of deregulation, network development and expansion ensured growing demand and the production side looked healthy. Australia's total exports of line, transmission and broadcasting equipment increased by 330% during the early 1990s, peaking at AU$ 416 million in 1997-98. Australian produced exports of switching and data communication equipment also increased rapidly, peaking at AU$ 414 million in 1995-96. Unfortunately, with the end of local monopsony purchasing and with no specific development policies in place, local production has faltered.

Employment in Australia's telecom and broadcasting equipment manufacturing industry reached almost 8,300 in 1993, but declined to just over 5,000 (or by 38%) between 1993 and 1999. Over that same period, the number of telecom and broadcasting equipment manufacturing businesses operating in Australia declined from 140 to just 73 (or by 48%), and industry income declined from AU$ 1.9 to AU$ 1.5 billion. Cable and wire manufacturing is also in decline.

As a result, Australian-produced exports of line, transmission and broadcasting equipment have declined since the mid 1990s – from AU$ 378 million in 1997-98 to AU$ 225 million in 2000-01, or by 40% (see Figure IV.2.1). Similarly, switching and data communication equipment exports have declined from AU$ 414 million in 1995-96 to AU$ 267 million, or by 36%. Australia's deficit on trade in line, transmission and broadcasting equipment expanded from AU$ 630 million in 1997-98 to AU$ 1.9 billion in 2000-01 (almost 200%), while the deficit on trade in switching and data communication equipment increased from AU$ 373 million to AU$ 2.4 billion (or by 545%).

Figure IV.2.1 Composition and Balance of Trade in ICT Equipment, Australia 1990-91 to 2000-01 (AU$ million)

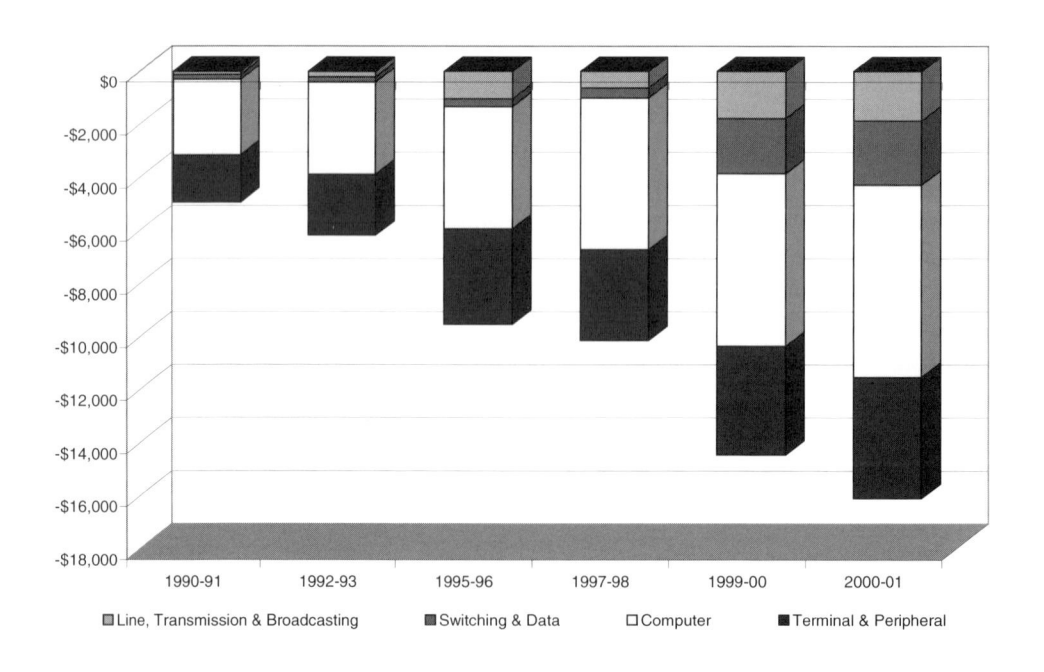

Source: Houghton (2001: 15)

It is much more difficult to track production and trade in communication related software, but anecdotal evidence suggests similar fortunes. The introduction of competition reshaped the local communications software industry, with Australian suppliers seeking to build business with new entrants into the telecom market and use this as a springboard for international expansion. There have been a number of success stories, but the concern among industry players is that, driven by financial markets and extensive foreign investment, Australian carriers have become risk-averse and are increasingly looking to the United States for their requirements. Richard Favero (2001: 54), CEO of Soprano argues that,

The carriers' mentality is that to buy from the USA is a low risk option. Telstra, Optus, Vodafone – they all look to the USA, at the risk-taking carriers, and copy what they are doing. Ten or 15 years ago the Australian industry led the world in many segments of the telecom market – now we don't want to, or can't afford to.

Australian innovations are being taken up and developed overseas. Two well known cases are illustrative. The Australian Photonics Cooperative Research Centre has spun off a number of innovative businesses, including Indx. Indx was sold to JDS Uniphase Corporation, the leading fibre optic component maker in the United States, in late 1997. Drs Skellern and Weste started Radiata in 1997, using radiocommunication technology originally developed and patented by the Commonwealth Scientific and Industrial Research Organisation (CSIRO) and Macquarie University. In November 2000, US-based Cisco Systems bid AU$ 567 million for the 89% of Radiata it did not already own. It was the first major purchase by Cisco in Australia and allowed Cisco to acquire wireless local area network technology. Cisco took over the technology licences.

At the same time, some of the major players have been reducing their activities in Australia. During the early 1990s, IBM and Alcatel had been Australia's leading ICT equipment exporters, with IBM accounting for around half of Australia's information technology equipment exports and Alcatel for almost half of Australia's communication equipment exports. In the mid 1990s, IBM Australia sold its manufacturing facility at Wangaratta in Victoria to Bluegum, which was established by venture capitalists as a contract manufacturing operation. IBM placed its local manufacturing requirements with Bluegum on a contract basis. Alcatel soon followed suit, contracting much of its manufacturing requirements to Bluegum. The change was significant, with the contract manufacturer having a domestic market rather than export focus. In mid-2000, contract electronics manufacturer, Solectron, bought the Bluegum Group, acquiring its manufacturing and office sites in Wangaratta, Sydney, Melbourne and Singapore. Faced with a downturn, Solectron closed the Wangaratta plant in early 2001. While this was playing out, Alcatel moved its Asia-Pacific base from Sydney to Shanghai.

An International Perspective

Putting Australia's position into an international perspective is instructive. Among OECD countries, the enormous contribution of Nokia and Ericsson to communication equipment exports from Finland and Sweden is clear. The index of revealed comparative advantage in communication equipment for Finland in 1999 was 6.05 and for Sweden 4.76 (see Figure IV.2.2).[7] The next highest was the Ireland at just 2. At the opposite end of the scale, Australia had a revealed comparative advantage index value of 0.28; and only Portugal, Norway and Japan experienced greater declines in revealed comparative advantage between 1990 and 1999.

Figure IV.2.2 Revealed Comparative Advantage in Communication Equipment, 1990 and 1999

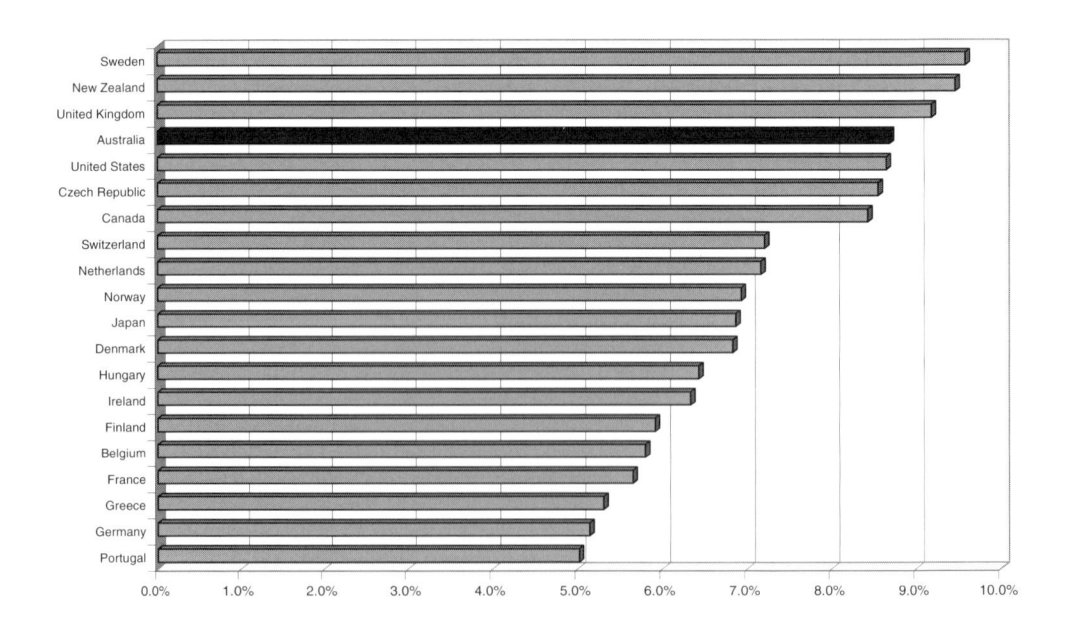

Source: OECD FTS Database <www.sourceoecd.org>, author's analysis

Australia is widely seen as a leading user of ICTs, with fixed and mobile phone penetration rates, and Internet take up in businesses and homes among the highest in the world (see Figure IV.2.3). In 1999, Australia ranked fourth among OECD countries in terms of the ratio of ICT expenditure to Gross Domestic Product (GDP) – behind Sweden, New Zealand and the United Kingdom. Australians spent the equivalent of 7.2% of GDP on ICTs in 1992, rising to 8.7% in 1999.

Australia's recent growth and productivity performances have also been relatively good. OECD (2001c) estimates of the increase in GDP per hour worked, adjusted for the business cycle, show that South Korea, Ireland and Luxembourg had the highest rates of labour productivity growth in the 1990s. Ireland, Australia, the United States, Greece and Germany experienced an acceleration in labour productivity growth during the late 1990s. Ireland and Finland also experienced the most rapid increases in multifactor productivity growth during the 1990s, with strong acceleration during the latter half of the decade in Ireland, Finland, Belgium, Australia, Canada and the United States. Some analysts of productivity growth in the United States and Australia have concluded that the use of ICTs is as, if not more, important for productivity improvement than is production.[8]

Figure IV.2.3 Ratio of ICT Expenditure to Gross Domestic Product, 1999

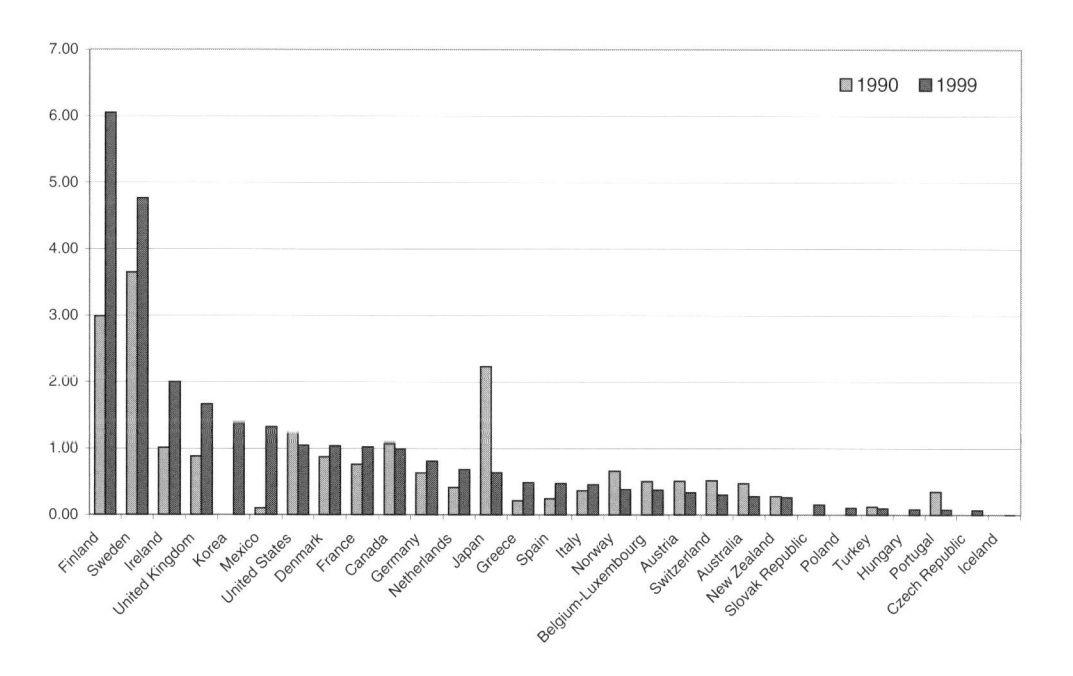

Source: World Information Technology and Services Alliance (2000)

Nevertheless, Australia's ICT trade deficit continues to expand at an alarming rate. In 2000-01, total imports of ICT equipment into Australia cost AU$ 17.7 billion – up from AU$ 5.58 billion a decade earlier. ICT equipment now accounts for around 16% of Australia's total merchandise imports. To put this into perspective, in 1999-2000 Australians paid AU$ 3.94 billion for food imports, AU$ 4.2 billion for textiles, clothing and footwear imports, AU$ 7.7 billion for non-industrial transport equipment (principally motor vehicles), AU$ 1.4 billion for civil aircraft, AU$ 7.5 billion for fuels and lubricants, AU$ 3.6 billion for chemicals and pharmaceuticals, and AU$ 3.2 billion for books, toys and leisure goods.

Australia's ICT equipment imports (excluding software, services and content) cost more than imports of cars and fuel combined, and more than imports of food, textiles, clothing, footwear, civil aircraft, chemicals, pharmaceuticals, books, toys and leisure goods combined. Can we afford this?

There is some evidence that perhaps we cannot. Australia's formerly strong record on ICT adoption has recently flagged. For example, in July 1995 Australia ranked seventh among OECD countries in terms of Internet hosts per 1000 population, but by July 2001 Australia's ranking had slipped to tenth; in 1998 Australia ranked ninth among OECD countries in terms of Web sites per 1000 population, but by July 2000 Australia's ranking had slipped to thirteenth; and in 2000 Australia ranked thirteenth among OECD countries in terms of penetration of broadband – with 0.59 adopters per 100 population, compared to an OECD average of 1.96 and South Korea's 13.9 – but by June 2001, Australia's ranking had slipped to sixteenth. While not conclusive, these trends are suggestive of an emerging problem.

Where To From Here?

There is little sign of significant change in policy in Australia. The conventional wisdom is that it is the use of ICTs that matters; not their production. To a large extent, of course, that is true. However, it is not an either-or choice. There is no reason why Australia could not be a leading-edge user *and* producer – as are Finland, Sweden, South Korea and the United States. OECD analysis shows that some of the major ICT producing countries have enjoyed rapid productivity improvements during the 1990s – such as Ireland, Finland and South Korea. What is clear is that by vacating ICT production Australia is creating a significant import burden. There are obvious benefits from specialisation and trade, and no country should seek to balance trade line-item by line-item. But with declining terms of trade and a declining dollar, it is going to be increasingly difficult for Australia to afford to be a leading-edge user of ICTs. Early signs of falling behind on a number of ICT adoption indicators suggest that Australia's failure to produce ICTs may be undermining its ability to use them.

Information Societies: Towards a More Useful Concept

Knud Erik Skouby

INFORMATION SOCIETY PLANS

Almost every industrialised and industrialising state has, since the mid-1990s produced one or several plans for the Information Economy or the Information Society. They followed the United States 'Agenda for Action' (Information Infrastructure Task Force 1993); the European Commission's 'White Paper on Growth, Competitiveness and Employment', the Bangemann Report (European Commission 1993); and the Japanese report on 'Reforms Toward the Intellectual Creative Society of the 21st Century' (Ministry of Posts and Telecommunications 1994).

The plans show a high degree of political and economic attention to the development of information and communication technologies (ICTs) with the assumption, explicitly or implicitly stated, that they will have a decisively positive socio-economic impact via the development of a 'new economy'. A closer look at these information society programmes reveals that they are mainly traditional industrial policy programmes dressed up in new clothes in the sense that they address the problems and potentials of the traditional strongholds of different countries (Henten et al. 1996). This indicates that, whereas the restructuring effects of ICTs on today's social, economic and technical systems are beyond dispute, the character of these effects is not very well understood. We do not have a firm theoretical basis for analysing or predicting the effects of developments in ICTs.

A THEORETICAL FOUNDATION

The terms Information Economy, Information Society, New Economy and Network or Networked Economy have been used to encompass a wide range of loose ideas, processes and implications (Bell 1973; Toffler 1980; Negroponte 1995). Most of the work in this area is characterised by deterministic and even naïve technological visions informed by few theoretical insights. Work that does have a solid theoretical foundation is mostly kept within the boundaries of academic institutions. This is so in the case of the seminal work by Fritz Machlup (1962) who began a discussion about the information economy, arguing that a growing proportion of Gross National Product can be attributed to information activities and that a dominant part of the work force is engaged in information-related activities.

This work challenges traditional General Equilibrium Theory by emphasising the importance of increasing returns (Arthur 1994), but it addresses only a limited aspect of the implications of developments in the new technologies. A distinguishing feature of ICTs is that they play an important role in the value chain, not only within the ICT sector itself, but across the economy. Changes in the value chains have a combined influence on consumer behaviour and on production including their organisation. The resulting changes in the allocation of resources in society is often referred to as the information technology version of the information society (Duff 2000). It puts the emphasis on the technologies of information processing, storage and transmission rather than on knowledge production and communication flows. This is a common conception of the information society which highlights the informatisation of organisational processes and its implications.

THREE ASPECTS OF THE INFORMATION SOCIETY

The observation that human development broadly is dependent on the development of the technologies and institutions of social communication is neither new nor original. The relationship between communication and other social structures was considered long before more recent discussions about the information society. Three main aspects can be distinguished (Garnham 1998). First, communication increasingly becomes dependent upon the mobilisation of and access to scarce resources. This leads to a need to understand how control is structured over these resources, but may also suggest that communication is a primary explanatory variable of these relationships. Second, all social communication depends upon and is shaped by technology leading to a search for how these technologies are shaped within a wider social and historical context. Third, the development of systems of social communication has been promoted by, and accompanied by, a class of communication experts.

Three rather different theoretical traditions are associated with each of these aspects. Harold Adams Innis (1950; 1951) and Bell (1973) provide examples of the first aspect. Innis has been described as one of the first and most influential media determinists. He argued that changing forms of communication lead to changes in the nature of society. Although Innis stressed the interdependence of the development of communication and general socio-economic development, the tradition he inspired came to stress communication as the primary explanatory variable. This was epitomised in McLuhan's (1964) statement: 'The medium is the message'. In this view, the technology of communication ultimately governs socio-economic development in a one-dimensional way.

The second aspect is associated with the techno-economic paradigm tradition developed by Christopher Freeman and his colleagues (Dosi et al. 1988). This tradition argues against mechanistic economic models and for an evolutionary approach which stresses the interaction between environment (natural, built and institutional) and innovation as the basic nature of the techno-economic relationship (Freeman 1982). Innovations or systems of innovations are characterised according to their potential for changes in the techno-economic paradigm that have profound transformational effects throughout the economy. This provides a framework for analysis that provides insight into the potential restructuring effects of ICTs. However, the evolutionary diffusion processes are described as a 'general system dynamic' which underpins the 'expression' of a techno-economic paradigm and the relative cost structure of production (Freeman 1982). As a result, this approach does not provide a tool for understanding the relation between structures of innovation and the character of ICTs.

The third aspect is associated with the work of Manuel Castells (1996; 1997; 1998). The basic claim is that the industrial society is being transformed by a new mode of production; informational capitalism. The consequences of this transformation are explored for the social dimensions from mass communication to global power restructuring. The transformation is analysed using a labour theory of value framework with its virtues and weaknesses. A major weakness in this context is that it is inherently technologically deterministic. For example, it leads to the claim that ICTs have a direct impact on the socio-economic totality by creating a 'culture of real virtuality' (Garnham 1998).

THE NEED FOR A DEMONSTRATION
This characterisation of some of the dominant theories of the information society suggests a stylised fact (or assumption). Most theories of the restructuring effects of ICTs on social, economic and technical systems do not fully explain the nature of the changes that are underway. William Melody's efforts to address this deficit clearly stand out (see also Miles and contributors 1990). Melody's point of departure was neither an apocalyptic vision nor a technologically deterministic analysis, but rather reflected an understanding that changes in the telecom industry opened the possibility for profound socio-economic changes and that there is a close interdependence between these two sets of changes (see Melody 1975; 1990a; 1996a,b; 1999b).

He recognised that, while ICTs predominantly are shaped and developed as a response to corporate needs, they can also be used for broader public goals such as greater participation in the processing of information, the production of knowledge and the sharing of meaning. The shaping of telecom reform is crucial to the potential of this process and an information society is understood as one where the possible benefits of new ICTs are increased and the risks of loss and harm are reduced (Melody 1996c). It follows from this definition that the development of the information society can only meaningfully be analysed as a unique construction in each country.

As a stylised fact, the information society is seen as being constructed by two interdependent key components: the telecom facility system, and by information content and communication services. The telecom system is a critical component and establishing it is a far more complicated task than simply establishing a superhighway or a broadband network. Ultimately, however, it is the system's capacity to accommodate new and increased requirements for future services that opens up the potential for major benefits. This involves a number of issues from design of network standards for components and terminals, to intellectual property rights, privacy and security and, not least, development of a skills base which is crucial for the application of new services. These applications lead to complex restructuring of organisations and other institutional changes. All this occurs within highly dynamic structures. Melody's great achievement has been to develop an adequate framework for analysing these developments empirically.

This framework calls for an analysis where the supply side is made up of the technical capacity including equipment, telecom infrastructure and services terminals and skills and content. The demand side is comprised of applications in organisations (professional use involving services, skills, organisational and sectoral reforms) and in households (demand or need, skills, income, changes in habits and reallocation of resources) (Melody 1996c: 252-3). Each element on the supply side and the demand side is characterised and compared.

CONCLUSION

This framework and methodology has been applied with very interesting results in a set of studies for the Danish Telecom Agency (Melody 1999c; 2000; 2001c). The information infrastructures in different countries are analysed using indicators such as Internet services development, preparation throughout the economy for applications of new services, and the expansion of bandwidth capacity. The results have drawn attention to the fact that the development of the information society is not only a question of international technological and structural trends, but also of priorities and investments specific to each country.

Rather than a theory of the totality of the restructuring effects of the ICTs on the social, economic and technical system, Melody seeks to establish an empirical demonstration of the impact of ICTs and of the conditions necessary to realise an information society where broader public ends, such as greater participation in the processing of information, the production of knowledge, and the sharing of meaning, are achieved. This approach has been successful in the sense that it has been used within the political and administrative systems in Denmark to develop policies and procedures for reactions to the challenges and potentials suggested by developments in the new technologies and services (Telestyrelsen 2000).

Evolving the Information Society in the Caribbean: The Paradox of Orderliness

Roderick Sanatan

Introduction

Colonies of profit can tell a story of bypass of the local loop of development in order to establish external links and markets. It is a paradox of telecom development that the new satellites of ageing empires must now shift their policies and their markets if the information society is to take hold. This contribution considers the major shifts in the policies and markets to the start of the 21st century and points to the most important directions and priorities for future policy. The main argument is that new governance institutions are vital to support the emergence of a distinctive information society in the Caribbean and that these institutions can only emerge as a result of the destabilisation of existing system orderliness.

Information Society Developments

The changes in the telecom and broadcasting infrastructure and in the regulatory apparatus have been considerable over the past decade and they have built on the earlier experiences of a highly monopolised industry structure.

Telecom infrastructure in the pre-Caribbean federation years resembled the traditional technology system of microwave links, old copper and coaxial cables, and large earth station transmitters. There was a similar infrastructure girding most of the Caribbean, except for the Bahamas and Belize. Under various licensing conditions, foreign direct investment in the telecom sector was attracted, leading to separate operators (handling domestic service and international service). Investment in optical fibre networks, including a regional digital grid during the 1990s, encouraged investment in high technology systems located in ribbons in some countries. This stimulated links with computer and satellite systems. This has enhanced the capacity of the Caribbean to be connected to the rest of the world and in the 1980s Jamaica led the way with the Digiport in Montego Bay. Intra-regionally, there have been a few spirited efforts to connect the region and to access the global radio spectrum. Wireless services, and especially cellular services, are likely to enable a greater reach of new systems and broader citizen access to networks of the 21st century.

Telecom regulation generally comes under Wireless Telegraphy Ordinances which treat services as a commodity. Regulation was based on special licensing regimes that found it difficult to focus on the potential of the new technologies for improved spectrum use and the advantages of greater bandwidth, new computer interfaces and gateways for global trade. The legal basis of telecom regulation has yet be reformed to accommodate the unsettled foray of Caribbean telecom into the provision of services as an international trading tool. In the 1990s, various Caribbean States have used fair trading instruments to settle disputes over the competitive provision and use of telecom equipment. Greater challenges lie ahead in order to accommodate the right to access services and networks and Public Utilities Commission-type regulation has provided an arena for arbitration between competing telecom suppliers. There have been constitutional challenges aimed at identifying the right to free expression and speech and the right of access to the infrastructure as a means to exercise such freedom. Growing consumer and citizen awareness of such rights is expected to lead to new legislation, but the net effect so far is that the old telecom legislation has yet to catch up with the fast moving actions of citizens and entrepreneurs. The regulatory system of the past was the domain of a Ministry of Works, whereas there are now shifts towards the introduction of Policy Advisory Units within ministries in recognition that telecom is a matter for a ministry of trade.

At the regional level, two organisations provide the axis of new telecom initiatives. CANTO, a grouping of regional operators, started in the early 1980s in Trinidad and Tobago, and has addressed technological issues and served as a lobbyist for private and government owned telecom operations. This organisation has successfully pursued alliances to influence global equipment purchases that favour its shareholders. The Caribbean Telecommunication Union (CTU) is a decade old, and was a creature of regional CARICOM policy. It has made strides in enabling multilateral rules to be negotiated for the Caribbean telecom region, in training, and in developing policy guidelines for the new regulatory and business environment.

At the close of the 20th century, the Caribbean policy makers initiated a process of advocacy in the heartland of the international system, through the CTU and with support from the World Bank. Several countries in the region had acceded to the World Trade Organization's Special Agreement on Basic Telecommunications, which assumed a roll-out of competitive services, systems and practices from 1998. In the International Telecommunication Union, the Caribbean consistently secured a seat at the policy making Council (Saint Lucia holds the seat, 1998-2002), and the Caribbean has also influenced decisions within the region and the positions of international lobby groups.

The broadcasting sector (radio and television) also plays an important role in contributing to the infrastructure for the information society. In the late 1970s, community radio was developed, and there was the establishment of a Communication School at the University of the West Indies in Jamaica. There were early experiments with regional private television and the growth of independent production houses. Regional broadcasting now competes with international television stations, and cable television has been established. There have been attempts to create an institution to handle broadcasting regulation with industry representation. In addition, the rise of local production facilities for film and television has occurred. Public opinion programmes have grown in popularity and public service broadcasting has a stable citizen response. The growth of private radio ownership, sometimes through interlocking media cross ownership, has also increased the diversity of content that is available.

Over the past 25 years, there has been a major shift in the capacity for human resource training at high levels in law, policy, business and engineering as applied to telecom and in technical fields. The CTU played a major role in providing this training, as did Cable & Wireless Training Centres and international and regional organisations. However, there is growing impatience in the region with the rate at which a new orientation to capacity building for the new information and communication technology environment is occurring. The goal of developing services activity accounting for more than 60% of the Gross National Product of the Caribbean economy will require a quantum leap in skills development.

Education and Training for Social Equity

In 2002, Trinidad and Tobago completed a survey of the utilisation of information technology by households. The results suggest that the market is not spreading the potential benefits of advanced ICTs evenly and that there is a need for policy direction. For instance: upper income elite are not ICT-oriented; lower income and rural populations are disadvantaged; secondary school graduates account for 50% of ICT users; two-thirds of households use the Internet two or three hours daily; less than one-third of users are engaged in e-commerce; and nine-tenths of households do not have computers at home.

Governments, and particularly ministries of education, are faced with the difficult decision of which technologies to select for different levels of education and distance learning. The questions they must grapple with include the extent of access (how accessible is a particular technology for learners; how flexible is it?); the cost structure of each technology and the unit cost per learner; the kinds of learning that are needed and the instructional approaches that will best meet these needs. Additional issues include questions about the best technologies for supporting teaching and learning, interactivity and user-friendliness supported by the technology, the organisational requirements and barriers to use, and the novelty of the technology and its capacity to support the rapid production or implementation of learning materials.

There is a deep gulf between the traditional education system and the system required to support demand in the 21st century with its emphasis on knowledge, technical progress, innovation and creativity. Governments agree that to increase national competitiveness, there is a need for more and more skilled people and that there needs to be closer links between the worlds of education and of communication. In addition, education in the future requires greater autonomy, administrative responsibility, experimentation and close links with the community. There is a risk of growing inequality between the minority trained to manage the future and the majority who are excluded from the dynamic progress of modernity. An emphasis needs to be given to social integration, compensation for the underprivileged and policies aimed at checking the tendencies of the market that lead to segmentation of the population.

Deregulating the telecom sector has paid rich dividends in terms of new services, new skills and faster economic growth. Nevertheless, although the new technologies are being absorbed within our organisations and we are enjoying the benefits of new services in our personal lives, the adverse impact of technology on some people's lives must be managed. The new technology may improve livelihoods and enrich society overall, but it also creates a great deal of disruption in the lives of many people. If this disruption is not managed effectively, the full potential of new technologies is likely to remain unfulfilled.

Unfortunately, the telecom deregulation policy has been developed with little consideration of the necessary corresponding labour policy. In many industrialised countries, regulators undertake deregulation to stimulate economic growth. Adverse social impacts have been felt outside the framework of telecom policy. In the large economies, such as the United States and the United Kingdom, the disruption of workers' lives is not very apparent or visible as long there is the capacity to absorb displaced workers. However, the de-linking of labour policy from regulatory policy plays out very differently in smaller economies with high unemployment rates. The ability of these economies to absorb displaced workers is much weaker and there is greater potential for social upheaval in the wake of telecom deregulation in economies such as those of the Caribbean.

The positive and negative consequences of telecom deregulation for labour are well documented (Hudson 1997b). New technologies and deregulation have led to large-scale restructuring of the telecom sector and many skills have become obsolete while new skill requirements have emerged. Many telecom operators have downsized by 30% or more in the post-deregulatory era. Some of the workers in the middle-age groups are most vulnerable and their plight raises the spectre of shattered lives and an inability to return to the labour market. These disruptions impose a high cost on society as these people are likely to suffer more physical and mental illness than those in employment.

To learn from the experience of telecom deregulation it would be prudent to consider ways of linking regulatory policy to labour policy. In this way, it may be feasible to avoid some of the costs of social disruption. The development of a labour policy can contribute to a social dialogue in which workers, union members, customers and citizens can participate with their governments and telecom firms in establishing new policies.

Conclusion

International trends in the emergence of information societies require the engagement of Caribbean policy and market institutions. Issues of political governance are being considered as the Internet spreads to support new forms of e-government services. There are growing demands for improved citizen participation and more efficient public systems for the delivery of goods and services. This is leading to shifts in the organisation of the regional innovation system to accommodate National ICT strategic plans and new policy frameworks, as well as a new legal framework for e-government services and new organisations to support innovative activities through tele-centres, non-governmental organisation support for trade initiatives, and programmes for the agriculture and education sectors.

The capacity to generate, circulate and absorb knowledge as a sustainable resource is a central challenge for the development of the Caribbean information society. New institutional practices are needed to support the establishment of a property rights system, to take advantage of the availability of new spectrum capacity and to manage the social processes of change (and dislocation) in the information societies that emerge in the region. In order to progress it will be necessary for system orderliness to yield its traditional growth path to accommodate a brave new world in the Caribbean that is much more intensive in its use of advanced ICTs and the content of the digital age.

Revealing the Ties that Bind:
Property and Propriety in the Information Age.

Oscar H. Gandy, Jr.

INTRODUCTION

William Melody's fundamental contribution to the study of communication is based on his consistently argued claim, that we cannot understand the characteristics of communication, and the information commons it supports without examining the nature of the institutions that bring it into being and determine its shape. Among the most important institutional arrangements that Melody (1987b) has suggested we should consider are those that emerge from time to time to establish and enforce the system of property rights necessary to the efficient operation of a market. The ways in which systems of property rights develop are not well captured by the economic theories that Melody has criticised so often during his career. Indeed, as numerous critics remind us, the assignment of rights reflects the exercise of power as well as a desire to guarantee that its unequal distribution remains fundamentally unchanged. The establishment of property rights in information represents an increasingly troublesome concern for governing bodies because the commodification of information has become such a central feature of the global economy (Preston 2001).

It is the intangible nature of information itself that makes the establishment and management of property rights such a troublesome enterprise. Economists have attempted to draw distinctions between what they refer to as the public and private goods components of an information commodity. The tangible, or material character of information goods is readily understood in terms of the books, tapes and disks upon which the information can be stored, bound, boxed and distributed for sale in stores, or directly to the home through the mail. These are the private goods, and they can be understood as private property because of the relative ease with which an individual can exercise control over their use. The information that is recorded on these media, however, is far more difficult to control. Indeed, the fact that the information can be reproduced and shared, given away, or even sold to other individuals almost without limit, helps to define its character as a public good.

THE INFORMATION COMMODITY

Understanding the ways in which institutions have developed in order to bring the public goods aspects of information commodities under the control of technical systems and the rule of law remains a critical concern of scholars who have followed Melody's lead. Understanding how those institutions help to reproduce structural inequalities within social systems is no less important a concern, but is much less well understood.

In writing about the nature of information markets, Melody (1987b) suggested that there were two paths that entrepreneurs within communication and information markets might pursue in the search for maximum profits. The first was associated with the maximisation of output, and the widespread distribution of the commodities to consumers at minimal cost was the means by which profits might be ensured. An alternative strategy was based on limiting output and restricting distribution to those consumers who were willing to pay high prices for privileged access. The development of legal, technical and, to an extent not well understood, culturally-based institutions that enabled the management of intellectual property would still be necessary if either strategy were to succeed.

A third strategy combines the first two in a way that information entrepreneurs hope will support the extraction of still more profit from the communication market. Segmentation and targeting of consumers depends upon the use of marketing techniques to create an illusory expansion of diversity and the individualisation of supply within the information market. The output of information goods would expand, but 'personalisation' would justify an elevation in the price of virtually indistinguishable goods.

BALANCING PRIVACY RIGHTS AND INTELLECTUAL PROPERTY RIGHTS

The realisation of these goals depends, however, on the collection and processing of more and more information about individual consumers. Concerns about the loss of control over the use of information about their tastes, preferences and resources has led to the development of a set of institutional responses that include efforts to establish property rights in personal information. The struggle to find a balance between privacy rights and intellectual property rights has emerged as a critically important site for understanding the contradictions in the development of capitalism in the Information Age (Cohen 1996). However, the resolution of those struggles is unlikely to do much to reduce the substantial inequalities in access to information that always seem to accompany adjustments in the market, or, in the expansion of marketplace rationales into spheres that had been governed by a different logic or goal, such as the maximisation of public welfare.

Segmentation and targeting can be understood as strategic resources that support discrimination within markets. Advertiser-supported media are especially sensitive to the differential values that are associated with the demographics of their audiences. Within markets, discrimination on the basis of race, gender or age is often justified on the basis of economic efficiency (Gandy 2000). Within the social, cultural and political realms, the basis for evaluation might include considerations of equity, fairness and social justice, although discrimination may be said to be 'rational' in these discussions as well. Indeed, the process through which neo-classical economists have established the consideration of efficiency as more important than a determination of fairness within the public sphere is itself a subject that demands scholarly reflection.

Melody often admonished his readers to pay attention to the ways in which the development of markets and regulatory institutions might affect the nature of inequality in access to information. In reflecting on the development of telecom policy in the United States (Melody 1989), he underscored the need for theory and research that would make sense of the changes that would accompany deregulation and increased competition in the delivery of telecom services. He felt that it was also important for researchers to understand the ways in which interested parties were able to influence the development of both the technical systems and the regulatory infrastructures that would come to redefine what we now understand universal service to mean in practical terms.

Recent debates about the nature and extent of the 'digital divide' risk confusing access to technology with access to the *capabilities* that information and knowledge might bring to different communities (Preston 2001). Recent surveys have identified a substantial segment of the public that does not have Internet access because they do not believe that there is much of value for them. Their needs and interests largely have been ignored because the estimates of their long-term value as consumers are below some minimal level.

Unfortunately, the segmentation of consumers into groups on the basis of their estimated value to advertisers or investors has a host of unanticipated, or ill-considered social consequences that are unlikely to be overcome by greater access to technology. Among these consequences is an enhanced sense of difference that supports even greater polarisation along race, class and ideological lines (Sunstein 2001). The segmentation and isolation of groups of people in physical space is reinforced by their isolation in the social space of information flows. While Sunstein (2001) sees this isolation as an unintended consequence of the exercise of consumer sovereignty, others recognise it as the result of strategic action. When this isolation and resultant polarisation increases the efficiency with which the manipulation of public opinion and engagement with political debates can be achieved, the harmful consequences for the operation of democratic systems may be substantial.

Conclusion

Some of the consequences that are generated by a process of segmentation and targeting based on assessments of value may be understood to flow from the absence of certain kinds of communication, as well as from exposure to particular messages. Populations and subgroups that are valued less within social systems are either provided with low quality material, or they are ignored entirely. To the extent that our competence as citizens and as consumers is shaped by our engagement with arguments that we might disagree with or do not understand, our isolation denies us an opportunity for growth. People who are bypassed, or merely ignored, cannot develop through engagement with the unfamiliar. This is a system that amplifies deviation and validates predictions of failure.

Melody's invitation for us to examine the ways in which social institutions are formed, and then to assess the consequences that flow from the operation of those institutions, is an invitation that ought not be refused. There is much to be learned about the spread of neo-liberal ideas and policies. There is even more to be learned about ways in which the information market will shape, and be shaped by, the management of intellectual property rights and the rights to personal information. We are fortunate that William Melody provided the motivation, opportunity and guidance to so many of his students and colleagues to ensure that the path will be well-marked.

IV.6

Critical Infrastructure Protection in the Information Age

Peter S. Anderson

INTRODUCTION

A new theme emerging in the information age is critical infrastructure and, in particular, information infrastructure. Infrastructures are indispensable for human welfare, not only because of the important economic, social and other benefits they provide, but also because of the consequences for society-at-large when they fail to meet expected service requirements. Critical infrastructures consist of physical and information-based facilities, networks and assets, which, if disrupted or destroyed would have a serious impact on the health, safety, security or well-being of citizens or on the effective functioning of governments and industries. They include, but are by no means limited to, telecom, energy, banking and financial, transportation, water and sewage, healthcare, government and emergency systems.

Historically, many of these infrastructures were physically segregated. However, with rapid changes since the 1970s in technology, national regulatory practices, market conditions and industrial realignments, critical infrastructures have progressively converged. Technological advances have also enabled significant automation in the operation and control of critical infrastructures.

In our information age, information infrastructure has emerged as one of the most important critical infrastructures because it now lays the foundation for managing and integrating all other critical infrastructures as well new forms of communication, information exchange and commerce.

CONVERGENCE AND THE CRITICALITY OF INFORMATION

Convergence within the computer and telecom technology sectors is also challenging underlying concepts of traditional infrastructures. For example, within the telecom industry, the Public Switched Telephone Network (PSTN) traditionally consisted primarily of a narrowband, mature, switched telephone network designed and scaled primarily to support voice communication with data overlaid on separate networks. Increasingly, public telecom infrastructures are consisting of networks of circuit-switched networks interoperating and converging with broadband, packet-based Internet Protocol (IP) networks and associated applications.

Electric power utilities, for example, are expanding their use of information systems and interconnecting previously isolated networks because of competition, reductions in staff and operating margins, ageing proprietary systems and the need to integrate national and even continental power grids. Further, as with the telecom sector, as new players enter the power generation and distribution markets, existing utilities are being required to offer open access to their transmission systems and integrate new subsystems into an ever growing complex power management system where different players have to communicate in real time in order to carefully balance power demand and supply arrangements. Simultaneously, many utility companies are moving away from using their own private network infrastructures and towards widespread dependency upon public telecom facilities to integrate transmission and distribution control centres and corporate networks.

Of course, dependency upon public network infrastructure is not unique to the electricity sector. In the transportation sector virtually all traffic control systems rely upon public telecom infrastructure. Similarly, in the financial sector, much of the electronic fund transfers and trading transactions are carried over public networks, as are links used by producers and suppliers to lower costs through just-in-time manufacturing. Businesses of all kinds regard the ability to exchange information internationally across single, multi-site virtual enterprise networks overlaid on public networks as a strategic necessity.

The same pattern holds for the provision of government services. In the United States, over 95% of government communication is carried over public information networks. In Canada, the federal government directly controls only 10% of its infrastructure, with the remainder supplied by the private sector. These arrangements not only support basic administrative services, but military as well as important public safety services. In particular, public commercial mobile cellular technology is now perceived by most emergency management organisations as a strategically important solution to traditional problems of incompatibility and interoperability among agencies' private radio networks and as a crucial bridge between wireless systems and the PSTN. Moreover, commercial mobile wireless services offer this interoperability without the added costs of establishing and maintaining agency-specific networking arrangements.

The resulting convergence of voice and data applications is leading to the evolution of hybrid networks that combine infrastructures of different jurisdictions and disciplines with those of public wireline and wireless carriers. Such infrastructure arrangements increasingly support mission critical functions ranging from seismic monitoring, to weather and tsunami public warning, to disaster situation reporting and facilitating appeals for assistance. Such examples illustrate how essential societal functions progressively are becoming entangled in an interdependent network of critical infrastructures, where each infrastructure is required for the effective operation of the other, and whose management and overall quality control is simultaneously becoming increasingly decentralised, less coordinated and exceedingly complex.

Vulnerability of Critical Infrastructure

Not surprisingly, these rapid advances in interconnectedness have created major challenges for protecting critical infrastructures. In today's global environment, national security is measured in both economic and military terms, and a nation's social advancement and world competitiveness rely upon efficient, robust and secure information, electrical power, transportation and other critical infrastructures.

The increased interdependency fostered by Critical Information Infrastructure (CII), combined with greater operational complexity, have made critical infrastructures particularly vulnerable to a variety of potential threats, including natural hazards, cascading failures due to human error and technical problems as well as new forms of cyber mischief, crime, terrorism and warfare. Each of these threats can result in severe service degradation or outright infrastructure failure.

The pace of technological change and the drive to automate control systems are aggressively challenging society's ability to design and implement necessary safeguards, including appropriate hazard detection, prevention and mitigation standards and practices. The vulnerability created by these gaps affects not only utility services, but also databases and systems that maintain vital confidential and/or proprietary information in all sectors.

Many of our most critical systems are highly vulnerable to damage from earthquakes, extreme weather and other natural hazards. Even when they are not physically impacted, sudden demand surges during crises can foster blackouts, brownouts and/or service congestion, leading to loss or denial of service. Similar scenarios can take place through deliberate or accidental human action. The CII has become especially vulnerable to fun-seeking hackers, criminals and even deliberate cyber attacks from nation states and terrorists. Every day, computer viruses and worms move rapidly across the world-wide Internet destroying data and overloading systems with superfluous e-mails, shutting down government, industry, academic, community and even private residential systems. Cyber-crime is becoming a growing transnational phenomenon, making prosecution extremely difficult. It is even perceived as a threat to national security, and in its most virulent form, cyber-war is now ranked in between nuclear and conventional war by the United States government as having one of the highest levels of threat impacts.

Protection of Critical Information Infrastructure

While physical restoration of the CII can often be completed quickly, even the most temporary failures can result in longer-term harm. They can seriously undermine public and business confidence in electronic commerce and government initiatives. The human and economic costs associated with recovery or initiating new mitigation strategies is enormous. The value alone of lost business and productivity is now measured in billions of dollars from each world-wide virus attack, and even the largest software vendors are hard pressed to keep up with security enhancements.

As important as our infrastructures are, many legal, institutional, economic, social and even conceptual issues continue to challenge protection efforts. Securing information infrastructure requires significant ongoing capital investment and evolving expertise, as well as coordination with other infrastructure sectors. Fortunately, these requirements have been identified world-wide already as a result of international planning and coordination efforts in the attempts to alleviate potential Year 2000 (Y2K) computer date rollover problems. Many factors contributed to successful organising efforts, including a universally recognised potential threat; a fixed deadline for reducing the risk and preparing contingency plans; compelling political and economic reasons for government and non-government interaction, and a shared knowledge base of common technical problems and solutions. Most importantly, Y2K provided, for the first time, a comprehensive view of international interdependence brought about by networked systems.

However, it also revealed as much about the differing perceptions of risk associated with CII consequences, variations in the protective actions that countries are prepared to initiate, and in the scope of participation that is considered necessary.

Some consider CII to be primarily a national security issue that needs protection measures to be directed by law enforcement, military and intelligence services. Representatives of businesses and of industrial sectors often view criticality in terms of what they need to conduct business and strategically protect proprietary interests. The public sector wants to reduce cost and improve efficiencies delivering services online, while protecting the privacy of citizen records.

Vendors and service providers may view risk in terms of new market opportunities to introduce a range of value-added security services and products, including technical support, software and hardware enhancements (encryption, firewalls, access control systems, etc.). The public wants assurances that financial and other electronic transactions are secure, and that appropriate control mechanisms are in place to prevent objectionable material reaching children.

Conclusion: Towards Practical CII Protection
One of the key features of our networked environment is that individuals, corporations and governments all share a responsibility in securing this environment. While not all of the potential residual benefits of Y2K efforts may have been widely garnered, countries are moving beyond this event to establish longer term CII protection strategies. Some of these initiatives were catalysed by the 11 September 2001 terrorist events.

In Europe, Germany, the United Kingdom, The Netherlands and other countries are putting in place CII programmes to better educate enterprises and the public. The United States has established a new Critical Infrastructure Assurance Office to carry out functions relating to protection of information systems for critical infrastructure, including those functions assigned to the new Office of Homeland Security. Canada has folded similar responsibilities into a new civilian agency, the Office of Critical Infrastructure Protection and Emergency Preparedness, that combines protection from and response to threats involving national critical infrastructure with the need to respond to other more traditional hazards. Such an all-hazards approach has both administrative and operational advantages. Among other things, it recognises that threats of natural and human-induced disasters also pose threats to critical infrastructures. It also provides a single focal point for coordinating national planning and response efforts.

Regardless of what approaches countries pursue, all will necessitate a continuing dialogue to promote mutual understanding of public and private sector interests and concerns, as all stakeholders strive to meet the objectives of protecting critical infrastructures increasingly through non-regulatory solutions. In the coming years, CII protection could very well become the fertile ground for spawning new public policy paradigms.

Box IV.6.1 Critical Information Infrastructure Protection

PRODUCT DESIGN AND IMPLEMENTATION

Vendor product development and testing cycles are decreasing, creating or leaving exploitable vulnerabilities; infrastructures may have fundamental security design problems that cannot be quickly addressed; vendors produce software with vulnerabilities, including those where prevention is well-known and computer source code often is not required to find vulnerabilities; the sophistication of attacks and intruder tools is increasing and many are designed to support large-scale attacks. Using these automated tools, intrusions from remote systems can be achieved in a matter of seconds; Internet attacks can be easy to launch, are often low risk and increasingly hard to trace. During a confrontation with Iraq in 1998, widespread intrusions into US Army, Navy, Airforce and other systems were discovered with no clear indication of how long they had been penetrated, where the intrusions were coming from or what information had been compromised.

INFRASTRUCTURE INVESTMENT AND MANAGEMENT

In a competitive environment, the need for rapid innovation and the lack of a clear return on investment for specialised critical infrastructure-protection features often preclude risk reduction considerations during design and implementation phases; information networks are becoming globally integrated and widely distributed among numerous stakeholders, whose control over network functions extends beyond national boundaries, making overall quality control complex, difficult to achieve, sustain and even monitor; many users are willing to accept higher risk of security deficiencies in exchange for greater technical and other efficiencies associated with advanced technologies.

AWARENESS AND TRAINING

The vast majority of CII intrusions result from exploitation of known vulnerabilities or configuration errors; intruders do not have to be well-trained since tools, knowledge and access to expertise are widely available over the Internet. However, the overall effectiveness of intrusion is increasing as knowledge is passed on to less knowledgeable intruders. The capabilities needed for initiating a global information infrastructure attack are no more than a networked personal computer and an e-mail programme; organisations trying to prevent intrusions are usually constrained by a shortage of qualified system and network administrators and information security staff. End-users are often left to train themselves; new entrants may not possess the same level of knowledge as incumbents about system capabilities, potential vulnerabilities or risk reduction measures.

Policy

Despite many lessons learned, these have not automatically led to a consolidation of knowledge; in many countries, there is no single authority or integrated programme for fostering innovation and new strategic approaches and there is little coordination across infrastructures. Public and private responsibilities for CII protection are evolving; many countries have yet to consider the Internet as a critical infrastructure; and in liberalised markets, governments are moving away from regulating new service markets. The international scope makes risk reduction strategies complex, and difficult to implement and enforce.

Trust and Information Sharing

While experience demonstrates the benefits of information sharing, widespread information sharing remains a significant problem. Liability and confidentiality concerns about disclosure of proprietary infrastructure data continue to deter firms from sharing information with governments, especially where there is the prospect of governments being forced to disclose such information under domestic access to information legislation.

Technology Determinism, the State and Telecom Surveillance

Peter Shields

Introduction

The importance of assessing the relationship between technology determinism and institutional power is a recurring theme in William Melody's writings. Technology determinism is a perspective that views technical innovation as driving society. That is, the relationship between technology and society is regarded as linear and mono-directional. For instance, Melody (1973b) convincingly shows how technology determinism, functioning through the natural monopoly concept, supported a regulatory regime that insulated, preserved and extended the market power of AT&T, the dominant telecom carrier of the day in the United States. As he put it, 'acceptance of the concept of technology determinism ... has had a devastating effect on the approach to regulation adopted by regulatory authorities... . It has narrowed the scope of analysis of public policy makers to encompass only changes within the established institutional structure' (Melody 1973b: 170). Similarly, he demonstrated how the rampant technology determinism that infuses information society policy statements of national governments, international organisations and corporations, privileges regulatory strategies and resource commitments that would benefit major telecom supplier firms and countries (Melody 1996c).

Following Melody's lead, this contribution assesses how the relationship between technology determinism and institutional power has played out in the domain of state telecom surveillance, a relatively neglected area of telecom policy studies. For a decade, concerns have been raised in the United States that the 'telecom revolution' and the emergence of the network economy are undercutting the state's surveillance capabilities. Policy initiatives were launched in response to this ostensible crisis. These initiatives led to intense debate between law enforcement agencies and their allies, on the one side, and industry actors and civil liberty groups, on the other. The technology determinism, which is at the heart of this debate, has functioned to narrow the scope of policy analysis by obscuring the ways in which developments in criminal justice policy and associated changes in the state have conditioned policy initiatives. The law enforcement establishment has benefited most from this state of affairs.

Policy Initiatives in the United States

Since the early 1990s, law enforcement agencies have argued that the rapid deployment of fibre optic cable in telecom networks, the explosive expansion of mobile telephony and the Internet and the proliferation of strong private sector encryption technology are threatening to erode their long-standing capabilities of intercepting and monitoring electronic communications. Without appropriate regulatory responses, their argument runs, drug traffickers, terrorists and the like will be able to operate anonymously and with impunity in virtual havens with devastating effects for public safety.

Regulatory responses were not slow in coming in the United States. After several years of dogged lobbying by the Federal Bureau of Investigation (FBI), Congress enacted the Communications Assistance for Law Enforcement Act (CALEA) in 1994. CALEA, for the first time, 'hardwires' the surveillance interests of law enforcement agencies into the design of telecom networks and services; telecom carriers, both landline and wireless, must now engineer their networks and services in such a way that law enforcement agencies can continue to wiretap. The implementation of CALEA has not been smooth due to efforts by the FBI to use the legislation to significantly expand its surveillance capabilities. This includes, for example, its demand that cellular phone companies provide law enforcement with location-tracking information on demand.

On the encryption front, the Clinton Administration pressed for adoption of its Clipper Chip or key recovery initiative throughout the 1990s. The aim of the initiative was to guarantee law enforcement officials access to a set of 'spare keys' that could be used to unlock encrypted electronic messages when authorised to do so. The plan stalled in the face of intense opposition from industry actors and civil liberty groups.

With respect to the Internet, the FBI has disclosed that it has been using Carnivore, a surveillance system that is installed at the suspect's Internet service provider to scan all-incoming and outgoing e-mails. While the system can be used to perform fine-tuned, court-approved targeted searches, reportedly it is also capable of sweeping searches, potentially enabling the agency to keep tabs on all network communications. Civil liberty groups opposed the deployment of Carnivore on the grounds that the FBI should not be trusted with what amounts to *carte blanche* authority when it conducts searches on the Internet.

There have also been efforts to internationalise some of these initiatives. For example, the FBI has pushed for the international adoption of CALEA. In the early 1990s, the FBI held regular meetings with its counterpart agencies in European Union (EU) Member States with the goal of incorporating elements of CALEA into European law. Their collective efforts resulted in an EU Council of Ministers resolution, adopted in January 1995, that mirrored the FBI's demands. Shortly afterwards, the EU Council agreed a Memorandum of Understanding, which extended the January agreement to non-EU countries that chose to sign. Nations interested in participating were told to contact the General Secretary of the EU Council or the Director of the FBI. And in response to pressure by the signatories, the International Telecommunication Union adopted a resolution in 1997 that called for priority to be given to the harmonisation of technical requirements to make law enforcement interception possible (see Statewatch 1997).

Paralleling these developments, the Clinton Administration engaged in a sustained diplomatic effort to persuade EU Member States, members of the G-8 and the OECD to adopt a global key recovery encryption system fashioned after its Clipper Chip proposal. The initiative was abandoned in 1998.

In short, for a decade, United States law enforcement agencies have struggled at the national and international levels to maintain and, in some ways, to enhance their telecom surveillance capabilities. The struggle raises some important questions: are law enforcement agencies emerging as major players in the control arrangements that govern the design and evolution of telecom networks? If so, what are the implications for the communicative activity that takes place over these networks? The outcomes of the struggle, and therefore the answers to these questions, are far from certain. The modest goal here is to demonstrate that it would be a mistake to view this struggle as being driven solely by the rapid diffusion of telecom technologies.

Loss of Control and Technology Determinism

Much of the policy debate concerning CALEA, key recovery encryption, and Carnivore is premised on a jarringly simple logic: the problem is a given; only the means to its solution are in doubt. First, the problem. For law enforcement officials, as well as for many public policy makers and journalists, 'loss of control' has been the dominant narrative. The basic story line is that the telecom revolution has plunged state surveillance into crisis; recent and continuing advances in telecom have allowed organised crime to leap ahead in its contest with law enforcement. Without remedial action by industry and government, it is argued, these new technologies will bring about a *de facto* repeal of the existing telecom surveillance authority conferred upon law enforcement agencies. A comment by former FBI Director, Louis Freeh, exemplifies much of the policy discourse:

> ... new and advanced telecommunications technologies ... have come on line and others will soon. They gravely impede or totally prevent court-approved surveillance... . Without an ability to wiretap, the country will be unable to protect itself against foreign threats, terrorism, espionage, violent crime, drug trafficking, kidnapping and other crimes. Indeed, we may be unable to intercept a terrorist before he sets off a bomb... . Unable to arrest traffickers smuggling in huge amounts of drugs that will cause widespread violent crime and death (Freeh 1994).

The focus in this discourse is on the loss of state control and its consequences, as well as on the technical change that has supposedly precipitated this loss. A solution to the problem is embedded in the story: the state must regain control. Since the problem is essentially a technological one, the solution must lie in the technical domain. CALEA, key-recovery encryption, and Carnivore, it is argued, will allow law enforcement to close the technology gap on criminals. As a result, state control over criminal activity will be re-established.

Many industry actors and civil liberty advocates have challenged the recent surveillance initiatives of law enforcement agencies. The challenges take at least three forms. Accepting the loss of control narrative, the first kind of challenge focuses on what are perceived to be the unacceptable costs of the initiatives. For example, it is often argued that the initiatives will obstruct or distort technological progress, impair the security of telecom systems, and reduce the competitiveness of American-owned hardware and software companies in foreign markets. Equally as often, it is argued that the initiatives inevitably will result in the erosion of civil liberties. The second kind of challenge begins to question the loss of control theme but stops short of providing an alternative narrative. For example, some critics have argued that there is little or no empirical evidence to support the claim that new technology routinely has hamstrung law enforcement's ability to intercept and monitor electronic communications. The third challenge combines elements of the first and second. Accepting that the state's loss of control claim may be valid with respect to telecom networks, some argue that this is more than offset by developments in thermal imaging, facial and behavioural recognition systems and DNA testing.

Most of the arguments outlined above contain grains of truth. However, the basic problem is that the general acceptance of the loss of control theme, and its attendant technology determinism, has led to a fundamental misunderstanding of the state's recent initiatives. Specifically, the stress on loss of control, and on the technical innovations that have supposedly resulted in this loss, greatly understates the degree to which the state has actually structured, conditioned and even enabled (often unintentionally) the kinds of organised criminal practices that state telecom surveillance is supposed to help control. That is, by characterising the state as purely reactive, the loss of control theme obscures the ways in which the state and other social forces have helped to create the very conditions that have generated calls for new electronic surveillance powers.

THE WAR ON DRUGS AND THE LOGIC OF ESCALATION

The claim, then, is that the loss of control narrative conceals more than it reveals about the forces that have propelled the recent telecom surveillance initiatives. The following provides a sketch of an alternative narrative that places the agencies of the government front and centre.

With the passing of the Soviet Union from the historical stage, concerns about organised crime joined with terrorism to dominate the domestic and international security agenda of the United States. This shift in priorities is reflected in the fact that law enforcement has been the fastest – and one of the only – areas of federal government expansion in the last decade or so. The state's ongoing War on Drugs has been the key factor driving this expansion (Andreas 1999). Characterised by the language, strategies, and tools of military deterrence, the supply-side approach is premised on the notion that the best way to solve problems of drug abuse and addiction is to prohibit the supply of illicit drugs. It has been very evident that this approach has failed miserably; both the supply of drugs and levels of abuse and addiction remain high in the United States. Moreover, the collateral damage associated with the supply-side approach has been staggering (Bertram et al. 1996). In spite of this dismal record, the policy response to this failure has been to escalate the supply-side approach by getting tougher. The War on Drugs in the United States illustrates both the power and the limits of the state; even as the state fails to deter the illicit drug trade, there is no illicit drug trade without the state.

The dynamics of the supply-side approach have played out in the domain of state telecom surveillance. As the state stepped up its War on Drugs, the ability to wiretap was portrayed as a key supply-side tool. As former FBI Director, Louis Freeh put it: 'Court-ordered wiretapping is the single most effective investigative technique used by law enforcement to combat illegal drugs' (Freeh 1995). Law enforcement's fixation with the anti-drug offensive is reflected in official wiretap data. Since 1990, the majority of reported wiretaps have involved drug-related investigations, ranging from 60% of all applications in 1990 to 75% in 2000 (Administrative Office of the United States Court 2001).[9] This is in the context of a sharp increase in the overall number of reported wiretaps. Leading law enforcement officials offer these statistics, and other body count numbers – number of drug traffickers captured, amount of drugs seized and destroyed, and so on – as evidence of their success, even as the drug supply flows unabated.

Many of the technologies associated with the telecom revolution have presented businesses in the illicit economy with opportunities for greater efficiencies. For example, drug traffickers have used cell phones, pagers and encryption-enabled phones to better coordinate supply and distribution activities as well as to more efficiently evade law enforcement (Constantine 1997). It can be argued that law enforcement's more intensive use of wiretapping as a supply-side tool provided drug traffickers with an incentive to rely on telecom technologies that are widely publicised as being difficult to tap.

The policy debates on CALEA, key-recovery encryption, and Carnivore depict these developments as a major loss of state control. Assuming the moral correctness of the supply-side approach, the problem is viewed as a technological one; advances in telecom are enabling drug traffickers and other criminals to circumvent the law. CALEA, key-recovery encryption and Carnivore are portrayed as defensive responses that will help restore control. This is misleading. It glosses over the fact that the state's failed supply-side approach to the illicit drug trade has created the conditions that have led to the calls for these surveillance initiatives. It is the very existence and enforcement of supply-side controls that have made it necessary for many drug-traffickers to try to circumvent them by using new telecom technologies. It is this dynamic, not technical innovation *per se*, that has called forth the surveillance initiatives.

CALEA was enacted and Carnivore has been deployed, while the key-recovery encryption initiative floundered. CALEA and Carnivore, themselves partly products of supply-side escalation, can be viewed as visible signs of the state's resolve that may well create the conditions for further escalation. For example, in the late 1980s and early 1990s, drug-trafficking organisations used cellular phones, in part, because they could evade law enforcement telecom surveillance more efficiently. As law enforcers met this challenge, with advances in interception technology and the passage of CALEA, the more sophisticated drug traffickers began to use cloned cellular phones to conduct their business. By the time investigators identify a violator who is using a cloned phone and follow the traditional path of gaining court-authorised permission for a tap, the violator has moved on to the next cloned phone, thus staying one step ahead of law enforcement (Bocchicio 1997). Drug traffickers who respond to law enforcement supply-side techniques with more sophisticated methods provide a rationale for better supply-side tools. Law enforcement officials can thus simultaneously praise their progress (the passage of CALEA) and point to the emergence of a formidable new enforcement problem – cloning of cell phones – which in turn is used to justify further regulatory measures. Escalation, in other words, feeds upon itself.

Conclusion

Following Melody's example, I have shown that technology determinism narrows the scope of policy analysis to encompass only those changes within the established institutional structure. In the debates over telecom surveillance initiatives, technology determinism, functioning through the loss of control narrative, has served to deflect critical attention from the failed supply-side approach to the problem of the illicit drug trade. This has benefited those institutional interests that have gained most from this approach – the law enforcement establishment.

The alternative narrative may add a fresh policy-relevant perspective to the debates on recent state telecom surveillance initiatives. For example, the loss of control narrative suggests that some erosion of civil liberties may be a necessary cost as the state battles to regain control so that it can once again protect public safety with confidence. The alternative narrative suggests that it may be more accurate to view any erosion of civil liberties that may occur as yet another instance of collateral damage resulting from the War on Drugs. The narrative also suggests that a fundamental re-evaluation of drug policy in the United States would have important implications for the state's telecom surveillance policy.

The attacks on the World Trade Center and the Pentagon in September 2001 have greatly intensified the debates over the state's telecom surveillance powers. Congress has passed the USA-Patriot Act of 2001, which significantly enhances law enforcement's wiretapping capabilities. It also removes or reduces judicial oversight from a number of wiretap procedures. The debates on this legislation and other legislative proposals are taking a familiar shape: law enforcement agencies and policy makers are stressing a loss-of-control theme as the justification for more telecom surveillance powers. Questions about the role of the state and other social factors in shaping the 'new' threat are being pushed into the shadows amid the struggle to regain control. The loss of civil liberties is being viewed by many as a necessary sacrifice in this struggle.

IV.8

Opportunities and Risks for India in the Knowledge Society

B. P. Sanjay

INTRODUCTION

There is euphoria in India and the rest of the world because many people are enjoying the benefits of the information society. The visions of Arthur C. Clarke and Marshall McLuhan are invoked to suggest that we are living in a global village. These visions emphasise a great faith in the democratising and equalising potential of new information and communication technologies (ICTs). This contribution considers the risks and opportunities associated with these visions, which portray societies as shifting towards service or knowledge-based economies. This shift is based on the premise that all societies move from being agrarian to industrial to information societies. This may be the case for a few countries, but it is not the case in many countries including India.

THE INDIAN KNOWLEDGE SOCIETY

The enthusiasm of our policy makers is promoting efforts to create new knowledge societies. This is reflected in an overwhelming focus on strengthening the telecom infrastructure and promoting the use of ICTs in all sectors. The government of India has made five promises to the people: freedom from hunger, development of social structure, development of physical infrastructure, a national water policy and the fulfilment of an information technology mission. The government's goal is to use its agencies to give a boost to the ICT sector. A national task force on ICTs has been established which aims to ensure that all villages are connected by an information superhighway and that every telephone booth becomes a fully-fledged information centre. In May 2000 the government appointed a working group on 'IT for the Masses' with a goal of enabling both the middle classes and the poor to benefit from the opportunities provided by ICTs. The intentions of the central government are shared by many other state governments which are vying with one another to provide incentives to attract investment, which it is hoped, will encourage development initiatives and help to alleviate social and economic problems.

It is important for students of communication and development to reflect upon the last few 'development decades'. The euphoria about the potential of ICTs can be compared to the rising aspirations with respect to initiatives in the past. The industrialisation and urbanisation models embedded in the modernisation paradigm are examples. The critique of this paradigm by Beltran (1975), Melody (1977), Smythe (1981) and others needs to be invoked to understand the consequences, intended or unintended, of initiatives that are undertaken following this line of reasoning.

The revolutions in India, green and white, are examples that demonstrate the benefits of the application of technology to boost grain and milk production. These examples show that growth that is not accompanied by equity does not lead to the alleviation of problems for the vast majority of people. Alienation from land, marginalisation and migration continue to affect their lives. The Indian people face the dilemma of contending with a plethora of problems and of coping with the demands and pressures of globalisation. Amartya Sen (1998: 8; see also 2000) views the situation in this way:

On balance, there are major gains to be made in globalisation. But if a country has globalisation at the highest possible speed and pays no attention to lack of social opportunity, illiteracy and lack of health care, it is creating problems for itself. In that case the blame lies not with globalisation but with concomitant policies with which it is being married. Globalisation needs to be put in a broader context of social and economic policies.

The Indian government is concerned about the creation of social opportunities but opinions differ as to whether these should result from the application of political will or of the trickle down benefits of the ICT paradigm. The track record of other countries suggests that we should not rely on the trickle down strategy. It is a myth to argue that we have been living in the knowledge society, only in the recent past. All societies have been information or knowledge societies. What has changed significantly is the manner in which the information is collected, stored, processed and disseminated. The information and communication patterns we see today are influenced to a large extent by the advantages that have accrued historically to the former colonial powers. The core-periphery notion or hinterland economic model (Innis 1951; Watkins 1982) helps to understand the role of telegraphy, the railways and other connecting technologies. Questions have been raised by representatives of developing nations about the imbalances and biases in the development of these technologies. Similar questions have been asked about the implications of ICTs for biases in the media.

Notwithstanding the potential biases and risks associated with the patterns of technology development and use in the periphery, increased attention is being devoted to using new ICTs to solve the problems of developing countries. This thinking influenced policy makers and the then Prime Minister of India, the late Shri Rajiv Gandhi, who incorporated telecom and computing into a mission-oriented strategy for development. This initiative paid some dividends. It is possible for some people (at least) to use world-class communication facilities albeit at a high price. Access is mainly an urban privilege. In the telecom development sector many global partners are involved and the stakes are very high leading to instances of large-scale corruption. A liberalised market model is being promoted together with reforms aimed at setting up regulatory mechanisms, disinvestments of state-owned institutions and the introduction of cost-oriented tariffs.

The Consequences and Risks

It is important to reflect on the consequences of this shift towards investment in ICTs in light of the fact that many information indicators show that the diffusion and access to ICTs are very low and that high levels of illiteracy and unaffordable services further accentuate this. Some agencies are setting up community media and information centres to address this problem. One state government (Andhra Pradesh) has promoted information kiosks, which enable access to the Internet, but the consequences of these initiatives need to be considered within the context of globalisation. Developing countries, based on their colonial experience, have embraced many of the latter's institutional structures with the consequence that the mode of knowledge production is less relevant to developing countries' requirements. A key feature of emerging knowledge societies is the broadening of production on a spatial basis, a trend that may simply emphasise existing biases in knowledge production and application. India is a paradox because its capacity in many ICT-related production areas is comparatively stronger than in many other developing countries, but much of the research supported by scientific institutions separates the production of new knowledge from its application in the domestic context.

The notion that open science generates knowledge that can be shared through open exchange is changing significantly. There are major questions as to whether India's scientists can access knowledge on an equitable basis as intellectual property rights are extended to new sources of digital information. The present system of knowledge production and dissemination is based on an intellectual property regime with certain disadvantages for the developing world and there are also issues of the extent to which the flows of new knowledge will be policed and regulated to curtail access to some kinds of information by countries like India. There has been a push by Indian stakeholders to ensure that India is part of the new regimes for intellectual property rights protection that are being negotiated in the World Trade Organization and world intellectual property rights fora, but there are doubts about the consequences of these moves. Pharmaceuticals and biotechnology are significantly affected by this evolving regime. In the pharmaceuticals industry, there are concerns that drug prices may rise to international levels. In the biotechnology industry there are concerns that indigenous knowledge bases will be exploited and that the necessary knowledge base to develop the new 'green gold' resides in scientific laboratories protected by intellectual property rights in the northern industrialised countries. These risks suggest a bleak scenario as a result of the further development of the knowledge society in India as well as globally.

The Consequences and Opportunities

Set against these risks are the opportunities created by the availability of ICTs. The information infrastructure can be used to implement sustainable development initiatives. Many poverty alleviation programmes, such as the projects initiated by the M. S. Swaminathan Foundation in Pondicherry to develop educational information villages, are underway. Although these projects are not free from certain structural limitations which make it difficult to expand beyond their current scale of operation and to address some grass roots difficulties, they do provide illustrations of the benefits of ICTs. Mansell and Wehn (1998) emphasise the importance of capacity building strategies embedded in new approaches to education which take advantage of advances in ICTs but which also recognise the value of traditional face-to-face community based learning. In India ICTs have been used to support vocational training, and engineering colleges are being restructured to meet the skill requirements of the ICT sector.

The opportunities seized by the Indian software industry reflect government strategy. When the United States government sought to impose non-tariff barriers on the industry, offshore operations in India gained momentum. Successful companies are competent to work in the global market environment, but the educational opportunities rest with the few despite the rapid dissemination of the Internet and an e-mail culture.

Conclusion

Many believe that those representing Indian institutions will have the capacity to push for a level playing field on the world scene as far as access to technology and the relevant knowledge bases are concerned at the same time as they foster the development of local knowledge and ICT applications. However, this will depend on other factors such as international trade relations and whether the government and other stakeholders can avoid becoming victims of the ICT fetish. India's resilient features and strengths in terms of its social organisation, its cultural resources and its vast reservoir of knowledge workers should not be frittered away as a result of greater than necessary participation in the global knowledge society.

Infrastructure Development and the Digital Divide in Asia

Meheroo Jussawalla

INTRODUCTION

In an era of terrorist activities, tightened security, reduced air travel, looming recession and unemployment, the potential for large investments in the information and communication technology (ICT) infrastructure does not appear promising. This problem is very significant for the emerging economies of the Asia Pacific region where the war in Afghanistan means reduced exports to the United States, less foreign direct investment and reduced access to venture capital as a result of higher risk and political uncertainty. The trend is towards greater protection of domestic markets, with an emphasis on the regulatory regime. William Melody (1999a) argued that the diversity of East Asia may make it impossible for the Anglo-Saxon model of telecom reform to be applied in all Asian countries. Despite this diversity, however, telecom reform and infrastructure investment are resulting in higher telephone densities in the region as a whole and this is supporting hopes that investment will provide a basis for bridging the various digital divides. This contribution examines recent developments aimed at strengthening the telecom infrastructure in the region based on investment in the 'Internet economy' and new wireless networks.

THE INTERNET ECONOMY

The members of the Association of South East Asian Nations (ASEAN) Plus Three have diverse economic and political regimes but they are home to over 500 million people with a combined Gross Domestic Product of US$ 700 billion. If China, Japan and South Korea are taken into account, this region could encompass a giant trading bloc covering one-third of the world's population with a GDP of US$ 7 trillion, although this is not likely in the near future.

Asia has made strong inroads into the world Internet economy which is expected to exceed one trillion dollars by the end of 2002, as estimated by Accenture, a US-based consulting firm. Hong Kong, Singapore, Malaysia and Taiwan have invested vast sums of money in teleports, cyberports, cybercities and technology parks to advance the use of the Internet and e-commerce. South Korea has taken the lead in using broadband technologies for electronic data exchange and storage. Internet users in the region reached about 37 million by 2001, as compared with Europe's

30 million (Senmoto 2001). The 'digital divide' within and between the countries in the region raises the question of the public interest. Should the state monopolies that provide communication services continue and does the state have a positive role in bridging the divide? Western monopoly providers achieved universal service in a relatively stable technological environment, but Asia's service providers have offered sophisticated services to metropolitan areas without meeting the basic needs of the remote areas (see Melody 1990a). The state-owned monopolies have been, or are in the process of being, privatised or they are undergoing structural changes to introduce greater liberalisation.

THE POTENTIAL OF WIRELESS NETWORKS

Wireless communication is spreading like wild fire in the Asian countries, but it is costly for low-income countries. These services are contributing to a widening of the regional digital divide between Japan and South Korea, and their neighbours. Nearly nine million users in Japan use the DoCoMo or I-Mode cellular phones, giving NTT 25% higher revenues than from its land-based microwave service. According to *Business Week* (2000), the global market for Internet-ready cell phones is expected to increase to one trillion dollars by 2005. Competition between Japanese, South Korean and Taiwanese manufacturers of cell phones has reduced the cost per subscriber and, as China enters the same market, the advantages of economies of scale will further reduce prices. In Japan in October 2001 the 3G (third generation cellular telecom system) was rolled out. As the wireless revolution enters a new phase in Asia, the potential for its rapid deployment is promising, although there may be a problem because of the shortage of spectrum. Asian countries are seeking a fairer way of allocating the broadband spectrum. This natural resource is important because, as newer technologies are introduced, the demand for its use is exploding (Jussawalla 1994). The licence fees charged for use of the broadband spectrum are creating huge financing problems for suppliers and, in Europe, the spectrum auctions were mismanaged and failed to improve efficiency or to enhance competition (Melody 2001b).

The promise of 3G is that users will surf the net on wireless notebooks and watch video clips on their telephones. In Japan, the I-Mode is equipped with cameras so that pictures can be e-mailed directly from the telephone. The major change is that in 2002, no one knows from which location on the Internet a search originates. With the web-on-the-go, there are base stations whose locations are precisely known. There is great pressure on licence holders of 3G to roll out the service and to market it in a competitive environment (Jussawalla 2001). Broadband Internet access and Internet access figures provide a benchmark of the progress of countries in the region towards establishing an advanced infrastructure (see Table 4.9.1). Comsys (UK) estimates that 25% of Asia's one billion households will be in the market for broadband using digital subscriber line or wireless broadband services by 2010 (*Broadband Asia* 2000).

Table IV.9.1 Broadband Penetration in Asia, 2000

Country	Internet Users (million)	Broadband Users (thousand)	Broadband Penetration %
Taiwan	3,474	217	6.2
Singapore	1,988	79	4.0
China	5,217	68	1.3
South Korea	9,157	3,491	38.1
Hong Kong	3,259	359	11.0
Australia	3,205	76	2.4
Japan	18,590	636	3.4

Source: eAccess Ltd, IDC Research 2001.

CHINA'S INFRASTRUCTURE DEVELOPMENT EXPERIENCE

The recent experience of China – as one of the potentially largest growth markets for all aspects of ICTs in the world indicates that the process of infrastructure development is influenced by a variety of endogenous and exogenous factors. China has the second largest market in the world for telecom equipment. It invested US$ 100 billion in its ninth Five Year Plan between 1995 and 2000 to upgrade and extend its fibre optic landlines and digital exchanges. Internet connections have been installed under the direction of the Ministry of Information Industry (MII) since 1998 in 43 cities to form the Chinapac network. MII also plans to connect 1,000 universities to the CERN (China Educational Research Network).

China was admitted to the World Trade Organization (WTO) in November 2002 and will have to make major changes in its economy over the first three-year round of negotiations. It will have to provide market access so that suppliers from other countries can reach its 1.3 billion consumers. At present foreign direct investment and participation restrictions are set at 40% under the China-China-Foreign (CCF) policy – or Zhou Zhong Wai – and this will have to be reduced. Drastic reductions in tariff and non-tariff trade barriers will also be necessary in return for which Chinese goods, services and capital will gain greater entry into foreign markets, fuelling its rise as a world economic power.

Combined imports and exports now amount to US$ 475 billion per year, making China the world's seventh largest trading nation (Dorgan 2001). However restrictions remain in place on the activities of foreign suppliers. For example, in November 2001, the government announced that it will charge every foreign broadcaster US$ 100,000 annually for the use of television channels on its satellite systems (Greenberg 2001). This gives the Government the power to switch off channels that state censors deem unacceptable. In 2001, after protracted negotiations, the BBC won approval to broadcast its news service to embassies and hotels and AOL-Time Warner was given approval to serve the province of Guangdong. News Corporation and Turner Broadcasting will have no difficulty in paying the fees as their advertising revenues are in the billions of dollars.

Media protection in China is an offshoot of the Government's fear of the role of media in East Germany towards the end of communist rule. China's regulators may be learning from the experiences of the European National Regulatory Authorities and they may seek to ensure the accountability of industry players so that they contribute to social and economic objectives (Melody 1999a). Chinese satellites have excess capacity and the MII can earn revenues from foreign broadcasters. But this new ruling may exacerbate the digital divide as countries like India, Malaysia and Thailand will have to pay a costly broadcasting fee which may not be justified by their assessment of the benefits.

In the Chinese market, two million cellular phone users are being added every month and 14 million pagers are being imported annually in addition to the domestic manufacture of pagers. In 1994 a cell phone in China cost US$ 2,000 but by 2002, the cost had declined to $200. China Mobile has awarded a contract worth US$ 40 million to Siemens to extend its wireless network and a new telecom giant, China Telecommunications Satellite Group Corporation, involving Chinasat and the Asia Pacific Satellite Company in Hong Kong, has been authorised to provide telecom services. Although the mobile phone market is expected to prosper, the road to the next generation 3G services may be a long one for China (Asia Tele.com 2001).

In spite of the rapid deployment of ICTs there is a substantial digital divide within China. Workers in Shanghai earn eight times the national per capita average income, and a rural worker earns only an average per capita of US$ 166 annually. The poverty belt stretches from Yunnan in the south to Xingiang in the north (Jussawalla 2001).

CONCLUSION

Political and social uncertainties continue to plague the emerging and advanced economies of Asia. The digital divide may not be the same as in other regions and policies may differ in terms of the strategies devised to convert the digital divide into a digital dividend. All the economies in the regions are continuing to increase their investments in ICTs. A rising tide may not raise all boats at the same time, but the trend is clear. The promise of the digital age is coming closer to fulfilment for the low-income countries of Asia. However, even in a wealthy economy like Canada, Melody (1993b) argued that there is an imperative for a telecom infrastructure policy as a defence against loss of sovereignty. In Canada's case there is the threat of competitive entry by American-owned firms and its economic, social, cultural and political implications. Internet service demand is exploding in Asian countries, but there are restrictions on its use as a result of China's fear of a loss of sovereignty and Singapore's concerns about a cultural invasion.

The hope that infrastructure development, combined with market reforms and regulation, will contribute to improved growth prospects and to reducing the digital divide has been strengthened by the resolution of the G-8 country ministers in Okinawa, Japan in July 2000. Ministers agreed that the affluent nations would help to bridge the global digital divide through initiatives to stimulate the transfer of technology, capital and human resources to the underdeveloped regions. But the 'missing link' remains an unsolved problem for international policy makers. There is also opposition from some non-governmental organisations, labour unions and other groups as was witnessed at the meeting of the G-8 ministers in 2001 in Genoa. The terrorism crisis since September 2001, suggests that digital divide issues may again be placed on the back burner of world affairs.

Linking Information, Technologies and the Consumer Interest

Supriya Singh

I met William Melody when I began working at the Centre for International Research on Communication and Information Technologies (CIRCIT) in 1990. The study of information and communication technologies (ICTs) became central to my work and my interest in consumers was strengthened as a result. Melody encouraged me to study money, information and technology as part of my research at the Centre and to link disparate theoretical frameworks.

Money, Marriage and Information

Melody saw the relationship between my work on banking and deregulation and the study of ICTs, before I did. I had come from a background in Sociology and Anthropology, where the study of information was undeveloped. Moreover, I was approaching banking from an historical perspective and had not as yet linked the developments in banking with other industries in Australia or internationally.

Telecom conferences in Australia and overseas in the early 1990s included few sociologists. These conferences were full of technologists praising technologies – some in the market and some yet to be developed. Economists and lawyers dominated the debates. The telecom industry was also a very male world in Australia. In India it was worse. The discussions in the telecom field also assumed a Western context where there was a telephone in nearly every household. At CIRCIT we were introduced to scholars and international institutions focusing on developing countries, but this was very much the exception. Despite our best intentions, every now and then I felt that my experience of telecom in India was not being taken into account. After all, my family had waited nearly three years for my mother in Dharamsala to have a telephone at home. This finally happened because a friend spoke to someone high up. When the phone came, my mother distributed sweets in the neighbourhood. Where did that experience fit into our discussions of universal access to the telecom network?

The multi-disciplinary and multi-cultural perspectives at CIRCIT in the early 1990s meant that meetings were never dull. These discussions helped to change my thesis. I started out examining changes in consumer relationships in banking because of deregulation. The first few interviews ensured that money and marriage became the focus. Deregulation was not as important for consumers as it was for bankers. However, work at CIRCIT helped place information and technology at the centre of my thesis on 'Marriage Money: The Social Shaping of Money in Marriage and Banking' (Singh 1997).

This transformation would not have happened without constant exposure to discussions about the nature of information and technologies. There still are few attempts to connect the study of money and information at the consumer level. The important question of how the new ICTs shape and are shaped by the nature and use of money continues to receive little attention. There is a gap between theories of media and money. Information has an important role linking each of these theoretical frameworks. People use different forms and channels of money partly because the kind of information yielded fits the requirements of their activities in their cultural contexts (Singh 1999). As money becomes more and more defined at the domestic level by its information, the management of money becomes more entwined with the control of money. The days of sitting around the kitchen table with the cheque butts and bills are now being replaced with the use of financial software. Hence the new technologies in changing the ways in which money is managed have the potential to change the power relationships revolving around money in marriage.

INFORMATION AND THE CONSUMER INTEREST

Melody was also very encouraging regarding initiating a forum on information and the consumer interest at CIRCIT. The forum brought together academics, consumer activists and regulators. The forum ran from 1991 to 1998 and resulted in many friendships and alliances. The public interest has been a passion in Melody's work. In his remarks to initiate the forum in September 1991, he spoke of the relationship between information, market choice and market efficiency.

Consumer groups are necessary to make markets function more efficiently in an imperfect world. They act as information providers and advocates of consumer interests in obtaining unbiased information and in establishing conditions for access to information (Melody 1991a: 1).

He went on to make the point that 'consumer advocacy of information ... provide[s] the most essential ingredient for effective social control of monopoly power' (Melody 1991a: 2). Without information there can be no successful monitoring and accountability of public policy.

In many bureaucracies, information is the currency of power. Thus "consumer" advocacy of information is just as essential to participatory democracy and government accountability for achieving non-market goals as it is to achieving corporate accountability and market efficiency (Melody 1991a: 3).

Melody warned that information, in itself, is not a 'good'. Information can mislead; it is costly to obtain; and it may not be used properly. He concluded:

Serious research and analysis must be undertaken of the markets, consumers, suppliers and regulators to determine where the greatest information deficiencies ... are. Clear identifications of the information desired, its form, timeliness and distribution are all important to developing a strategic approach to information advocacy. There must be attention to processes, e.g. access to information, representation in decision making fora to substantive information needs and to effective communication (Melody 1991a: 3).

Conclusion: The Users' Perspective

This focus on information and the consumer interest developed into an emphasis on the users' perspective in the study of ICTs. In the early 1990s, there was some lip service given to this, but the discussion in conferences, in policy debates, and in academic work in Australia was nearly all on the study of technologies and the economics of information. Melody was responsible for the early emphasis in our work on the demand side. This focus was strengthened as we heard one international speaker after another emphasising that the future lay in a focus on demand, rather than on the policy of building the technology and rolling it out.

We used this focus on the users' perspective as our starting point in many studies including examinations of the use of ICTs in the home; e-mail and effective corporate communication; the development of electronic commerce for small businesses; gender and Internet use; deaf people's use of ICTs; evaluations of consumers' use of government electronic service delivery; and equity and access in learning technologies.

The story of effective communication is different when told from the perspectives of providers and users. The need to keep the multiple stories in mind has been the challenge in linking user research to the design, production and marketing of the new ICTs. Similarly, in terms of policy effectiveness, placing the user at the centre results in different kinds of monitoring and analysis. Melody introduced us to ways of examining the use of ICTs that draw upon many disciplines and perspectives and the linking of different disciplinary frameworks for the study of information has been enormously rewarding.

Theses on Informatisation

Jörg Becker

When the self-understanding of science is guided by the concept of critique, the main concern is to restrain people from dominating others. Most theoretical discourses in the social sciences take a contrary position: despite all their differences, systems theory, radical constructivism, discourse analysis, postmodernism and constructs such as socially-sustainable technology assessment, have in common an inability to deal conceptually with the categories of dominance and power. It is paradoxical that the following theses – which are indebted to a 'critical' science – are regarded by most academics as being less important than they are in the political or economic spheres, where the categories of dominance and power are well-known.

- The information and communication technology (ICT) industry (data processing, telecom, and the media) exhibits an exceedingly rapid rate of technical change, and an equally large diversity of application possibilities. This gives rise to ICT's convergence in terms of labour, capital and everyday life.

- The application possibilities of ICTs in the civil sector are so diverse that a spin-off from the military to the civil sector can no longer be assumed. The success of Japanese ICT initiatives based on civil resources, and the efforts of the United States military sector to invest in ICTs illustrate the dominance of the civil sector, and the relatively insignificant spin-offs from the civil to the military sector.

- ICTs enable major shifts away from electro-mechanical production. These lead to significant savings in material and energy costs. Due to these shifts, new divisions of labour are occurring world-wide and the importance of raw materials from the 'Third World' is decreasing.

- The production and distribution of ICTs requires capital and knowledge leading to economic concentration and the strengthening of transnational corporations (TNCs). The economic dynamism at the international level promotes company take-overs and mergers and collapses. Governments are actively involved in this process of change.

- ICTs facilitate the restructuring of national and international labour markets. The potential of ICTs to drive automation promotes structural unemployment and, because of the declining share of wages in production costs, also enables the return of production from low wage countries to the centres of economic activity.

- ICTs support the integration of R&D, design, production, resourcing, storage, administration, marketing and sales at the international level. The consequence is integration at the centres of production and truncated production at the peripheries.

- The dynamism of ICT innovation is promoting changes in professional qualifications in the fields of planning, design, team work, coordination and control. Industrial structures are based more intensively on information. Information-based industries rob the periphery of its former comparative cost advantages (especially wage costs). This explains the growing importance of intellectual property and human capital for international organisations in their negotiations on the so-called liberalisation of electronic services.

- ICTs have the potential to improve the instrumental quality of products, that is, to make them more accurate, more safe, more precise, etc. The periphery can compete less and less with such high-tech products on the global market. Following, however, Max Horkheimer's (1947) distinction between human and instrumental reason, it is an open question whether the centre or the periphery will develop towards a more human or inhuman direction.

- ICTs link the services and goods-producing sectors so closely that a separation between the 'service society' and the 'goods producing society' is analytically inaccurate and less meaningful.

- ICT innovation reacts in a unique way to the internationalisation of capital, while also favouring it. The increasing global (electronic) money supply is the technical and monetary precondition for the periphery's growing foreign trade debt.

- The internationalisation of capital and information flows favours differentiation on the periphery with a few winners (South East Asia) and many losers (Black Africa).

- The capacity of computers to accumulate information grants ever-greater economic status to the distribution and planning of global information flows just as Karl Marx saw the importance of distinguishing between industrial and traded products.

- As a result of the (technically possible) commodification of information, the regulation mechanisms in national economies are changing fundamentally. Economies are increasingly regulated by the relationship of information to social organisation.

- Deregulation and liberalisation are inaccurate terms for the industrial restructuring made possible by ICTs. Increasingly, national quotas are regulating global ICT and content trade structures.

- The commodification of information is giving rise to new forms of privatised information. The unequal distribution inherent in this privatisation is phasing out the state in the fields of child rearing, education, culture, science and communication and the public domain is being dismantled.

- The commodification of information is leading to concentration promoting the trend towards global cultural homogenisation. At the same time, it is strengthening cultural defences against this trend. ICTs contribute to the internal and external growth of structural heterogeneity. The drastic upheavals in Eastern Europe would have been inconceivable without participation in the international information flows. But the nationalist and ethnic eruptions in Eastern Europe are an historically late expression of the struggle for an independent cultural identity. The 'culturalisation' of politics is one of the most serious consequences of the internationalisation of information flows.

- Structural heterogeneity as a result of social change associated with greater use of ICTs is reflected in technology forecasts that are more and more inaccurate.

- The informatisation of global society is speeding up and becoming more all-embracing. The control mechanisms of companies, economies and countries are less predictable and reliable. Systems are becoming more unstable and vulnerable but there is no evidence of new political structures that might be able to deal with this greater risk.

There is little intellectual effort to differentiate between various technologies. The extent and depth of changes in the global society that are associated with informatisation exceed everything that is being claimed for biotechnology, gene technology or new materials. A task of academic research and teaching is to promote discourse in the public domain. The social sciences are no longer fulfilling this task. Computing science has assumed this function. Exciting theoretical issues are being discussed in this field. For instance, what is language? Can the activity of the human brain be depicted? What is information? Is there such as thing as artificial intelligence? It may be that computer scientists lack a background in the social sciences and philosophy, but their enthusiastic readiness to debate is refreshing.

V

Bias...

Sally Wyatt

Paschal Preston

Edward Comor

Sung Woon Cho

Peng Hwa Ang
and James A. Dewar

Robert E. Babe

Vincent Mosco

Anders Henten

Bias...

Rohan Samarajiva, Robin Mansell and Amy Mahan

Bias may seem an unusual title for a section. But it should not surprise those familiar with the work of Harold Adams Innis, the Canadian political economist, economic historian and communication scholar. Almost a quarter century ago, William Melody and his colleagues at Simon Fraser University in Canada organised a conference and edited a book on the legacy of Innis (Melody et al. 1981). The intersection of geography, history, economics and political science where Innis' work is situated, according to Hall (1998: 506), has proved conducive to fruitful work by Melody as well as by many of his colleagues, as is evident from the contributions to this section.

Innis' concept of bias refers to an emphasis on one aspect of something, to the neglect of another. Space-biased media, for instance, tend to neglect the dimension of time. The contributors to this section, whether they explicitly draw on Innis or not, refer to aspects that are shielded from view by conscious design or by theories and frameworks that are biased. Paschal Preston, Edward Comor and Cho, Sung Woon see Innis' and Melody's work as having tremendous potential for compensating for the impairments (Lindblom 1990) that affect inquiry.

Sally Wyatt's contribution is about theories and conceptions that shield as much as they illuminate. Hers is a story of teaching, of ideas being challenged, of impairments being reduced and of knowledge being passed on. There is also a parallel narrative about the impaired efforts of social scientists and others to grasp the social transformations that we are living through. These ideas are explored in greater detail not only by the other authors in this section, but also in other sections of this book.

Paschal Preston sees Innis' later, explicitly communication-focused, work as a starting point for analysis of information society issues, but calls for painstaking empirical work that addresses contemporary forms of technology, information and communication. He might have used Innis' (1923; 1930/1962) own research on the fur trade and railway (a relatively neglected part of the Innis legacy that is examined by Cho) as illustrative of his observations. In his call for concrete analysis, Preston foreshadows the argument with which Anders Henten ends this section. Preston shares with Henten, and with Melody, the view that there is no fundamental distinction between developing and industrialised countries. Preston describes the current literature on information societies as a reincarnation of the communication and development theses of the 1950s (Lerner 1958). The understanding of all countries as being in the process of development, rather than reaching a state of development is one that is also found in Melody's (1981b: 11) work.

Preston and **Edward Comor** both explore the paradox of information: more information everywhere but less knowledge; more channels for communication, but less interaction. Preston does not explore the causes of this paradox, but implies that something akin to an 'iron triangle' of forces has given rise to a plethora of analytically unsupported writing about the emerging trends of information economies. Comor touches on the processes through which information is made into knowledge. Behind his observations on the importance of learning what information to pay attention to and what information to ignore, is the concept of attention as a scarce commodity, perhaps the one truly scarce commodity. In his early writing on children's television, Melody (1973a) addressed the production or aggregation of attention into audiences by the media.

Comor, Mosco and Preston, along with Babe, share a sense of pessimism that also pervaded Innis' later writings, perhaps most eloquently expressed in the reference to wisdom and insight appearing in the twilight of civilisation: 'Minerva's owl begins its flight only in the gathering dusk' (Innis 1951: 3, citing Hegel). Preston sees the need for ideas that will help to forge the 'good society'; Comor sees a possibility of reducing the accumulation of monopolies of knowledge that hold back the resolution of long-term problems; and **Vincent Mosco** looks to a new convergence of labour and consumer interests to change the world. Babe, echoing Innis' (1951) concerns about industrial society, wishes to see the extrication of humankind from the price system that he argues is threatening the survival of the human (and other) species. It is interesting to juxtapose these analyses and prescriptions with those offered by Melody. In his case, it may be argued that pessimism is understated, if present at all, and that the remedies are less sweeping. As Preston points out, Melody drank not only from the well of Innis but also from that of John R. Commons. The sweep of his analysis comes from north of the 49th parallel, but the pragmatic reform orientation has its roots in the American Midwest.

Cho, Ang and Dewar offer an explication of some of the key Innisian ideas. **Ang, Peng Hwa** and **James Dewar** shed light on some of the policy issues that are likely to arise from the ongoing developments centred on the Internet. They do so by looking back in time at the invention and social adoption of the printing press, a technology that occupied the attention of Innis as well as McLuhan (1962). Their contribution draws from a workshop that included not only Eisenstein (1980; 2000), the pre-eminent scholar of the printing press in the West, but also Kang (2000), an expert on early Asian printing technologies and associated social changes. **Cho, Sung Woon** explores the relations between the economy and communication, drawing from the early economic work of Innis as well that of Du Boff (1980; 1983; 1984), an economic historian whose work was drawn on by Melody (1985c). Mosco also sees the relation between the economy and communication as being of great importance. He notes that both Melody and Dallas Smythe, another Canadian who made a significant impact in Washington as Chief Economist at the Federal Communications Commission at the time that television broadcasting was being introduced, contributed greatly to advancing our understanding of the inter-relationships of economy and communication.

Smythe and Melody were great friends and colleagues. Their commonalities extended beyond their service as Chief Economists of the FCC (separated by several decades) and as Chairs of the Department of Communication at Simon Fraser University (in succession). They also shared an interest in the economics of audiences. The differences in their treatment of this one concept shed important light on the nature of Melody's approach. In his book on *Children's Television*, Melody (1973a) asks the question 'what is bought and sold in the television industry?' The answer is audiences. Melody takes this significant finding and translates it into policy proposals for the reform of children's television (see also, Melody and Ehrlich 1974). Several years later, Smythe (1977; 1981) explicated the audience as the commodity that is bought and sold in communication industries. In his case, the audience commodity was the core concept of late 20th century capitalism, and audiences were seen as creating surplus value in the Marxian sense. Melody opts for a concrete analysis and the implications for reform, while Smythe moves to abstraction and grand theory. This friendly divergence is found also among the contributors to this section and to this book as a whole.

Robert Babe, who began his academic career steeped in institutional economics like Smythe and Melody, now writes from an ecological perspective. His first thesis is that the emerging information economy is intertwined with the price system and shares its space bias, as discussed by Innis (1956). Interpreting the concept of bias to refer both to what is emphasised and paid attention to, and what is hidden and ignored, Babe goes on to develop five arguments to show that the information economy, intertwined as it is with the price system, is destructive to the environment. His theses are directed to the information economy as such, but they are also a general critique of the price system. Would the threat to the environment be less, or more, or no different, if the cluster of activities described as the information economy had not arisen?

Focusing on the development domain, **Anders Henten** poses a series of questions about apparent inconsistencies in Melody's writings. How can Melody be critical of the activities of transnational corporations while, at the same time, actively promoting sector reforms in developing countries that increase the spread of communication infrastructures? Does this not increase the vulnerability of these countries to penetration by transnational corporations? He answers these questions by showing that Melody is, in fact, consistent. Henten argues that Melody's conclusions flow from concrete analysis, not grand theory; and that as a result, he can support sector reform without being inconsistent.

Henten notes that Melody's positions do not fit neatly into conventional right-left classifications. For instance, Melody has not been a defender of government ownership, especially when such ownership appears to stifle innovation and the efficient supply of services. But he has been an equally vehement critic of the view that markets are the solution to everything. Markets are very useful instruments, but they are only as good as their institutional design. In his writing and speaking on regulation, he has taken issue with others such as Littlechild (1984: para 4.11) who have proposed a highly constrained role for regulation: that of 'holding the fort' until competition arrives.

Henten's observation of apparent contradictions within the body of work of a single author and the 'reconciliation' of those contradictions, has an interesting parallel with that of a question asked by Albert Hirschman, best known as the author of *Exit, Voice and Loyalty* (Hirschman 1970), that Lindblom (1988) answers at length in the form of a compilation of articles. The question was how Lindblom had come from incremental policy making to the apparently radical argument of *Politics and Markets* (Lindblom 1977) (incidentally, a book that Melody used in his teaching).

Lindblom's (1988: 11) answer appears apposite to the question at hand.

Do I believe that the political and social world is in such good shape that it needs only incremental improvement? Indeed not. ... Do we therefore need drastic change? Indeed we do. Given, however, the existing political structures of the ostensible democracies, there is little hope of getting it except through long glacial sequences of incremental changes. ... Wars and catastrophes aside, it looks as though anyone who wants drastic change will do best to promote rapid incremental change cumulating into drastic change. His prospects are poor, but ordinarily worse if he takes any other route. Incremental policy making is weak, often inefficacious, inadequate to the problem at hand; and the control over it often falls into the wrong hands. It is also usually the best that can be done. Such a view of incrementalism, not the buoyant view of it that commentators often attribute to me, is not at all difficult to reconcile with the critical writing on democracy and market.

Melody has learned from, and contributed to, many traditions of social theory, but his core allegiance has always been to the institutional economics of Veblen (1899/1994), Commons (1959) and Mitchell (1913/1970). It is intriguing that it is Henten, a European political scientist several degrees removed from the intellectual milieu of the American variant of institutionalism, who chooses to develop his analysis around these foundational aspects of Melody's intellectual project.

When assessing and analysing specific situations and developments, it is far from sufficient – if not erroneous – to deduce outcomes from general theory. The specificities of different situations must be taken into account. General theories should be applied, but they should be used as tools to understand specific situations (Henten, in this section).

This is perhaps the key insight that can be taken from this section. The world is complex, and it appears to be increasing in complexity. Instead of an absolute test of truth and theories of everything, we can get by with the criterion of 'practical adequacy' (Sayer 1992: 65-71) and less than grand theory.

We need theory to help us see what is shielded by various biases, but beyond theory we need concrete analyses to help us see at least some of the biases of our own. It is only through this balance between abstraction and empirical inquiry, between theory and praxis, that we successfully can navigate the knife's edge between technological determinism, where all is preordained, and post-modern ruminations that allow everything to be criticised, but nothing to be done.

C is for Convergence (and Communication, Content, and Competition)

Sally Wyatt

INTRODUCTION

I first met William Melody in the summer of 1986. He was interviewing me for the position of research associate with the Economic and Social Research Council's (ESRC) Programme on Information and Communication Technologies (PICT) in the United Kingdom. Melody had arrived at the ESRC in 1985 from Simon Fraser University in Canada to direct PICT. I had left Canada in 1979, and had been working at SPRU – Science and Technology Policy Research at University of Sussex since 1980. SPRU was, and is still today, a large research institute. I had worked on many topics while at SPRU, including the measurement of technological competitiveness, technology and the domestic division of labour, the protection of intellectual property rights and technology transfer, but I had never undertaken any work on information technology (IT), as it was called at that time in SPRU. I fancied a change, so applied for the job of PICT research associate, to work with Melody in selecting and managing the six PICT centres. Before the interview, I did some reading and talked with some SPRU colleagues who did know about information technology and whose proposal had already been selected as one of the first three PICT centres.

My main questions were: what is so special about IT? Is it any different from other technologies with which I was more familiar, such as those for oil exploration or for domestic work? What challenges does it pose to understanding innovation, work and everyday life? What theoretical tools do we need to understand it? What questions does it raise for social theory?

I do not remember all of the answers, but one has stayed in my mind, perhaps because it is an answer to them all: convergence. Ian Miles, one of my SPRU colleagues, explained it in the following way.

New IT, often defined as the convergence of computing and telecom, is made possible by the increased power and reduced cost of information-processing via microelectronics. Modern computing and telecom ... treat data in digital form. This facilitates the process of convergence, as the same data can be processed by many devices and

media. Analysis of this potential is crucial to understanding IS
[Information Society] (Miles 1988: 7).

I probably reproduced a form of this technicist definition of convergence during the interview in response to a question about why, even though I had no experience of doing research about information technology, I wanted to work with PICT. I must have done something right in the interview, however, as I was offered the job. Thus began a very steep learning curve.

Communicating Convergence

What I learned from Melody and others in PICT was that this technical view on convergence was rather partial and limited. Convergence could mean a great many other things, though it was not always defined by people who wrote about it. At the very least, convergence could also refer to the coming together of hardware and software, of mass communication and personal communication and of the policy instruments for controlling these technologies. Convergence was not only the technical merging of computing and telecom but also an economic and industrial restructuring of these two industries which hitherto had very distinct characteristics in terms of market structure, conduct and performance. It was hoped that the monopolistic powers of the large telecom companies would be challenged by their encounter with the more competitive environment of the computing industry. While Melody certainly made a major contribution to challenging the monopolistic position of AT&T, global market forces were too much even for him. The information and communication technology (ICT) industry remains characterised by oligopoly at the beginning of the 21st century.

I learned even more from Melody about convergence. This part of the story relates to the use of the C for communication in the PICT title. My former colleagues in SPRU such as Ian Miles and Christopher Freeman emphasised the technology and the potential of IT as a new techno-economic paradigm (Perez 1983), which would give rise to whole new sectors as well as affecting all other areas of economic activity. A new techno-economic paradigm alters relative costs of inputs and outputs and thus the conditions of production and distribution for both old and new products. It also involves the emergence of a new 'common sense', a new best-practice set of rules and customs for designers, engineers and managers which differs fundamentally from that of the previous paradigm.

Interesting and important as this is for understanding long-term economic changes, what Melody and some of my other new PICT colleagues pointed to was the content of the information and the importance of its communication. Not only did a change in techno-economic paradigm encompass the production and use of microelectronics and telecom in a wide range of industries but it also stimulated a recognition of the importance of information and communication processes in economic and social life. Attention needed to be paid to the changing and growing role of information services: the emerging ones, which we called interactive or value added network services back in the 1980s; and the more traditional information services of the mass media, publishing, library, education and postal delivery.

While working with PICT I was also thrust into debates about the information society. For Daniel Bell (1973), one of the features of the 'information society' was indeed the centrality of information as an organising principle. While Melody was always the first to emphasise the importance of information in social and economic life, he reminded me that it had always been thus.

People working in long-established and well-settled sectors of society as education, libraries, printing, consultancy, administration, and the entire bureaucracies of every organisation in the world were suddenly reclassified as part of the information sector and transformed into pioneers in the progressive and futuristic information society (Melody 1996b: 313).

Melody introduced me to the complexities of understanding and measuring information as a commodity. Drawing on the work of Charles Read and the Information Technology Advisory Panel (ITAP) (1984) report, Melody was scathing in his critique of neo-classical economics for treating information as perfect and costless. Everything we know about institutions and the economy as a whole suggests otherwise, even if our conceptual tools for dealing with imperfect, and sometimes very costly, information were themselves not always adequate. Just because something is difficult to measure is not a reason for pretending that it is not there or does not need to be measured. One of the ambitious, cross-centre PICT projects was entitled Mapping and Measuring the Information Society.

A few years after both Melody and I had left PICT, I found myself teaching many of these ideas in the Department of Innovation Studies at the University of East London. In one of my courses, entitled, Technology, Information and Consumption, his presence was keenly felt. Translating these ideas about convergence for undergraduate consumption was often a challenge for both the students and me and of course the shifting and contested nature of the term convergence had to be addressed each and every time I taught the course. PICT had as part of its remit the training of junior researchers, but the ideas went beyond postgraduate and PhD training and were taken up in many undergraduate programmes.

I now find these ideas about convergence reappearing in my work, which examines the ways in which people interpret the advantages, disadvantages and uncertainties of particular health treatments. In this research, we recognise that people have access to multiple sources of information and thus it is important not to reify the new, the Internet (Henwood et al. 2001). We aim to analyse the significance of different media and sources of health information in the discursive production of 'risk narratives' as constructed by both producers and consumers of health information. Convergence helps us to understand the multiple media that people draw upon, the multimedia form of some of the new media and the relationship between content and medium.

My work with Melody was primarily about managing a large research programme. Nonetheless, I remember him best as a teacher. As Henry Adams (1907/1990) said, 'A teacher affects eternity; he can never tell where his influence stops'. Melody helped me to understand the complexity of convergence, which I have since passed on to my own students and which continues to inform my own research.

Knowledge or 'Know-less' Societies?

Paschal Preston

> The conditions of freedom of thought are in danger of being destroyed by science, technology, and the mechanisation of knowledge ...
> (Harold A. Innis 1951: 190)

DECEPTIONS OF DOMINANT DISCOURSES

Since the 1980s, the dominant economic and political discourses have tended to characterise the present era as one of radical, if benign, transformation. Such discourses mobilise a common set of terms to describe the transformations that are said to be underway. These include: 'the information society' or 'the knowledge economy' or 'the technological society', or indeed, 'the techno-culture'. Yet when we look beneath the glossy surface of such slogans to seek some enlightenment about the nature, direction and causes of socio-economic change, not to mention the potential for alternative paths of future development, we are generally disappointed. We confront a profoundly grey and dull cluster of chaotic concepts, linear conceptualisations and some extraordinary extrapolations (speculations) that are being used to define the role and meaning of technology or information in societal change. We are greeted by a heady cocktail of speculative 'dreamware' based on techno-centric analyses of clusters of technological innovations. Or we find idealised conceptualisations of the distinctive features of information as resource or product. These are usually laced with a strong dose of doctrinal prescriptions, especially those celebrating the idealised virtues of the 'invisible hand', the 'naked cash nexus' or the sovereignty of the consumer.

Beneath the gloss on so many technocratic strategies or guides to the national, European or global 'way to the information society', we find a subsidiary and subliminal marketing campaign on behalf of the producers of new technology products and services. Not only is information relegated to the margins and subsumed under the primacy of the 'technology' imperative, but the wider use and consumption of new information and communication technologies (ICTs) are prescribed as both *end* and *means* of economic and social development. We meet a 'born-again', fundamentalist version of the linear modernisation theory of the 1950s. New ICTs are deemed to operate not only as the universal 'magic multiplier' or tool to drive socio-economic development, they also become a core indicator of societal development (Preston 2001).

The foregoing highlights a poverty or implosion of meaning, a veritable 'imaginative failure' as well as a void of values. These are found at the heart of the rhetoric advanced by our dominant political and economic elite with regard to the changing roles and features of technology, and especially information, in contemporary social development. These features exist despite a quantitative explosion of information and communication overload. This is manifest especially in the specialist knowledge domains addressing the fundamental changes in economic, managerial and policy making processes and practices.

This particular realm includes the surge of contributions to public discussions of the 'new economy' and the rise of the Internet over the 1995-2000 period. We have witnessed the publication of a vast number of books, articles, and radio and television coverage celebrating the emergence of the 'new economy' and the information age. This wave of publication amounts to a distinctly new multimedia publishing niche; a virtual information sub-sector in its own right. This niche is replete with its own superstars in the form of gurus and high priests, each out-bidding the other with lofty promises of technology-based plenitude and bliss. But, much like the claims of prophets of earlier times, these promises are vacuous when it comes to grounded analyses of 'what's really going on' in material terms, not least with respect to how different socio-economic interests may survive, develop and prosper in our times.

The quantitative explosion of information about the 'new economy' has not been matched by qualitative advances in public debate or understanding of important structural changes in technology, information and related shifts in economic structures or policy processes. Nor has it been matched by robust debate on the alternative forms, or fundamentally different paths, of socio-economic or cultural development that may open up for citizens of democratic polities. Indeed, the contrary is the case. We are confronted with a classic case of more is less when it comes to grounded knowledge of the distinctive features and strategic contours of change in the economy. In this realm, we confront an especially impoverished or distorted version of the public sphere. Reputation and status seem strongly correlated with the degree of hype and speculation being pedalled and with the intensity of each author's refusal to test key hypotheses. Many prominent techno-gurus proclaim the demise of the old media in the face of the new but their predictions rely on simplistic assumptions about substitution effects. Distinction in this genre is negatively correlated with efforts to produce empirical analyses of socio-economic processes and sustained, critical engagement with the accumulated knowledge-base of prior research.

These discourses amount to a particular manifestation of information overload: a quantitative explosion of data, but a diminution in the level of understanding of what is really going on. The same criticism applies to alternative models of socio-economic development centred around maximising the use and adoption of ICTs. Indeed, when it comes to public understanding of the key features and potential directions of change relating to the knowledge economy, there is the ironic prospect of eliminating any potential for democratic choice and decision making. As models to guide or inform our future paths of socio-economic development, the imaginative reach of such technocratic discourses rarely extends beyond the cul-de-sac of an information-consuming, but 'know-less society'. We appear to be 'lost in the void of information' – to borrow a phrase from that high priest of post-modern theory, Jean Baudrillard (2000).

Towards Grounded Knowledge

The above summarises a comprehensive and sustainable critique of fundamental blind spots in the content and method of accounts of the role of technology and information in the process of socio-economic change (Preston 2001). In this contribution, I consider alternative approaches and methods and offer some conceptual resources for a more grounded analysis by focusing on an important stream of work which contributes to a robust knowledge-base for technology, information and communication studies: a diverse Canadian school of pioneering research within which William Melody's work is located. This body of work provides a starting point for alternative approaches and methods to prevailing orthodoxies (Preston 1994). This contextualisation of Melody's work must be qualified by acknowledging the formidable and distinctively international dimensions of its range, influence and mode of operation. The lineage of this work includes J. E. Cairnes (1870; 1873) through to Thorstein Veblen (1898/1961) and John. R. Commons (1959).

In all areas of socio-economic and cultural analysis it is increasingly recognised that we live in technology-tempered times. There is little agreement on how to define or conceptualise the roles of technologies as drivers of socio-economic or cultural change. For one Canadian theorist, the answer was categorical: 'the medium is the message'. Technological change holds the key to understanding other aspects of historical change. Marshall McLuhan's fundamentalist message of the 1960s has strongly influenced the dominant code, grammar and content of contemporary discourses surrounding new ICTs. His fame and influence have been re-born in the era of Internet. Indeed, he has been canonised as patron saint of the wired generation. His ghost haunts newer disciplinary fields such as cultural studies, whose founders explicitly distanced themselves from the techno-centric musings of McLuhan's earthly existence. This influence is manifest, for example, in the content as well as the operational devices of the influential postmodernist theorist, Jean Baudrillard.

Thanks in part to the critique provided by Melody (1999d), it is recognised that McLuhan represents one particular diversion in the Canadian tradition of research on technology and communication. McLuhan not only overstates the technological moment of the socio-economic and cultural change complex, his focus and method preclude him from providing a detailed analysis of such relationships. His work focused on the individual-media-machine relation, ignoring social and institutional contexts. As in the case of his contemporary counterparts, this limitation of focus or method 'didn't stop him from leaping to conclusions about institutions, the direction of human development, or anything else' (Melody 1999d: 376).

There is another stream of pioneering Canadian work that leads to much more productive concepts and insights relevant to present concerns. Harold Adams Innis' (1950; 1951) work addressed the intersection of technology, commerce and information – including its cultural components. Innis attended to systematic empirical methods and addressed sociological concerns; 'in his writings are found bits of geography, history, economics and political science', and the core of his theory 'lies at the point where they intersect'. It represents an 'intellectual voyage' worth taking and a 'rich lost continent awaiting exploration' (Hall 1998: 506).

Although he died before his main work was fully complete and his writings are often elliptical and fragmentary, Innis is recognised as an inspiring intellectual figure by researchers across a range of social science disciplines. Indeed, many of Melody's writings signal how Innis' work provides a productive starting point for researchers concerned with the political economy and spatial dimensions of new ICTs and the changing role of information. Innis' work provides a subtle and dialectical platform for understanding the distinctive character and role of technology in the process of socio-economic change. His distinctions between time- and space-biased communication provide a fruitful entry point for contemporary analyses of the spatial dimensions of change (Melody 1987b: 1322-24). Indeed, Innis' writings on changing systems of communication and their linkages to changes in social and political power, provide many pointers to the sources, limitations and biases of the hegemonic discourses surrounding new ICTs and information.

These are only starting points, however. Reflecting on insights from the relevant research is necessary to minimise the fashion for re-inventing the wheel that is so prevalent in contemporary discourse. But such reflection does not provide a royal road to a robust understanding of our times. This is because the very forms and categories of technology, information and communication, and the interactions between them, are dynamic and changing according to the temporal or spatial context of their development (Melody 1987b). Such starting points must be appropriated and developed through conceptual and empirical work that is: 1) attuned to the most pressing research questions and their particular socio-economic, political and discursive contexts, and 2) capable of crossing established boundaries of the social sciences and humanities fields. This is precisely the systemic, if challenging, road to research and knowledge that Melody (1985a; 1987b) demonstrates in his research and which he champions in his role as leader and facilitator of research.

We confront a tendency to conflate the categories of information (and knowledge) with technology and to confuse the inter-relations between them. This is manifest in many of the technocratic and policy discourses that undergird the information society initiatives that have emerged since the early 1990s. This conflation is quite pervasive. It is also evident in the allocation of resources within organisational settings, including those of those fonts of knowledge, the universities. In a recent case, a university's management responded to financial restraints by proposing to cut 50% of a Communication Department's journal holdings. The department's much larger expenditure on computers was not touched. The techno-obsessive thinking was that access to a technology tool is more sacred than access to a traditional resource of learning, knowledge stored in journals. Yet technology is no substitute for the latter, as Melody (1985b: 7-8) warned many years ago.

In the face of the conflationary tendencies, Melody's work is a particularly fruitful resource. He provides many stimulating insights into the differences between the categories of information and knowledge, and their relation to the technology category. He has suggested how (new) technology may be defined as a particular type of embodied knowledge or as a codified sub-set of the overall stock of knowledge (Melody 1987b: 1317). He has considered the nature and role of societies' shared knowledge (Melody 1993b: 66-68). This work is useful in addressing the obsessively sacred status accorded to technology in our present culture. But it is in his applied work on the frameworks of information society policy that Melody (1996a; 1996b) makes his most compelling contributions. These should be compulsory primers for all consultants and technocrats before they engage in the production of information society policy reports.

Robust analyses of contemporary social and economic change require subtle and sophisticated understandings of the changing roles and characteristics of information. This requires that we challenge what C. Wright Mills (1959/1970) identified as the tendency to diminish the importance of historical analysis. This syndrome is evident in new economy discourses and in the mystifying babble of boundless information frontiers that helped to fuel the dot.com bubble. It points to the importance of theoretical work, which aims to offer an archaeology and a reworking of the categories of information and knowledge both before and since the advent of capitalist modernity. What is required is a theory-building project that is empirically grounded and attentive to the empirical complexities of changing institutional forms and diverse categories of information resources and products.

In sharp contrast to McLuhanite techno-centrism and methodological individualism, Innis' work is a 'rich continent' and provocative starting point for historical analyses. Here, too, Melody's writing and his leadership of research have contributed to a grasp of the changing institutional dimensions of information and communication services in the modern era. His intellectual voyage in exploring the role of information in the evolution of economic thinking has drawn attention to the distinctive socio-economic roles of different categories of information (Melody 1985c; 1987b). His work offers a nuanced understanding of the importance of the 'information commons' and the role of public communication institutions, an aspect that is rare in information society policy discourses and in the work of other economists. In Melody's (e.g., 1985c; 1990a; 1993b) work we also find sophisticated and empirically-grounded analyses of the limits of the 'invisible hand', not least in the domains of information and communication services; these serve to fracture the cosy slogans of neo-liberal rhetorics.

Knowledge Matters

The prevailing orthodoxies that steer the contemporary information society policy initiatives that were summarised above are framed as visionary strategies for socio-economic development that take account of the implications of technological and information-related trends. Yet at their core, these initiatives represent a failure of political imagination, a confusion of the ends and means of social development and a conservative politics.

The nihilistic language of much post-modern theory captures the evacuation of politics and the general void of values, which are at the heart of these developments. Post-modern theory matches the trajectory of real world developments much better than the idealised contours of the 'coming' information society so confidently promised in the work of Daniel Bell (1973). But neither the naïve optimism of the latter nor the apocalyptic pessimism of former accounts for our current condition. These texts do not provide the intellectual resources to challenge orthodoxies or to effect a radical shift towards a robust vision of 'the good society'. Yet, knowledge and ideas do matter in the struggle for the just and the good society. We are not yet completely lost in the void of information nor are we locked into the iron cage of a deterministic technological logic. There are rich veins of intellectual resources that provide alternatives to prevailing orthodoxies. The extent to which these and other such resources will be harnessed and appropriated to develop socially cohesive, futures projects is, as always, a matter of politics and practice.

When More is Less:
Time, Space and Knowledge in Information Societies

Edward Comor

INTRODUCTION

Beginning in the 1960s, social scientists and others began to conceptualise the future in terms of a dawning information society. What this has meant and the policies related to it have changed with emerging economic needs, political developments and technological potentials. But information society policies also have been driven forward by shared mythologies, powerful interests and scant empirical evidence (Webster 1995; Huws 1999). While this has escaped the attention of most, the writings of William Melody have been important exceptions.

The claim that widespread use of information and communication technologies (ICTs) will facilitate economic development for the majority is based on a number of assumptions. More information available to more people, it is thought, would facilitate better, that is, efficiency-enhancing, decision making in more parts of the world. Furthermore, as the world's economy is increasingly interconnected, it will become more competitive and, as a result, efficiencies in production, distribution and consumption will emerge. More wealth and better living standards thus will be attainable for more people. In sum, new technologies, according to this mainstream mythology, will allow real markets to become more like neo-classical textbook ideals 'where markets are frictionless and operate under conditions of perfect information' (Melody 1985c: 524).

Most social scientists and policy makers appear not to be interested in winnowing the potentially correct from the patently false components of this model and grasping that such economic theories are, in fact, *theories*. Melody recognises this phenomenon as a complex reflection of predominant power relations. As the World Bank and other international organisations are now beginning to accept, the implementation of neo-liberal policies since the 1970s and the accompanying dissemination of ICTs has not produced development for all. In fact, the world's poor have been getting poorer and the rich, richer (UNDP 1999). Beyond the questionable assumptions associated with the information society ideal, how we think about this society and how this way of thinking shapes policies affecting the lives of billions of people around the globe constitute more pressing concerns.

In assessing information society issues in such broad conceptual *and* real life terms, Melody's work clearly has been influenced by the writings of the early 20th century political economist, Harold Adams Innis. In Melody's (1981b) introduction to a collection that he co-edited honouring Innis, the latter's concepts of time, space and monopolies of knowledge are emphasised. I revisit these as a means of contextualising Melody's writings and, in keeping with his political concerns, challenging predominant mythologies and stimulating an appreciation of the role of power in sustaining them (Melody 1981b).

Monopolies of Knowledge

Compounding the theoretical problems facing mainstream economists is the fact that understanding and, subsequently, formulating policies involving information-related developments are inherently problematic. This can be appreciated when we try to assess or measure the main component in such analyses – information. The commonest means of assessing information is to view it as a component of individual and group knowledge (that is, what is 'known'). Information, in this context, is the raw data from which knowledge is constructed. But what precisely is the relationship between information and what is known? More information does not necessarily lead to more knowledge. As Melody indicates, for some, more, under prevailing conditions, may well result in less.

We would be hard put to demonstrate that the quantum leap in communication technologies, and the vast increase in communication and information transfer that now takes place using these technologies, have led to an increased understanding of human and social affairs ... . [Indeed,] improvements in communication have ... contributed to an increase in the complexity of economic and social relations, introduced new elements of uncertainty, had negative effects for some people, increased class disparities and in certain instances debased our information and communication currency (Melody 1990a: 28).

Information does not become knowledge as a result of some kind of innate and progressive mechanism through which the more information we have, the better our decisions will be (as in the neo-classical concern with perfect information). Instead, as Melody understands, the mechanisms used by individuals and cultures to process information into knowledge are mostly learned. Such filtering and interpreting capacities have been referred to as conceptual systems (Carey 1975: 45) and these are shaped by socialisation processes involving various institutions, organisations and technologies that mediate norms of thought and behaviour. Not only do we learn what to attend to and what to ignore, we also learn how to interpret or make sense of the information received.

It is in the context of this essential but often under-assessed process that Melody's awareness of what Innis calls monopolies of knowledge is so very important. For Innis and Melody, this concept refers to control over not only what information is made available but also to the dominance of particular ways of interpreting it. *Structurally*, a monopoly of knowledge implies the production and distribution of particular kinds of information instead of others and differential access based on technological and other factors (for example, information that can generate profits instead of information in the service of other pursuits). In a capitalist market system, for example, in which the public service model has been banished to the policy periphery, access to wealth is a primary determinant of who gets what information. *Culturally*, a monopoly of knowledge refers to the norms shaping how information is processed into what is known. At this level of analysis, what is realistic and unrealistic, imaginable and unimaginable, are framed through both socialisation processes and the information available to people as a result of prevailing structural conditions.

For Melody, predominant thinking about and policies related to the information society are being directly influenced by a contemporary (and deepening) monopoly of knowledge. It is a monopoly characterised by a particular conception of the future involving new technologies and a mythological market system. This monopoly of knowledge has been perpetuated by the world's powerful at the expense of the relatively weak and it is facilitated by the construction of information highway infrastructures involving massive investments, political and economic pressures, and a commercial agenda in which particular kinds of information from particular sources tend to dominate discourse and debate.

BIAS

Significant and widespread communication technology developments influence how people organise themselves politically, economically and socially. Such modes of interaction shape individual associations and identities. In conjunction with their implications for entrenching or challenging monopolies of knowledge, new communication media entail certain biases. Biases, broadly speaking, are organisational and conceptual orientations most generally expressed in terms of the two most fundamental indices of human existence – time and space (Melody 1981b: 5-7).

Innis' (1951) discussion of bias of communication (involving core institutions, organisations and technologies as nodal points through which what we know and how we know are produced and reproduced) is one of his more important and influential theoretical contributions. A communication technology for Innis may facilitate control over space (or territory) as a necessary pre-requisite to increasing control over time (involving duration and sustainability). Radio, television, and now the Internet, for example, can be assessed as technologies that have been increasingly structured to serve advertisers and marketers. As such, capitalism has been sustained through the widening and deepening of marketplace relations involving, in this instance, the promotion of consumerism. In another analytical light, such attempts to control space could lead to a decline in the ability to control time. The globalisation of commercial radio, television and Internet technologies since the beginning of the 20th century through their promotion of consumerism – with its requisite propagation of short-term and individualistic thinking – may well undermine the ability of a culture to make the long-term and collective commitments needed to survive. The recognised but seemingly irreversible spectre of ecological collapse is just one of the more obvious examples of this.

For Melody, already dominant interests and ways of thinking are able to extend their control of the world through the application of contemporary ICTs to military resources, flexible production strategies, and efforts to open up markets. But this understanding that new technologies play crucial roles in the struggle to control time and space should not be read as some kind of technological determinism. For Innis and Melody, both historical contexts and the cumulative effects of how people communicate through a broad range of media over any given time and in any particular place are not reducible to the characteristics of a given technology, organisation or institution. Instead, as the examples noted above indicate, a comprehensive assessment of history is required to elaborate the influence of given technologies, organisations and institutions and to delineate future policy options. Indeed, this is precisely what Melody has demonstrated through his work. Again and again, he applies the concepts of time and space as heuristic tools, as means of escaping and subsequently redressing those monopolies of knowledge shaping information society developments. Rather than embracing the information society as the path toward some kind of ideal global village, Melody's writings reveal mythological constructs, complex power relations, and real world potentials to use new technologies for the good of the many rather than just the few.

Conclusion

In the context of early 21st century political economic conditions, ICTs are likely to extend the dominance of the already powerful (Comor 2001). Melody's writings contain suggestions of strategies to redress the deepening imbalance. In response to recent national and international policies obsessed with the rapid building of information infrastructures, he stresses the need for governments to pursue policies in terms of their particular circumstances and to focus on the development of the skills and intellectual capacities needed to take advantage of them. This entails a conscious effort to resist the smoke and mirrors of forging ahead with infrastructure supply before demands and capacities are clearly addressed. 'If government policy makers succumb to the siren song of the suppliers,' warns Melody, 'it will inevitably lead to inefficient investments, unbalanced growth and the cultivation of an elite information class in societies characterised by increasing divisions between the information rich and poor' (Melody 1996c: 259). It may be extrapolated that efforts to control space through ICTs before local potentials, vulnerabilities and needs have been identified must be resisted through the ultimate sovereignty of the nation state over domestic developments – in effect, a government's (and people's) control over space as a means of better controlling the future.

The monopoly of knowledge over information society developments thus must be challenged through the carefully articulated needs of citizens, workers, small businesses and other interests whose fates may appear to be out of control. But the potentials of new technologies to serve the needs and desires of people rather than powerful vested interests, according to Melody, will involve the use of space to regain control over time. The tendencies generated by existing biases and the complex relation between information and knowledge are implicitly or explicitly dealt with in Melody's (e.g., 1990a: 30) writings on the information society. 'The public interest', he states, 'requires that the diffusion of the new opportunities be planned and implemented at a pace which minimises the losses imposed on those who cannot benefit from them, and is accompanied by programmes to help the potential victims of change become beneficiaries of it'.

William Melody's work on information society developments reflects an awareness of, and an extraordinary ability to apply, Innis' concepts of monopoly of knowledge and time- and space-bias. This application is important because Melody demonstrates through these heuristic tools that what is thought to be feasible or realistic today – since it largely reflects a biased way of processing information into knowledge – may well serve to buy time and deepen the powers held by the already powerful. As such, the seemingly rational application of particular economic ideals in which 'more is more' may serve to exacerbate existing disparities and cultural problems, making future political and economic crises more probable and less correctable. As Innis pointed out, the cumulative tendencies of monopolies of knowledge and related biases perpetuate often unconsciously constructed barriers to the long-term resolution of systemic problems. Melody, in his ability to historicise information society developments using accessible and applicable abstractions has produced a body of work that compels us to pause, question entrenched assumptions, and re-think how we want to move forward, collectively and democratically.

The Telecom-Economy Nexus:
Innis and Du Boff Revisited

Cho, Sung Woon

INTRODUCTION

The telecom sector has been undergoing profound changes around the world. Technological progress has lowered the barriers of time and space. Institutional reforms have resulted in ever-greater contributions to national economies. Demand from individuals and businesses has become increasingly sophisticated. With its capabilities of governing and guiding the activities of agents, telecom has become the strategic underpinning of modern society.

As telecom-related services have become important media in modern society, the focus on point-to-multipoint associated with mass media has gradually shifted to point-to-point. The social-science study of telecom, however, lags behind the rapidity of change of the object of study. The field of telecom studies has tended to produce numerous mosaic stories, especially in the case of institutional reform of telecom. Attempts to systematically comprehend the phenomenon have failed adequately to identify its dynamics. Furthermore, policy research tends to focus on immediate issues, neglecting long-term consequences.

Telecom is fundamentally a connecting mechanism. It requires broader, context-driven research (Cho 1998). Understanding the telecom phenomenon in the context of economic activities is imperative. However, linkages between economic activities and communications (telecom, in particular) have not received adequate attention, with the significant exceptions of the work of William Melody (e.g., 1985c; 1990a; 1996b), Richard Gabel (1969), David Gabel (1987), and Dallas Smythe (1981).

Long before the recent wave of institutional reform, Harold Adams Innis and Richard Du Boff conducted significant studies on communication and its long-term social and economic effects. This contribution examines some relatively neglected aspects of their research in relation to research on institutional reform.

HAROLD ADAMS INNIS' PERSPECTIVE

The significance of Innis to the field of communication has mainly been seen through *The Bias of Communication* (1951) in which he attempted to reinterpret the entirety of Western civilisation related to the transformation of communication media. Innis, was first and foremost an economic historian whose early work was on the emergence of Canada as a nation state from the perspective of political economy. Later, Innis extended his analysis beyond any specific country or region. The later Innis articulated the preconditions for the existence of systems in space and time in terms of the dialectically related concepts of control over space and control over time. Control over space is related both to the territorial extension of control by a system and to the degree of organisation of the means of maintaining territorial control by the system. Similarly, control over time is related both to the systematic intensity of an agency over time and to the adaptability or flexibility of the agency in response to changes in its environment. The dichotomy is somewhat arbitrary and has been challenged. The concepts were developed from his studies of the Canadian staples trade, a part of his work that is relatively little known.

Although the notion of two Innises may be misleading, on balance, there is value in a focus on the early Innis. Two major works of the early Innis – *A History of the Canadian Pacific Railway* (1923) and *The Fur Trade in Canada* (1930/1962) – are instructive for the examination of the influence of communications in the shaping of social systems. According to Innis (1923), the pace and direction of the growth of Canadian civilisation were largely dominated by the communicative aspects of its physical characteristics: the geological formation, the climate and the topographical features. As a result, the country was divided into three drainage basins. According to Innis,

Early civilisation was confined by these limits to three distinct areas. The Canadian Pacific Railroad was tangible evidence of the growth of civilisation beyond these boundaries (Innis 1930/1962: 2).

Civilization had developed almost alone. It had grown and expanded beyond the boundaries set by topographical features. Politically these sections were united but economically the barriers proved to be of a character which tested severely and almost to the breaking-point the union which had been consummated (Innis 1923: 74).

Innis provides meticulously detailed accounts of how the development of communication facilitated the staples trade. Canada developed in directions and at a pace permitted by such communication media as waterways and railways. Canada's evolution was bounded by the possibilities of effective communication. Changes in the technology of communication influenced the transformation and extension of the country.

The existence of Canada, according to Innis, was tied to certain features of the landscape relevant to the staples trade. Boundaries – whether national or regional – were not tied to the land but rather tied to the mechanisms of communication. In Innis' view, the media of communication do not simply constitute a causal nexus but are an integral element in the way distinct realities arise out of the economic activities. He noted that the utilisation and the deployment of communication media are central to economic development. He argued that communication technologies are the most important building blocks for the shaping of social systems. At the same time, he recognised that economic incentives and market forces have powerful influences on the development of communication media. It should be emphasised that Innis was unique among his contemporaries in recognising the strong interrelationship and interdependence between economics and communication and in adopting the long-term historical approach for the study of communication.

RICHARD DU BOFF'S PERSPECTIVE

Du Boff's object of study was the influence of modern communications on the formation and development of economic institutions. Du Boff examined the impact of the earliest form of telecom, the telegraph, on the early economy of the United States. Du Boff (1980: 459, 60) claimed that the business revolution of the mid 19th century occurred because of 'technological advances of the 1840s... the railroad and telegraphy'. Du Boff (1980: 463) explained that 'the discovery of the railroads as the nation's first big business has overshadowed the role of telegraph industry, which preceded the railroads ... in holding out the promise of wider market reach ... '. The telegraph and the railroad developed on the same geographical lines and common commercial interests were the basis of their reciprocal relationship.

Ultimately, each was necessary for the other: telegraphs without railroads would have found customers, but social savings would have been less as installation of telegraph poles and lines would have been costlier withoutpreviously cleared railroads right-of-way ... ; and demands for telegraph services would have grown more slowly in the absence of the mass-distribution and mass-production revolutions the railroads did so much to unleash (Du Boff 1983: 255).

The major customers of telegraphy were profit-seeking organisations that operated in competitive environments. Even though the development of the market was constrained by the capacity of communication networks, the development of communication was what made it possible for the exploitation of economies of scale to become an institutionalised practice.

[The telegraph] influenced the structure of the economy itself through subtle links that connect technology and markets. The impact of the telegraph on allocative efficiency and markets was intermingled with contemporary changes in transportation, scale of production, and general technical progress (Du Boff 1984: 254).

On the other hand, the connecting mechanism of telecom also promoted mass production: 'The telegraph, in tandem with the railroad, opened the way toward such cost savings, which virtually invited the centralization of executive powers [of firms]' (Du Boff 1983: 266).

Du Boff's main focus was on the impact of communication on the formation of economic institutions, and he drew out the long-term consequences of communication technologies. 'Increasing market size helped "empire builders" widen initial advantages which at first may have been modest' (Du Boff 1983: 270). In other words, he claimed that communication technologies tend to concentrate market power in the hands of a few dominant firms which adopt the new communication technologies.

In summary, telecom was the most vital element in the formation and spread of nation-wide business practice in the United States in the mid 19th century. Although transportation (railroad) has been credited as the driving force of economies of scale, telecom (telegraph) proved to be, according to Du Boff, as important an element. Du Boff demonstrates with Innis, the contribution that a context-driven understanding of telecom network development can make.

Conclusion

The premises of the Innis and Du Boff projects, that communication and information activities are carried out within social systems at both the economic and political levels, have contemporary and global relevance. Their work, and especially that of Du Boff, illuminates endogenous relationships existing within a single system. Yet, the fundamental connecting nature of communication can extend beyond the boundary of a given state or system, as Innis showed.
The principal institutional artefacts of capitalism have been, in many instances, created by technological advances. Thus, the histories of business and of technology cannot exist in isolation if they are to remain vital areas of inquiry. The insights of Innis and Du Boff show us that long-term and context-driven perspectives are necessary.

Back to the Future of the Internet: The Printing Press

Ang, Peng Hwa and James A. Dewar

INTRODUCTION
It is a truism that the Internet is a new medium with a revolutionary impact. To what can it be compared? Might an apt historical analogy help in illuminating the destiny of the Net? The printing press, which created the world's first truly mass medium, is a good analogy (Dewar 1998). This contribution summarises the findings of a gathering of experts on the potential impact of the Internet as seen through this analogical lens.[10]

GOVERNMENT INTERVENTION
Policies lag technology. Intuitively, this makes sense; problems caused by technology are what give rise to policies. In the case of printing, governments in both Europe and China adopted *laissez-faire* positions regarding printing and publishing even when printers published vituperative propaganda against foreign governments. In China, as late as the 17th century, there were no printing regulations. Printers brought out books that portrayed rebels as heroes. In Britain, the Crown granted printing licences to the guilds. There were no licensing fees because the government did not regard the nascent printing industry as a source of revenue. In fact, private individuals gained little financial benefit by writing. Only when governments were directly threatened or challenged did they react; even then, typically, it took a lot to provoke a response. In contrast, modern governments are significantly more interventionist.

PARADIGM CHANGE IN INTELLECTUAL PROPERTY
The modern copyright regime evolved over a hundred years from the late 17th century in Europe. In England, chaos reigned in the printing industry as printing licences lapsed and publishing moved overseas, out of the reach of the English Crown's jurisdiction. There were arguments that authors should not have their works protected. After all, if an author could be content after producing one creative work, what incentive was there for more? New technology is again challenging an extant paradigm of copyright and a similar rhetoric of paradigmatic crisis is being evoked. In England, intellectual property protection began with regulation by the guilds, which is a form of self-regulation. The Statute of Anne of 1709 turned guild regulations into civil law. Over the next three-quarters of a century, self regulation was replaced by the modern copyright law.

Before the 18th century, European legal notions of property were typically confined to real (short for corporeal) estate and material objects. The evolution of copyright law augmented property law with the concept of intellectual property (incorporeal estate). Unlike other forms of property, intellectual property is not held in perpetuity.

It is noteworthy that the current paradigm that emerged in Britain in the form of the 1774 copyright law was seen as counter to the interests of the largest concentration of capital among the stakeholders, the London book publishers. A concern about the ongoing policy process on digital era intellectual property rights is that there are too few voices *against* strengthening property rights. Copyright is a limited monopoly but a monopoly nevertheless. Too strong a regime in favour of rights holders disadvantages users in the short run and society at large in the long run.

The policy lesson is that a focus on the *process* of new paradigm creation is more fruitful than theorising the form that that paradigm will take. The new paradigm will evolve gradually through a series of landmark legal decisions. The Napster dispute on the legality of sharing music files made possible by the technology is important in this context.

Policy Opportunities

Three broad policy areas where government might play a role in the intellectual property field are access, authentication and archiving.

Access

Governments historically in both Europe and Asia did not give much weight to access to printed materials. Only when education was deemed to be important for society did governments pay attention to the need for access to books. In both China and Korea, the more enlightened governments sent books to the counties. In China, the Ming dynasty sent printed Confucian texts, classics and philosophical books to every prefecture and county (Reed 2000). In the case of the Internet, the link to education has been made very quickly. Just as the printing press engendered literacy, the personal computer engenders digital literacy. Policies to promote digital literacy, therefore, are justified.

Authentication

The advent of printing did not immediately make scribes obsolete. Written texts were considered to be more 'true' or 'authentic' than printed texts. Part of this thinking is explained by Heidegger's (1982) notion of the 'connection of the hand and the word'.

In Korea, it was widely believed that writing by hand, especially of religious materials, edified the writer (Kang 2000). The printing press was thus viewed with scepticism regarding its validity, legitimacy and even spirituality. The issue of authentication was most significant for letters of credit and paper money. Anti-fraud and anti-counterfeiting measures by governments were put in place. Similar government action will be required to alleviate fraud and counterfeiting in the Internet environment.

Archiving
There was concern historically that the printed page would not be as durable as the traditional vellum (treated animal hide) used in writing. Today, the concern is that the Internet leaves less evidence for historians (Sherman 2000). Just as technology has made it possible to archive paper, technology may well be developed to archive Net content.

Implications for Governance and Markets
Modern bureaucracy would not have developed without the printing press. Printing technology facilitated the development of codes and laws, which could be more widely disseminated. It also made possible the use of forms, or standardised ways of government-citizen communication. Although printing may have led to the strengthening of central authority, it also strengthened the rule of law. For the first time, citizens had easy access to the laws of the land. For example, arbitrary actions by tax officers were made more difficult. Similarly, it is likely that the potential of the Internet to make laws and administrative decisions more accessible may make government more transparent. However, the Internet could also lead to the strengthening of central authority.

Printing increased the production of ephemera. However, it also lowered the price of books and promoted literacy. Pamphlets in the 16th, 17th and 18th centuries spread political and economic ideas in Europe, laying the foundation for the Enlightenment. Ephemera may be the price to pay for the availability of materials on the Net.

The printing press played both a unifying and fragmenting role. Printing standardised languages but also reinforced local dialects. Printing fostered national languages and contributed to the evolution of national identities. Similarly, the Internet is likely to lead to a greater standardisation of language. The Internet allows geographically dispersed minority groups to assert common identities.

The scientific revolution was enabled by postal communication. It allowed a more rapid exchange of ideas, as in the case of e-mail in recent times. Perhaps e-mail will be the biggest benefit conferred by the Internet. In 19th century Britain, when the postal service changed from a luxury service with variable pricing to a universal service with fixed pricing, the volume of use exploded. Letters subsidised newspapers in the early days of the postal system. Newspapers were 85% of the postal weight, but only 15% of the costs. Similarly, the current Internet tax moratorium subsidises Internet ventures.

Perhaps the greatest impact of the printing press on business was the standardisation of practices that previously had to be memorised or reinvented. In Europe, from the 16th century onwards, there were many books describing how to run a business. The use of forms standardised business practices, thereby increasing uniformity and decreasing transaction costs. In Europe, double entry accounting was an important tool. Better information improved the chances of survival for businesses. Similarly, more transparency as a result of greater availability of information on the Internet may allow a better chance of success for viable business models.

The printing press enabled goods and services to be offered at fixed prices. Historically, letters were full of questions about market prices in different regions. The Internet, with its ability to capture detailed information on consumers, allows opportunities to price discriminate. The online retailer, Amazon, has attempted to price discriminate based on the user's personal information and past purchases.

New forms of media create opportunities for new advertising methods. Advertisements appeared in the early books; they were a revenue source. Publishers no longer have to insert advertisements in books in general, but it is unclear whether advertising will provide adequate revenues to support Internet businesses.

Paper money was used in China from around the 10th and 11th centuries. It began with IOU notes but was replaced by silver when silver became widely available in the 1600s through trade. This is a curious quirk in history; for whatever reason, perhaps fraud, China regressed from paper money to metal money, instead of moving to lighter materials. Europe began to use paper money from the 18th century. Like the Chinese, the Europeans began with IOUs and letters of credit, which gave rise to paper money. The history of money suggests that it will probably take some time to make digital money secure. Today, e-money moves through secure channels among closed user groups. This movement parallels the earliest use of letters of credit and IOU notes.

Diffusion and Commercialism

The different diffusion rates of the printing press in Europe, China and Korea may be explained by factors such as the cost of capital or barriers to entry. Censorship was not a major cause of slower diffusion. To be sure, there was some censorship in Korea and China. In their attempts to build a Confucian society that maintained the status quo, kings and scholars printed books that advocated the Confucian order. In China, there were episodes of book burning and one king, Qianlong, conducted what is probably the world's most thorough house-to-house search for proscribed literature. However, both China and Korea experienced long periods of minimal censorship. The same Qianlong who conducted the search sponsored the breath-taking 36,000-volume, *The Complete Works of Four Treasuries*, in which 300 scholars summarised some 3,500 Chinese classics. In contrast, the printing industry diffused in Europe in the face of censorship.

Commercialism expedited diffusion of both the printing press and the Internet. In Europe, mass demand for printed matter and opportunities for profit spurred the diffusion of the printing press. The early printers were the world's first capitalists (Eisenstein 2000 and see 1980). The contrast between China and Korea strengthens the argument: the printing press diffused more quickly in China because of commercialism. In Korea, there was no commercial basis for the widespread use of the movable type printing press (Kang 2000). The Internet took off when the dot.coms were allowed to develop.

Concluding Comment

Historical analogies have limits. Complex and intertwined variables make isolating the effects of printing difficult. This is also the case in attempts to isolate the effects of the Internet.

# The 'Information Economy', Economics, and Ecology

Robert E. Babe

INFORMATION ECONOMY

William Melody (1987b: 1330) remarked that *all* societies, past and present – including 'the oral traditions of the most primitive tribes' – are or have been rich in information. He added, however, that in the 'developed' West, information and communication have changed. No longer does communication take place primarily outside markets; rather, the institutionalisation of information-generating organisations, and technological change (most, recently interactions among advances in computing and telecom), have induced ever-heightening commodification of communicative processes.

Fritz Machlup's 1962 book, *The Production and Distribution of Knowledge in the United States*, went a long way in directing economists' attention to the importance of markets for information. In that tome, Machlup estimated that in 1958 nearly 29% of output and 32% of employment in the United States were accounted for by knowledge industries. Several years later, Marc Porat (1976) announced that the information sector of the United States economy in 1967 had increased to about 46% of Gross National Product. He proclaimed that the United States was no longer primarily an agricultural economy, nor an industrial economy, but an Information Economy.

Policy makers in the United States and elsewhere responded quickly. After all, if information is central to the generation of wealth, then it had better be more strictly commodified, or so the thinking went. Governments, therefore, became keen on tightening and enforcing more vigorously intellectual property legislation. Even genes are now subject to copyright and patents in order to stimulate bio-technology firms and industries. Furthermore, governments have deregulated hitherto monopolised markets providing transmission services, and have made them subject to rivalry. Also they have introduced, to varying degrees, markets in cases where information had previously been provided freely or at low cost (public service broadcasting, public education, public data banks). As well, encryption technologies and ways of segregating and identifying information users so they can be charged directly for accessing information have been encouraged. Governments have also supported information highway infrastructures, anticipating that the production and exchange of digitised, electronic information will become increasingly important as the years go by.

Innisian 'Bias'

Melody also refers, approvingly, to the Canadian economic historian, Harold Adams Innis, who, according to Melody (1987b: 1322), 'observed that any medium of communication is "biased" in its tendency to permit control over extended periods of time or over extended geographical space'. For Innis, inherent physical properties of every medium predispose it towards carrying certain types of information, and not to carrying certain other types. This notion of inherent selectivity, or bias, has been extended or applied to technologies generally (by McLuhan 1962, for instance), and to languages by Carroll and Whorf (1964).

It is important to note that Innis (1951: 8) regarded the price system as being a particularly space-biased mode of communication. Quoting Mirabeau, he wrote: 'The two greatest inventions of the human mind are writing and money ... the common language of intelligence and the common language of self-interest.' In fact, Innis (1956) saw the price system as penetrating and breaking asunder such time-binding, communal institutions as families, cultures and religions.

The Price System and Innisian Bias

Innis' recognition that money, or the price system, is an important mode of communication is certainly in accord with the thinking of mainstream economists. According to F. A. Hayek (1945: 525), for example, prices are 'quantitative indices (or "values")'. Every index or price, Hayek proposed, *is* concentrated information, representing the significance of each scarce resource relative to all others. Prices permit autonomous economic agents to adjust strategies 'without having to solve the whole puzzle [input-output matrix] *ab initio*'.

In fact, a large portion of the economics literature describes the purported effectiveness of the price system in communicating relative values; it also addresses certain obstacles to the effective functioning of that system (monopoly, externalities, uncertainty, public goods and so on). However, as Melody observes, the mainstream discipline has not addressed the price system in terms of Innisian bias, that is, it has not asked what types of information the price system systematically marginalizes or excludes, nor the consequences of those exclusions.

Here, I take up Innis' implicit challenge – to address the biases in the price system, and thereby identify properties of the Information Economy expected to result from its undue reliance upon this biased mode of communication. I do this from the standpoint of ecology.

Ecology and the 'Biases' of the Price System
Five arguments are presented here to support the claim that the Information Economy, emblematic of a heightening in the commodification of information, is inherently destructive to the environment. This destructiveness is due to the selectivity or inherent Innisian bias of the price system.

Time
The price system is biased with regard to time. In Innis' terms, it is 'present-minded'. With regard to the past, it is axiomatic that 'bygones are forever bygones'. In other words, regardless of sunk costs, decision-makers following the dictates of the price system try to maximise the discounted stream of *future* earnings.

Likewise, however, the future too is trivialised. Assuming a 10% discount rate, US$ 1,000 thirty years hence are worth only US$ 57.31 today! Built into the heart of our monetary system of representation, then, is a sloughing off of both the past and the future.

Because they rely so heavily on the price system, then, we can expect information economies to denigrate considerations of continuity, community and tradition. According to ecologist David Suzuki, however, an awareness of and identification with the past is necessary for deep ecological awareness. Suzuki (1997) writes that aboriginal peoples, who possess profound ecological awareness, look to seven generations in the past (as well as in the future) before taking decisions.

Likewise, we can expect that information economies will be very cavalier about pollution, resource depletion and species extinction, simply because, according to their predominant mode of symbolisation, the future matters so little.

Exclusions
Not everyone or everything is privileged to register preferences in the price system. Systematically excluded or marginalised are the poor, the young, the unborn, trees, whales, insects and indeed all non-human species. The price system, then, is both an anthropocentric system of valuation, and an exclusive system in which the wealthy are given a much louder voice than the poor, and in which future generations are accorded no direct voice at all. Again, this contrasts with aboriginal cultures where other animal species are regarded as kin, and where attempts are made to listen to and speak for their interests (Knudtson and Suzuki 1992).

We would therefore expect information societies to create and tolerate environmental conditions dangerous to the poor. As the Bruntland Commission (World Commission on Environment and Development 1987) emphasised, however, poverty is itself an immense environmental issue, endangering the lives of rich and poor alike.

As well, societies governed by the price system may be expected to rob future generations of their birthrights to clean air, clean water and non-toxic soil, and to cause plant and animal species to become extinct at alarming rates.

Individual Valuations
Economic theorists have emphasised that the price system takes into account the preferences of individuals. A system of valuation based on individual maximisation, however, gives little or no accounting for group or collective well-being.

From an ecological perspective, life on this planet is characterised by total interdependence. Suzuki (1997: 130) writes: 'You and I don't end at our finger tips or skin. We are connected through air, water and soil. ... We *are* quite literally air, water, soil, energy and other living creatures'.

Consider briefly just the first element in Suzuki's list. Air is, of course, well recognised as a medium of communication. Air carries sound through condensations and rarefaction. Also, it transmits odours, informing sentient creatures of their surroundings through their sense of smell. Air can become visible when pollutants in high density are spewed into it, again informing us of industrial or other activity. Often air carries invisible pollutants, including radioactivity; but that too is communication, as recipients of such messages, can grow sick and die.

But for Suzuki (1997: 32, 37), air is a medium of communication in yet another, and far more profound sense. He writes:

We are [completely] embedded in air, all of us caught together in the same matrix. Air is a physical substance; it embraces us so intimately that it is hard to say where we leave off and air begins. ... Air is always within us and is as much a part of our bodies as any tissue or organ. We are a part of the air, which in turn is a part of all green plants and every other breathing creature.

In terms of Innisian bias, by systematically failing to transmit information reflective of radical interdependence among all organisms, the price system and the

Information Economy based on it, can be expected to cause hedonistic individuals to disregard the effects of pollution when making their wealth-maximising decisions, even though these actions poison all living creatures, including themselves, through continuous contamination of the air, water, and soil.

Knowledge

Individual preferences are based at least in part on knowledge. It is difficult, of course, to prefer something if one is ignorant of its existence.

In terms of ecosystem interactions, however, human knowledge is overwhelmed by ignorance. E. O. Wilson (1992) estimates that of all species extant on Earth, scientists have managed just to name perhaps 10%. Simply identifying a species and naming it, of course, is but a first step in learning about its interactions with other species. What we do not know, we cannot name; and what we cannot name, we cannot value. According to Wilson's estimate, then, 90% of the species on the Earth today carry no monetary representation, which is to say they are not valued by the price system. They are 'worthless' according to that system of valuation – even though individually or in combination these species contribute to the capacity of the ecosystem as a whole to sustain human and other forms of life.

In terms of Innisian bias, we would expect an Information Economy founded on the primacy of the price system to lead to alarming rates of species extinction. Indeed, estimates are that annually 20,000 species are rendered extinct.

According to other systems of valuation, for example those of indigenous peoples, by contrast, Nature as a whole is deemed sacred, to be of inestimable value. That valuation affects profoundly the nature of human interactions with the ecosystem by those holding that valuation.

Exponential Growth

Finally, the price system misrepresents the ecosystem in yet another way. Money, and indeed information of all types, can grow exponentially, seemingly without limit, through 'the magic of compound interest'. But the Earth is finite. Human population, human consumption of non-renewable natural resources, stockpiles of radioactive materials and other wastes, cannot increase indefinitely. Even in principle, however, the price system can give no indication of the limits of growth. This is because prices symbolise only relative, not absolute, values; prices, therefore, are silent with regard to the size of the economy relative to, and supportable by, the biosphere.

We would expect societies governed by the price system, then, to engage in uneconomic growth, that is to increase production and consumption well beyond the point where harms from this growth outweigh the benefits.

These five factors do not exhaust the problematic nature of the price system as an information system connoting value. It is an 'amoral' system of information that does not disclose violations of human rights and destructive environmental practices that go into the production of commodities. It may cause media, funded by advertising, to self-censor material unfavourable to the business community, including stories on environmental malpractices.

Conclusion

The Information Economy has been justly criticised on a number of fronts – for increasing inequalities both at home and abroad through user-pay principles, for eroding privacy and other civil liberties, for threatening indigenous cultures and so on. In this contribution I have argued that we should view it also as threatening human survival, because the price system upon which the Information Economy is premised is inherently biased in the information it is capable of carrying.

Rather than attempting to commodify increasing aspects of human life, thereby representing their value by prices, efforts should be made to extricate as far as possible human activities and nature from commodity exchanges and the price system. This would be in explicit recognition that humans and all other species share a common future.

Bridging the Gap: Processes of Communication and Institutions of Political Economy

Vincent Mosco

INTRODUCTION
In his contribution to a book honouring his colleague and friend Dallas Smythe, William Melody singled out the concerns of Smythe and others that 'concentrated corporate wealth and power corrupts the flow of information to the general public. This prevents the real value of the citizenry from arising and a true efficiency and consumer choice from being achieved' (Melody 1993b: 71). In conclusion, Melody praised Smythe for having 'prepared the ground upon which following generations can build. In the 'information society' of the future, it will be even more fundamental to understand the relations between the institutions of political economy and the processes of communication' (Melody 1993b: 80).

These words cut to the heart of Smythe's enduring achievement, but they also apply to Melody himself. For among the most important of the many contributions that Melody has made to the study of communication are his analysis of corporate concentration in the communication industry, his concern for its impact on the public interest and his effort to bridge the gap between the political economy of society and its communication processes. This essay takes a small step toward honouring Melody's legacy by addressing the twin processes of digitisation and commodification in communication. It further suggests how these are propelling the expansion and concentration of integrated national and global communication companies and concludes by considering the implications for a new politics of citizenship.

DIGITISATION AND COMMODIFICATION
Digitisation refers to the transformation of communication, including words, images, motion pictures, and sounds, into a common digital language. It provides enormous gains in transmission speed and flexibility over earlier forms of electronic communication which were largely reliant on analogue techniques. Current media myths, including those claiming the end of history, the end of geography and the end of politics, are based, in part, on the leap from digitisation to the view that the world of atoms is morphing into a virtual utopia. This is a serious mistake because it neglects to recognise that digitisation takes place in the context of, and greatly expands, the process of commodification or the

transformation of use to exchange value in communication. The expansion of the commodity form provides the context for who shapes the process of digitisation and for determining how it is applied.

Digitisation is used first and foremost to expand the commodification of information and entertainment, specifically by enlarging markets in communication products, by deepening the commodification of labour involved in the production, distribution and exchange of communication, and by creating markets in the audiences that receive and make use of electronic communication. The contemporary media landscape results in large part from the mutual constitution of digitisation and commodification.

Digitisation expands the commodification of communication content by extending the range of opportunities to measure and monitor, package and repackage information and entertainment. This vastly expands the process of delivering audiences of viewers, listeners, readers, movie goers and telephone and computer users, to advertisers. In essence, companies can package and repackage customers in forms that specifically reflect both their actual purchases and their demographic characteristics. A similar extension of commodification applies to the labour of communication. The replacement of mechanical with electronic systems once eliminated thousands of jobs in the printing industry as electronic typesetting did away with the work of linotype operators. Today, digital systems allow companies to expand this process by eliminating jobs and deepening managerial control over work across the communication industries.

The combination of digitisation and commodification and the growing integration of communication sectors into a consolidated electronic information and entertainment arena explain much of why there has been an unprecedented acceleration in mergers and acquisitions. Communication systems in the United States are now largely shaped by a handful of companies including Microsoft, AT&T, General Electric-NBC, Viacom-CBS, Disney-ABC, and AOL-Time Warner. There are others, including non-United States firms like Bertelsmann which owns Random House publishing and Vivendi, the French telecom giant. Indeed, each of these firms has a significant transnational presence through outright ownership, strategic partnerships and investment.

National communication systems have also experienced the acceleration of concentration. For example, in just a few years, the Canadian arena has come under the domination of four firms. These include BellGlobemedia, formed from the merger of Canada's largest telecom firm (Bell Canada), its largest private television network, CTV, and its major national newspaper, *The Globe and Mail*. Rogers Communication brings together Canada's largest cable television company, its second largest mobile telephone firm and the country's major newsweekly magazine. CanWest Global resulted from the merger of the second largest private television network and Canada's largest newspaper group. Finally, Quebecor combines cable, tabloid newspaper and multimedia interests to form a giant across the English-French divide. The combination of growing concentration and diminishing regulation leads some, like Sunstein (2001), to fear that the media landscape is becoming little more than a commercial space with less than adequate room for diversity and the clash of ideas so vital to democracy.

The transformation, however, is far from complete. Canadian communication firms, like their counterparts in the United States and elsewhere, face enormous pressures for even further regional and global integration (Mosco and Schiller 2001). Moreover, media concentration often does not produce the synergies that companies anticipate and sometimes results in content that fails to attract audiences. Digitisation is not a flawless process and numerous technical problems have slowed its development.

The Retreating State

More importantly, we can observe deeper political contradictions. Contemporary neo-liberalism is founded on the retreat of the state from critical areas of social life, including the communication arena where the state historically was directly involved in building infrastructure, setting technical standards, regulating market access and directly providing services. According to the neo-liberal view, such functions are best provided by the private sector with minimal state involvement. Aside from the ideological commitment to this perspective, neo-liberalism aims to customise state functions, to tailor them to suit business needs and thereby avoid the challenges that the vision of the state as a universal or public space, open to a wide range of contestation, once posed. But the communication arena demonstrates that it is not so easy to reach this goal.

One of the most significant of what are typically presented as narrow technical concerns is standardisation. Digitisation only succeeds to the extent that common technical standards are used to harmonise the processing, distribution and reception of digital signals. It is one thing to translate audio, video and data streams into digital packets; it is quite another to ensure their flawless flow through global information grids. In order to accomplish this, a wide range of standards for equipment necessary to process signals and for managing the data flows through networks is essential. Achieving such agreement is normally difficult because competitors are reluctant to cooperate since it requires sharing information which is increasingly valued in its own right and is central to success in developing new technical systems.

Capitalism has traditionally dealt with this problem by establishing government agencies or private-public partnerships that might serve as independent standards arbiters. However, in recent years, private businesses, in keeping with a neo-liberal agenda, have stepped up the effort to shrink government involvement in standards issues by setting up private or quasi-public standards organisations. But, as disputes over the Internet Corporation for Assigned Names and Numbers (ICANN) demonstrate, these are actually only displacing tensions and contradictions. As a result, seemingly technical questions are caught up in political economic maelstroms that impede or slow the process of global technological development. However, the alternative, returning to genuinely public national or international regulatory authorities, a central feature in the expansion of communication before neo-liberalism took hold, invites turning this arena, widely recognised as critical to capitalist expansion, into a highly contested terrain (Lessig 2001).

This problem is not only evident in the struggle over standards, it has marked debates about how to expand access to technology in order to build markets and about how to ensure some measure of privacy to create consumer confidence in the technology. The overall crisis in the dot.com and telecom industries, and the yawning chasm between the massive glut of high-speed, long haul capacity and the shortage of high-speed, local access connections needed to gain access to cyberspace, can be traced directly to the almost religiously driven neo-liberal strategy that the market would do a better job of regulation than traditional forms of state intervention. With no political or social policy check on investment decisions, cemented into law in various forms, companies went on a long-haul building binge that resulted in a glut of telecom capacity and widespread corporate failures. In one year, June 2000 to June 2001, more than 100,000 jobs disappeared from the United States communication industry. And the promise of universal access to broadband communication remains just that (Romero 2001). Meanwhile, in another demonstration that the 'new economy' is not all that new, and that the role of the state is still a contested issue, a Canadian federal government task force recommended in June 2001 that up to four billion Canadian dollars should be spent to expand broadband access in Canada. Is this evidence of backsliding from the neo-liberal orthodoxy or just a bailout of failing telecom and computer firms? Whatever the answer, the recommendations and responses to them demonstrate the tension over the role of the state.

A similar conundrum shapes the issue of privacy. The drive to use communication and particularly the new media of cyberspace to expand commodification inevitably leads to the commodification of personal identity. The production and distribution of information about consumers and workers takes on a value related to, but distinct from, the value of their purchases and their labour. The threat to privacy is intrinsic to the commodification process. Consequently, the fight for personal privacy is part of a wider struggle against the expanding commodity. All of this reflects a fundamental contradiction besetting the media business: the conflict between the need to build consumer trust necessary to turn the Internet into a universal market tool and the need to commodify, through the use of deepening surveillance, whatever moves over the Internet, including personal identity.

Novel Convergences

The complex politics of digitisation, commodification and concentration, leads directly to conclusions about the politics of convergence and helps us to draw an important conclusion about what Melody called the relationship between communication processes and the wider political economy. There is no need to repeat familiar and banal platitudes about technological and institutional convergence. Rather, consider a different type of convergence which is energising debate about the potential for a new cultural politics. The recent world-wide anti-globalisation protests are grounded in a powerful and unprecedented understanding of the convergence of labour and consumption. These movements focus on the links, indeed the convergence, between the commercial brand, so central in the media, and the exploitation of labour. Convergence does not just mean plugging a cable modem into a personal computer, it also means the global convergence of labour and consumption practices which, in a multi-mediated world, drive home for the many what only a few understood over a century ago.

Commodity production makes transparent the divide between knowledge workers and the unskilled; it also brings together consumers and makes transparent the divide between them and those who have little. In essence, it enhances the possibility to unite the politics of labour, which, as Denning (1996) reminds us, energised social movements of the first half of the 20th century and the politics of consumption, which drove much resistance in the second half, to create a politics of citizenship which transcends both labour and consumption with the active construction of a democratic world order. Following Melody's unflagging drive to bridge the gap between communication processes and the wider political economy of society, we can pursue with greater confidence the concrete connections between communication, the convergence of labour and consumption and the politics of citizenship.

Concrete Analyses Versus Abstract Deduction

Anders Henten

INTRODUCTION: INCONSISTENCIES ON DEVELOPMENT?
Throughout his academic career, William Melody has taken a keen interest in the role of communication in broader social development. Melody has focused a great deal of his attention on economically related development trends. However, he has always situated economic development in broader political, cultural and technological contexts.

An interest in economic and social development and in developing countries is not surprising for a Canadian building on the tradition of Harold Adams Innis. In his analyses of the staples economy of Canada, Innis demonstrated how dependent Canada was on the British economy, and later, on the United States. In a tribute to Innis, Melody (1981b: 4, 11) wrote: 'Canada is still very much a staple economy; it still is a region at the margin of western civilisation'; in the same comment, he went as far as to state that 'Canada finds itself in the anomalous position of being the world's most modern developing country'.

A similar dependency theory was applied to the analysis of transnational corporations and their use of new information and communication technologies (ICTs). In the footsteps of Innis, who analysed the implications of the means of transportation and communication for the exploitation of natural resources, Melody (1991b: 37, 39) examined how new and enhanced telecom systems may 'provide an efficient system for sucking out the economic benefits and opportunities that otherwise would be generated in the region'. He concluded that 'if they [the developing countries] buy into these technologies, most will be committed to a long-term dependence that will contribute to continuing short-term balance-of-payments deficits and virtually permanent constraints on their domestic economies'.

In the 1970s, Melody was involved in research on the role of communication in development. His premise was that 'a lack of communication, or a failure of communication, *can* be a barrier to development. But it does not mean that the introduction of a new communication technology facilitates, or even an increase in communication will necessarily *stimulate* development' (Melody 1977: 40).

Is this positive, yet highly qualified, assessment of the contribution of communication to development consistent with Melody's critical perspective on the role of communication infrastructures and the activities of transnational corporations? And how does the critical view of transnational control of communication infrastructures fit with his later work on regulatory structures to facilitate the development of communication infrastructures and services, including the creation of conditions to attract foreign capital?

Concrete Analyses

The answer is that it fits very well: Melody has been internally consistent. Melody (1977: 25) stated that, 'The effects of an expansion of communication depend ... upon the many ... interrelated and interdependent factors that constitute the environment within which the expanded communication takes place. In certain circumstances, an expansion of particular kinds of communication may be detrimental to development'. He emphasised that 'the effects of communication depend upon the particular, and often unique, characteristics of society within which communication takes place'.

A concrete analysis of concrete situations is, therefore, essential. When assessing and analysing specific situations and developments, it is far from sufficient – if not erroneous – to deduce outcomes from general theory. The specificities of different situations must be taken into account. General theories should be applied, but they should be used as tools to understand specific situations. This is a very important premise in Melody's research and teaching. It is not limited to his work on development; all his work shows evidence of its application.

Melody's methodology leads to sometimes surprising conclusions. One cannot, as with some orthodox researchers, predict beforehand the conclusions of his research. Melody often finds himself opposing, and being opposed by, the predominant points of view, whether orthodox liberalism or leftist generalisations. His ideal is to review all the relevant factors at the concrete level and transcend abstract deductive analysis.

The theoretical basis for this ideal is found in institutional economics. Melody's work is in the tradition of American institutional economics with John R. Commons and Melody's own mentor, Harry Trebing, as major figures. This strand of institutional economics values concrete analysis and does not seek to confirm or deny any particular thesis in advance of analysis.

Melody is critical of neo-classical economic theory as it is taught in many university departments. He is critical of the dogmatism and orthodoxy of theoretical work in this tradition and of the value of the supporting econometric analyses. This does not mean that concepts and tools are not taken from neo-classical economics. But Melody believes that neo-classical analyses exclude too many relevant factors and neglect the essential dynamism of phenomena.

An advocate of multidisciplinary research, Melody has been instrumental in setting up and supporting multidisciplinary research programmes and centres throughout the world, most recently in Denmark and The Netherlands. Strict disciplinary specialisation is seen, at best, as narrowing analysis and, at worst, a dead end that yields no usable conclusions.

Elements of Analysis

Melody's research adheres to the tenets of holism, heterodoxy and evolutionism in institutional economics – although he is unlikely to use these terms. Melody (1977: 38) commends 'the systems approach, [under which] communications can be viewed as a system with many components. The communication system can be examined as one component in a larger system of national development'. The analysis becomes concrete when it involves many different aspects, because reality – the object of analysis – is certainly multi-faceted.

Institutions that crystallise interests and power structures in society are among the most important aspects to be analysed. It is also important to view markets as institutions. This is why Melody often emphasises that liberalisation and competition are means to achieve certain ends, not ends in themselves. The market does not exist in a natural state that may only be distorted by political acts. The market is an institution, constructed by societal interests.

These are some of the major positions that may be discerned from a close examination of Melody's work. His endeavours exemplify the importance of focusing on the concrete conditions for change. Melody makes no fundamental distinction between economically developed and developing countries. All countries are affected by the same global trends. However, this does not mean that policies should be identical. The key lesson is that specific conditions require concrete analyses. The appropriate policies must be designed on the basis of the findings of concrete analyses, not read off a general theory.

VI

What...

Roger **Silverstone**

Anthony **Smith**

Gaëtan **Tremblay**

Werner A. **Meier**

Elizabeth **Fox**
and Silvio **Waisbord**

Binod C. **Agrawal**

Marc **Raboy**

John D. H. **Downing**

Joseph **Turow**
and Rivka **Ribak**

VI

What...

Amy Mahan, Robin Mansell and Rohan Samarajiva

This section is concerned with the *What* – the information wares that are bought and sold in the marketplace and that are circulated under arrangements that do not depend on the price mechanism. The 'what' concerns the conditions for the circulation of knowledge – from production, to distribution, to consumption. This theme was present in William Melody's (1977) early work on the mass media and the economics of access to the marketplace of ideas. It characterises his elaboration of the dimensions of freedom of speech questions that arise in the context of the media. Who has freedom to speak, about what, and to whom? He addressed this issue in his analysis of the conditions necessary for cultural development. This is the common thread that runs throughout this section.

The developers of public policy, he argued, must attend to technological transformations, the shifting sites of public access to communication networks and to cultural products, and the associated transformations in industry structure, nationally and globally. Melody's analyses of the dynamic interplay of these developments are closely linked to his work on regulatory reform and to his critiques of the emerging information society. From the 1960s, the technical convergence of the media, computing and telecom industries was becoming increasingly apparent. Melody examined these developments in the light not only of the potential for market failure, but also in terms of the potential for opening new spaces for the expression of distinctive cultures and traditions.

The implications of the changing structure of the media industries for the way content is appropriated by audiences are addressed through the lens of policy reform. Melody emphasised the economic incentives facing media producing firms and he examined the market-led advertising and the public service broadcasting models. Where he found evidence of market domination or practices that he argued were not in the public interest, he called for public policy reform.

Melody's influential book, *Children's Television: The Economics of Exploitation* (1973a), is still in use today. Working in collaboration with Action for Children's Television (ACT), an American advocacy group, Melody asked, 'Should special protections be provided to insulate children from direct advertising designed to stimulate their consumption desires so that they would become active lobbyists for the merchandiser within the family?' (Melody 1973a: 4). He considered whether the broadcast industry's claims of financial harm as a result of the withdrawal of advertising targeted at the potentially lucrative children's market were founded on fact. His investigation showed that these claims were vastly overstated. He advocated in testimony before the Federal Communications Commission (FCC) that the elimination of advertising deemed to be harmful to children could be promoted without significant financial hardship to the industry and with minimum negative consequences.

Melody's view of developments in the media industries is complementary to Dallas Smythe's understanding of the institutional dynamics of markets for the production of media content under capitalism. In his article, 'Communications: Blindspot of Western Marxism', Smythe (1977) argued that the economic incentives of producers were organised to exploit audiences by making them do the work necessary to consume commodities of all kinds. Smythe (1981: 111) claimed that the 'role of the market for audiences, produced by mass media and bought by advertisers, has been totally ignored'. When audiences are influenced (or 'educated') by the ideological messages embedded in cultural products, they become a valuable asset for the media industry firms. Smythe suggested that countries should erect 'cultural screens' as a form of policy to protect themselves from these commercial products. In contrast, Melody advocated country-specific strategies of reform to change the economic incentives facing the commercial media and to improve the performance of public service broadcasters. His analyses of the economics of the media industries extended to the cable and satellite television industries. His work in this area was motivated by a search for institutional structures and practices that converge to a greater degree with the public interest.

The Internet Age is marked by digital technologies, convergence and multimedia content delivered over multiple platforms. The Internet also enables relatively convenient replication that may be construed as infringement of the copyright of the owners of digital information. In response to these developments, Melody has been concerned about the changed economic incentives that govern and shape the behaviour of media producing firms. Melody has argued that it is feasible to win some measure of protection for the diversity of ideas and of freedom of expression through policy measures that stimulate competition in the marketplace of ideas. Even in the face of growing numbers of suppliers, regulation is necessary to ensure that economic imperatives do not take precedence over social obligations. Melody

(1990a: 22) maintained that cultural products are influenced by institutions: 'These institutional constraints do not deny creativity and discretion so much as channel it in particular directions. Some of the most creative programming is channelled into advertising'.

Melody has always differentiated between policy mandates imposed on public service broadcasters and private broadcasters, on the one hand, and government capacity to implement those policies, on the other. In his 1986 Neil Matheson McWharrie Lecture on the Canadian Broadcasting Corporation's (CBC) contribution to Canadian culture, he asserted that Canada has the 'best communication policy statements of any nation', but that they are 'the idealistic aspirations of Canadian policy-makers rather than statements of purpose that will be made operational in practice' (1987a: 290-1). He suggested that the CBC had been hamstrung by problematic management decisions and that the Canadian Radio-television and Telecommunications Commission (CRTC) was ineffective in implementation: 'The issue is not so much one of private commercial interests insidiously undermining the public interest, as it is public service broadcasters losing sight of their mandate, and government policymakers and regulators failing to implement the noble principles that are so often enshrined in words, but missing in action' (Melody 1988: 280).

The justification for regulating media industries is the obligation to ensure that non-market objectives are articulated and addressed (Melody 1978; Cave and Melody 1989; Melody 1990b). Broadcast regulation is connected to the management of the radio frequency spectrum as a scarce resource. According to Cave and Melody (1989) broadcast markets have always been subject to government oversight or public financing. Broadcasting organisations implement their own preferences and biases regardless of whether they are located within the public or private sector.

The contributors to this section are concerned with policy objectives and rationales for regulation of the media industries. Their discussions draw upon experiences in national contexts including Canada, India, Israel, Switzerland, the United Kingdom, and the United States, as well as Latin America. They acknowledge that media content is now produced for circulation within global networks, but they point to distinctive patterns of content production and variations in policy priorities in the light of specific institutional histories. In some cases, they emphasise reform of extant media institutions; in others, they stress opportunities for the emergence of alternative media.

In his contribution, *Roger Silverstone* calls for a fundamental re-examination of the rationale for media regulation. We regulate, he argues, because the media are part of our lives – they enter the private spaces of the home and they influence our understandings of the world and the meanings we construct about others and ourselves. Silverstone suggests that it is necessary to think carefully about how regulation affects media producers and influences our experiences of geographical space and social relationships. He calls for consideration of what might constitute 'proper distance', that is, the knowledge of another person that is consistent with enabling responsible and caring action. He argues that the way the media constitute and mediate our lives may be inconsistent with an ethically appropriate 'proper distance'.

Anthony Smith claims that there is little understanding of what was intended historically by support of institutions such as the British Broadcasting Corporation (BBC), despite continuing deliberations about the mission of public service broadcasters. Traditionally, the broadcast media were subject to control in the public interest. This took the form of prohibiting certain content that was deemed to be harmful, and promoting other content that was thought to contribute to national well being and social cohesion. Smith observes that public service broadcasting sought to 'fill in the gap between citizen and consumer' and assesses the possibilities of recapturing the public-service ethos. Like Silverstone, he emphasises the need for a moral stance, one that acknowledges the role of the media in assisting in the construction of a shared agenda. He foresees institutional changes in the media that may lead to the emergence of public information, even in the face of the cacophony of images and messages that now constitute our mediated environment.

With the intensification of global distribution of media content facilitated by the use of satellite, cable television, and now the Internet, media regulation and copyright protection are no longer solely of national concern (Ó Siochrú et al. 2002). Historically, most supranational issues have been dealt with through bilateral agreements or multilateral regimes. Melody examined trade in cultural products and advocated more effective public policy at the international level. He observed that 'television programming that is specifically designed for the precise purpose of responding to international or global market conditions, and not to the particular domestic conditions of any country, must be different – perhaps substantially different – than the programming produced for the domestic market in any particular country' (Melody 1988: 267). There are major differences in public service objectives that are given priority in different countries. In Australia, for instance, the 'tyranny of distance' is a key issue; in Canada, language and bilingualism are important; in Latin America, the role of church ownership of the media is a consideration; and in the United States, the educational role of public service sometimes has been emphasised. Media policy must therefore accommodate diversity of objectives. In the globalising market for information commodities this is easier to aspire to than to achieve. Melody (1988: 270) observed that 'if one seeks programming diversity within one's country that is responsive to a variety of specific domestic conditions and issues, there is likely to be disappointment upon learning that the incentives of national public service programmers may be moving away from that objective, towards the objective of success in global market'.

The problems of international governance are addressed by *Gaëtan Tremblay*. He goes to the heart of the problem created by the conflicting values that influence media production and consumption in global and local markets. He asks, 'how can we preserve cultural diversity while opening markets to encourage technological innovation and stimulate commercial exchanges? What is the right balance between political intervention and market rules?' This issue is very important in the light of the recurrent and mounting pressures within the World Trade Organization negotiations to bring cultural production within the scope of trade in services agreements. Tremblay favours an international policy environment that recognises the peculiarities of the cultural industries. Any new trade regime should give weight to both commercial and cultural objectives. Tremblay draws attention to Melody's consistent view that markets are, in fact, social institutions; they can be constructed and shaped to favour a variety of goals and outcomes.

Werner Meier takes up the theme of the globalisation of the media industries through the lens of media ownership. The industrial structure of the media affects who may access the marketplace of ideas. In an oft-cited article, 'Communication Policy in the Global Information Economy: Whither the Public Interest?', Melody (1990a: 20) stated that '... the public interest has been seen essentially as preserving the conditions of "independent" reporting, not a diversity of information services and viewpoints'. As media abundance in terms of channels and distribution alternatives has emerged, Melody has contested the argument that this implies increased media diversity. Concentration of ownership continues to matter and it requires scrutiny. Meier notes the passing of the political economy turn in media research as the attention of researchers has shifted from analysis of the supply side of the market to analysis of consumption. Studies of the active audience and the mediation process are revealing but as Meier suggests, there is a continuing need for detailed and critical analysis of the ways in which media conglomerates are accumulating power.

The terrain of media structure, ownership and policy is covered by **Elizabeth Fox** and *Silvio Waisbord* in the context of the changes in Latin American broadcasting markets. Fox and Waisbord show that there has been no coherent policy coordination between the countries in the region with the consequence that 'global capital and programming moves easily into weaker and smaller markets with low production, and more aggressively in partnerships with local powerhouses into advertising-rich countries with large, actual or potential, audiences'. Tracing the early history of public service broadcasting in the region and the forces of globalisation, this contribution highlights the power of resistance within the region to the hegemony of Hollywood. Local production of content has been a constant and there have been successes in export markets. The Latin American 'patchwork quilt' of media production, consumption and export is influenced strongly by factors such as per capita income, diffusion of technologies and expenditure on advertising. These authors are pessimistic: '... globalisation signals the consolidation of commercial media systems and the end of alternative models'. But, they are also hopeful that policy makers can influence the market.

The unequal development of the media industries and diverse patterns of media consumption are evident in India. In his contribution, **Binod Agrawal** considers the divides between those in the South Asian region who are excluded from participating in emerging information societies and those who are not. He argues that policy makers are indifferent towards measures that might facilitate greater equity in the distribution of the potential benefits of digital infrastructures. He calls for a vision of a distinctive Indian information society that can guide coordinated policy action. He notes that although much of the policy debate juxtaposes the views of those who fear the consequences of global developments and those who welcome it, there is a paucity of research on the nature of, and the contradictions in, the way the media and other information products are being accommodated or resisted in people's lives.

Marc Raboy addresses the themes of globalisation and paradigmatic change in the media environment. He examines the role of regulation in facilitating media and communication governance, arguing that regulation can help to secure access to content and alternative means of communication, and that it can support efforts to create opportunities for citizens. Raboy sees the need to revise government policy continuously in the light of the changing dynamics of the market, which are blunt instruments at best. Continuous reassessment of available means of mobilising production of media content that is responsive to public interest considerations is necessary. Policy must enhance access to information that is valued not just by consumers, but also by citizens. Raboy gives priority to devising new forms of governance that take issues of cultural development and democratisation issues into account. The stakeholders that are most successful in developing innovative approaches to governance, he suggests, are the transnational media companies. For inclusive governance, the other collective groups in society will have to follow suit.

Melody (1990a) argued that there are deep and complex connections between the way information is generated and exchanged in any given society and the organisation of industry. When there are changes in the modes of information production or exchange, we must examine the potential for new biases and new distributions of power to emerge and their consequences for firms and other organisations.

The characteristics of information generation and dissemination affect the nature of markets and the structure of industry, as well as the competitiveness of firms, and the prosperity of regions and nations. They affect the international structure of organisations, ranging from corporations to government agencies, political parties, universities, trade unions, libraries and volunteer groups. The implications of the changes now taking place ... affect the characteristics of essential information and communication networks both for individuals and organizations (Melody 1990a: 26).

John Downing claims that it is no longer meaningful to refer to a universal concept of public service broadcasting. In this respect his position is similar to that of Anthony Smith. Downing is more concerned however, with whether the new technological developments, in conjunction with earlier generations of technologies, open up spaces for the emergence of 'contrahegemonic' media. Downing recounts a number of initiatives, including Independent Media Centres and micro-radio, that offer the potential for creative production of media to contribute to democratic participation. He observes that relevance and watchability are no longer necessarily in conflict. Declining production costs enable developments that may help to support the 'public's ability to amass power to achieve secular, just, pro-human purposes'. But Downing is cautious in his expectations because the extreme right can appropriate the new media spaces. The social scientist's obligation in his view is to examine how the new media (and the old) are being appropriated and to assess the consequences for citizens.

The final contribution in this section by *Joseph Turow* and *Rivka Ribak* cautions against the tendency to treat the Internet and the World Wide Web as undifferentiated phenomena. They argue that many comparative studies oversimplify and fail to acknowledge that these media are fundamentally associated with identity formation. This process is highly differentiated. Turow and Ribak examine two discourses about the Internet and the Web. The first, an essentialist approach, foregrounds the technological aspects and draws conclusions about the common experiences of users. The second, a relativist perspective, emphasises local identity and social practices. They suggest that neither is helpful in examining what happens when the Internet enables 'encounters between local cultures ... in the context of transnational political and economic interests regarding the new technology'. Adopting a 'world systems perspective', they raise issues about asymmetries in the interpenetration of cultures and how these, in turn, may influence how various populations create and resist new meanings and identities.

The challenge that Turow and Ribak set out is a very appropriate. The research and policy challenge, they claim, is that of 'relat[ing] people's attitudes and that which takes place locally, to the national and global sociopolitical system' – a statement that resonates with Melody's lifelong concerns.

Regulation and the Ethics of Distance: Distance and the Ethics of Regulation

Roger Silverstone

INTRODUCTION

The locus of our regulatory concern needs to shift. In the new media world, a world that still includes old media, and old but yet resistant values driving institutional processes of mediation, the concern with markets, competition, and content needs to be rethought. This is not only because of the decline of spectrum scarcity, or the incapacity of national governments to control international flows of information and communication, but because new media are challenging what it means to be human, through their increasing salience as both information and communication resources, and, as such, as crucial components of our relational infrastructure and our social life.

Just as William Melody (1999b) argues in a recent article that the issue of human capital is the key to the unlocking of the information economy, I want to suggest in this equally short piece, that an understanding of what it is to be human is the central question underlying and, in the final analysis, regulating the development of the mediated world in which more and more of us live, and by which almost all of us are affected. Marshall McLuhan (1964) suggested that media, all media, were extensions of ourselves, and although this perhaps makes more sense now than it ever did, it leaves untouched the thorny question of what we are, and of how what we are in turn affects the way in which media emerge and develop. It fails to register mediation as either a social or a political process. In other words, the humanity or inhumanity at the heart of the processes of mediation is left unexamined; it is presumed to be unproblematic.

Similarly, regulatory discourse rarely examines why regulation should take place in the first place. Its presumptions about public interest, freedom of expression, rights to privacy, competition policy, intellectual property and the like presume an ordered or at least orderable world, and indeed a world that would benefit from deliberative, and presumably accountable, regulation. The main beneficiary of such regulatory impulses and practices is the citizen, in his or her public and private life. These citizens need to be protected against the depredations of untrammelled vested interests, be they commercial or imperial. They need to be given freedoms to speak and to be heard; they need to be given freedoms of choice. They need to be consulted on how regulatory policies are formed and implemented (Collins and Murroni 1996).

But who is the citizen these days? And how has his or her status as a citizen been affected by the media, both old and new, both broadcast and interactive? In what ways do our media enable or disable our capacity to relate to each other as citizens, but also as human beings? In what ways do they enable or disable us as ethical beings in our relationship to the world?

Home ...

In an earlier essay (Silverstone 1999) I argued that almost all our regulatory impulses, those that engage with the ownership of media industries, on the one hand, and those that concern the welfare of the family, on the other, are between them concerned with the protection of home. What links them is a preoccupation with *content*: with the images, sounds and meanings that are transmitted and communicated daily, and over which regulators increasingly feel they have little control. Content, they say, is king. What appears on the page or on the screen, what is represented, especially in its consistency or inconsistency, its decency or indecency, its intrusiveness, is deemed to be important precisely because it has been allowed to cross the threshold, seeping into private spaces and private lives. This was, of course, the impetus for the earliest attempts at content regulation, in the Hays Code, for the cinema. But these anxieties and the regulatory attempts to manage them have become more insistent as 20th century media migrated away from public to private screens, and from shared sitting rooms to solitary bedrooms.

Banal though it may seem, the media are seen to be important because of the power they are presumed to exercise over us, *at home*, a power that no amount of audience research can quite completely deny, and of course which most of us believe, one way or the other, naturally to be the case. Competition policy is as much about such breaches of personal security and domestic integrity – of the rights of the person and the personal – as it is about cross-media ownership and the future of public service broadcasting and the public sphere. Indeed, it is precisely the private which is at stake in the discussions and deliberations on the latter.

And yet while regulators struggle to control and direct, to label and to licence content, parents and families struggle over a personal and private culture, shaping and protecting the domestic spaces where public and private moralities are supposed to coincide. This is a struggle for control, a struggle which propagandists, advertisers, television schedulers and portal designers well understand. And it is a struggle which parents understand too, as they argue with their children over time spent online. It is a struggle which at least in part defines, across lines of age and gender, the particular politics of individual households.

Regulation is, then, a private as well as a public matter. It takes place in frontrooms as well as in debating chambers, in the cut and thrust of discussions over viewing habits, as well as in international debates over v-chips and trans-border media flows. In both these environments what is being fought over are the rights of, and control over, representation: of the availability of, and access to, the continuities and consistencies of both the immediacy and the flow of images and narratives. And in those representations what is at stake are the rights to define a relationship: between what is known and not known, between what is valued and not valued, between what one believes to be the truth and what one suspects is a falsehood, and between what one lays claim to and what one can discard in one's relationship to the rest of the world. What is at stake, in these moments and mechanisms of regulation is, essentially, a moral order.

... AND AWAY
As we become increasingly dependent on the mediated word and image for our understanding of what takes place beyond our front door; as everyday life, in its taken-for-granted ordinariness, becomes inseparable from the mediations that guide us through it, and connect or disconnect us from the everyday lives of others; how the media position us, or enable us to position ourselves, become crucial.

As citizens we are expected to take responsibility for, and to act responsibly in relation to, ourselves, our neighbours and also the strangers amongst us. Such expectations have been, arguably, undermined by (among other things) a century of electronic mediation, which has led to increasing privatisation and individualisation. The dominant trope in the analysis of 20th century public life has been its erosion: the palpable lack of care, the paradoxical lack of communication, has been revealed in increasing alienation from the formal processes of politics and engagement in public life; perhaps not for all, but for many, especially in the wealthy and highly mediated democracies of industrial society.

These societies, equally it goes without saying, are becoming increasingly connected to each other. What imperialism once enforced, globalisation now enables, or indeed requires: a mutuality of increasingly highly stratified economic and financial structures and processes; a shared but still massively and unevenly discomforting physical environment; a political space that no longer knows, nor much cares about, national boundaries and territorial sovereignty; networks of information and communication that shrink social and cultural space and time to the size of a handset.

In this context, and taking the broadest sweep, problems of regulation become problems of governance, in which order and accountability are dreamed about on a global scale, and at the level of states and transnational non-governmental organisations. Foreign and domestic policy converges. Somehow even these dreams depend on a notion of citizenship, though a transcendent one, but they still require an engagement with the human – and they challenge it too. However, they leave untouched and unexamined, for the most part, the individual in his or her humanity, in his or her sensibility. In what ways, if at all, can or should this humanity be affected by our regulatory impulses and institutions? In what ways should this humanity (or its lack) inform and affect our attempts at regulation and governance?

Early commentators, both utopian and dystopian, on the emerging late 19th century wireless and telegraphic space recognised the implications of what has subsequently come to be known as the double life of media and communication: that they separate as well as connect. This paradox inevitably calls the lie to any contemporary notion of the media's role in what is called the death of distance. It raises the question of isolation and not just privatisation – and isolation of both the individual and of the group. It also raises the question of the illusion of connection: that in our mediated innocence, in our mediated naïveté, we are unable to recognise how imprisoned we are, how easily blinded we are, by the mediations that apparently link us together.

As I have argued elsewhere (Silverstone 2002 forthcoming) there is often quite a fundamental confusion in much of the writing on the geography of new media. Time-space distanciation, or time-space compression, even ideas of the network society, suggest a profound and misleading elision between two kinds of distance: the spatial and the social. It is presumed in these discussions that the electronic mediation of physical or material connection provides at the same time, social, cultural or psychological connection. The technologically-enabled transformation of time and space which marked the entry into the modern world certainly provided new conditions and possibilities for communication, communication that provided connection despite physical separation. Yet the contradictions at the heart of such communication become even more profound the more we insist that electronic mediation brings no penalty when it comes to understanding and caring for the other. Indeed, when we insist, on the contrary, that our world view is now global in its reach. That there is no escape. That nothing can be hidden, nothing can be, or is, ignored. But of course it can.

My point is that distance is not just a material, a geographical or even a social category, but it is, by virtue of all of these and as a product of their interrelation, a moral category. The overcoming of distance requires more than technology and indeed more than the creation of a public sphere. It requires what I have called 'proper distance' (Silverstone 2002 forthcoming). Proper distance is the critical notion that implies and involves a search for enough knowledge and understanding of the other person or the other culture to enable responsibility and care, as well as to enable the kind of action that, informed by that understanding, is in turn enabling. We need to be close but not too close, distant, but not too distant.

Proper Distance

The media have always fulfilled the function of creating some sense of proper distance, or at least they have tried, or claimed to be able, to do so. In the reporting of world events, the production of news, the fictional representation of the past, the critical interrogation of the private lives of public figures, the exploration of the ordinariness of everyday life, what is involved, in one way or another, is a negotiation between the familiar and the strange, as the media try, though always imperfectly, to resolve the essential ambiguities and ambivalences of contemporary life.

Yet such mediations have tended to produce, in practice, a kind of polarisation in the determinations of such distance. The unfamiliar is either pushed to a point beyond strangeness, beyond humanity; or it is drawn so close as to become indistinguishable from ourselves. And, it should be said, there is also very little sense that we are the objects of the others' gaze, that how *we* are seen and understood by those far removed from us also matters; we need to see and understand that too.

We find ourselves being positioned by media representation as so removed from the lives and worlds of other people that they seem beyond the pale, beyond reach of care or compassion, and certainly beyond reach of any meaningful or productive action. Technology has a habit of creating such distance, and the bureaucracies that have been built around technologies have in the past, and with cataclysmic effects, reinforced this sense of separation and alienation, this immorality of distance. This is certainly and obviously the case in times of conflict, but it is rarely far away even in peace.

Per contra the representation, just as frequent and just as familiar, of the other as being just like us, as recoupable without disturbance into our own world and values has, though perhaps more benignly, the same consequence. We refuse to recognise not only that others are not like us, but that they can be made to be like us. What they have we share. What they are we know. They are as they appear in our documentaries and in our advertisements. Such cultural neo-imperialism represents the other side of the immorality of distance, in its refusal to accept difference, in its resistance to recognising and to valuing the stranger.

In both cases, we lose a sense of both the commonality and difference that should inform the ethics of how we live in the world. Either way we lose the capacity effectively to grasp both what we share and what we do not share as human beings. The irony of the electronically mediated century just passed, in which we have come to believe that the immediate and the visible are both necessary and sufficient to guarantee connection, is that this apparent closeness is only screen-deep.

Distance can, therefore, be proper (correct, distinctive and ethically appropriate) or it can be improper. If improper distance can be, and is, created, *inter alia*, through the mediations that electronic technologies provide for us, then it follows that we can use the notion of *proper* distance as a tool to measure and to repair the failures in our communication with and about other people and other cultures and in our reporting of the world, in such a way as our capacity to act is enabled and preserved (Boltanski 1999; Silverstone 2002 forthcoming). And it follows too that we can use it as a way of interrogating those arguments, most recently in the analysis of the supposed miraculous capacity of the Internet, that mistake connection for closeness, and closeness for commitment, and which confuse reciprocity with responsibility.

It is with the convergence between the public and the private, the personal and the social, that the notion of proper distance seeks to engage, since it is at this interface, perhaps increasingly confused and confusing, where social beings, citizens real or manqué, need both to confront a moral agenda that is appropriate to the conditions of its mediation and to confront the mediated world which defines and constrains how the other person appears to us – as through a glass darkly.

Conclusion

Regulation has always been a technical activity. To suggest that it should also be a moral one has its dangers. Yet these dangers need to be confronted. What is missing so often in the regulatory discourse is the question: regulation for what, and for whom?

The focus on content, on media as representational technologies, is in many ways atavistic. It brings back concerns that many had thought long since buried in the analysis of mediation: concerns with ideology, effects and false consciousness, even. Yet media are nothing if they do not convey meanings, and even if we can (and we can) negotiate those meanings for ourselves, and distance ourselves from those meanings we find unacceptable or unpalatable, in the absence of others – both other meanings and other realities – our perceptions of the world cannot but be increasingly and consistently framed by what is seen and heard through screens and audio-speakers.

The multiple negatives of the last paragraph are intended – and intended to be instructive. There is inevitably and necessarily a need for caution in any kind of moral position lest it be seen as, or become, moralistic. So it needs to be understood that the present argument is not for a new kind (or even an old kind) of censorship. On the contrary, at issue are the presumptions and preconditions for our understandable (perhaps even natural, at least sociologically speaking) concern for regulation. Perhaps it is time to recognise that regulation should not just be concerned with the protection of our own securities and of those we hold dear or for whom we have some formal, familial or even national, responsibility.

Regulation should address the wider and, I have suggested, much deeper issue of our relationships to others, to those for whom we have no formal responsibility, to those who are distant in space or culture, the strangers amongst us, our neighbours abroad; but for whom our basic humanity requires that we should care. This is of course a tall order. However, it suggests a shift, and one that it might well be argued is long overdue. It involves a shift away from regulation as narrowly conceived in the minds and practices of parliaments and councils, towards a more ethically oriented education, and towards a critical social and cultural practice which recognises the particular characteristics of our mediated world. We once upon a time taught something called civics. It is perhaps time to think through what civics might be in our present intensely mediated century.

Our regulatory impulses need to be both informed and moderated by these concerns. Citizenship requires responsibility and to exercise such responsibility well and thoroughly in turn requires the need to be able to see the world and to see through our media's limited and inadequate representations of it. In this sense, as well as reading, we might need to regulate, against the grain.

VI.2

In Search of the 'Shared Moment'

Anthony Smith

Introduction

Have we come irrevocably to the end of the discourse of 'public service', which was attached so firmly to much of the communication institution of the mid-20th century? Is it possible that the beliefs and ideals that went with public service can be revivified in our current media environment? The notion of public service helped at first to sanitise what seemed to be an inevitable monopoly in broadcasting, especially in geographically small countries; then, when commercial competition started up in radio and television, it came to mark the contrast between what people were thought to want and what they might be induced to accept, in their own higher interest and for their own protection. It filled in the gap between citizen and consumer.

Throughout their history the communication media have given rise to an evolving dialogue between the optimism of technological prediction and the pessimism of cultural prophecy. This dialogue has generated a vast international literature as well as a complex history of national administrative practices. We have in the decade of the 1990s crossed the threshold into a whole new phase of this dialogue, as well as of the practices – as the ramifications of the multimedia age have begun to reveal themselves. The old institutions are rapidly evaporating and even the reasons for their existence are rapidly fading from our minds. Essentially, the culture of radio and television (and to a declining extent cable and satellite) was built upon the intimation of a large undifferentiated audience, usually bounded by a national identity, who were brought together electronically and without specific payment, to share an experience. The Internet, on the other hand, presents itself to an unpoliceable mass of audiences, not linked by anything other than the happenstance of surfing or the individual subscription to a particularism. The 'shared moment' enjoyed by the early audiences of broadcasting, which made the domestic environment the location of a collective, regional or national, citizen identity has given way to a discord of haphazard loyalties.

Older Generation Public Service

The development of the 20th century's media coincided with a series of administrative experiments in forms of public service around the world. In the

United States, a Federal Communications Commission evolved by stages, taking to itself a series of largely negative and preventative responsibilities in respect of the as yet unknown impact of the mass media of radio and television. Its duties revolved around the vague sense that in the electronic media there lay at stake a 'public interest, convenience and necessity'. Cinema, too, found itself embraced by public institutions in many places, concerned with policing representations on the screen of social relationships, protecting children from certain kinds of knowledge, upholding images of correct conduct between classes and generations and safeguarding the production of indigenous images where these were threatened by foreign competition.

Not only entertainment but other new technologies seemed to require visible governing institutions, belonging morally to nation or society or public. The airways, the telephone system and, in due course, trains, electricity and energy were thought to be so fundamental, so infrastructural, so supportive of all other sectors of economy and society that they could not simply be permitted to function as owned enterprises, outside the ultimate control of public authorities operating on behalf of the wider society. Forms and styles of regulation furnished political agendas with their principal controversies for many decades.

By the end of the 20th century the ideologies which sprang from public service institutions were wearing thin and it was possible for a Democratic Party administration in the United States and a Labour government in the United Kingdom both to offer little more than social compassion in place of institutional development in public service. The Clinton foray into socialised medicine rapidly petered out; the balanced budget took precedence over welfare. As far as the Labour Party, free of Clause Four, was concerned, the means of production, distribution and exchange were never again to be socially owned, or so it seems. In the information and entertainment media the available abundance had defeated the public service imagination. In France the main mass channel was simply sold off into the private sector and there was talk of selling off another one of the four. In the United States the triad of networks had given way to a mass of cable and satellite channels and to much else. In the United Kingdom the BBC had transmogrified itself into a 'management' where once it had seen itself as a vast *atelier*. By this means it had saved itself from the Conservative administration in the mid-1990s, and convinced them, for the time being, that the licence fee, the only truly socialised charging system for electronic media, was worth retaining for the BBC.

At the turn of the century it had become impossible for an older generation of public service broadcasters even to explain what they had meant by public service broadcasting, a system of broadcasting that prevented as it presented, that offered delight and instruction in order to displace the materials which would, it was believed, fill the airways were the medium wholly or substantially in private hands. Those private hands were no longer attached to people who shared the ideals of public service while earning a crust in the private sector. A generation of small independent television companies which had sprung up in their hundreds across Europe (now in the ex-communist East as well as the West) were in the possession of people who saw glittering markets for media materials opening up. They devised entertainment formats that could be sold across boundaries and across continents, devoid of local allusiveness. The most universal reservoir of common allusion is sex and the moral barriers were duly swept away.

Reconstructing Policy Ideals

Public service had always entailed suggesting to listeners and viewers that something on offer was better for them than something they might have been tempted to switch to themselves. Thus the Light Programme in the 1940s was there to coax listeners from Radio Luxembourg, and in the 1960s Radio One was introduced to overcome the propensity of the young to turn to the illegal pirate radios. BBC-2 was awarded to the BBC because the commercial channel was believed by those in authority to be debasing public taste. By the end of the 20th century the notion of such a possibility had been evacuated from the official mind.

Public service had grown alongside a particular range of technologies and a matching range of ideologies. It drew also upon a tradition of service and a sense of social duty on the part of those who ran the institutions and produced the content, that harked back to empire and to the age of missionaries. The beliefs and attitudes about the nature of society and kind of service society required were not unique to the media; they were present of course in education and in the church but also in such bodies as the Post Office and the providers of utilities, any institution responsible for equal, continual, guaranteed and universal provision of a good or service. The BBC became for a considerable time – in some sense still – the world's supreme example of its kind. It depended upon a complex machinery of motivation on the part of twenty thousand individuals, selected, socialised, trained and indoctrinated into the slowly evolving attitudes that composed the public service mentality.

One cannot over-emphasise the differences in mindset between the provision of television in a closed three- or four-channel environment and the advent of multi-channel choice, even though the latter remains subject to 'light touch' forms of regulation. Though it could be and was described, in slightly sneering tones in the

1970s, as a form of social control, as a subtle means of painless hegemony and false consciousness, it extracted from those who lived by it special forms of social idealism. The cynicism of commercialised culture was largely absent. Political pressure was vigorously withstood, though not always with complete success. Commercial motivation was institutionally treated as improper. Advertising was not merely absent, it was immoral, especially where public information was concerned. The purpose of entertainment was still to educate or at least to edify. Audience size had the status of being something that a producer had seriously to consider; it did not circumscribe the entire nature of a programme. Audience measurement had not yet become the chief determinant of the environment in which programme commissioning took place. That gradually came about during the 1980s and 1990s and in the era of subscription cable and where satellite service has become a staple.

With privatisation the cultural experience of broadcasting has itself altered, with a change in the whole manner by which the audience is sought and addressed. The public space, in which the discussion of broadcasting regulation has always taken place, has somehow seemed to shrink. But, at the same time, cultural bureaucracy has been de-legitimised in all its forms. The continuing public service institutions have all had to re-construct their *raisons d'être* in full public view while searching for new terms in which to justify their existence. In the United Kingdom the Arts Council, to take one example, has performed this task awkwardly, but the BBC proceeded to carry off the shift in its own consciousness extremely effectively; government willingly accepted its view of how it was intending to function in the abbreviated public realm and rewarded it with the allocation of further channels in the filling of which its role would appear more 'commercial' than public service. The BBC succeeded in preserving the licence fee under the Thatcher government after this substantial self-realignment and internal managerial transformation. The United Kingdom's Channel Four underwent its own drastic change during the same decade of the 1990s when it took on the role of selling its own advertising and turning ITV into a rival where previously it had been a kind of partner. The French too have reviewed their entire system and went further than any other of the European broadcasting administrations by selling off their main mass channel while suggesting that the same thing might be done with a second one. No broadcasting system in the world in the era of media abundance resembles what it was, in terms of its physical shape and in the way it announces itself to its audience.

The changes we see around us in the media world are generally ascribed to the exigencies of new techniques and technologies (which all share the characteristic of multiplying the outlets available), but the changes are equally derived from new prevailing economic precepts. Almost every country has come to accept that its future financial success depends on the endless creation of new markets for new commodities which, in turn, depend upon the endless re-development of public tastes and needs. The great national terrestrial channels all survive but on the basis of new identities within a feverishly competitive market of channels. Private capital, demanding freedom to operate internationally and with minimal constraint, has come to impose its own diktats and prevailing political attitude suggests that these should be accepted as legitimate.

One highly illustrative incident in the United Kingdom was the shifting of the main news on ITV from 10 to 11 p.m. in 2001. This was a great test of the extent to which public service concerns still held sway in the commercial sector of television: for the regulatory authority had long ago stipulated that the bulk of the population should be enabled to see one major news bulletin a day within peak hours. The resulting programme had for decades been something which the main commercial channel always pointed to as proof of its public service credentials. Despite vigorous protest in Parliament the change went ahead, only to be followed by the BBC's decision to shift its 9 o'clock news to 10. The purpose of the first change was to rescue advertising revenue and the argument of the BBC was that it felt it had to give itself the same scheduling opportunity as a competitor. The 'shared moment' had had its day. A wave of take-overs within the commercial sector has taken place, where once the entire sector had been constructed by public authorities to provide every region within its own locally owned company. There is no space between the competitors in this marketplace, no space for any redundancy of provision. The attention of every viewer available is urgently required for commercial exploitation or to justify the revenue of the non-commercial competitor.

Conclusion

The process of change has much further still to go. But already one can see the glimmerings of an internal contradiction or at least of a positive new horizon. For the world is evolving a single shared agenda, what one might call the post-September 11th agenda. There is a clear set of internationally shared dilemmas, with regional and national versions. This was not the case during the Cold War, nor during the years of its immediate aftermath. There is an urgent need now to understand things which neither West nor Islam had felt were necessary to take in, each about the other. There are the outcomes of the war against terrorism to absorb into the political bloodstream, whatever the interim results of those conflicts. There is a fresh sense of duty, international duty which spills back into domestic programmes, affecting migrants and refugees, education, welfare, religion and the economy. There are tasks of absorption and socialisation which are urgent if further conflict is to be forestalled. The case for 'shared moments' has a new and compelling momentum and one that is unlikely to be evaded or ignored.

Looking back on the public service media ethic one sees an important bifurcation; on the one hand, people believed that audiences had to be protected against certain images and messages and, on the other, that they had to be manipulated into absorbing other messages. The former tended to prevail and the endless studies of the effects of violence and 'bad language' are the evidence of an obsessive concern to protect. But the latter was also important for it meant the creation of materials which passed with a equal understanding and equal emotional pleasure into a multitude of minds. From the boundless multiplicity of messages of today new homogeneous understandings must be derived. One cannot help but feel that a way will be found, not a way of excluding, but a way of making coherent, of legitimating some of that which we are learning and discarding some of the rest. We will never go back to a few clear streams of news and information but out of the chaos of messages those institutions that are in a position to play a shaping role will inevitably emerge and take on the mantle of international public information. Those existing institutions that cave in to the pressures now will not play that eventual shaping role. Those that stick it out will.

VI.3

Global Media and Cultural Diversity

Gaëtan Tremblay

Introduction

William Melody is best known for his work on telecom reform. While his commitment in the broadcasting field has been more sporadic and his writings less numerous, they nevertheless have been significant and remain deeply inspiring for scholars in the field. Reading his material again quickly convinced me that Melody addressed most of the major issues that are still relevant today to the analysis of broadcasting policy. His institutional approach is as appropriate as ever to diagnose the problems and to put forward thoughtful solutions.

My purpose in this contribution is to illustrate how Melody's definitions of problems and theoretical and methodological choices with respect to the analysis of broadcasting policies more than ten years ago remain pertinent to current studies. I cannot put aside my personal understanding of Melody's thought and I must extrapolate from his writings in order to render a 'Melodian' interpretation of contemporary issues.

The main concern of our times regarding broadcasting, and more broadly, the exchange of cultural products and services at the international level, is what type of system should govern their world-wide circulation. Melody (1978; 1988) and Cave and Melody (1989) addressed these questions through the lens of international television and the implications of European satellites and the regulatory issues that these developments raised. Refusing the mechanical solutions of neo-liberalism, Melody sought answers by applying the principles of a classic institutional approach. In his view, the rule of the market helps to escape the heavy weight of vested interests and stimulates innovation. However, markets are but social institutions and political intervention is required to guarantee equal access and real competition, among other aims.

The questions I want to discuss from a 'Melodian' perspective include: How can we preserve cultural diversity while opening markets to encourage technological innovation and stimulate commercial exchanges? What is the right balance between political intervention and market rules?

MARKETS, TECHNOLOGICAL INNOVATION AND POLITICAL INTERVENTION

In his early work, Melody (1978) argued for the necessity to preserve individual freedom of speech and diversity of sources of information through: 1) competition within and between the media; and 2) specific rights of individual access to the media. Since the end of the 1970s the distribution facilities of cable and satellite have hugely increased and the number of radio and television channels has soared.

Technological innovation has opened wide avenues and created new opportunities, and scarcity is no longer the predominant characteristic of audio-visual markets. Has this fundamentally changed the fact that in a *laissez-faire* marketplace 'the inherited conditions will differ among the different participants?' Given these conditions, then 'if the international economic system is to operate to the mutual advantage of all trading nations, it may be necessary to establish certain terms of trade that to some countries will be restrictions' (Melody 1978: 220).

Freedom is at the core of Melody's thinking in this area. And open markets provide the arena where various initiatives can compete in their search to meet consumer demand. However, to guarantee real freedom to everyone, Melody is ready to accept, and even proposes imposing constraints on market functioning in certain circumstances and sectors. 'In the broadcast industries in particular, certain regulatory functions cannot be totally eliminated' (Cave and Melody 1989: 224), even if critics rightly recognise that the regulatory bodies often tend to share the interests of the industry they regulate.

Some believe that fibre optic cables, satellite distribution and the Internet now provide equal access to the means of expression that democracy requires. But many statistics show this to be wishful thinking. While these technologies are more and more available, individual and collective inequalities remain regarding access to and the use of cable and satellite services or the Internet. The distribution of computers among various social classes and nations reveals large discrepancies.

In short, if technological development offers opportunities for social innovation and markets provide the best mechanism to challenge vested interests, social equality must be addressed at the political level. But what kind of regulation is needed and is desirable? The answer of course varies from time to time and from place to place. One way to assess this question is to consider the supply and demand for regulation, following the work of Stigler (1971). Another is to undertake comparative analysis. Melody has used both approaches in his work.

Globalisation and cultural diversity

If broadcasting systems are designed and operated so as to ensure social equality, they are also often expected to work in such a manner as to achieve cultural objectives. Melody (1988: 270) addressed this in discussing the future of satellite television in Europe.

> Will global television programming help overcome nationalist programming differences and lead to programming designed to unite us all by emphasising cross-national common cultural values and the flowering of diversity? Or will it lead to programming designed to serve an artificial bland, homogeneous set of values that represent no one and offend no one, that is, a destruction of diversity to serve only the lowest common denominator?

His answer deserves an extensive quotation.

> If the objective is to promote pan-European broadcasting specifically directed to common European interests, the more restrictive model may be more appropriate. The EEC proposal of minimal regulation does not really promote pan-European Television. It promotes global television. The dominant source of programming will be almost certainly the US, and programme production by European producers and broadcasters will be directed not to common European themes, issues and values, but to those of the competitive, commercial global market. There is nothing uniquely European about it, as a casual observation of current pan-European television quickly demonstrates. Under the model of more restrictive regulation, the programming is much more likely to reflect the claimed objective of promoting television programming with a common European cultural dimension (Melody 1988: 276).

The challenge remains the same at the beginning of the third millennium. Free trade agreements and on-going discussion at the World Trade Organization are pushing towards more liberalisation, including the cultural sector. Cultural exchanges, like economic exchanges, are stimulating and should be promoted. But the main danger still lies in the hegemony of a few dominant actors controlling the production and distribution of the most significant part of cultural products.

Global culture is following the path opened by economic globalisation. It usually evokes superficial consumer products, and is often perceived as a threat to national and local cultures. The acceptance of universal individual and collective rights could be seen as a positive outcome of the globalisation process. If the universalisation of human rights is to be promoted, it appears to most experts that cultural diversity is a collective heritage that must also be protected.

Culture is vital to democratic life where the major arena remains the nation state. Democracy is 'government for the people by the people', as represented in popular texts. It is a 'one man, one vote' formula. But true democracy must also include 'one person, one voice'. And to achieve that, a society must care about its cultural and communication system in order to guarantee equality in access to information and the possibility of expression. This is true for news and for norms and values, and opinions and ideas.

Culture is as essential to the survival of a society as a military system of defence or the security of agricultural provision. Culture is at the core of social solidarity. People must agree on norms and values, and share feelings, models and ideals, in order to live together. To play their role as social mediators, artists and creators of all kinds should be deeply connected to their community.

However, it has to be recognised, at the same time, that cultural vitality also depends on contacts with other cultures. Interchanges should be encouraged to maintain the dynamism of different cultures. In this respect, to ensure cultural development, openness is as much needed as protection.

For the culture and communication sectors, the State must intervene to guarantee equality of access, artistic freedom, education of the public, heritage protection and the connections between the creators and their community. The policy instruments developed by the Welfare State do need to be submitted to reassessment and new tools, more appropriate to the new context, should be invented. In the Age of the Internet and modern electronic networks, content quotas are no longer very effective measures to protect and promote local and national cultural products. A new system is required.

In a global world, regulation at the national level is no longer sufficient. Regulation at the international level is increasingly needed. From an economic perspective, it is accepted that States must agree to rules that guarantee conditions for fair competition. States should also play a similar role in the cultural field to preserve conditions for content diversity. This should be considered a basic requirement which is as important to cultural development as antitrust legislation is to economic competition.

The main question may be summarised as follows: if culture, information and education cannot be reduced to mere commodities, how can international exchanges be regulated in order to allow as much free trade as possible while, at the same time, protecting and fostering cultural identities in a pluralistic world? It is essential to establish another point of reference than the market to assess the value of a cultural product. It is equally important that a new regulatory system at the international level takes this complimentary reference point into account.

Unfortunately, we do not know much about the dynamics of cultural development and this makes it difficult to specify exactly how this can be achieved. More research is clearly needed, and such research should take into account the basic characteristics of culture. Fundamentally, even for commercial products, culture is meaning expressed through shared symbols.

There are three basic policy options: promoting free trade applied equally to cultural commodities; creating a clear distinction between culture and commerce; and, giving specific recognition to the peculiarities of the cultural industries and adopting an adapted regime which, at the same time, respects the cultural and commercial objectives of these industries. The first option does not recognise the nature of culture. Given the complexities of reality, the second seems impossible to achieve. The third option then should be pursued through compromises that take into account the many contradictions involved in regulation to achieve protection and openness, competition and social cohesion, exchange value and use value, and commodity production with a variety of meanings.

Conclusion

William Melody is a citizen of the world. He has lived and worked in many countries located in different continents: Australia, Canada, Denmark, the United Kingdom, The Netherlands, and the United States. He has had the opportunity to gather the information needed to develop a comprehensive understanding of various communication systems and societies. He has been very well equipped to conduct comparative research and he has put it into action, in many cases, including the broadcasting field. Comparative analysis is central for researchers who adopt an institutional approach. If institutions matter, their social and cultural differences must be taken into account in social scientific studies as well as in political strategies. Cave and Melody's 1989 article comparing the British, Canadian and American regulatory systems is a model for students in the field.

Historical and comparative approaches are equally seminal for an understanding of social, economic and cultural phenomena. Historical analysis provides us with insights into the uniqueness of every society and with a certain sense of necessity. Comparisons give us insight into the relativity of things and allow us to highlight the real similarities and real differences.

Cultural diversity is certainly a largely shared value. But it is understood in various ways and it does not have the same meaning in Canada, Europe, Brazil, the Middle East or China. It is the academic community's duty to contribute to a better understanding between people and comparative research is a good way to achieve this. Furthermore, the outcomes of such research can also help political leaders in their efforts to find the most workable solutions to the need to balance the goals of economic efficiency, social justice and cultural expression.

VI.4

Media Ownership – Does It Matter?

Werner A. Meier

INTRODUCTION

> Le travail scientifique, ne se fait pas avec les bons sentiments, cela se fait avec des passions. Pour travailler, il faut être en colère. Il faut aussi travailler pour contrôler la colère.
> (Pierre Bourdieu[11])

According to William Melody, the greatest threat to freedom of expression in the United States or elsewhere is the possibility that private entrepreneurs will always tend to monopolise the marketplace of ideas in the name of economic efficiency and private profit (Melody 1978). As a result of economic conditions or circumstances, access to the marketplace of ideas is restricted to a privileged few. Twenty-five years ago, when Melody made this statement, only 37 cities out of 1,519 in the United States had two or more daily newspapers. By 2000, the number had decreased and the one-newspaper town had become the national norm (Sterling 2000: xvi). In 1996, the number of the cities with two or more dailies declined to 19 or 1.3% of all American cities (Compaine and Gomery 2000: 9). Fewer owners have control over more newspapers and their circulation, and most of the media have been absorbed by large conglomerates, 'families' or chains.

In addition to ownership concentration of the mass media industry, content provision, packaging and distribution have also 'become a standardised production and marketing process in which the messages communicated are constrained and directed in both quantity and quality to meet the economic imperatives of that process' (Melody 1978: 219). What are the implications of this? The result is that what most people hear and see in the mass media is remarkably uniform in content and world-view (Neuman 1991: 130). Giddens goes even further when he calls for 'the democratising of the democracy'. He criticises the untamed power of media owners:

The media...have a double relation to democracy. On the one hand ...
the emergence of a global information society is a powerful democratising
force. Yet, television, and the other media, tend to destroy the very public

space of dialogue they open up, through relentless trivializing, and personalizing of political issues. Moreover, the growth of giant multinational media corporations means that unelected business tycoons can hold enormous power (Giddens 1999: np).

MISSING EMPIRICAL EVIDENCE

What does it really mean if 'ten colossal vertically integrated media conglomerates dominate the global media market' (Herman and McChesney 1997: 52)? What is the real harm of conglomerates, group ownership and the concentration of financial, political and social power in the hands of only a few firms? What standard of ownership concentration is economically and politically appropriate and what is socially acceptable?

The implications of alternative standards are controversial in regulatory circles, in popular public policy debates, as well as in communication and media policy studies. The question for media and communication studies is whether a meaningful contribution to a profound public policy debate can be made on the problem of media ownership and concentration.

The first paradox is that very few scholars do research on this issue in a holistic manner. Few complain about the missing analyses and debates within the scientific community. As Sterling (2000: xvii) observes, 'Surprisingly little research has been done – only marginally more than we could draw on two decades ago. Too much is assumed or anecdotal, merely suggesting results from ownership changes'. Compaine and Gomery (2000), editors of *Who Owns the Media* do not agree with this observation about neglect. Gomery (2000: 507) argues that 'no research in mass communication can ignore questions of mass media ownership and the economic implications of that control'. Unfortunately, mainstream communication researchers are not very often able, and not very often willing, to analyse the implications of media ownership and concentration. McQuail (1992: 116) argues 'despite the amount and ingenuity of research, it is hard to avoid the conclusion that it has failed to establish clear general effects from monopoly conditions on the balance of cost and benefits, in performance term. Where there is evidence, the effects seem to be quite small'. According to Picard (2001: 66), the primary reasons for the absence of research in this area is the lack of adequate data and funding.

The problem of media ownership and concentration is perceived quite differently from a political economy perspective. In this context, the mass media industry is said to play a significant role in legitimating inequalities in wealth, power and privilege. When the control of the flow of information, knowledge, values and images is concentrated in the hands of those who share the power of the dominant class, the ruling class will establish what is circulated through the mass media in order to reproduce the structure of class inequalities from which they benefit. The mass media industry is crucial for the creation of reliable information, knowledge, ideology and propaganda in contemporary capitalist societies. As Strinati (1995: 137) argues, its structure of ownership and control are equally crucial. Marxist 'critical studies' claim that the mass media 'assume an all-encompassing conspiracy by monopolist' (Gomery 2000: 507). Political economists like Golding and Murdock (1997) see the relationship between ownership and control as an indirect and mediated one. Control is not always exercised in a direct way, nor does the economic structure of media institutions always have an immediate impact on their output. Mainstream communication researchers criticise the conspiracy theories of the media on theoretical as well as on empirical grounds, arguing that political economists' views are supported only by anecdotal evidence.

The most common assumption is that the owners of the media influence the content and form of media content through their decisions to employ certain personnel, by funding special projects, and by providing a media platform for ideological interest groups. In the United Kingdom, Curran and Seaton (1997) conclude that the national press generally endorses the basic tenets of the capitalist system – private enterprise, profit, the free market and the rights of property ownership. In the United States, according to some media observers and scholars, a small group of powerful owners of six to ten media conglomerates, control what is read by the population, what people see and hear – or do not read, see and hear. Concerns are expressed about increasing corporate control of mass mediated information flows and about how democracy can function if the information that citizens rely on is tainted by the influence of mega-media (Bagdikian 2000; McChesney 2000; Herman 1998).

Overall, the implications of media ownership and concentration on a global scale are as follows. The global interlocking of the media industry and traditional corporate power creates a powerful cartel, which in turn encourages the spread of certain values (for example, consumerism, shareholder value, individualism, egoism, etc.). There are strong incentives for the displacement of the public sphere with commercial infotainment, reality shows and trivialised news programmes. This strengthens a conservative 'common sense' view of the world, eroding local cultures and communities.

Media Power's Expansion to Political Power

The economic strength of media conglomerates increases their position in society so that they become powerful institutions with substantial political power. According to Bagdikian (2000: viii) the largest media giants have achieved alarming success in writing the media laws and regulations to favour the interests of their corporations rather than the interests of the general public. In Europe and the United States, many cross-media ownership rules have been relaxed or have disappeared with the rise of a *laissez-faire* ideology within parliaments, governments and regulatory bodies. In the United States, '[w]here the FCC once had stringent ownership controls concerning radio and television stations most are gone and the rest have been liberalized' (Sterling 2000: xvi). The Federal Communications Commission once believed that programming diversification was necessary to maximise public service. It was argued that the greater the number of independent broadcasters, the greater the chances for achieving the desired diversity. Rules restricting common ownership of broadcast stations, and of broadcast stations in combination with other media forms, were adopted (Tillinghast 2000: 77). But media regulators have actually stimulated the ownership concentration process. In the United Kingdom, for example, a law, intended to restrain concentration, was manipulated into a Newspaper Preservation Policy under which in practice preservation meant, not less, but more, concentration of ownership (Tunstall 1996: 378).

As a consequence of the increasing influence of the media conglomerates on public opinion, there is little substantive coverage of the spectacular media deals in terms of the perceived effects of these deals. In most cases, journalists are directly affected but they do not report their own concerns (probably because of internal pressure). Media owners are keen to advertise the advantages of horizontal, vertical, diagonal and international concentration. State agencies play down the potential risks and threats of media conglomeration for the public sphere, in particular, and for democracy, in general.

Conclusion

Communication researchers should ask some basic questions. Why is it important to analyse the complex media ownership pattern in the United States, Europe and elsewhere? Why consider only who owns the media – should the role of managers and journalists also be examined? What does the assembling of available ownership data tell us? Should we examine media concentration from market and public sphere perspectives? What can we learn from the application of both political economy and institutional economic perspectives, and from corporate media and media power approaches? What are the relevant data and how can we access these data? We need to analyse and evaluate the implications of changing patterns of ownership for media content, the economy and audiences.

The giant media owners are an important subject for research in order to asses what they do with their acquired financial power via their media outlets and content platforms (Cranberg et al. 2001). Since the government role as regulator has declined substantially over the years in Europe and in the United States, we need to analyse the changing power relation between government, regulatory bodies and a converging and booming media industry. An overview of a converging field is essential to assess how interlocking contracts and ownership agreements influence the content of the media.

Research is needed to assess political outcomes and alternative ways in which the media can be made more accountable to all the mediating institutions of civil society. This is a project that would seek to transform the corporate media industry into an independent media trust that would strengthen the public media system to secure both the public interest and democracy. To cite John Dewey: 'Talk of democracy has little content when big business rules the life of the country through its control of the means of production, exchange, the press and other means of publicity, propaganda and communication'.

Latin American Media:
A Long View of Politics and Markets

Elizabeth Fox and Silvio Waisbord

INTRODUCTION

The Latin American model of commercial broadcasting superficially is quite similar to that developed in the United States. This model consists of privately-owned, commercially-financed radio and television stations with one or more large companies controlling a significant market share. Early American investments in Latin American radio and television stations facilitated the adoption of this commercial broadcasting model, and the region's media were internationalised many decades before globalisation became a buzzword in political and academic circles.

Paradoxically, the Latin American media were both unregulated and highly controlled. The ruling elite demanded economic growth and political stability, satisfied by a docile commercial broadcasting system under their political thumb (Fox 1997). In some countries, alongside precocious commercialisation, nationalism also shaped how the media developed. Factions within governments and progressive social movements pushed for increased state control of domestic radio and television in order to ensure domestic content and national, rather than foreign, ownership. These nationalist measures were largely successful when motivated by the need for increased political control of the media but largely unsuccessful when motivated by considerations of public service or preserving national culture (Waisbord 1995).

EARLY PUBLIC SERVICE

Government censorship quickly became the norm in Latin American broadcasting. The state imposed controls on the political content of the media through censorship, licensing, and government paid advertising. State interference in the media began early, for example in Brazil in the 1930s under Vargas, in Argentina during the *decada infame*, and in the first years of radio in Peru.

In some countries, radio, and later television also were seen as ways to integrate new populations into the culture or economy of the country. In 1924, for example, the Mexican Government set up a radio station in the Ministry of Education. Ten years later, President Lázaro Cárdenas (1934-1940) donated a radio receiver to all agricultural and workers' communities to enable them to listen to the courses, book reviews and concerts transmitted by the government radio station.

Some of these earlier ideas about public service broadcasting resurfaced in the late 1950s and early 1960s. Development communication focused on the use of broadcasting to provide education, information and modern values to the 'traditional masses'. UNESCO, the Alliance for Progress, and the Organization of American States funded communication equipment and programmes to use the mass media for health, education, rural development and family planning.

In 1966 Colombian President Carlos Lleras used foreign aid to set up an educational television programme to complement regular classroom programmes. In 1968 the Mexican government launched Telesecundaria, an open-circuit educational television system for secondary schools. Efforts at educational and public service broadcasting flourished as long as foreign financing and domestic political support were forthcoming. When funds and support dried up, public services languished in the backwaters of official bureaucracies.

The endorsement of free market economies by the dictatorships that swept Latin America in the 1970s further spurred broadcasting's commercial as opposed to its public service growth. When authoritarian governments were able to forge a close relationship with national broadcasting industries, strong media monopolies developed. This was the case in Brazil and Mexico where domestic broadcasters grew powerful under the protection of strong, authoritarian states. Brazil's rulers worked closely with private radio stations that they censored and, in part, directly controlled, and later with commercial television, notably TV Globo, which they helped create and had no need to control. The Brazilian media eventually proved the stronger partner; outlasting the military and successfully rolling their loyalties over to the civilian governments that followed (Sinclair 1999). The relationship between government and the media in Mexico was the natural outgrowth of the radio broadcasters' early bond with the state and, in some cases, ownership by the country's political leaders.

Where the bond between broadcasters and the state was not possible, domestic broadcasting industries remained politically weaker and generally more fragmented. Peru, Argentina, and Chile have been paradigmatic cases of fragmented broadcasting industries. In Peru major swings in policy between *laissez-faire* and government intervention thwarted the consolidation of a strong domestic broadcaster. The most radical of these swings occurred between 1968 and 1980 under a nationalist military government that expropriated the media companies. In 1980 a civilian administration returned broadcasting outlets to their previous owners, hardened against government intervention and operating largely without competition.

Fragmentation of media ownership in Argentina began when the military who came to power in 1976 were unwilling to privatise the television stations that the Peronists had expropriated in 1974. The military distrusted the private media and preferred to spread the control of television and radio stations among the branches of the Armed Forces. The Menem government finally privatised the stations in 1989. The fragmentation of the Chilean broadcasting industry largely resulted from the decision to place television channels under state- and church-run universities rather than under the private sector. After General Pinochet's brutal take-over in 1973, the military kept the media under strict control and censorship, while, at the same time allowing commercial growth.

In the early to mid-1980s the Latin American military dictatorships started showing cracks, and the transition to democracy gained momentum. As civilian regimes replaced military ones, the region's media experienced significant transformations at many levels – technological, legal, policy, content, ownership and financial.

GLOBALISING FORCES

The globalisation process that profoundly reshaped media structures and dynamics world-wide in the 1990s did not spare the region, although privatisation, liberalisation and deregulation were not new to the region. Latin American media had long been open to international capital and programming flows and was dominated by commercial principles. What the globalising push of the 1990s did was to tip the balance further in the direction of the market, without downplaying, let alone eliminating, the role of the state and domestic politics.

The widespread introduction of technological innovations is a necessary starting point to analyse how globalisation relates to sweeping changes in Latin American media. Whereas some media technologies and industries declined, others exploded. More people gained access to television and radio sets than ever before while the region experienced one of its worst economic and social crises in contemporary history. The explosion in the number of radio and television households and the existence of 35 million video cassette recorders and two million satellite television subscribers suggest a media landscape substantially different from that of the early 1980s.

By the late 1990s cable had become a dynamic sector. It is estimated that there are more than 15 million subscribers in the region, a small number compared to the industrialised countries, but 20% of a total of 81 million television households. Cable television reaches over 50% of television households in Argentina, 25% in Chile and Mexico, and less than 10% in Brazil. Predictably, distribution patterns are socially stratified. In a region with persistent and deepening social inequalities, cable audiences are concentrated mainly among upper- and middle-classes.

These technological developments underpin policy decisions that shaped fundamental transformations in the organisation and operation of the media industries. These include: the formation of multimedia corporations; the decline of family-owned companies; the articulation between local, regional and international capital; the intensification of cross-regional trade of money and content; and the increase in the production and export of television programming.

During the 1990s the participation of state and public interests in the media shrank and market principles consolidated. Privatisation became the policy *du jour* in the television industry. Governments in Argentina and Mexico auctioned state-owned television stations that had been nationalised in the early 1970s. In Chile, private capital was authorised to bid for television licences, historically in the hands of universities. Private ownership was permitted in Colombia where before the state controlled television. The private sector also benefited from the new era of abundance of electromagnetic spectrum. The vast majority of the new radio and television frequencies were awarded to private bidders, and only a few to public organisations and governments.

These changes did not fundamentally alter some of the traditional dynamics of the media sector, most notably the lack of wide participation of civil society in the decision making process and, ultimately, in access to media organisations. Political democratisation did not bring a process of genuine democratisation of media ownership, content or control. Nor has public accountability become an integral part of the process by which media licences change hands. Public officials approached the politics of privatisation as a mechanism for political and economic gain. The old system in which the state had an all-pervasive role in the media, and especially in ownership, changed, but the *pro quid quo* of personal favours and clientelism remained unchanged.

The removal of cross-media ownership restrictions and the liberalisation of new media industries were other catalysts in a process of rapid concentration of information resources and consolidation of media corporations. Highly concentrated media companies are hardly new to the region. Televisa and Globo already held quasi-monopolistic positions in Mexico and Brazil, respectively. Policy decisions towards the end of the 1990s accelerated the process of concentration, in flagrant contradiction to constitutional rules banning the formation of monopolies and oligopolies in media industries. Policies opened new media sectors and strengthened the position of already dominant local groups. Argentina's Clarín Group and Colombia's RCN and Caracol received the plums of the privatisation of television stations in their countries. Privatisation also enabled companies with diverse industrial interests to move quickly and aggressively into television. Mexico's Elektra Group, for example, formed Azteca in its successful bid for state-owned Channel 13.

Cable and satellite television also entered into the fold of dominant companies. In Uruguay firms that controlled open television branched into cable. In Argentina and Brazil, where cable development was originally fragmented in numerous mom-and-pop companies, larger companies swallowed smaller companies, spearheading an intense and rapid process of concentration. The result was the formation of duopolies: the Clarín Group and CEI Group in Argentina and Globo and TVA in Brazil.

Regional media powerhouses took the lead in the development of satellite television. Approximately 30 satellites cover Latin America. Optimism about growing numbers of subscribers stimulated the launching of two regional satellite services in the mid-1990s. Both feature an alliance between global technology and media behemoths and the largest producers and owners of television in Latin America. Western media groups provide satellite connections, large international operations and extensive film and television archives; Latin American partners provide domestic experience and popular local programming.

A handful of companies now control the majority of media interests in Latin American countries. Most markets are dominated by two media behemoths: CEI and Clarín in Argentina, Globo and SBT in Brazil, Televisa and TV Azteca in Mexico, Venevisión and TVC in Venezuela. These large media companies from larger markets have inroads in medium-sized and smaller countries.

United States cable powerhouses such as TCI and Liberty Media have been particularly interested in expanding into countries with high, actual or potential numbers of subscribers and television households. Argentina has become a regional launching pad for pay-television business. The 1994 Argentina-United States trade agreement of reciprocal investments paved the way for the entry of

American investors. The 1995 Cable Law initiated important changes in Brazilian pay television. By increasing foreign ownership to 49%, the law shook off Brazil's tradition of media protectionism and attracted the interest of global companies.

Latin America also has been affected by the world-wide phenomenon of global financial companies entering media markets. Goldman Sachs, Citibank and the buyout firm Hicks, Muse, Tate & Furs own substantial media interests and programming sources. In need of capital to bankroll acquisitions, maintain expansion, and keep ahead of competitors, domestic groups reached out for capital from financial firms. Citibank's dominant position in the Argentine media, for example, followed the decision of the Menem administration in the early 1990s to privatise state-owned companies. One of the major creditors of Argentina's public debt, Citibank, was able to trade public debt titles for public interests.

The formation of conglomerates coupled with media globalisation accelerated the transition from family to corporate ownership of media companies. The removal of protectionist legislation, the easing of the circulation of global capital, higher barriers to entry in media markets, and the need for large amounts of capital to finance conglomerates made the long term survival of family ownership impossible.

Local Content

Far from reinforcing Hollywood's historical pre-eminent position as the *lingua franca* of Latin American television, more demand for television programming has resulted in some interesting developments. The number of domestic and regional television hours has increased remarkably throughout the region. The decrease in costs of video technologies and production inputs removed important obstacles that, particularly in the early days of television, discouraged local productions and overwhelmingly favoured cheaper American imports. Television stations and networks, particularly in metropolitan areas and large markets, now own state-of-the-art studios.

Local productions are not cheaper than Hollywood fare. Still, networks, and stations' preferences for local shows encourages local production. Local content consistently performs better than regional or American productions in audience ratings. Only in countries where the market is too small to cover costs and one-hour episodes of foreign productions command between US$ 500 and US$ 800, do imported shows tend to predominate.

Finally, local productions offer the opportunity to reap gains in ancillary markets. The opening of international markets in the 1990s and the expansion of demand for Latin American content (mainly tele-novellas) were important incentives for local production. The exportability of content has been a constant concern for Televisa, Globo and Venevision, companies that in the late 1970s and in the 1980s were trailblazers for regional producers around the world. Lately, other companies based in medium-sized audio-visual markets also have successfully exported their productions.

As a region, Latin America confirms the conclusion that markets with a substantial number of television households coupled with large advertising investments and gross national products offer better conditions for the development and consolidation of a domestic audio-visual industry than those without. As some authors have concluded, these factors are the comparative advantages that account for the dissimilar development of media industries across markets. Brazil, for example, offers more propitious conditions for the consolidation of an indigenous audio-visual industry than Panama or Nicaragua.

By reducing the role of the state and removing restrictions preventing or limiting foreign participation, globalising policies deepened disparities among media markets in the region. Globalisation contributed to the consolidation of a three-tier structure formed by large producers and exporters of audio-visual content based in Brazil, Mexico and Venezuela; medium-sized producers and exporters in Argentina, Chile, Colombia and Peru; and modest producers with virtually no exports in Bolivia, Central America, Ecuador, Paraguay and Uruguay.

If global patterns of television flows need to be understood as a 'patchwork quilt' (Sinclair et al. 1996), Latin American television suggests that flows inside regional and geolinguistic markets also need to discriminate among complex inflows and outflows. There is not a single, dominating centre that exports content to the rest of the region but a Latin patchwork quilt, formed by multilayered flows of capital and programming. Intra-regional trade of television shows and formats, and ownership and production partnerships among regional and global companies suggest that globalisation is not unified in terms of programming or capital flows. Instead, it is a highly uneven process that affects each media market differently.

Conclusion

Global capital and programming moves easily into weaker and smaller markets with low production, and more aggressively in partnerships with local powerhouses into advertising-rich countries with large, actual or potential, audiences. Not all regional media companies are on an equal footing vis-à-vis globalisation. To some, globalisation has been a boost to business; to others, globalisation has facilitated the entry of powerful competitors and challenges. The trajectories of Globo and Televisa show that securing a dominant position at home through extensive horizontal and vertical integration and close contacts with political powers is fundamental for regional and global expansion.

Globalisation exacerbates pre-existing characteristics and accentuates differences. It facilitates the expansion of already dominant media companies in domestic, regional and international markets. While large countries now produce a substantial amount of televisual content, smaller countries continue to experience enormous difficulties. Globalisation augments regional programming traffic due to the rising demand for more television hours created by the explosion in the number of cable and satellite channels.

After decades of governments promoting state-owned media, threatening private owners with nationalisation, and toying with projects for media reform, globalisation signals the consolidation of commercial media systems and the end of alternative models. But states and governments are hardly the losers in globalisation. They are still able to keep the media on a short leash by negotiating the terms of business practices and defining the workings of media markets. In contrast with past decades of authoritarianism and state-owned media, they no longer control broadcasting stations or overtly restrict media content. They are still able to pull the levers that define the conditions under which businesses operate.

Markets and states, business and politics, local and international forces long have been intertwined, locked in a more confrontational or more peaceful relation depending on the politics of day. Domestic politics are not accessory to global dynamics but, as it has been since the early beginnings of Latin American broadcasting, continue to be fundamental mediators and articulators in the interaction between national and supranational forces.

Towards an Information Society: The Need for a Policy Perspective

Binod C. Agrawal

INTRODUCTION

In this contribution I synthesise some of the dominant paradigms of change and the social implications of the rapid expansion of communication and information technology (ICT) and telecom services. I call for clear policies to steer the societies in India and South Asia in a desirable direction.

COMMUNICATION: CHANGING SCENARIO IN BROADCASTING

The most visible and perceptible change can be observed in the field of television and radio, where one out of three households in India has access to television and almost every household has a radio. Twenty years ago, total television ownership in India had not reached even three million and only one out of 80 households had access to television. Only the government-owned black and white television channel was accessible in selected urban and rural areas. Radio ownership in India had achieved greater penetration, particularly after the transistor revolution.

The reach of television has increased as a result of satellite and cable television distribution systems, and now more than 70 colour television channels owned by both private and government-supported corporations are on offer. Radio has been privatised, but private investment in radio programming remains limited. Information, both news and entertainment, continue to be invisibly regulated and controlled by government policies and local conventions that have evolved over several decades. Radio listening and television viewing, and especially the consumption of indigenously produced cinema, have been the prime movers of social change. People, by and large, whether political workers, social scientists, or technocrats and technologists, consider television to be an important means of mobilising change. In this respect, the expansion of television has helped to accelerate the process of change and is leading to the adaptation of life styles. This process is punctuated by the arrival of new material goods from international markets as a result of privatisation and the globalisation of the Indian economy.

Television has, to some extent, influenced the daily routines of the viewers who are no longer bound by sunrise and sunset to regulate their daily routine. There seems to be a major shift from a broadly agrarian to an industrial and information society. Changes are also evident in several social domains of Indian life where food habits, clothing, leisure, recreation, mode of travel and inter-personal communication have undergone modifications.

Three issues are being debated in various academic, political and social circles where fears have been expressed about the 'homogenisation of the multilingual and multi-ethnic cultures', 'undesirable western cultural influences due to transnational satellite television' and 'increasing consumerism and individualisation'. However, the sporadic observations generated by a limited number of research initiatives and cross-regional comparisons do not permit definitive conclusions about the implications of the changes that are occurring. There is no clear direction of change although there is a fair amount of change visible among the rich as compared to the poor. In spite of all the technological expansions, individualised television viewing, a preference for 'Direct to Home' television has remained extremely limited as compared to collective and family viewing of television. Much remains to be understood about the nature and growth patterns of television viewing and, so far, access, rather than ownership, has been emphasised by policy makers. It seems there is a lack of will and effort to understand the cultural process of broadcasting and to develop concomitant policy guidelines to chalk out directions for desirable culturally compatible societal changes.

INFORMATION TECHNOLOGY: RISE AND FALL

The most remarkable and visible signs of change that have steered the Indian economy can be seen in the domain of the information technology and computing industries. The rise and fall of information technology companies and education and job opportunities were pervasive across the country in the decade of the 1990s. This period saw a rapid rise in economic gains, the large-scale migration of young people in search of new opportunities mostly to the United States, and the appearance of innumerable information technology companies, educational and training institutions and placement services. Suddenly, in recent years, there has been an upsurge in international travel. By the turn of the century, equally important was the decline of all these developments due to a global recession which has adversely affected further investment in the ICT industry or the 'new economy'.

Pervasive ICT applications have penetrated, and continue to penetrate, all walks of Indian life and have begun to influence the daily lives of the people. Formerly extremely difficult to access, civic and administrative data such as centuries-old land records are now quickly accessible via computers. Jobs that took several months to complete, now take a few hours when the work is computerised. Services are faster such as in the case of simple receipts or railway reservations which are now available in the form of computer printouts. The process of computerisation is underway in earnest in various sectors including administration, business, education, services and the manufacturing industry. This has certainly made life easier in India for a good number of people in both urban and rural areas. Computer automation also has its mystical influence on many people who believe that tampering with information and cheating have been reduced as a result of automation.

The long-term influence of these developments has yet to be assessed or deeply understood. However, the champions and enthusiasts of information and communication technology and the business leaders are all vigorously pushing the idea of the information society. Many believe that ICT solutions are the panacea for all the social, political and economic ills of society. Yet, it is undeniable that educated youths, and elderly men and women, have begun to invest time, energy and money to become computer literate and to gain mastery over information technology. Information technology, by and large, has a small number of individual owner users as compared to a large number of users who access the services in cyber cafés, private institutions and in the public domain. This suggests the direction in which the future of the information society in India will move. Current policies and government efforts are helping to achieve improved access more than to promote ownership of ICT, though clear policy guidelines have yet to be formalised. Whether such efforts will lead to major structural changes and steer the very fabric of Indian civilisation has yet to be seen.

TELECOM: RAPIDLY CONNECTING PEOPLE

Since the 1980s, more than any South Asian country, India has taken a long leap in communication, information technology and telecom services. The floodgate of convergence technology has submerged the entire nation. In any nook and corner of India, whether on urban streets or on dusty village roads, one can access a telephone to reach out to anywhere in the world. More than ownership of the telephone, access to the telephone as a shared utility and service is important, but it is essential that it be available at a continuously declining cost. Telephones have helped to overcome the literacy barrier as illiterate rural women can communicate with their spouses who are working elsewhere using public phones. The innovations of the pager and the mobile phone added to ever-increasing communication access for a few owners of such facilities. Increased telecom access and the growth in the availability of mobile phones with value added services have brought a quick death of pager services in India. These rapid changes are also influencing the very social fabric of the Indian cultural life and the business and organisational ethos that were previously quite immune to external pressures.

The telecom sector continues to grow rapidly, especially since the privatisation of the telecom sector in India. This has created a need for trained workers and increased the service sector requirements within the country leading to the creation of new educational institutions to cater to the need for specialised training. The outcome seems to be horizontal sharing of information among people over a much larger geographical region. This could lead to a gradual decline of vertical communication between information 'haves' and information 'have nots' in the country. Current policies are helping to promote healthy competition and the expansion of services, but without a vision of the future of the Indian society, this needs to be carefully reviewed with the goal of giving equitable access to the large majority of people.

Conclusion: Policy Perspective

Societies in South Asia, according to many observers, continue to be impervious to major technological changes. The multiple images that appear of South Asia are of an historical continuity of several millennia with multiple religions and highly stratified and linguistically diverse social groups. Communities generally continue to maintain a high level of autonomy and to live within their own created worldview. Changes in the social milieu and in communication patterns, in information technology and telecom services are expected to have diverse effects. This can be seen very clearly even by casual observers. South Asian society is clearly now divided between those who are part and parcel of the newly emerging information society and the large majority who are untouched by the benefits of ICTs and telecom services. Policy makers remain somewhat indifferent towards creating a policy for the equitable distribution of the benefits of the new technologies and services. Policy efforts remain a patchwork in response to demands by people for measures to protect them from the onslaught of the communication revolution.

Most of the policy efforts so far by the government are in response to multinational pressure, especially the international agencies and loan giving institutions. Policy reforms have somewhat ignored the cultural and economic reality in the country. These efforts, without doubt have helped to encourage the rapid privatisation of communication, information technology and the telecom sector, but without much serious thought about their overall impact on the South Asian societies, especially India. There is a serious need for analysis within the framework of a vision of the future information society that one would like to have. This should help to formulate policy within the framework of the democratic constitution of India.

Media Policy and the Public Interest

Marc Raboy

INTRODUCTION
In the courses I have been teaching on media policy over the past ten years or so, I typically begin by having students read William Melody's 1990 article, 'Communication Policy in the Global Information Economy: Whither the Public Interest?' Reacquainting myself with this piece each Autumn, I am always amazed at how forward-looking and synthetic it is. Melody looked at media policy as a global domain that cuts across national, transnational, local and regional fields, and posed the fundamental question of a global public interest. His groundbreaking work in this area continues to act as a beacon.

Perhaps it was his parallel interest in the media and the telecom industry that made Melody one of the first to anticipate the emergence of a new global communication environment, which would require a reframing and refocusing of communication policy issues. As old institutions and practices were revamped, new ones would need to be invented, but the overarching issues remained the same. Regulatory frameworks, in particular, would need to be retooled in the light of new phenomena such as economic liberalisation, technological convergence and the erosion of the power of state authorities. But the goals that these regimes had been conceived to achieve would remain in place as long as societies continued to consider them valid.

GLOBALISATION AND NEW REGULATORY PARADIGM
In an era marked by the multiple challenges of globalisation, attempts to define and promote public policy with respect to communication are typically met with scepticism. Globalisation refers here to a context marked by a diminishing role of national governments, increasing transnational concentration of corporate power, the shrinking of constraints of time and space, challenges to conventional thinking about identity, the emergence of new global networks, and the progressive establishment of a new political system of global governance. One of the clichés of this era is that the emergence of a world media system has rendered attempts to regulate media at the national level obsolete. This is still far from a *fait accompli*, and debates over the changing role of the nation state with respect to media are ongoing everywhere. Less apparent but increasingly present in public and

academic debates, are the signs that the global media system is generating its own unique new forms of influencing communication.

In a broad historical perspective, however, what is really new here? Radio, in its infancy, held out much the same promise that is attributed to the Internet today. In order for it to function appropriately, the leading national governments of the day had to meet together and negotiate a series of international agreements specifying the use of the radio spectrum. They allocated its resources to the trust of designated authorities. These authorities then established various types of rules and regulations appropriate to meeting specific public policy objectives.

What distinguished that era from the present one is that radio (and later, television) was regulated according to a logic marked by channel scarcity. Today's media environment is characterized by information abundance. Rather than indicating that media policy is no longer necessary, information abundance and the new problems it generates, require us to think in terms of a new media policy paradigm.

In this new paradigm, regulation still has a role to play in ensuring equitable access to distribution markets for producers and consumers, and in ensuring that the means of communication can be channelled towards social and cultural objectives. Consider the new meaning that needs to be given to one of the classical goals of communication regulation – a concept fundamental to much of Melody's work – *access*.

Access is one of the key concepts of models that see communication technologies as instruments of social and cultural development. In general, this requires mechanisms to ensure accessibility to channels of production and distribution for all those capable of rallying a minimal public, increasing interactivity in the relations between creators and their publics, and providing for feedback that can ultimately result in corrective measures.

To illustrate the complexities of thinking about access, consider what happens when conventional broadcast media and telecom technologies converge. The notion of access has traditionally meant different things in broadcasting and in telecom. In the broadcasting model, emphasis is placed on the receiver, and access refers to the capacity to choose from the range of content on offer. In the telecom model, emphasis is on the sender, and access refers to the capacity to use the means of communication to send messages. Within these two models, public policy and regulation have been recognised as necessary social measures for guaranteeing access.

In the new media environment, a hybrid conception of access is necessary, and public policy will need to promote a model of communication that combines the social and cultural objectives of established institutional forms – not only broadcasting and telecom, but also libraries, the education system and so on. Realising the social and cultural potential of new media requires ensuring maximum access for people to the means of communication *both* in their capacity as receivers and as consumers of services *and* as producers and senders of messages.

A policy model directed at maximising the potential of post-convergence media should therefore address the following: how to ensure access to both available content and the means of communication; how to balance universal services and costs that can be left to users; how to guarantee free choice and fair access; how to distinguish between public communication and private information; how to promote both cultural and economic development; how to situate the user as both citizen and consumer; and how to facilitate both public participation in society and an improved quality of life.

These issues would once have been addressed in each country at the level of a national regulatory authority. The new environment, however, is characterised by the fact that communication policy is no longer 'made' at any clearly definable location, rather, most significantly it is made across a range of sites (see Raboy 2001). Specific policy issues, such as copyright or rules governing property transactions, or Internet regulation, migrate from one level to another, often typifying the flashpoint of conflicts between jurisdictions. Global organisations, such as the World Trade Organization, have superseded national bodies as supreme instances of policy definition and enablement. Exclusive multilateral clubs, such as the OECD or the G-8, impose their own agendas on other non-member economies without being democratically accountable to their own national constituencies. International trade accords, such as the North American Free Trade Agreement, further constrain the capacities of participating states – while, paradoxically, the nation state continues to be the main location for media and communication policy debate.

Effective Policy Intervention

This complex and multifaceted general structure makes it extremely difficult to intervene effectively in the new policy environment to promote access or other policy goals. The overriding issue in communication policy is thus the issue of *governance*: how and where will decisions about the future evolution of the system be determined and, crucially, who will be involved?

Approaches to communication governance traditionally have spanned the spectrum from the authoritarian to the libertarian, with a broad middle ground covering such institutions as public service broadcasting, post, telephone and telegraph administrations and commercial media (see Golding 1998). In practice, virtually every modern communication system in the world developed within a regime that was circumscribed and characterised by some degree of national regulation. This is now in flux.

'The changing structure and role of the media needs serious analysis and reconceptualisation', Melody wrote in a contribution to a Canadian research project in 1994.

Within this broader framework the media can contribute to cultural development and democratisation. But if the focus of analysis is constrained to the traditional notion of public service broadcasting and attempts by national regulators to force transnational corporations to promote local culture, it will be attempting to impose yesterday's institutional structures on tomorrow's information society
(Raboy et al. 1994: 99)

The new institutional structures are not yet clear, but it is clear that they will involve a range of actors and will transcend national borders. Something akin to a global civil society may well be emerging, but for the moment its links to power and influence are tenuous. At this point, the only actor that has been managing to pursue an agenda with anything approaching consistency is the transnational private sector and concrete policy developments at every level are still being driven essentially by economic concerns.

New media have opened the possibility for unprecedented freedom of expression and information flow. However, if we are not careful, freedom from state control will be replaced by an even more insidious form of corporate control. Unlike state control, corporate control is first of all structural; it is built into the architecture of information systems, by designs intended to maximise the possibility for efficient and streamlined profit-taking, rather than effective uses (Lessig 1999).

A regulatory model for communication governance is the appropriate policy choice for promoting a new global approach to defining the public interest with respect to the media. This raises the question of the legitimacy of intervening in a sector which ought, by definition, to be free. There is not necessarily a contradiction between regulation and the value of freedom. It all depends upon what is regulated and how one decides to regulate – as well as on the basis upon which regulation is justified (Hoffmann-Riem 1996).

Conclusion

As Cave and Melody (1989) pointed out, the main justification for regulating communication is that regulation provides an opportunity for meeting non-market public policy objectives. This is especially important in a context where the meeting of such objectives has to be spread across a range of organisations within the complex world system that we have today.

In general, the role of regulation should be to promote the public interest with respect to the media and communication on an ongoing basis, and with regard to specific issues. This is too fine a job to be done by governments in the course of their general activities. It cannot be left to the media organisations themselves, for they necessarily have vested interests. The marketplace is too blunt an instrument. Citizens can individually, and through their collective organisations, articulate expectations, but they have no power for implementing these. What is the solution?

Thinking on this question tends to generate new variants on an old theme: terms like self-regulation and co-regulation seek to express what is essentially the hybridisation of the classical regulatory process based in a state-sanctioned, more or less independent public agency. In the new media environment, regulation will have to be negotiated between a range of actors, including state, corporate and civil society representatives. The point is that, in the sphere of communication, there will always be some form of regulation. To imagine things otherwise is at best naïve, as Melody might have put it.

VI.8

Radical Media Projects and the Crisis of Public Media

John D. H. Downing

INTRODUCTION

My initial purpose in this contribution is to propose that the endless e-mails circulated in recent years in the United States exhorting recipients to save the Public Broadcasting Service (PBS) and the National Public Radio (NPR) from their demolition by Congress are akin – along with the sacralisation of the British Broadcasting Corporation (BBC) – to playing a string quartet as the Titanic is sinking,[1][2] with the exception that, if the 1997 movie version is to be believed, those musicians were attempting to assert the dignity of cultural achievement in the teeth of the haphazardness of human life, whereas these desperate laments are simply in denial of the effective evaporation of what they are seeking to defend. To mix my metaphors furiously, we are invited to surround and defend an empty Trojan horse.

There are numerous voices that have evidenced my case in relation to public radio and television in the United States, most notably McCourt's (1999) richly detailed study of National Public Radio and Public Radio International, and Starr's (2000) case studies of struggles to push public television to fulfil its national mandate. McCourt (1999: 104) sums up the situation with an admirably pungent comparison.

Like the Catholic Church in the Middle Ages, the CPB [Corporation for Public Broadcasting] remains an overarching, if often ineffectual, authority. Rather than on holy writ, its mandate is based on the heated subjectivity of politics and the cold objectivity of dollars and demographics.

Thus, there is every reason to look elsewhere for creative contrahegemonic media, particularly to the radical video movements of various countries and to what is sometimes called community radio, but also, most recently, to the Independent Media Centres (IMCs) that first sprang up during the anti-World Trade Organization (WTO) movement in Seattle in November 1999 and have since become an international phenomenon. There is, moreover, a fundamental argument from a human rights principle for ensuring that digital information opportunities do not become the virtually exclusive property of the already privileged (Mansell 2001).

The term 'contrahegemonic' is drawn from a broadly Gramscian and Benjaminian conceptual framework. Beyond this, there are different versions and indeed visions of how such contrahegemonic media do and should operate in practice. Three of these are: the counter-information model (Baldelli 1977; Hammond and Herman 2000); the Bakhtinian model (1968/1984) of earthy and ribald popular cultural expression; and the public deliberation model developed by Habermas (1996).

Such media cannot be what public broadcasting has been at certain points in the past in Britain or in the United States, as though we were merely called upon to replace a new toner cartridge in the same printer. But these movements and their media exist, there is every reason for them to grow, and effective strategies to foster and multiply them need to be developed as a pressing priority.

A Personal Historical Note

Along with others, whether in, or like myself, out of the Leicester University Centre for Mass Communication Research and the Birmingham University Centre for Contemporary Cultural Studies, I cut my critical media researcher's teeth in the early 1970s on attacking the BBC. My focus was the almost comprehensive failure of BBC television to represent, with either respect or accuracy, British wage-workers' strikes for improved pay and conditions and, even more so, the situation or aspirations of people of colour in Britain (Downing 1980). The BBC did not perform noticeably any better than its regional commercial competitor television channels. And while it did not convey quite the racist and anti-labour viciousness of the majority of the press, its constructive achievements were few and far between.

People of colour rarely surfaced on BBC television, and when they did, it was normally in stereotypical roles and without voice, at least in any meaningful sense of the term. This was as true of Black South Africans and Zimbabweans desperately fighting their despicable regimes as it was of young Black people trying to survive in Britain's discriminatory labour market and against a militantly hostile police force. Racist politicians who took it as their mission to amplify popular racism, such as the late and much unlamented Enoch Powell, were given by contrast a huge amount of voice (Downing 1975). I compared BBC and other journalists of those days to the legendary weasel frozen motionless with fear when face-to-face with a fox, so emasculated were their responses to the racist demagogue.

Strikers were regularly depicted as a purely sectional interest, their battles with their employers having no possible beneficial outcome for wage-workers and their families in the rest of the economy. The role of government as of the BBC news professionals was supposedly to hold the ring as disinterested arbiters. Now this was the BBC, long before it turned itself into its current manifestation as a wham-bang global marketing operation.

If we turn our attention to PBS in the United States, albeit always a poor stepchild in comparison, then some may defensively hark back to its significant role in developing the Watergate affair to the point where it became understood as the crisis it was, and so cobble together an argument that it is a cultural beacon in peril.

Yet as a convenient index of why that argument will not work, we can take KLRU, the PBS station in Austin, Texas. As of 2002 KLRU had an enlightened and energetic Executive Director, and a number of pleasant and dedicated staff. But what did it do? It saturated us with increasingly lame 'British Comedies', ever limper Masterpiece Theatre productions bought from the BBC and continuing versions of *Austin City Limits*, now in its third decade and a money-spinning show whose logistics must have long ago stopped offering any challenges. This was no surprise. Market-force fundamentalism is not only an economic policy, but before that it is a way of life, a hegemonic regime of truth that necessarily excludes as it frames.

So what is it that we are trying to defend when we rush to circle the wagons around PBS? Or the BBC? Whatever the achievements of public broadcasting in the past and even the present, we are now in a different place and time. And the question inevitably is, where can we and should we go from here in order to produce and diffuse *high quality* media as *effectively* as possible?

What is 'High Quality'?

The hitherto unbridgeable chasm between aesthetically pleasing and culturally significant video is closing up and classic formulations such as García Espinosa's 1969 essay 'For An Imperfect Cinema', are no longer as urgently needed as they were when first made. In that essay, he vigorously challenged the ideology of technical 'perfection' as arbiter of cinematic quality, especially to the point where the budgets of dispossessed groups meant they could never imaginably make films supposedly worth watching. Brazilian *cinema novo* director Glauber Rocha (1995/1970: 89) equally attacked the pretensions of the left: 'The Tricontinental filmmaker should burn the theories that the neo-colonialist left tries to impose on us'.

Most recently Hamilton (2000) has reinvigorated this argument, urging that absolute priority should be given to alternative media that require no professional expertise to create, and warning against the snares of professionalisation. I do not follow Hamilton's exclusive emphasis on the simplest, preferring rather to envisage a spectrum running from the non-professional to the professional, but his emphasis, like Mansell's (2001), on the urgency of *widespread* public media empowerment is nonetheless tremendously important.

In an era of digital cameras and editing stations, however, with prices reducing constantly, the production of technically fluent video – lighting, sound, framing, montage, and so on – presents many fewer challenges of a purely financial nature. This is not to say that jump-cuts and other ruptures of canonical procedure should be ironed out, nor is it to say that producing a tough film on a difficult subject means the film-makers can live or do it without money. And beyond finance, political repression may also levy an extremely severe toll.

Nonetheless, accidental visual distractions and dislocations due purely to lack of finance are now more avoidable. For a public culturally inured to a certain level of glitch-free visual expression, this often matters, because it interferes with their appropriation of the textual content. While video- or film-makers may both chafe under this and also challenge it in creative and provocative ways, we cannot pretend our learned visual culture is otherwise. Art videos that seek specifically to re-orient our culture of visuality as though that by itself were a contrahegemonic moment, are perfectly valid and simultaneously, self-indulgent within and for a select community. Seepage outside that community is almost certainly the thinnest of trickles.

Content quality and watchability no longer have to be horses straining in different directions. The proliferation of film and video production courses in colleges, universities, cable access centres, community groups and schools means that at least elementary media-making skills are becoming far more widely diffused than ever in the United States, and similar trends are evident in a growing number of countries. Admittedly there are many shortfalls, not least the tendency towards a gender-divide in public video-making in favour of young males, who in turn have often glued themselves to hegemonic formats such as shoot-em-ups and worse still, violence against women. But their capacity to develop beyond that point is not necessarily packed in permafrost.

What is 'Diffusing Effectively'?

And so to distribution. For all the endless hours spent in low-to-no-budget production/editing/mixing, the final ratio of those hours to the number of times when (and people by whom) the video is subsequently watched, is a ratio mostly at the misery end of asymmetrical. The obverse of the dominance of the distributors in Hollywood, the networks and the multiservice operators, is the abysmal lack of distribution for the films and videos made from within the general public. Not all of them, by any means, deserve extensive distribution. But the following account from Juhasz's (1995: 216-7) notable study of AIDS-theme videos made in the United States gives some sense of the headache.

When factoring an AIDS video into the already small network of alternative distribution companies willing to distribute low-budget, progressive, educational video, things become even more difficult ... Most alternative AIDS tapes require some complex interweaving of these particularized distribution networks ... . Furthermore, the people who most need to see AIDS tapes ... are the disenfranchised members of our society who are not going to be reached by even the methods of progressive distribution ... which means nothing less than labour-intensive, pro-active strategies that take the tape to the people that need it ... . This means phone calls, follow-up, letter campaigns, follow-up, then long train rides to hard-to-find agencies, a small audience, and then, finally, few of the institutionally accepted markers of success ... . A *successful* screening finds a tape playing to fifteen members of an HIV support group or women's club, the tape introduced by the makers and then discussed afterward.

There are alternative approaches. Video documentaries can be taken out on the road. This can be a particularly powerful combination of distribution, exhibition and, most importantly, of debate and possibly ensuing activism following screening, but the process is tremendously time-consuming and – the more the locations – physically exhausting.

A different approach to the problem is taken by Rodríguez (2001) in her *Fissures In The Mediascape*. There she argues from a case study of women making videos in a poor *barrio* in Bogotá, that it is very mistaken to assume that only a nationally distributed video or film has validity – that only very large numbers of viewers are an acceptable index of meaningfulness. She instances from her own study in Bogotá how younger members of the *barrio* community, often somewhat scornful of their elders as still bound to rural ways, switched to a very new and from-the-gut respect for them once they became involved in filming the parents' stories of their harsh transition to urban life.

This is an important corrective to the 'huge audience' fallacy, which tends to lead to defeatist and fatalistic attitudes that go well beyond the 'pessimism of the intelligence' of which Gramsci once wrote. At the same time, there is no reason to lurch to the opposite pole and deny absolutely the value of international, national and regional distribution agencies and networks.

Critics may point to the limited nature of this form of distribution, and query whether classroom or other screenings outside a formal educational setting represent anything very significant. Yet to define the impact of working in higher education or in community or religious social action groups as a form of self-indulgent solipsism seems to me an unwarrantedly masochistic, almost suicidal judgement, that sociologically goes well beyond the evidence. There seems to be an audience assumption lurking unstated, safely disguised behind the shrubbery of academic analysis, namely that the capillary and molecular transformation of cultural life is equivalent to nothing happening at all. It represents a definition of media audiences curiously insulated from the analysis of social and political movements (Downing 2000).

A further network of distribution in the United States is constituted by cable community access centres. These centres cannot be trumpeted as automatic purveyors of compelling video visions. About a third of Austin's access programmes are from religious sources, mostly with no content beyond the politically quiescent, and the rules of the game have meant that syndicated racist neo-nazi programmes such as *Race and Reason* have also been part of the fare. But these centres do now exist, around 300 of them across the United States, and are part of the media landscape, even if potential could be much more interestingly realised than it has been. Whole series of Deep Dish TV programmes on the 1990-91 Gulf War, on the AIDS crisis, on the quincentennial of Columbus' invasion, on racism and imprisonment in the United States, and on many other topics, have found their way on to screens in localities nationally as a result – material that never could have found its path on to the mainstream broadcast networks.

In other countries some opportunities still exist, albeit flawed, such as Australia's Satellite Broadcasting Service, a multicultural channel operating since the late 1980s, and Canada's Aboriginal Peoples Television, seriously deprived of funds in the later 1990s, but still operating. And though public broadcasting internationally is experiencing problems, while it still lasts it would be foolish to ignore the sporadic spaces that it opens up.

Other Developments: Micro-Radio and IMCs

Micro-radio (Sakolsky and Dunifer 1998; Soley 1999) is the most recent expression in the United States and elsewhere of the much longer-running phenomenon usually referred to as 'community' radio (Girard 1992) and evinced in the World Association of Community Radio Broadcasters (AMARC) conferences <www.amarc.org>. The term 'community' is extremely fuzzy, but, in this instance, covers radio stations not beholden to government, private capital or other authoritative bodies. Some of the first low-power radio experiments were those conducted in Tokyo in the early 1980s (Kogawa 1985) and there are reckoned to be micro-stations numbering in some hundreds in the United States.

There was a battle for years with the National Association of Broadcasters (NAB), the American television networks' industry association, concerning their licensing. The Federal Communications Commission (FCC), having for years acted as the NAB's police arm in threatening and closing down these micro-stations, has moved to permit their licensing as long as they have not already been broadcasting without FCC approval. The point of these stations in heavily populated areas is that they can reach, and serve as a forum for, a relatively large but still locally-bound public. This network of tiny open-microphone stations in urban areas contains the potential to engage a variety of voices either rejected or corralled by major radio operations, now typically in the hands of mega-corporations. However, a variety of forces are jumping aboard this bandwagon, in the United States particularly, the religious right.

A major development, however, in 2001 was the emergence of Independent Media Centres (IMCs), with the Seattle IMC dating its origin to the massive protests against the World Trade Organization at the end of November 1999 (Downing 2001). To illustrate the rapid proliferation of IMCs, as of the end of 2001, 70 were operating in countries around the world <www.indymedia.org>. This figure represented an approximate 40% rise over December 2000, even though a handful had ceased operating over that year. While clearly they are still an overwhelmingly North American phenomenon, nonetheless this was a phenomenal growth rate. The organisational dynamism and imaginative use of a whole raft of media technologies in the IMCs make them one of the most potentially promising radical media developments anywhere.

Conclusion

The flood of small-scale radical media, past and present, constitute a contrahegemonic public sphere. They have done so on many levels, from German anti-nuclear media in the 1980s to the diaper-headscarves of the Mothers of the

Plaza de Mayo in Buenos Aires, from *dazibao* on Beijing's Democracy Wall in 1978 to Russian guitar-poets such as Vladimir Vyssotskii. They can be referred to collectively, but cannot be homogenised in either production, text or impact. Their consequences typically have been most visible at the height of social and political movements, but perhaps most pivotal when invisible, at the moments they have kept the tiny flames of contestation dancing when repression *and* cynicism *and* common sense alike dictated them to be a derisory, even suicidal, self-indulgence. Rather than lamenting what may be disappearing as public media, we need to investigate as thoroughly as possible the massive tapestry of contrahegemonic media, or citizens' media, and their relation to contested social movements.

Most illustrations of alternative media are in some sense hostile to capitalism, state repression, religious hierarchy, religious or economic fundamentalism, patriarchy, or sovietism. But we must also acknowledge the energy, insight and weight of radical rightist media in the public sphere. Three complications of this complex arena deserve to be flagged. First, these media and their backers are very far from being in synch with each other. Second, they are not all apocalyptic in tone, and this includes a number of the Christian fundamentalist operations. And, third, a pivotal question, yet to be properly researched, is the character and significance of the links between these extreme rightist forces and the more conventional right. A connecting thread among rightist media is that they represent the contrary to what C. B. MacPherson (1973) called 'developmental' power, which he contrasted with exploitative (or 'extractive') power. Developmental power signifies the public's ability to amass power to achieve secular, just, pro-human purposes. Extreme-right small and not so small-scale media have this in common; that they are not in the empowerment business but in the enslavement business. We wildly mischaracterize alternative media if we do not incorporate these too into our priorities for analysis. Small may not be beautiful, but it is surely able to subvert, for good or for ill.

VI.9

Towards a World System Perspective on Cross-National Web Research

Joseph Turow and Rivka Ribak

INTRODUCTION
The World Wide Web as a term and as a phenomenon embodies a number of fundamental tensions. The Web's reach is technically world-wide, but in practice it is accessible only to a small proportion of the planet's population. Its subject matter travels globally but is by necessity experienced locally. Moreover, language barriers and content filters actually hamper different populations from confronting, or linking to, different content. The World Wide Web is, in reality, neither world-wide nor a fully interconnected web.

Our purpose in this contribution is to gain insight into the dialectic between the Web's global and local faces by constructing it as a dialogue that is anchored within transnational political and economical bearings. We begin by outlining two views – the essentialist/universalistic and the social constructionist – that underlie opposing ways to understand the global Web. We then argue that neither of these perspectives recognizes the multi-levelled struggles that are taking place in many societies that define Web technology simultaneously in terms of local cultures and world markets. Finally, we suggest that a 'world system' perspective can be helpful in pointing toward ways to contextualise a society's technological development and human practice within global political and economic parameters.

CROSS-NATIONAL UNDERSTANDING OF THE WEB
Essentialist/universalistic research assumes that technology has inherent features that affect people and societies in predictable and inescapable ways. Such research studies note that the Web's basic components – computers, monitors, network connections – can be seen everywhere, as can the browsers, search engines, chat rooms and instant messaging systems that link millions of surfers world-wide. It is therefore concluded that the whole world is exposed to the same Web (an *essentialist* claim) and that effects, problems and solutions, are built into the technology and are generalisable to virtually all locales – a *universalistic* claim (Buckingham 2000).

The obverse, relativist, view is that the applications of technologies, and the social problems and solutions they raise, are constructed through social practice.

Investigations of the early reception of, for example, the telephone, radio and television in the United States and elsewhere suggest that, although they have distinctive technological features, the social meanings and controversies around these features developed over time through elaborate interactions among various constituencies and regulatory regimes (Marvin 1988; Silverstone and Hirsch 1992). From this perspective, the Web, in particular, subverts any attempt to construe it as a fixed variable. Because it changes over time, a user cannot surf 'the same' Web twice. Because it is (re)constructed differently through multiple languages and Web pages in various places, users from different cultures might realistically visit wholly separate virtual villages and neighbourhoods. Finally, because it is interactive, the Web allows for intertwined and mutually constitutive relationships between medium, text and consumers, audiences or users.

The most consistent herald of the essentialist/universalistic view is the commercial market research industry. Companies such as Ipsos-Reid, Roper Starch, and Taylor Nelson Sofres release a flood of commercially generated data about the Web that shows up in the press, especially the online press.[13] They identify the national populations as distinguishable less in terms of their indigenous beliefs and practices and more in terms of ownership and exposure, blending all into universal consumers who might be enticed to buy goods or information from a Web site once they gain access to it (Turow 2001). Similar assumptions show up in much United States academic writing on Web marketing or Web privacy without specifying that the real focus of interest is a specific manifestation of the phenomenon available to particular segments of American society (see Brin 1998; Wind and Mahajan 2001).

The contrasting, relativist, view can be found at the heart of almost all studies that involve close observation of populations' use of new media as well as in a growing number of cross-national academic surveys of media use. Sonia Livingstone (1998; Livingstone and Bovill 2001), for example, emphasises the importance of the socio-political and economic contexts in relation to an important project on young people and the changing media environment in Europe.

THE NEED FOR A THIRD VIEW

What both the essentialist and relativist perspectives have in common is their reluctance to explore encounters between local cultures and the Web in the context of transnational political and economic interests regarding the new technology. This limitation may seem clear in the case of essentialist thinkers, who privilege the Web's global impact with little attention to local context. But relativists also wear blinkers when it comes to understanding the interplay of the local with the transnational, even when conducting comparative analysis.

Livingstone (1998: 445), for example, practically rules out the possibility of cross-cultural research where countries are structurally interdependent or where one country may disproportionately influence the other when it comes to the adoption and arrangement of new media. She argues that 'to make ... comparisons [between countries] manageable in practice, the research should be restricted to modernized, western countries which are undergoing related sociopolitical changes; overlarge national differences would prevent observations interesting in one country being informative for another'.

The upshot of this guiding principle is that the dominant interest in reporting the results is on cross-national comparison without cross-national influence. In fact, four of the five studies presented in a *European Journal of Communication* issue devoted to the 12 country project headed by Livingstone (1998) treat the countries they compare as unrelated entities. They ignore the fact that many are geographically close to one another, many share languages and cultural products, and all belong to a European Economic Community that is developing pan-continental rules about electronic commerce, Internet privacy and a host of other activities that affect life on the Web.

Ironically, the only article that departs from this hermetic approach is one that compares the most geographically distant place in the study, Israel, with Denmark and France. The piece is concerned with 'how globalisation becomes embedded into the lives of children and adolescents in three very different countries' (Lemish et al. 1998: 554) and the authors conclude that 'the meetings between the global and the local can be those of coexistence and conflation rather than assimilation vs. isolationism'. While insightful, their analysis is nevertheless limited by blinkers regarding key questions that have been outside the province of the relativistic perspective: Where does the 'global' originate? What forces lie behind its interpenetration of the local? Does that interpenetration take place differently in countries that have substantially different socio-political and socio-economic environments?

A World System Perspective

To understand what a society's people think and do about the Web and why, we must contextualise its technological development and human practice within broad political and economic parameters. And, indeed, international economic competition is part of the contemporary Web in terms of both software and hardware. The developing relationships recall the core-, semi-periphery and periphery categories that Wallerstein (1984) and Skocpol (1984) have used in describing the hierarchy of the world system.

The Internet was developed by the American military and scientific establishments; its graphical Web interface was invented at an American university. Core-country corporate leaders such as Microsoft, Intel, AMD, and 3Com have situated outposts strategically in different parts of the world that reflect different positions on an innovation/cheap labour continuum. They mine nations in the core (in Europe and Japan) and the semi-periphery (in parts of Asia and South America) for their ability to contribute cutting-edge knowledge about hardware and software. They use countries at the periphery for their supply of inexpensive, stable and compliant manufacturing conditions. Independent firms in all regions vie to provide the large companies with component parts as well as to export their own innovations to Web-linked consumers (Kellerman 2000).

What is especially interesting about these relationships is that people in the semi-periphery often find it most profitable to create software and hardware that do not necessarily speak to their own practical and ideological concerns; instead, they address their products to their most prominent markets. Web privacy, security and child surfing, for example, are topics that have generated huge investments by consumers and Web firms in core regions. Firms in the semi-periphery must monitor these sensibilities, keeping up on debates regarding regulatory solutions and technological fixes that take place in front of United States regulatory agencies, the European Commission and within academic circles. This blurring of national and cultural boundaries is compounded by the large European and American polling organisations that aim to help global advertisers target Web users around the world. Their demographic and lifestyle categories, defined at the Euro-American centre of the global system, but increasingly relevant in its semi-periphery and even parts of its periphery, render traditional political distinctions obsolete.

These neo-colonial relationships between core countries, on the one hand, and semi-peripheral and peripheral countries, on the other, point to a neglected field of inquiry about the negotiation between the Web's global political economy and its local social construction. For example, if a semi-peripheral society emphasises high-tech exports that cater to Web needs in the United States and is surrounded by American popular culture about Web issues, should we expect that its members share the same sense of the Web's power, and its potential and problems, as members of the United States society?

This question implies propositions regarding comparative research that are quite different from the ones that Livingstone posits about the comparison of core countries. Here the emphasis is on sharply different socio-economic conditions (core vs. peripheral or core vs. semi-peripheral) and often sharply different political and cultural circumstances. It would undoubtedly be wrong, however, to assume from the outset a totalising influence of core countries on their suppliers. World system theorist Robertson (1997: 72) has noted that in contemporary capitalism the complex issues involved in formulating all sorts of social identities are bound up in complex interactions of global, often market-related, forces with local, also often market-driven, influences. He calls this 'the universalisation of particularism and the particularisation of universalism'. It suggests that cross-national studies of attitudes and actions around the Web must be alert to the flows of influence from many directions, at many levels, and across time.

The world system perspective has proven to be a useful lens for comparative analysis of parents' and youngsters' attitudes toward the Web in Israel and the United States. We started our project with an awareness that the positions of the two countries within the world system are strikingly different. The international economic and military influence of the United States places it at the core of the world system. Israel's regional military power, relatively high per capita income, and knowledge-based economy, places it between the edge and the centre, or at the semi-periphery, of the global hierarchy.

The two nations also have very different traditions of individualism, personal privacy and government and business responsibility. Yet Israel is interpenetrated by an American agenda on these issues. The country produces hardware and software for American (and, by extension, world) markets that must take US-based views on the topics into account. With relatively few Web sites in Hebrew, Israeli Web users navigate to sites based in the United States and communicate through applications, using software and hardware that (wherever produced) map onto an American ideology in general and concerns about privacy, in particular. Moreover, national press coverage and entertainment programming about the Web centre on American sensibilities regarding information disclosure and translate controversies over United States government and business into local parlance.

The world system perspective sensitises us to the following question: In the face of the countries' very different traditions of individualism, personal privacy and institutional responsibility, to what extent, and how, does Israel's US-centred (and somewhat export-oriented) business and media agenda find its way into individual Israelis' views and actions on those topics when it comes to the Web? This question certainly cannot be answered definitively through an initial foray into cross-national survey research. Whether and what portions of society are changed, how much, and what resistance there is to 'imported' views is a topic that requires comparative ethnographic field explorations, historical analyses and longitudinal studies.

While clearly complex, the topic of transnational influences is fascinating and important. The challenge that the world system perspective raises especially with respect to countries outside the core, but also to countries within it, is to relate people's attitudes and that which takes place locally, to the national and global socio-political system. That, metaphorically and practically, is what 'the Web' is really about.

Epilogue...

Economics of Infrastructures: The Ultimate Challenge?

Rolf W. Künneke

CHALLENGE

William H. Melody is the founder of the Economics of Infrastructures Programme of the Delft University of Technology, established in September 1997. He saw the Economics of Infrastructures as a new academic discipline that is distinct from traditional Public Utility Economics. His long and rich experience in this field, both as an academic and as a practitioner, is reflected in his innovative approach. Not surprisingly, many of the aspects of Melody's life work celebrated in this *festschrift* are evident in the design of the programme at Delft. The distinctive features of Melody's approach to the Economics of Infrastructures are:

- His generic approach to infrastructures. Traditionally infrastructures have been approached as distinct industrial sectors with fundamentally different technological and economic characteristics. Conversely, Melody puts emphasis on the commonalties with respect to regulatory regimes, network economics, industrial structures, consumer needs, national interests and public service obligations.

- His wish to contribute to solving real-world problems. The liberalisation processes of various infrastructures poses a broad range of policy challenges, including long-term dynamic efficiency, sustainable competitive market structures, the position of residential customers, and economic equity in a globalising economy.

- His wish to look beyond the traditional technologically determined infrastructures exemplified by physical networks of wires, pipelines, roads, waterways and others. In his view, information based networks with distinctive economic features constitute the infrastructures of the 21st century. Virtual networks replace physical networks.

- His aversion to traditional neoclassical economics. As Trebing, his academic mentor, remarks in this collection: 'Throughout his work he never hesitated to examine the shortcomings and abuses inherent in the application of neo-classical economics to the problems facing society'. Instead, Melody relies on Institutional Economics, which is much closer to the complexity of real world problems.

- His strong belief in interdisciplinary approaches. Economic allocation processes in infrastructures are influenced by technological design, regulation and market-related processes. Hence, understanding the economics of infrastructures requires an interdisciplinary approach that includes technology, law, policy and economics. The qualifications of the staff of the Economics of Infrastructures Section are reflective of this approach: they have backgrounds in physics, law, political science, and of course, economics.

- His inclination to contribute to the diffusion of knowledge, beyond his students in Delft. In this vein, he has developed courses for telecom regulators, with a specific focus on the problems and needs of developing countries; served as editor of the well-known journal *Telecommunications Policy*; and established LIRNE.NET an Internet based initiative to enable and stimulate the exchange of knowledge of the regulation of liberalised infrastructure industries.

Melody also established a tradition of annual international conferences on aspects of economics of infrastructures at Delft. Their themes, summarised in the remainder of this contribution, reflect the major research interests of the Economics of Infrastructure Programme.

INFRASTRUCTURES OF THE 21ST CENTURY

The ongoing process of world-wide infrastructure reform is the result of complex interrelations between changing technologies, market structures and institutional arrangements. In addition to the contributions of the individual elements, interrelations among them create innovative functions and even new infrastructures, enhancing socio-economic performance and creating new regulatory requirements.

Advances in information and communication technologies (ICTs) are an important driver of technological change in infrastructure industries. Traditional infrastructures such as transportation and energy now rely heavily on ICTs, among other reasons to improve system performances, enable individual pricing, allow for service based costing, and introduce new services such as road pricing and virtual utilities. Virtual utilities are small-scale power producers that combine their facilities using ICTs, enabling a more significant market position. The ICT infrastructure itself, which includes telephony and Internet, has proven to be very innovative in terms of new technologies (for example, wireless technologies) and customer services. But even beyond that, it has engendered an entirely new infrastructure: the information infrastructure. Information, or 'anything that can be digitised – encoded as a stream of bits' (Varian and Shapiro 1998: 3), is distributed through ICT infrastructures, and it is processed into knowledge by formal and informal institutions such as universities, research and development departments of firms or informal networks of researchers. Hence information infrastructures consist of technological and institutional networks that generate knowledge-based products and services that often have public-goods characteristics. For this reason regulation of these new infrastructures is desirable.

Rapidly changing market structures are another source of infrastructure reform. Adjacent to network-based regulated activities, there exist a wide range of commercial activities subject to market provision. Traditional infrastructure products such as electricity, gas, telecom and rail transport are supplemented or improved by newly developed services that contribute to a higher customer satisfaction. Vertically integrated infrastructure firms are forced to unbundle, and are looking for new synergies. Possible new business strategies include horizontal integration with comparable activities in other infrastructures (the multi-utility approach), or globalisation. But there are also opportunities for newcomers with technical expertise (for example, maintenance, metering, billing) or leveraging an existing customer base (for example, petrol stations selling electricity). The new market structures and customers' needs yield different technical and regulatory requirements for future infrastructures.

Telematics and the Economy of Information Societies

The key ambition is to understand the characteristics of the evolving new telematics-based networked economy and to assess implications for policy and strategy. These implications become visible in emerging flexible networked organisations, their linkages with electronic marketplaces, and in the new 'rules of the game' for competition and collaboration arising within chains of supply and demand. One starting point is the evolving new electronic marketplace, new trading relations and their implications. In the new economy the limits of markets are extended and the structure of markets and the conduct of trade are changing. The development of telematics networks has many economic aspects, such as viability and critical mass, market and industry structure, market attractiveness, and the potential for radical innovation in services and production. These and other influences will strongly affect firm strategies and government policies concerning investment in infrastructure, R&D priorities, innovation in new products and services, organisational choice and the quality of life.

Epilogue

CONVERGENCE

The sharp delineation between infrastructures was often thought of as a 'natural' consequence of the highly specific network structures in these sectors. Electricity cables could be used for one purpose alone, that is, the transmission of electrical energy. Correspondingly, electric or telecom wires, water and gas pipes, or railroad tracks determined the services the operators of these networks were able to offer. Technology seemed to be the decisive factor characterising these sectors. The economics of these infrastructures had common characteristics in that they were associated with various kinds of market failures, for instance, natural monopoly and positive externalities. Consequently, there was no room for competition or rivalry. For this reason distinctive institutional structures were established for each of these infrastructures. Institutions supported distinct technologies; the technologies justified distinct institutions.

The liberalisation of infrastructures has made the demarcations appear less rigid than commonly assumed. As one of its constituting features, liberalisation separates the operation of facility networks from other activities such as the provision of services. Generally the facility networks remain regulated monopolies whereas other activities in the value chain may develop into competitive markets. This offers new business opportunities. Although the technology remains more or less the same, railroad companies can become telecom operators, water companies can sell electricity, energy firms can not only combine gas and electricity, but also engage in activities such as insurance or banking services. Unexpected new suppliers such as environmental organisations, supermarkets, petrol stations or even churches may emerge. This blurring of the boundaries of different infrastructure services is referred to as 'convergence of infrastructures'. There are three specific fields of interest under this rubric:

- *The nature of convergence:* In addition to physical networks, there are newly developing virtual network economies, both on the demand and supply side. Therefore, it is expected that convergence will be part of a fundamental turning point in the technical and institutional development of infrastructure industries.

- *New business approaches:* Based on synergies attributed to convergence, new business approaches are being developed. Traditional infrastructure industries are disintegrating, but, at the same time, new opportunities for reintegration are emerging beyond the traditional business. For example, grocery stores, environmental organisations and trade unions are offering utility services, whereas traditional infrastructure firms are engaging in new activities such as credit cards, insurance, or shoe sales.

- *Regulatory challenges:* Government policies and regulation have to adapt to the changing conditions. Is there still a need for sector specific regulation or should there be regulatory convergence? What are the consequences for the effectiveness of regulation or for the scope of competition policy?

BEYOND THE MARKET

By definition, infrastructure industries are important for the economy, polity and society. They are generally understood to be network industries, characterised by high capital cost facilities with long life spans, the existence of some bottleneck features and network externalities. These characteristics have been used historically to justify the need for public planning. However, the traditional public or private monopoly model for provision of infrastructure services has failed to yield sufficiently wide penetration or adequate service quality in many parts of the world. Even in countries such as The Netherlands where high penetration and good reliability were achieved, the sector is thought to have fallen short on innovation. During the current period of transition from monopoly to liberalisation, public planning has become the neglected factor. The recent crises of infrastructure – accidents in the railroad system in the United Kingdom and electricity shortages in California – constitute evidence that not all in the old order needs to be abandoned. In particular, there may be justification for focused public planning that does not distort market forces, but instead complements them.

The function of public planning is twofold in the new market-centric environment. On the one hand, it concerns the design of markets and, on the other, the design of safeguards for special cases of market failure that cannot be addressed by the basic design of markets. The latter is the more controversial aspect of public planning. The public interest is often associated with objectives such as universal service, reliability, safety and fair pricing. In this respect, two fundamental questions need to be considered: 1) *To what degree is regulatory involvement required to guarantee the supply of these services?* For example, fair pricing might be the result of competition, and reliability can be understood to be a precondition for competitiveness in a well functioning market. 2) *Does liberalisation necessarily engender a need for redefinition of the public interest?* In the electricity sector, for example, the provision of reactive energy has been only very recently discovered to be an important service that large-scale production facilities used to provide without much attention. However, in largely decentralised systems, reactive energy is more difficult and costly to realise. There is also some discussion as to whether the availability of sufficient network capacity can be achieved by market processes alone. There also may be further tensions between the public interest as nationally defined and as seen from European Union or global perspectives.

Epilogue

What are the appropriate mechanisms to address the public interest in infrastructure industries? To what degree will public planning be both appropriate and necessary for the 21st century and what will the appropriate policy instruments look like? There is a broad spectrum of possibilities ranging from government provision of infrastructure services to loose government supervision of private sector activities. Although these policies are not new, they must be readapted to the changing regulatory and market regimes of liberalised infrastructure sectors. Ideally, the policy instruments will support competition without providing opportunities for private investors to shift risks to the public sector. A final complicating factor is that public planning has shown a tendency to preserve the economic and technical status quo. Allowing for dynamic efficiency requires a flexible system capable of generating new solutions for old planning problems. In this vein, we might optimistically anticipate the obsolescence of the need for public planning as new infrastructure concepts are developed and deployed.

Regulation and Innovation

Liberalisation affects the economic, organisational and technical performance of network industries. Changes in the institutional set-up of infrastructure markets modify economic incentives with respect to the design and management of infrastructures. Changes in economic parameters have repercussions for the choice of the hardware and the technical organisation of complex systems. Network components have to serve new or different purposes and it may be necessary to develop new network concepts. New and incumbent firms spend large amounts of money to demonstrate that they have become sensitive to customers' preferences and, thus, seek to enhance the quality of their services and the choice available to their customers.

Under these changing conditions, the safeguarding of the technical integrity, the public interest, and the coordination and planning of the long-term transition of existing infrastructures to systems that adequately meet future demand poses new challenges. The ambitions for sustainable development are another area of attention. In some cases, the consequences of these shifts are evaluated positively. Yet, elsewhere, the results of real world deregulation are giving rise to doubts about the chosen means and ends.

There is insufficient understanding of these processes of change. There is a need to reassess the role and functions of regulation to shape markets in liberalised infrastructures in order to improve the socio-economic performance of these industries. Regulation must contribute to technical and institutional innovation in these vital sectors. Three aspects require attention:

- *Networks and Imperfect Markets:* Networks generally give rise to various kinds of market failures and market imperfections that demand regulatory intervention or coordination of activities. What are the consequences of liberalisation for the technical functioning of infrastructures and innovation in governance and technology? How do they influence their performance?

- *Networks and Externalities:* Network based infrastructures are of fundamental importance to facilitate activity in the future society. The questions here include issues such as the economic, social and technological requirements for next generation infrastructures; the needs of an information economy; the requirements for sustainable development; the need to develop adequate performance indicators, and the consequences of ongoing globalisation for infrastructure design.

- *The Limits of Regulation:* What are the prospects for a different scope of regulation, including sector specific regulation, general infrastructure regulation for converged utilities, or even competition policy alone that is based on commodified infrastructure goods and services? How do these regulatory approaches relate to the performance of sectors?

The applicability of various regulatory paradigms must be assessed in order to provide policy makers, regulators and the regulated industries with sets of lenses to *identify* and *select* the technical, organisational, economic and regulatory elements of the supply system that are relevant to their operation. This includes performance indicators such as quality, security, convenience, standards for market behaviour, routines for solving problems and the selection of technologies, procedures and rules for training people and advertising campaigns, etc. In contrast to the limited neoclassical paradigm of regulation, these approaches open up new possibilities for management and policy intervention, and for the interpretation and influencing of the behaviour of firms and customers in a regulated network sector.

Conclusion

From my vantage point as his close associate, it appears that the establishment of the programme at Delft was Melody's ultimate challenge to contribute to the basic needs of society through well functioning infrastructures. Under his leadership, the Economics of Infrastructures became a solid and essential element of the research and teaching programme of the Faculty of Technology, Policy and Management of the Delft University of Technology. But his scope of knowledge diffusion was much broader than the university itself. His many international publications were

Epilogue

not the sole vehicle. His genuine concern for the problems of developing, as well as industrialised, countries in reforming their infrastructure industries caused him to engage in extensive travel to make presentations at numerous conferences, workshops, seminars and training programmes. Even in his post-Delft period, it is certain that he will continue to pursue his research and teaching objectives with great success.

Notes

1. The views expressed here are those of the author and do not necessarily reflect those of the European Commission or any other organisation.

2. These observations are taken from notes made while the author was an external assessor in March 2000 for an interdisciplinary faculty at a university in Canada.

3. The views expressed in this article are those of the author and do not necessarily reflect the opinions of the ITU or its Member States.

4. Arctic Village is an Athabaskan Indian community on the Chandalar River in Alaska; Alice Springs is in the Australian Outback.

5. See also http://www.ofta.gov.hk/frameset/industry_index_eng.html and http://www.trp.hku.hk/publications.html. The only similar suggestion I am aware of was made by John Kay writing in the *Financial Times*, 29 November 2000.

6. This section draws on the work of Julian Wright of the Department of Economics at the University of Auckland, New Zealand.

7. Revealed comparative advantage is calculated as the ratio of the share of communication equipment exports in total merchandise exports for each country to the share of OECD communication exports in total OECD merchandise exports. A value of greater than 1 indicates a comparative advantage, and a value of less than 1 a comparative disadvantage.

8. However, some of the most rapid productivity growth during the 1990s was experienced by major ICT producing countries (for example, Ireland, Korea and Finland). Recent sectoral analysis of the late 1990s productivity surge in the United States shows that the six 'jumping sectors' were retail, wholesale, securities, telecom, semiconductors and computer manufacturing. Other sectors experienced minor productivity gains and losses which cancelled each other out, regardless of whether or not they were major users of ICTs (see McKinsey 2001).

9   These data refer only to court-approved wiretaps and do not report on 'national security' wiretaps conducted under the Foreign Intelligence Surveillance Act of 1978.

10 On 5-6 October 2000, the authors organised with the help of their respective home institutions, a conference on the impact of the Internet drawing on the historical analogy of the printing press, see http://www.rand.org/multi/parallels/, accessed 31 September 2001.

11 Pierre Bourdieu cited in his *Libération* obituary by Robert Maggiori. Available at: http://www.liberation.fr/quotidien/semaine/020125-000002195EVEN.html, accessed 12 April 2001

12 An earlier version of this essay was presented in January 2001 to the seminar Rethinking Public Media in a Transnational Era, held at New York University and funded by the Ford Foundation.

13 See <http://cyberatlas.internet.com> and <http://www.nua.com> for a good compilation of such data.

Bibliography

Abramovitz, M. (1986) 'Catching Up, Forging Ahead and Falling Behind', *Journal of Economic History*, **46**(2): 385-406.

Adams, H. (1907/1990) *The Education of Henry Adams*, Washington: Adams. (Reprinted New York: Vintage).

Administrative Office of the United States Court (2001) *The 2000 Wiretap Report*. Available at: http://www.uscourts.gov/ wiretap00/ 2000wttxt.pdf, accessed 11 February 2002.

Agre, P. E. and Rotenberg, M. (eds) (1997) *Technology and Privacy: The New Landscape*, Cambridge MA: MIT Press.

Allegiance Telecom (2001) 'In the Matter of Developing a Unified Intercarrier Compensation Regime', 21 August, CC Docket #01-92, Federal Communications Commission, Washington DC.

Alleman, J. and Noam, E. M. (eds) (1999) *The New Investment Theory of Real Options and Its Implications for Telecommunications Economics*, Boston: Kluwer Academic Publishers.

Andreas, P. (1999) 'Smuggling Wars: Law Enforcement and Law Evasion in a Changing World', in T. Farer (ed) *Transnational Crime in the Americas*, New York: Routledge, 85-98.

Arnbak, J. C. (1998) 'On the Dynamics of Access, Entry and Cost Issues in Electronic Communication Markets', invited paper presented at the 1998 EU Competition Workshop, European University Institute, Florence, 13-14 November.

Arnbak, J. C. (2000) 'The Dynamics of Access, Entry and Costs in Electronic Communication Markets', in C. D. Ehlermann and L. Gosling (eds) *European Competition Law 1998: Regulating Communications Markets*, Oxford: Hart Publishing, 85-104.

Arthur, B. W. (1994) *Increasing Returns and Path Dependence in the Economy*, Ann Arbor MI: University of Michigan Press.

Asia Tele.com (2001) '3G Veering?' *Asia Tele.com*, 1 September. Available at http://www.asiatele.com/, accessed 1 March 2002.

Asian Wall Street Journal (2001) 'Consumers Yawn at Dawn of 3G Future', *Asian Wall Street Journal*, 22 February.

Bagdikian, B. H. (2000) *The Media Monopoly: With a New Preface on the Internet and Telecommunications Cartels*, Sixth Edition, Boston MA: Beacon Press.

Bakhtin, M. M. (1968/1984) *Rabelais and His World*, Bloomington IN: Indiana University Press, Translated by H. Iswolsky.

Baldelli, P. (1977) *Informazione e Controinformazione*, Milan: Gabriele Mazzotta Editore.

Bar F., Cohen, S., Cowhey, P., DeLong, B., Kleeman, M. and Zysman, J. (2000) 'Access and Innovation Policy for Third-Generation Internet', *Telecommunications Policy*, **24**(6/7): 489-518. Available at: http://www.stanford.edu/~fbar/Publications/Access-TP24_6-7.pdf, accessed 11 April 2002.

Baudrillard, J. (2000) *The Vital Illusion*, The Wellek Library Lectures. New York: Columbia University Press.

Bauer, J. M. (2001) 'Spectrum Auctions, Prices and Network Development in Mobile Communications', paper for presentation at the 29th Annual Telecommunications Policy Research Conference, Alexandria, VA: 27-29 October.

Becker, J. (1983) 'Contradictions in the Informatization of Politics and Society', *Gazette (International Journal for Communication Studies)*, **32**: 103-118.

Becker, J. (1984) *Information Technology and a New International Order*, Bromley: Chartwell-Bratt.

Becker, J. (1994) 'Communication' in I. Hauchler and P. Kennedy (eds) *Global Trends: The World Almanac of Development and Peace,* New York: Continuum Books, 345-363.

Bell, D. (1973) *The Coming of the Post Industrial Society: A Venture in Social Forecasting,* Harmondsworth: Penguin.

Beltran, S. L. R. (1975) 'Research Ideologies in Conflict', *Journal of Communication,* 25(2): 187-193.

Beniger, J. R. (1986) *The Control Revolution: Technological and Economic Origins of the Information Society,* Cambridge MA: Harvard University Press.

Beniger, J. R. (1996) 'Who Shall Control Cyberspace?' in L. Strate, R. Jacobson and S. B. Gibson (eds) *Communication and Cyberspace: Social Interaction in an Electronic Environment,* Cresskill NJ: Hampton Press, 49-58.

Benkler, Y. (1998) 'Overcoming Agoraphobia: Building the Commons of the Digitally Networked Environment', *Harvard Journal of Law and Technology,* 11(2): 287-400.

Bertram, E., Blachman, M and Sharpe, K. (1996) *Drug War Politics: The Price of Denial,* Berkeley CA: University of California Press.

Binmore, K. (2001) 'Hong Kong Refines 3G bids', *South China Morning Post,* 26 March: M-12.

Blumenstein, R., Scott, T. and Greg, L. P. (2001) 'Telecom Sector's Bust Reverberates Loudly Across the Economy', *Wall Street Journal,* 25 July: A-1.

Bocchicio, A. R. (1997) 'Drug Enforcement Administration', Testimony before the House Judiciary Committee, Subcommittee on Crime, Washington DC, 11 September.

Boltanski, L. (1999) *Distant Suffering: Morality, Media, Politics,* Cambridge: Cambridge University Press.

Boxer, M. J. (1998) 'Remapping the University: The Promise of Women's Studies PhD', *Feminist Studies,* 24(2): 387-403.

Brin, D. (1998) *The Transparent Society: Will Technology Force Us to Choose Between Privacy and Freedom?* Reading MA: Addison-Wesley.

Broadband Asia (2000) 'Facts & Stats', *Broadband Asia,* May/June. Available at: http://optistreams.com/factsandstats2.htm, accessed 1 March 2002.

Buck, S. (2002 forthcoming) 'Replacing Spectrum Auctions with a Spectrum Commons', *Stanford Technology Law Review.*

Buckingham, D. (2000) *After the Death of Childhood: Growing Up in the Age of Electronic Media,* Cambridge: Polity Press.

Burgelman, J. C. (2000) 'Regulating Access in the Information Society', *New Media & Society,* 2(1): 51-66.

Burgelman, J. C. (2001a) 'How Social Dynamics Influence Information Society Technology: Lessons for Innovation Policy', in OECD (ed) *Social Sciences and Innovation – Information Society,* Paris: OECD, 215-224.

Burgelman, J. C. (2001b) 'Why the Social Sciences are Left Out in Info Society Policy' in OECD (ed) *Social Sciences for Knowledge and Decision Making – Information Society,* Paris: OECD, 163-168.

Business Week (2000) 'Wireless in Cyberspace', *Business Week,* 22 May. http://www.businessweek.com/2000/00_21/b3682029.htm, accessed 10 April 2002

Cairnes, J. E. (1870) 'Political Economy & Laissez-faire', Introductory Lecture delivered after appointment as Professor of Political Economy at University College, London. Reproduced in S. Deane (ed) (1991) *The Field Day Anthology of Irish Writing, Volume 2,* Derry: Field Day Publications.

Cairnes, J. E. (1873) *Essays in Political Economy: Theoretical and Applied,* London: Macmillan. Reproduced in S. Deane, (ed) (1991) *The Field Day Anthology of Irish Writing, Volume 2,* Derry: Field Day Publications.

Callon, M. (2002 forthcoming) 'The Increasing Involvement of Concerned Groups in R&D Policies: What Lessons for Public Powers?' in A. Geuna, A. Salter and W. E. Steinmueller (eds) *Science and Innovation: Rethinking the Rationales for Funding and Governance,* Cheltenham: Edward Elgar.

Calvin, W. H. (1992) 'De rivier die tegen de berg opstroomt' (The River that Flows Uphill), Amsterdam: Bert Bakker.

Carey, J. W. (1975) 'Canadian Communication Theory: Extensions and Interpretations of Harold Innis', in G. Robinson and D. Theall (eds) *Studies in Canadian Communications*, Montreal: McGill University Press, 27-59.

Carroll, J. B. and B. L. Whorf (eds) (1964) *Language, Thought and Reality. Selected Writings of B. L. Whorf.* Cambridge MA: MIT Press.

Castells, M. (1996) *The Information Age: The Rise of the Network Society, Volume 1*, Oxford and Malden MA: Blackwell Publishers.

Castells, M. (1997) *The Information Age: The Power of Identity, Volume 2*, Oxford and Malden MA: Blackwell Publishers.

Castells, M. (1998) *The Information Age: End of Millennium, Volume 3*, Oxford and Malden MA: Blackwell Publishers.

Cave, M. (2001) 'Managing Spectrum Efficiently: A Review for the UK Government', *info*, 3(5): 369-374.

Cave, M. and Melody, W. H. (1989) 'Models of Broadcast Regulation: The U.K. and North American Experience', in C. Veljanovski (ed) *Freedom in Broadcasting*, London: The Institute of Economic Affairs, 224-244.

Cave, M. and Valletti, T. M. (2000) 'Are Spectrum Auctions Ruining Our Grandchildren's Future?' *info*, 2(4): 347-350.

Charles, D. and Benneworth, P. (2001) 'The Regional Mission: The Regional Contribution of Higher Education. The North East', Universities UK, London. Available at, http://www.universitiesuk.ac.uk/bookshop/downloads/northeast.pdf, accessed 1 March 2002.

Cho, S. W. (1998) *The Dynamics of Institutional Reform in Telecommunications: Globalization, Liberalization and Regulatory Change*, New York: Garland Publishing.

Chubin, D. A. P., Rossini, F. and Connolly, T. (eds) (1986) *Interdisciplinary Analysis and Research*, Mt. Airy MA: Lomand Publications.

Coady, C. A. J. (ed) (2000) *Why Universities Matter,* Sydney: Allen and Unwin.

Coase, R. H. (1959) 'The Federal Communications Commission', *Journal of Law and Economics,* 2:1-40.

Cohen, J. E. (1996) 'A Right to Read Anonymously: A Closer Look at "Copyright Management" in Cyberspace', *Connecticut Law Review,* 28: 981-1039.

Collins, R. and Murroni, C. (1996) *New Media, New Policies,* Cambridge: Polity Press.

Commons, J. R. (1959) *Institutional Economics: Its Place in Political Economy,* Madison WI: University of Wisconsin Press.

Comor, E. (2001) 'The Role of Communication in Global Civil Society: Forces, Processes, Prospects', *International Studies Quarterly,* 45(3): 389-408.

Compaine, B. M. and Gomery, D. (2000) *Who Owns the Media? Competition and Concentration in the Mass Media Industry.* Third Edition, Mahah NJ: Lawrence Erlbaum Associates.

Constantine, T. A. (1997) 'Drug Enforcement Administration', Testimony before the Senate Judiciary Committee, Subcommittee on Technology, Terrorism, and Government Information, Washington DC, 3 September.

Cornford, J. (2000) 'The Virtual University ... is the University Made of Concrete?' *Information, Communication and Society,* 3(4): 508-525.

Cornford, J. and Pollock, N. (2002) 'The University Campus as Resourceful Constraint: Process and Practice in the Construction of the Virtual University', in M. R. Lea and K. Nicholl (eds) *Distributed Learning: Social and Cultural Approaches to Practice:* London, Routledge, 170-181.

Cranberg, G., Bezanson, R. and Soloski, J. (2001) *Taking Stock: Journalism and the Publicly Traded Newspaper Company,* Ames IA: Iowa State Press.

Cronin, F. J., Colleran, E. K., Parker, E. B. and Gold, M. A. (1991) 'Telecommunications Infrastructure and Economic Growth: An Analysis of Causality', *Telecommunications Policy,* 15(6): 529-535.

Cronin, F. J., Gold, M. A. and Lewitzky, S. (1992) 'Telecommunications Technology, Sectoral Prices and International Competitiveness', *Telecommunications Policy*, 16(7): 553-564.

Cronin, F. J., Colleran, E. K., Herbert, P. L. and Lewitzky, S. (1993a) 'Telecommunications and Growth: the Contribution of Telecommunications Infrastructure Investment to Aggregate and Sectoral Productivity', *Telecommunications Policy*, 17(9): 677-690.

Cronin, F. J., Colleran, E. K., Parker, E. B. and Gold, M. A. (1993b) 'Telecommunications Infrastructure Investment and Economic Development', *Telecommunications Policy*, 17(6): 415-430.

Curran, J. and Seaton, J. (1997) *Power Without Responsibility: The Press and Broadcasting in Britain*, 5th Edition, London and New York: Routledge.

David, P. A., Foray, D., and Steinmueller, W. E. (1999) 'The Research Network and the New Economics of Science: From Metaphors to Organizational Behaviours', in A. Gambardella and F. Malerba (eds) *The Organisation of Innovative Activities in Europe*, Cambridge: Cambridge University Press, 303-342.

DeGraba, P. (2000) 'Bill-and-Keep at the Central Office as the Efficient Interconnection Regime', Federal Communications Commission, Office of Plans and Policy (OPP) Working Paper 33, Washington DC.

Denning, M. (1996) *The Cultural Front*, London: Verso.

Dervin, B. and Shields, P. (1990) 'Users: The Missing Link in Technology Research', Paper for the Communication Technology Section Meeting, International Association for Mass Communication Research, Yugoslavia, Lake Bled, July.

Dewar, J. (1998) 'The Information Age and the Printing Press: Looking Backward to See Ahead', Santa Monica, CA: RAND. Available at http://www.rand.org/publications/P/P8014/P8014.pdf, accessed 8 March, 2002.

Dorgan, M. (2001) 'No title', Knight Ridder News Service, 10 November.

Dosi, G., Freeman, C., Nelson, R., Silverberg, G. and Soete, L. (1988) *Technical Change and Economic Theory*, London: Pinter.

Downing, J. D. H. (1975) 'The (Balanced) White View', in C. Husband (ed) *White Media, Black Britain*, London: Arrow Books, Hutchinson, 90-137.

Downing, J. D. H. (1980) *The Media Machine*, London: Pluto Press.

Downing, J. D. H. (2000) *Radical Media: Rebellious Communication and Social Movements*, Thousand Oaks, CA: Sage.

Downing, J. D. H. (2001) "Independent Media Centers," in M. Raboy (ed) *Global Media Policy in the New Millennium*, Luton: Luton University Press, 215-232.

Du Boff, R. B. (1980) 'Business Demand and the Development of the Telegraph in the United States, 1844-1860', *Business History Review*, 54(4): 459-479.

Du Boff, R. B. (1983) 'The Telegraph and the Structure of Markets in the United States, 1845-1890', *Research in Economic History*, 8: 253-277.

Du Boff, R. B. (1984) 'The Rise of Communications Regulation: the Telegraph Industry, 1844-1880', *Journal of Communication*, 34(3): 52-66.

Duff, A. S. (2000) *Information Society Studies*, London and New York: Routledge.

Dutton, W. H. (ed) (1996) *Information and Communications Technologies: Visions and Realities*, Oxford: Oxford University Press.

Dutton, W. H. (ed) (1999) *Society on the Line: Information Politics in the Digital Age*, Oxford: Oxford University Press.

Economist, The (1997) 'Ornamental alliances', *The Economist*, 26 April, 74-5.

Economist, The (2001) 'The telecoms begging bowl', *The Economist*, 5 May: 15.

Economist, The (2001) 'Opinion: A Crunch of Gears', *The Economist*, 20 September. Available at: http://www.economist.com/science/tq/displaystory.cfm?story_id=779391, accessed 14 April 2002.

Eisenstein, E. (1980) *The Printing Press as an Agent of Change: Communications and Cultural Transformation in Early Modern Europe,* Cambridge: Cambridge University Press.

Eisenstein, E. (2000) Presentation at the RAND/Nanyang Technological University conference 'New Paradigms and Parallels: The Printing Press and the Internet', October.

Ellul, J. (1990) *The Technological Bluff,* Translated by G. Bromiley, Grand Rapids MI: William B. Eerdmans Publishing.

Etzkowitz, H. and L. Leydesdorff, L. (eds) (1997) *Universities and the Global Knowledge Economy.* London: Pinter.

European Commission (1993) 'White Paper on Growth, Competitiveness and Employment: Challenges and Ways Forward into the 21st Century', COM(93) 700 final, Brussels, 5 December.

European Commission (2000) 'Proposal for a Directive of the European Parliament and of the Council for a common negotiating framework and for electronic communications networks and services' Art. 13 (ONP Framework Directive), COM (2000) 393 final, Brussels, 12 July.

European Court of Justice (1985) BT *Telex Case*, ECJ, case 41/83, 1985, Brussels: European Court of Justice.

Favero, R. (2001) *CommsWorld,* Roundtable: Communications Yearbook 2001, Sydney: Informa Publishing.

Federal Communications Commission (1968) 'Use of the Carterfone Device in Message Toll Telephone Service', 13 FCC 2d 420, Federal Communications Commission, Washington DC.

Federal Communications Commission (1983) 'MTS/WATS Market Structure Order', 97 FCC 2d 682, Federal Communications Commission, Washington DC.

Federal Communications Commission (1996) 'In the Matter of Implementation of the Local Competition Provisions of the Telecommunications Act of 1996', CC Docket No. 96-98, First Report and Order, FCC 96-325, Federal Communications Commission, Washington DC.

Federal Communications Commission (2001a) 'Implementation of the Local Competition Provisions in the Telecommunications Act of 1996; Inter-Carrier Compensation for ISP-Bound Traffic', CC Docket Nos. 96-98, 99-68, Order on Remand and Report and Order, 16 FCC Rcd. 9151, Federal Communications Commission, Washington DC.

Federal Communications Commission (2001b) 'In the Matter of Developing a Unified Intercarrier Compensation Regime', Notice of Proposed Rulemaking, CC Docket No. 01-92, 16 FCC Rcd. 9610, Federal Communications Commission, Washington DC.

Federal Communications Commission (2001c) 'In the Matter of Nondiscrimination in the Distribution of Interactive Television Services Over Cable', Notice of Inquiry, CS Docket No. 01-7, 16 FCC Rcd. 1321, Federal Communications Commission, Washington DC.

Focal Communications Corporation, Pac-West Telecommunications, RCN Telecom Services, and US LEC Corporation (2001) 'In the Matter of Developing a Unified Intercarrier Compensation Regime', 21 August, CC Docket #01-92, Federal Communications Commission, Washington DC.

Fox, E. (1997) *Latin American Broadcasting: From Tango to Telenovela*, Luton: University of Luton Press.

Freeh, L. (1994) Director, Federal Bureau of Investigations, speech to the American Law Institute, Washington DC, 19 May.

Freeh, L. (1995) 'FBI Wants Advanced System to Vastly Increase Wiretapping', *New York Times*, 3 November.

Freeman, C. (1982) *The Economics of Industrial Innovation*, Second Edition, London: Frances Pinter.

Freeman, C. and Louçã. F. (2001) *As Time Goes By: From the Industrial Revolutions to the Information Revolution*, Oxford: Oxford University Press.

Freeman, C. and Soete, L. (1997) *The Economics of Industrial Innovation*, Third Edition, London: Pinter.

Friedman, S. S. (2001) 'Statement: Academic Feminism and Interdisciplinarity', *Feminist Studies,* 27(12): 504-509.

Gabel, D. (1987) 'The Evolution of a Market: The Emergence of Regulation in the Telephone Industry of Wisconsin, 1893-1917', Unpublished PhD Dissertation, University of Wisconsin, Madison, 1987.

Gabel, R. (1969) 'The Early Competitive Era in Telephone Communication, 1893-1920', *Law and Contemporary Problems,* 34: 340-59.

Gandy, O. (2000) 'Audience Segmentation: Is it Racism or Just Good Business?' *Media Development,* 2: 3-6.

García Espinosa, J. (1969/1983) 'For an Imperfect Cinema', in A. Mattelart and S. Siegelaub (eds) *Communication and Class Struggle, Volume 2,* Bagnolet, France: International General, 295-300.

Garnham, N. (1998) 'Information Society Theory as Ideology: A Critique', *Society and Leisure,* 21(1): 97-120.

Geuna, A. (1999) *The Economics of Knowledge Production: Funding and the Structure of University Research,* Cheltenham: Edward Elgar.

Gibbons, M., Limoges, C., Nowotny, H., Schwartzman, S., Scott, P. and Trow, M. (1994) *The New Production of Knowledge: The Dynamics of Science and Research in Contemporary Societies.* London: Sage.

Giddens, A. (1999) 'Runaway World', *1999 Reith Lectures: Democracy.* At: http://news.bbc.co.uk/hi/english/static/events/reith_99/week5/week5.htm, accessed 14 April 2002.

Gieryn, T. (1983) 'Boundary Work and the Demarcation of Science from Non-Science', *American Sociological Review,* 48: 781-95.

GILC (2000) *Bridging the Digital Divide: Internet Access in Central and Eastern Europe,* report by Center for Democracy and Technology prepared for the Global Internet Liberty Campaign. Available at: http://www.cdt.org/international/ceeaccess/, accessed 1 March 2002.

Gillett, S. E. (1995) 'Connecting Homes to the Internet: An Engineering Cost Model of Cable vs. ISDN', Unpublished MBA Thesis, June, Massachusetts Institute of Technology Program on Internet and Telecoms Convergence. Available at: http://itel.mit.edu, accessed 22 February 2002.

Girard, B. (ed) (1992) *A Passion For Radio*, Montréal: Black Rose Press. Available at: http://www.comunica.org/passion/index.htm, accessed 11 April 2002.

Glaeser, M. G. (1957) *Public Utilities in American Capitalism*, New York: Macmillan.

Global Knowledge 2 (2000) *Transforming Governance*, Background Paper, Kuala Lumpur, Malaysia, March. Available at: http://www.globalknowledge.org.my/index_ main.htm, accessed 8 April 2002.

Goddard, J. (1994) 'ICTs, Space and Place – Theoretical and Policy Changes', in R. Mansell (ed) *The Management of Information and Communication Technologies: Emerging Patterns of Control*. London, ASLIB, 274-285.

Goddard, J. and Chatterton, P. (1998) 'The Response of Universities to Regional Needs', Institutional Management in Higher Education, OECD, Paris.

Golding, P. (1998) 'New Technologies and Old Problems: Evaluating and Regulating Media Performance in the "Information Age"' in K. Brants, J. Hermes and L. van Zoonen (eds) *The Media in Question: Popular Culture and Public Interests*, London: Sage, 7-17.

Golding, P. and Murdock, G. (eds) (1997) *The Political Economy of the Media. Volume I and II*, Cheltenham/Brookfield: Edward Elgar.

Gomery, D. (2000) 'Interpreting Media Ownership', in B. M. Compaine and D. Gomery, *Who Owns the Media? Competition and Concentration in the Mass Media Industry*. Third Edition. Mahah, New Jersey: Lawrence Erlbaum Associates, 507-535.

Greenberg, J. (2001) 'No title', Reuters News Service, 5 November.

Gruber, H. (2001) 'Spectrum Limits and Competition in Mobile Markets: the Role of Licence Fees', *Telecommunications Policy*, 25(1/2): 59-70.

Haas, E. B. (1990) *When Knowledge is Power: Three Models of Change in International Organizations*, Berkeley: University of California Press.

Habermas, J. (1996) *Between Facts and Norms*, Cambridge MA: MIT Press.

Hall, P. (1998) *Cities in Civilization: Culture, Innovation and Urban Order*, London: Orion Books.

Hamilton, J. (2000) 'Alternative Media: Conceptual Difficulties, Critical Possibilities', *Journal of Communication Inquiry*, 24(4): 357-78.

Hamilton, W. H. (1919) 'The Institutional Approach to Economic Theory', *American Economic Review*, 9(1): 309-318.

Hamilton, W. H. (1932) 'Institution' in E. R. A. Seligman (ed) *Encyclopaedia of Social Science, Volume 8*. New York: Macmillan, 84-89.

Hammond, P. and Herman, E. S. (eds) (2000) *Degraded Capability: the Media and the Kosovo Crisis* London: Pluto Press.

Hansen, P. and Melody, W. H. (1989) 'The Changing Telecommunication Environment: Policy Considerations for the Members of the ITU', Report of the Advisory Group on Telecommunication Policy, Geneva: International Telecommunication Union.

Hardy, A. P. (1980) 'The Role of the Telephone in Economic Development', *Telecommunications Policy*, 4(4): 278-286.

Hayek, F. A. (1945) 'The Use of Knowledge in Society', *American Economic Review*, 35(4): 519-530.

Heidegger, M. (1982) *Parmenides*, Frankfurt am Main: Klostermann.

Henck, F. and Strassburg, B. (1988) *A Slippery Slope: The Long Road to the Breakup of AT&T*, New York and London: Greenwood Press.

Henten, A., Skouby, K. E and Falch, M. (1996) 'European Planning for an Information Society', *Telematics and Informatics*, 13(2/3): 177-190.

Henwood, F., Wyatt, S. and Hart, A. (2001) 'Presenting and Interpreting Health Risks and Benefits: The Role of the Internet', funded by the ESRC Programme on Innovative Health Technologies, April 2001- March 2003.

Herman, E. S. (1998) 'The Propaganda Model Revisited', in R. W. McChesney, E. M. Wood and J. B. Foster (eds) *Capitalism and the Information Age*, New York: Monthly Review Press, 191-205.

Herman, E. S. and McChesney, R. W. (1997) *The Global Media: The New Missionaries of Corporate Capitalism*, London and Washington DC: Cassell.

Herzel, L. (1951) 'Public Interest and the Market in Colour Television Regulation', University of Chicago Law Review, 9: 802-816.

Hirschman, A. O. (1970) *Exit, Voice and Loyalty: Responses to Declines in Firms, Organizations and States*, Cambridge MA: Harvard University Press.

Hoffmann-Riem, W. (1996) *Regulating Media: The Licensing and Supervision of Broadcasting in Six Countries*, New York: Guilford Press.

Horkheimer, M (1947) *Eclipse of Reason*, New York: Oxford University Press.

Horwitz, R. B. (2001) *Communication and Democratic Reform in South Africa*, Cambridge and New York: Cambridge University Press.

Houghton, J. W. (2001) 'Australian ICT Trade Update 2001', Melbourne: Centre for Strategic Economic Studies.

Hudson, H. E. (1997a) 'Converging Technologies and Changing Realities: Toward Universal Access to Telecommunications in the Developing World', in W. H. Melody, (ed) *Telecom Reform: Principles, Policies, and Regulatory Practices*, Lyngby: Den Private Ingeniørfond, 395-404.

Hudson, H. E. (1997b) *Global Connections: International Telecommunications Infrastructure and Policy*, New York: Wiley.

Hudson, H. E. and Pittman, T. (1999) 'From Northern Village to Global Village: Rural Communications in Alaska', *Pacific Telecommunications Review*, 21(2): 23-35.

Huws, U. (1999) 'Material World: The Myth of the Weightless Economy', in L. Panitch and C. Leys (eds) *Global Capitalism Versus Democracy, Socialist Register 1999*, London: Merlin Press, 29-55.

Independent Commission for World-Wide Telecommunication Development (1984) 'The Missing Link: Report of the Independent Commission', Geneva: International Telecommunication Union.

Information Infrastructure Task Force (1993) 'The National Information Infrastructure: Agenda for Action', Washington, DC.

Innis, H. A. (1923) *A History of the Canadian Pacific Railway*, Toronto: University of Toronto Press.

Innis, H. A. (1930/1962) *The Fur Trade in Canada: An Introduction to Canadian Economic History*, New Haven CT: Yale University Press.

Innis, H. A. (1950) *Empire and Communication*, Toronto: University of Toronto Press.

Innis, H. A. (1951) *The Bias of Communication*, Toronto: University of Toronto Press.

Innis, H. A. (1956) 'The Penetrative Powers of the Price System', in M. Q. Innis (ed) *Essays in Canadian Economic History*, Toronto: University of Toronto Press, 252-272.

ITAP (1984) *Making a Business of Information, Information Technology Advisory Panel to the Cabinet Office*, London: HMSO.

International Telecommunication Union (2001) *African Telecommunication Indicators 2001*. Geneva: International Telecommunication Union.

Juhasz, A. (1995) *AIDS TV: Identity, Community and Alternative Video*, Durham, NC: Duke University Press.

Jussawalla, M. (1994) 'Sharing the Air Ways', *Asian Wall Street Journal Weekly*, September: 18.

Jussawalla, M. (2001) 'The Promise of 3G for Asia', *Pacific Telecommunications Review*, 23(1): 23-27.

Kang, S. (2000) 'The Printing Press in Korea', Paper presented at the RAND/Nanyang Technological University conference 'New Paradigms and Parallels: The Printing Press and the Internet', October. Available at: http://www.rand.org/ multi/parallels/SM/papersnav.html, accessed 8 March 2002.

Kay, J. (2000) 'No title', *Financial Times*, 29 November.

Kellerman, A. (2000) 'Phases in the Rise of the Information Society', *info* 2(6): 537-541.

Klein, J. T. (1990) *Interdisciplinarity: History, Theory and Practice*, Detroit MI: Wayne State University.

Klemperer, P. (2001)'What Really Matters in Auction Design', Discussion Paper, University of Oxford: Nuffield College. Available at: http://www.paulklemperer.org/ index.htm, accessed 8 April 2002.

Knudtson, P. and Suzuki, D. (1992) *Wisdom of the Elders*, Toronto: Stoddart.

Kogawa, T. (1985) 'Free Radio in Japan', in D. Kahn and D. Neumaier (eds) *Cultures in Contention*, Seattle, WA: The Real Comet Press, 116-21.

Lemish, D., Drotner, K., Liebes, T., Maigret, E. and Stald, G. (1998) 'Global Culture in Practice: A Look at Children and Adolescents in Denmark, France and Israel', *European Journal of Communication*, 13(4): 539-556.

Lemley, M. and Lessig, L. (2001) 'The End of End-To-End: Preserving the Architecture of the Internet in the Broadband Era', *UCLA Law Review*, 48(4): 925-972.

Lerner, D. (1958) *The Passing of Traditional Society: Modernizing the Middle East*, New York: The Free Press.

Lessig, L. (1999) *Code and Other Laws of Cyberspace*, New York: Basic Books.

Lessig, L. (2001) *The Future of Ideas: The Fate of the Commons in a Connected World*, New York: Random House.

Lindblom, C. E. (1977) *Politics and Markets: The World's Political Economic Systems*, New York: Basic Books.

Lindblom, C. E. (1988) *Democracy and Market System*, Oslo: Norwegian University Press.

Lindblom, C. E. (1990) *Inquiry and Change: The Troubled Attempt to Understand & Shape Society*, New Haven, CT: Yale University Press.

Littlechild, S. (1984) 'Regulation of British Telecommunications' Profitability', London: Department of Trade and Industry.

Livingstone, S. (1998) 'Mediated Childhoods: A Comparative Approach to Young People's Changing Media Environment in Europe', *European Journal of Communication*, 13(4): 435-456.

Livingstone, S. and Bovill, M. (eds) (2001) *Children and their Changing Media Environment: A European Comparative Study*, Hillsdale, NJ: Lawrence Erlbaum Associates.

Lundvall, B.-A. (ed) (1992) *National Systems of Innovation: Towards a Theory of Innovation and Interactive Learning*, London: Pinter.

Machiavelli, N. (1513/1966) *The Prince*, Translated by Daniel Donno, Toronto: Bantam.

Machlup, F. (1962) *The Production and Distribution of Knowledge in the United States*, Princeton, NJ: Princeton University Press.

Maggiori, R. (2002) 'Pierre Bourdieu: mort d'un sociologue de combat', Libération, 25 January. Available at: http://www.liberation.fr/quotidien/semaine /020125-000002195EVEN.html, accessed 12 April 2002.

MacKenzie, D. A. and Wajcman, J. (eds) (1999) *The Social Shaping of Technology*. Second Edition, Milton Keynes: Open University Press.

MacPherson, C. B. (1973) *Democratic Theory: Essays in Retrieval,* Oxford: Clarendon Press.

MacPherson, C. B. (ed) (1978) Property: *Mainstream and Critical Positions.* Toronto: University of Toronto Press.

Mansell, R. (2001) 'New Media and the Power of Networks', Dixons Chair in New Media and the Internet Inaugural Lecture, London School of Economics and Political Science. Available at: http://www.lse.ac.uk/Depts/Media/, accessed 5 March 2002.

Mansell, R. and Steinmueller, W. E. (2000) *Mobilizing the Information Society: Strategies for Growth and Opportunity,* Oxford: Oxford University Press.

Mansell, R. and Wehn, U. (eds) (1998) *Knowledge Societies: Information Technology for Sustainable Development,* Oxford: Oxford University Press published for the United Nations Commission on Science and Technology for Development.

Marvin, C. (1988) *When Old Technologies Were New: Thinking about Electric Communication in the Late Nineteenth Century,* New York: Oxford University Press.

McChesney, R. W. (2000) 'Commentary: The Political Economy of Communication and the Future of the Field', *Media, Culture & Society,* **22**(1): 109-116.

McCourt, T. (1999) *Conflicting Communication Interests in America: the Case of National Public Radio,* Westport CT: Praeger Publishers.

McGee M. C. (1980) 'The "Ideograph": A Link between Rhetoric and Ideology', *The Quarterly Journal of Speech,* **66**(1): 1-16.

McKinsey (2001) 'U.S. Productivity Growth, 1995-2000', New York: McKinsey & Company.

McLuhan, M. (1962) *The Gutenberg Galaxy: The Making of Typographical Man,* Toronto: University of Toronto Press.

McLuhan, M. (1964) *Understanding Media: The Extensions of Man*, New York: McGraw-Hill.

McQuail, D. (1992) *Media Performance: Mass Communication and the Public Interest*, London: Sage.

Melody, W. H. (1971) 'Interservice Subsidy: Regulatory Standards and Applied Economics', in H. M. Trebing (ed) *Essays on Public Utility Pricing and Regulation*, East Lansing MI: Michigan State University, 167-210.

Melody, W. H. (ed.) (1972) 'Applications of Computer/Telecommunications Systems', OECD Informatics Studies: Proceedings of the OECD Seminar, Paris: OECD.

Melody, W.H. (1973a) *Children's Television: The Economics of Exploitation*, New Haven NJ: Yale University Press.

Melody, W. H. (1973b) 'The Role of Advocacy in Public Policy Planning', in G. Gerbner, L. P. Gross and W. H. Melody (eds.) *Communication Technology and Social Policy: Understanding the New 'Cultural Revolution'*, New York: Wiley and Sons, 165-181.

Melody, W. H. (1974) 'The Marginal Utility of Marginal Analysis in Public Policy Formulation', *Journal of Economic Issues*, 8(2): 287-300.

Melody, W. H. (1975) 'Technological, Economic and Institutional Aspects of Computer/ Telecommunications Systems', in OECD (ed) *Applications of Computer/Tele-communications Systems*, OECD, Paris.

Melody, W. H. (1976a) 'Comment [on shortcomings of marginal cost]' in H. M. Trebing (ed) *New Dimensions in Public Utility Pricing*, East Lansing MI: Michigan State University, 205-214.

Melody W. H. (1976b) 'Comment [on the interrelationship between scale economies, pricing, and competition]' in H. M. Trebing (ed) *New Dimensions in Public Utility Pricing*, East Lansing MI: Michigan State University, 380-400.

Melody, W. H. (1977) 'The Role of Communication in Development Planning' in S. A. Rahim and J. Middleton (eds) *Perspectives in Communication Policy Planning*, Honolulu HI: East-West Center, 25-41.

Melody, W. H. (1978) 'Mass Media: The Economics of Access to the Marketplace of Ideas', in C. E. Aronoff (ed) *Business and the Media,* Santa Monica CA: Goodyear, 216-226.

Melody, W. H. (1980) 'Radio Spectrum Allocation: Role of the Market', *American Economic Review,* 70(2): 393-397.

Melody, W. H. (1981a) 'The Economics of Information as Resource and Product', in D. J. Wedemeyer (ed) Proceedings of the Pacific Telecommunications Conference (PTC '81) Honolulu HI, Pacific Telecommunications Council, C7-5-9.

Melody, W. H. (1981b) 'Introduction', in W. H. Melody, L. Salter and P. Heyer (eds) *Culture, Communication and Dependency: The Tradition of H. A. Innis,* Norwood NJ: Ablex.

Melody, W. H. (1983) 'Development of the Communication and Information Industries: Impact on Social Structures' paper for the Symposium on the Cultural, Social and Economic Impact of Communication Technology, sponsored by UNESCO and Instituto della Enciclopedia Italiana, Rome, 12-16 December.

Melody, W. H. (1985a) 'Implications of the Information and Communication Technologies: The Role of Policy Research', *Policy Studies,* 6(Oct): 1-11.

Melody, W. H. (1985b) 'The Information Economy: The Role of Public and Private Information', Annual Library Lecture, Polytechnic of Central London, 6 November.

Melody, W. H. (1985c) 'The Information Society: Implications for Economic Institutions and Market Theory', *Journal of Economic Issues,* **XIX**(2): 523-539.

Melody, W. H. (1986a) 'Dealing with Global Networks: From Characteristics of the International Market', COM-8 Conference on Dealing with Global Networks, Tilburg University, 30-31 October.

Melody, W. H. (1986b) 'Some Implications of Change in the Information Age', First Eugene Garfield Lecture, Strathclyde Business School, University of Strathclyde, Glasgow, Scotland, 27 November.

Melody, W. H. (1987a) 'The Canadian Broadcasting Corporation's Contribution to Canadian Culture', The Neil Matheson McWharrie Lecture for 1986, *The Royal Society of Arts Journal,* **CXXXXV**(5368): 286-297.

Melody, W. H. (1987b) 'Information: An Emerging Dimension of Institutional Analysis', *Journal of Economic Issues,* **XXI**(3): 1313-39.

Melody, W. H. (1988) 'Pan European Television: Commercial and Cultural Implications of European Satellites', in R. Paterson and P. Drummond (eds) *Television and its Audience: International Research Perspectives,* London: British Film Institute, 267-281.

Melody, W. H. (1989) 'Efficiency and Social Policy in Telecommunication: Lessons from the U.S. Experience', *Journal of Economic Issues,* **XXIII**(3): 657-688.

Melody, W. H. (1990a) 'Communication Policy in the Global Information Economy: Whither the Public Interest?' in M. Ferguson (ed) *Public Communication: The New Imperatives,* London: Sage, 16-30.

Melody, W. H. (1990b) 'The Information in Information Technology. Where Lies the Public Interest', *Intermedia,* **18**(3): 10-17.

Melody, W. H. (1991a) 'Information and the Consumer Interest', paper presented at the Centre for International Research on Communication and Information Technologies (CIRCIT) Forum on Information and the Consumer Interest. Melbourne: CIRCIT.

Melody, W. H. (1991b) 'The Information Society: The Transnational Economic Context and Its Implications' in G. Sussman and J. A. Lent (eds) *Transnational Communications: Wiring the Third World,* London: Sage, 27-41.

Melody, W. H. (1993a) 'Improved Telecommunication: Catalyst for Development?' Suva, Fiji, Paper for the Pacific Telecommunications Forum Seminar.

Melody, W. H. (1993b) 'On the Political Economy of Communication in the Information Society' in J. Wasko, V. Mosco and M. Pendakur (eds) *Illuminating the Blindspots: Essays Honoring Dallas W. Smythe,* Norwood NJ: Ablex, 63-81.

Melody, W. H. (1996a) 'Identifying Priorities for Building Distinct Information Societies', *The Economic and Social Review,* 28(3): 177-184.

Melody, W. H. (1996b) 'Policy Research in the Information Economy' in W. H. Dutton (ed) *Information and Communication Technologies: Visions and Realities,* Oxford: Oxford University Press, 303-317.

Melody, W. H. (1996c) 'Toward a Framework for Designing Information Society Policies', *Telecommunications Policy,* 20(4): 243-59.

Melody, W. H. (1997a) 'Interconnection: Cornerstone of Competition', in W. H. Melody (ed) *Telecom Reform: Principles, Policies, and Regulatory Practices,* Lyngby: Den Private Ingeniørfond, 53-66.

Melody, W. H. (1997b) 'Policy Objectives and Models of Regulation', in W. H. Melody (ed) *Telecom Reform: Principles, Policies and Regulatory Practices,* Lyngby, Den Private Ingeniørfond, 13-27.

Melody, W. H. (1997c) 'Universities and Public Policy', in T. Smith and F. Webster (eds) *The Postmodern University? Contested Visions of Higher Education in Society,* Milton Keynes: Open University Press, 72-84.

Melody, W. H. (1999a) 'Diversity in East Asia', *Telecommunications Policy,* 23(3/4): 211-12.

Melody, W. H (1999b) 'Human Capital in Information Economies', *New Media and Society,* 1(1): 39-46.

Melody, W. H. (1999c) 'Regulatory Trends and Developments in European Telecommunications, A Status Report of Progress in Telecom Reform', Telestyrelsen, Copenhagen.

Melody, W. H. (1999d) 'Review of "Marshall McLuhan: The Medium and the Messenger" by P. Marchand', *Information, Communication and Society,* 2(3): 374-377.

Melody, W. H. (1999e) 'Telecom Reform: Progress and Prospects', *Telecommunications Policy,* 23(1): 7-34.

Melody, W. H. (2000) 'Trends in European Telecommunication: A Status Report of Denmark's Progress in Telecom Reform and Information Infrastructure Development', Telestyrelsen, Copenhagen. Available at http://www.lirne.net/library/publications.php, accessed 5 March 2002.

Melody, W. H. (2001a) 'Performance Indicators: Measurement and Interpretation', Presentation at LIRNE.NET Telecom Reform course offered in collaboration with LINK Centre, Johannesburg, South Africa.

Melody, W. H. (2001b) 'Spectrum Auctions and Efficient Resource Allocation: Learning from the 3G Experience in Europe', *info,* 3(1): 5-10.

Melody, W. H. (2001c) 'Trends in European Telecommunication: 2001 Status Report of Denmark's Progress in Telecom Reform and Information Infrastructure Development', Telestyrelsen, Copenhagen. Available at http://www.lirne. net/library/publications.php, accessed 5 March 2002.

Melody, W. H. and Ehrlich, W. (1974) 'Children's TV Commercials: The Vanishing Policy Options', *Journal of Communication,* 24(4): 113-125.

Melody, W. H. and Mansell, R. E. (1983) 'The Debate over Critical vs. Administrative Research: Circularity or Challenge', *Journal of Communication,* 33(3): 103-117.

Melody, W. H., Salter, L., and Heyer, P. (eds) (1981) *Culture, Communication and Dependency: The Tradition of H. A. Innis,* Norwood NJ: Ablex.

Messer-Davidow, E., Shumway, D. and Sylvan, D. (eds) (1993) *Knowledges: Historical and Critical Studies with Disciplinarity,* Charlottesville VA: University Press of Virginia.

Miles, I. (1988) 'Information Technology and Information Society: Options for the Future', PICT Policy Research Paper No. 2, ESRC: London.

Miles, I. (2001) 'Rethinking Organisation in the Information Society' lecture presented at SOWING Conference *Regional Paths to the Information Society,* Karlsruhe 2-3 November; forthcoming 2002 in M. Rader and G. Schienstock (eds) *Work, Organisation and Social Exclusion in the Information Society,* Frankfurt: Campus Frankfurt.

Miles, I. (2002 forthcoming) 'Transformations of Information Society' in Theme 1.24 'Capital Resources Issue IV: Global Transformations and Futures: Knowledge, Economy and Society', published in UNESCO (ed) *The Encyclopaedia of Life Support Systems,* Oxford: Eolss Publishers.

Miles, I. and Contributors (1990) *Mapping and Measuring the Information Economy,* Boston Spa: British Library (LIR Report 77).

Mills, C. W. (1959/1970) *The Sociological Imagination,* New York: Oxford University Press (Reprinted Harmondsworth: Penguin).

Ministry of Posts and Telecommunications (1994) 'Reforms toward the Intellectual Creative Society of the 21st Century', Tokyo: Ministry of Posts and Telecommunications.

Mitchell, W. C. (1913/1970) *Business Cycles,* Los Angeles CA: University of California Press, reprinted New York: B. Franklin.

Mody, A. and Dahlman, C. (1992) 'Performance and Potential of Information Technology: An International Perspective', *World Development,* 20(12): 1703-1719.

Mosco, V. and Schiller, D. (eds) (2001) *Continental Order: Integrating North America for Cybercapitalism,* Boulder, CO: Rowman and Littlefield.

Negroponte, N. (1995) *Being Digital,* New York: Vintage Books.

Netherlands Ministry of Economic Affairs (2000) White Paper on Network Industries (in Dutch).

Nelson, R. (ed) (1993) *National Innovation Systems: A Comparative Analysis,* Oxford: Oxford University Press.

Nelson, R. and Winter, S. (1982) *An Evolutionary Theory of Economic Change,* Cambridge MA: Harvard University Press.

Neuman, R. W. (1991) *The Future of the Mass Audience,* Cambridge: Cambridge University Press.

Noam, E. M. (1998) 'Spectrum Auctions: Yesterday's Heresy, Today's Orthodoxy, Tomorrow's Anachronism. Taking the Next Step to Open Spectrum Access', *Journal of Law and Economics*, **56**(2): 765-790.

Nowotny, H., Scott, P. and Gibbons, M. (2001) *Re-Thinking Science: Knowledge and the Public in an Age of Uncertainty*, Cambridge: Polity Press.

OECD (2001a) 'Education at a Glance', Paris: OECD.

OECD (2001b) 'New Patterns of Industrial Globalisation: Cross-border Mergers and Acquisitions and Strategic Alliances', Paris: OECD.

OECD (2001c) 'Science, Technology and Industry Scoreboard: Towards a Knowledge-based Economy 2001 Edition', Paris: OECD.

Ó Siochrú, S., Girard, B., and Mahan, A. (2002) *Global Media Governance: A beginner's guide*, Boulder CO: Rowman & Littlefield.

Ostrom, E. (1990) *Governing the Commons: The Evolution of Institutions for Collective Action*, Cambridge: Cambridge University Press.

Oxman, J. (1999) 'The FCC and the Unregulation of the Internet', FCC Office of Plans and Policy Working Paper No. 31, Federal Communications Commission, Washington, DC. Available at: http://www.fcc.gov/opp/workingp.html, accessed 6 March 2002.

Parker, E. B, Hudson, H. E. et al. (1995) *Electronic Byways: State Policies for Rural Development through Telecommunications*, revised Second Edition, Washington DC: Aspen Institute.

Perez, C. (1983) 'Structural Change and the Assimilation of the New Technologies in the Economic and Social System', *Futures*, **15**: 357-375.

Perez, C. and Soete, L. (1988) 'Catching Up in Technology: Entry Barriers and Windows of Opportunity', in G. Dosi, C. Freeman, R. Nelson, G. Silverberg and L. Soete (eds) *Technical Change and Economic Theory*, London: Pinter, 458-479.

Picard, R. G. (2001) 'Relations among Media Economics, Content, and Diversity', in: *Nordicom Review*, **22**(1) June: 65-69.

Pisciotta, A. (1997) 'Global Trends in Privatization', in W. H. Melody (ed) *Telecom Reform: Principles, Policies and Regulatory Practice*, Lyngby: Den Private Ingeniørfond, 337-353.

Porat, M. (1976) *The Information Economy*, Stanford CA: Center for Interdisciplinary Research.

Preston P. (1994) 'Neo-liberal regulation and the smaller & peripheral economies: an institutionalist perspective', in Williams, H. et al (eds) *Telecommunication: Exploring Competition*, Amsterdam: IOS Press, 143-146.

Preston, P. (2001) *Reshaping Communications: Technology, Information and Social Change*, London: Sage.

Qwest (2001) 'Interconnection and Collocation for Transport and Switched Unbundled Network Elements and Finished Services', September. Available at: http://www.qwest.com/wholesale/downloads/2001/011017/77386_Issue_G_FD1.pdf, accessed 6 March 2002.

Raboy, M. (ed) (2001) *Global Media Policy in the New Millennium*, Luton: University of Luton Press.

Raboy, M., Bernier, I., Sauvageau, F., and Atkinson, D. (1994) *Développement Culturel et Mondialisation de l'Économie: un Enjeu Démocratique*, Quebec City: Institut Québécois de Recherche sur la Culture.

Rappert, B. and Webster, A. (1997) 'Regimes of Ordering: The Commercialisation of Intellectual Property of Industrial-Academic Collaboration', *Technology Analysis and Strategic Management*, 9(2): 115-130.

Reed, C. (2000) 'Printing and Publishing in Late Imperial China', paper presented at the RAND/Nanyang Technological University conference 'New Paradigms and Parallels: The Printing Press and the Internet', October. Available at http://www.rand.org/multi/parallels/SM/papersnav.html, accessed 8 March 2002.

Robertson, R. (1997) 'Social Theory, Cultural Relativity, and the Problem of Globality', in A. D. King (ed) *Culture, Globalization and the World System*, Revised Edition, Minneapolis, MN: University of Minnesota Press, 69-90.

Robins, K. (ed.) (1992) *Understanding Information: Business, Technology and Geography,* London: Belhaven Press.

Rocha, G. (1995) 'From the Drought to the Palm Trees," in R. Johnson and R. Stam (eds) *Brazilian Cinema.* New York: Columbia University Press [first published in 1970], 87-89.

Rodríguez, C. (2001) *Fissures in the Mediascape: An International Study of Citizens' Media,* Cresskill NY: Hampton Press.

Romero, S. (2001) 'Shining Future of Fiber Optics Loses its Glimmer', *The New York Times,* June 18, A1, A17.

Rothwell, R. (1994) 'Issues in User-Producer Relations in the Innovation Process: The Role of Government', *International Journal of Technology Management,* 9(5/6/7): 629-649.

Sakolsky, R. and Dunifer, S. (eds) (1998) *Seizing The Airwaves: A Free Radio Handbook,* Edinburgh and San Francisco CA: AK Press.

Salter, L. and Hearn, A. (1996) *Outside the Lines: Issues in Interdisciplinary Research,* Montreal: McGill-Queens University Press.

Samarajiva, R. (1996) 'Surveillance by Design: Public Networks and the Control of Consumption', in R. Mansell and R. Silverstone (eds) *Communication by Design: The Politics of Information and Communication Technologies,* Oxford: Oxford University Press, 129-56.

Samarajiva, R. and Henten, A. (2002) 'Rationales for Convergence and Multi-sector Regulation', Paper for presentation at the European Communication Policy Research Conference, Barcelona, 25-26 March. Available at: http://www.regulateonline.org, accessed 1 April 2002.

Samarajiva, R., Mahan, A. and Barendse, A. (2002) 'Multisector Regulation', Discussion Paper WDR 0203, World Dialogue on Regulation for Network Economies. Available at: http://www.regulateonline.org/dp/dp0203.htm, accessed 8 March 2002.

Sanatan, R. and Melody, W. H. (1997) 'Adapting to a Global Economy: Implications of Telecom Reform for Small Developing Countries', in W. H. Melody (ed) *Telecommunication Reform: Principles, Policies and Regulatory Practices.* Lyngby: Den Private Ingeniørfond: 327-334.

Sayer, A. (1992) *Method in Social Science: A Realist Approach*, Second Edition, London and New York: Routledge.

Schlager, E. and Ostrom, E. (1993) 'Property-Rights Regimes and Coastal Fisheries: An Empirical Analysis', in: T. L. Anderson and R. T. Simmons (eds) *The political economy of customs and culture: Informal solutions to the commons problem*, Boulder CO: Rowman & Littlefield, 13-41.

Schmitt, R. B. (2001) 'California Officials Justify Their Claims of Overcharges before Federal Mediator', *Wall Street Journal*, 9 July, A8.

Schumpeter, J. A. (1943) *Capitalism, Socialism and Democracy*, London: Allen and Unwin.

Schumpeter, J. A. (1961) *The Theory of Economic Development: An Inquiry into Profits, Capital, Credit, Interest and the Business Cycle*, Oxford: Oxford University Press.

Sen, A. (1998) 'Amartya Sen on Globalisation', *Pharma Link*, 2(3): 8, December.

Sen, A. (2000) *Development as Freedom*, New York: Anchor Books/ Random House.

Senmoto, S. (2001) 'The Broadband Revolution in East Asia', Paper presented to the Second Annual Conference on E-Commerce, East West Center, Hawaii, 29 October.

Sherman, W. (2000) Presentation at the RAND/Nanyang Technological University conference 'New Paradigms and Parallels: The Printing Press and the Internet', October.

Shy, O. (2001) *The Economics of Network Industries*, Cambridge: Cambridge University Press.

Silverstone, R. (1995) 'Media, Communication, Information and the "Revolution" of Everyday Life' in S. J. Emmott (ed) *Information Superhighways: Multimedia Users and Futures*, London: Academic Press, 61-78.

Silverstone, R. (1999) *Why Study the Media?*, London: Sage.

Silverstone, R. (2002 forthcoming) 'Proper Distance: Towards an Ethics for Cyberspace, in G. Liestøl, A. Morrison, and T. Rasmussen (eds) *Innovations*, Cambridge MA: MIT Press.

Silverstone, R. and Hirsch, E. (eds) (1992) *Consuming Technologies: Media and Information in Domestic Spaces*, London: Routledge.

Sinclair, J. (1999) *Latin American Broadcasting: A Global View*, Oxford: Oxford University Press.

Sinclair, J., Jacka, E. and Cunningham, S. (1996) 'Peripheral Vision', in J. Sinclair, E. Jacka and S. Cunningham (eds) *New Patterns in Global Television: Peripheral Vision*, New York: Oxford University Press, 1-32.

Singh, S. (1997) *Marriage Money: The Social Shaping of Money in Marriage and Banking*, Sydney: Allen and Unwin.

Singh, S. (1999) 'Electronic Money: Understanding its Use to Increase the Effectiveness of Policy', *Telecommunications Policy*, 23(10/11): 753-773.

Skocpol, T. (ed) (1984) *Vision and Method in Historical Sociology*, Cambridge: Cambridge University Press.

Slack, J. S. and Williams, R. A. (2000) 'The Dialectics of Place and Space: On Community in the "Information Age"', *New Media & Society*, 2(3): 313-334.

Smythe, D. W. (1977) 'Communications: Blindspot of Western Marxism', *Canadian Journal of Political and Social Theory*, 1(3): 1-27.

Smythe, D. W. (1981) *Dependency Road: Communications, Capitalism, Consciousness and Canada*, Norwood NJ: Ablex.

Soley, L. C. (1999) *Free Radio: Electronic Civil Disobedience*, Boulder, CO: Westview Press.

Spiller, P. T. and Cardilli, C. (1999) 'Towards a Property Rights Approach to Communications Spectrum', *Yale Journal on Regulation,* 16(1): 53-83.

Starr, J. M. (2000) *Air Wars: The Fight to Reclaim Public Broadcasting*, Boston MA: Beacon Press.

Statewatch (1997) 'EU & FBI Launch Global Telecommunications Surveillance System: "not a significant document" – UK Home Secretary', Statewatch bulletin 7(1), January-February. Available at: http://www.statewatch.org/eufbi/eufbi01.htm, accessed 8 March 2002.

Stavrou, A. and Mkize, K. A. (1998) 'Telecommunications Universal Service Policy Framework for Defining Categories of Needy People in South Africa', Durban: DRA Development.

Sterling, C. H. (2000) 'Foreword', in: B. M. Compaine and D. Gomery, *Who Owns the Media? Competition and Concentration in the Mass Media Industry,* Third Edition, Mahah, New Jersey: Lawrence Erlbaum Associates: xv-xviii.

Stevenson, G. G. (1991) *Common Property Economics: A General Theory and Land Use Application,* Cambridge: Cambridge University Press.

Stigler, G. J. (1971) 'The Theory of Economic Regulation', *Bell Journal of Economics,* Vol. 2 (1): 3-21.

Strinati, D. (1995) *An Introduction to Theories of Popular Culture,* London: Routledge.

Sunday Times (2001) 'We spent £10 billion too much', *Sunday Times* of London: 18 February.

Sunstein, C. (2001) *Republic.com,* Princeton, NJ: Princeton University Press.

Sutton, J. (1991) *Sunk Cost and Market Structure: Price Competition, Advertising and the Evolution of Concentration,* Cambridge MA: MIT Press.

Suzuki, D. (1997) *The Sacred Balance,* Toronto: Stoddart.

Telestyrelsen (2000) 'Denmark – International Discussion Forum', Copenhagen, 6-7. Available at: http://www2.tst.dk/uk/index_uk.htm, accessed 14 April 2002.

Telkom SA (2001) *Annual Report 2001*, Johannesburg.

Thorburn, L., Langdale, J. and Houghton, J. W. (2002) 'Friend or Foe? Leveraging Foreign Multinationals in the Australian Economy', Sydney: Australian Business Foundation.

Tillinghast, C. H. (2000) *American Broadcast Regulation and the First Amendment. Another Look*. Ames: Iowa State University Press.

Toffler, A. (1980) *The Third Wave*, London: Collins.

Trebing, H. M. (1988) 'A Critique of Economic Deregulation in the Context of Emergent Industry Structures in the United States', in N. Garnham (ed) *European Telecommunications Policy Research (CPR '88)*, Amsterdam and Springfield VA: IOS Publishers, 5-18.

Tunstall, J. (1996) *Newspaper Power*, London: Oxford University Press.

Turow, J. (2001) 'Children and the Web: Who's Telling Their Stories?' presentation to the National Academy of Sciences, Washington, DC, February.

UNDP (United Nations Development Program) (1999) *Human Development Report 1999*, New York: Oxford University Press.

UNDP (United Nations Development Program) (2001) *Human Development Report 2001*, New York: Oxford University Press.

Ungerer, H. and Costello, N. (1988) *Telecommunications in Europe*, Brussels: European Commission.

Ure, J. (2001) 'Feedback – licensing third-generation mobile: a poisoned chalice?', *info*, 3(1): 11-14. Available at: http://www.trp.hku.hk/publications.html, accessed 8 April 2002.

Valletti, T. M. (2001) 'Spectrum Trading', *Telecommunications Policy,* 25(10/11): 655-670.

Varian, H. R. and Shapiro, C. (1998) *Information Rules: A Strategic Guide to the Network Economy,* Cambridge MA: Harvard Business School Press.

Veblen, T. (1898/1961) 'Why is Economics not an Evolutionary Science?' in T. Veblen (ed) *The Place of Science in Modern Civilization and Other Essays,* New York: Russell & Russell, 56-81.

Veblen, T. (1899/1994) *The Theory of the Leisure Class: An Economic Study of Institutions,* London: Routledge, Thoemmes Press.

Veblen, T. (1904) *The Theory of Business Enterprise,* New York: Charles Scribners.

von Auw, A. (1983) *Heritage and Destiny: Reflections on the Bell System in Transition,* New York: Praeger.

von Hippel, E. (1978) 'Users as Innovators', *Technology Review,* 80(3): 31-39.

Waisbord, S. (1995) 'Leviathan Dreams: State and Broadcasting in South America', *The Communication Review,* 1(2): 201-226.

Wallerstein, I. (1984) *The Politics of the World-Economy,* Cambridge: Cambridge University Press.

Watkins, M. (1982) 'The Innis Tradition in Canadian Political Economy', *Journal of Political and Social Theory,* 6: 12-34.

Webster, F. (1995) *Theories of the Information Society,* London: Routledge.

Westerveld, R. (1994) 'Cost Effective Rural Communications Using Fixed Cellular Radio Access', in B. A. Kiplagat and M. Werner (eds) *Telecom and Development in Africa,* IOS Press: Amsterdam, pp 199-218.

Whitley, R. (1984) *The Intellectual and Social Organization of the Sciences,* Oxford: Clarendon Press.

Wilson, E. O. (1992) *The Diversity of Life,* New York: Norton.

Wind, J. and Mahajan, V. (2001) *Digital Marketing: Global Strategies from the World's Leading Experts,* New York: John Wiley.

Wolf, M. (2001) 'Comment: 3G treasure trove' *Financial Times,* 26 June 2001: 23.

World Commission on Environment and Development (1987) *Our Common Future,* New York: Oxford University Press.

World Information Technology and Services Alliance (2000) *Digital Planet 2000: The Global Information Economy,* WITSA, Vienna, Virginia. Available at: http://www.witsa.org/DP2000sum.pdf, accessed 7 March 2002.

World Trade Organization (1997) 'Fourth Protocol to the General Agreement on Trade in Services' Reference Paper, 15 February, Geneva: WTO. Available at http://www.wto.org, accessed 22 February 2002.

Acronyms

3G	Third Generation Mobile
ACT	Action for Children's Television
AMARC	World Association of Community Radio Broadcasters
ANATEL	Brazilian Telecom Regulator
AOL	America Online
ARPU	Average Revenue Per User
ASEAN	Association of South East Asian Nations
AT&T	American Telephone and Telegraph
AU$	Australian Dollar
B2B	Business-to-business
B2C	Business-to-consumer
BBC	British Broadcasting Corporation
CALEA	Communications Assistance for Law Enforcement Act (US)
CANTO	Caribbean Association of National Telecommunication Organizations
CARICOM	Caribbean Community
CBC	Canadian Broadcasting Corporation
CCF	China-China-Foreign (policy and financing model)
CCIR	Comité Consultatif International des Radio Communications (International Radio Consultative Committee), now ITU-R (see below)
CCITT	Comité Consultatif International de Télégraphique et Téléphonique (International Telegraph and Telephone Consultative Committee), now ITU-T (see below)
CD	Compact Disc
CELAET	Center of Latin American Studies of Economics of Telecommunications

Acronyms

CEO	Chief Executive Officer
CERN	China Educational Research Network
CII	Critical Information Infrastructure
CIRCIT	Centre for International Research on Communication and Information Technologies (Australia)
CLEC	Competitive Local Exchange Carrier
CPNP	Calling Party Network Pays
CPqD	National Institute of Telecom Technology (Brazil)
CPB	Corporation for Public Broadcasting
CPR	Communication Policy Research
CRTC	Canadian Radio-television and Telecommunications Commission
CSIRO	Commonwealth Scientific and Industrial Research Organisation
CTI	Center for Tele-Information (at the Technical University of Denmark)
CTU	Caribbean Telecommunication Union
DECT	Digital European Cordless Telecommunications
DG	Directorate General (European Commission)
DSL	Digital Subscriber Line
ESRC	Economic and Social Research Council (UK)
EU	European Union
FBI	Federal Bureau of Investigation (US)
FCC	Federal Communications Commission (US)
FUNTTEL	Technology Research Fund (Brazil)
G-8	Group of Eight (Britain, Canada, France, Germany, Italy, Japan, Russia and the United States)
GATS	General Agreement on Trade in Services
GDP	Gross Domestic Product
GILC	Global Internet Liberty Campaign
GMPCS	Global Mobile Personal Communications by Satellite
GSM	Global System for Mobile Communications
HEI	Higher Education Institution

Acronyms

IBM	International Business Machines
ICANN	Internet Corporation for Assigned Names and Numbers
ICT	Information and Communication Technology
IFRB	International Frequency Regulation Board
ILEC	Incumbent Local Exchange Carriers
IMCs	Independent Media Centres
IP	Internet Protocol
IS	Information Society
ISP	Internet Service Provider
IST	Information Society Technology
IT	Information Technology
ITAP	Information Technology Advisory Panel (UK)
ITU	International Telecommunication Union
ITU-D	ITU Development Sector
ITU-R	ITU Radiocommunication Sector
ITU-T	ITU Telecommunication Standardization Sector
IXC	Interexchange Carrier
KPN	Koninklijke PTT Nederland (Royal Dutch Postservices) Former Dutch PTT
LIRNE.NET	Learning Initiatives for Reforms in Network Economies
M&A	Merger and Acquisition
MCI	Formerly Microwave Communications Inc., then MCI, now Worldcom
MII	Ministry of Information Industry (China)
MIT	Massachusetts Institute of Technology
NAB	National Association of Broadcasters (US)
NPR	National Public Radio (US)
NPV	Net Present Value
NRA	National Regulatory Authority (or Agency)
NTT	Nippon Telephone and Telegraph (Japan)
OECD	Organisation for Economic Cooperation and Development
OFTEL	Office of Telecommunications (UK)

ONP	Open Network Provision
OPTA	Onafhankelijke Post en Telecommunicatie Autoriteit, Netherlands (Dutch Regulator)
PBS	Public Broadcasting Service (US)
PC	Personal Computer
PICT	Programme on Information and Communication Technologies (UK)
PSTN	Public Switched Telephone Network
R&D	Research and Development
RBHC	Regional Bell Holding Company
RCA	Radio Corporation of America
SIM	Subscriber Interface Module
SPRU	Science and Technology Policy Research, University of Sussex (UK)
TCI	Tele-Communications, Inc
TNC	Transnational Corporation
UMTS	Universal Mobile Telecommunication Service
UN	United Nations
UNDP	United Nations Development Program
UNESCO	United Nations Educational, Scientific and Cultural Organization
UNICEF	United Nations International Children's Emergency Fund
US$	US dollar
USAID	US Agency for International Development
USO	Universal Service Obligation
VoIP	Voice over Internet Protocol
VSAT	Very Small Aperture Terminal
WAP	Wireless Application Protocol
WB	World Bank
WHO	World Health Organization
WLL	Wireless Local Loop
WTO	World Trade Organization
Y2K	Year 2000

Contributors

Binod C. Agrawal, MSc, PhD, Wisconsin, is Director of the TALEEM Research Foundation, Ahmedabad. He worked for over two decades as Advisor at the Space Applications Centre, Indian Space Research Organisation (ISRO) where he pioneered the use of qualitative research methods for the Satellite Instructional Television Experiment (SITE) and led the SITE research and evaluation team. He is also the founding Director of the Mudra Institute of Communications, Ahmedabad (MICA), and of India's first professional teaching programme in business communication and advertising. He has lectured in universities in the United States and represented India in several international communication research forums. Recent publications include *Higher Education Through Television – The Indian Experience* (Concept Publishing 2000) and *Television in South Asia* (University Press of America forthcoming).

Peter S. Anderson is Director, Telematics Research Lab, Associate Director of the Centre for Policy Research on Science and Technology and Associate Professor of Communication at Simon Fraser University, Canada. His background is in the fields of telecom, media and information systems policy. He participates in the design and implementation of electronic communication and information systems for disaster management in collaboration with the United Nations, and scientific, government and non-government disaster management organisations and firms. He is the author of many publications and studies on communication policy, networking and planning. Professor Anderson also teaches accredited courses and supervises graduate research in emergency communication.

Dr Ang, Peng Hwa is a member of the Singapore Bar and Vice-Dean of the School of Communication and Information. He teaches and researches media and Internet law and policy. He has presented before and consulted for governmental, international and non-profit agencies on Internet-related legal issues in Singapore, Australia, Canada, Malaysia, Mongolia, the Philippines, South Korea, the United States, Belgium and Germany. He is a Board member of the Internet Content Rating Association, which is working to create an international standard for content self-labelling for the Internet. In 2000 and 2001, he spent a sabbatical at Harvard University and Oxford University.

Jens C. Arnbak completed graduate engineering studies in 1968 and PhD studies in 1970. He worked for eight years as an international civil servant in The Hague in support of satellite and other digital networks for joint political decision making by NATO countries. He was appointed Professor of Wireless Communications at Eindhoven University of Technology in 1979. Since 1986, he has held the chair of Tele-information Techniques at the Delft University of Technology, where he also held a part-time chair in the School of Systems Engineering and Policy Analysis from 1994 to 1997. He was appointed chairman of OPTA, the independent Dutch National Regulatory Authority in 1997, and is a board member of the Dutch Engineering Academy (NFTW). He is currently listed in *Who's Who in Engineering*.

Robert E. Babe holds the Jean Monty/Bell Canada Enterprise Chair in Media Studies, Faculty of Information and Media Studies at the University of Western Ontario, Canada. Since completing his PhD in Economics at Michigan State University, he has taught at several universities in both economics and communication departments, and has consulted widely on communication matters, appearing as an expert witness before Canadian tribunals. He is author or co-author of many books, including *Communication and the Transformation of Economics* (Westview Press 1995), *Canadian Communication Thought* (University of Toronto Press 2000) and *Cultural Ecology: Communication, Environment and Development* (University of Toronto Press 2002 forthcoming), and editor of *Information and Communication in Economics* (Kluwer 1994). In 1999, he received the Ontario Confederation of University Faculty Associations (OCUFA) Award for Outstanding University Teaching.

Johannes M. Bauer is Associate Professor in the Department of Telecommunication at Michigan State University where he also serves as the Associate Director of the James H. and Mary B. Quello Center for Telecommunications Management and Law. He joined Michigan State University in 1990 after receiving his PhD in economics from the Vienna University of Economics and Business Administration. From 1993 to 1998 he directed the Institute of Public Utilities and Network Industries at the Eli Broad Graduate School of Management, Michigan State University. He has published widely on issues of regulatory reform in telecom and energy policy, and is author or editor of five books, including *Walking a Thin Line in Infrastructures: Balancing Short Term Goals and Long Term Nature* (Delft University Press 2001) and *Telecommunication Politics: Ownership and Control of the Information Highway in Developing Countries* (Lawrence Erlbaum Associates 1995).

Contributors

Dr Jörg Becker is Honorary Professor of Political Science at Marburg University and Managing Director of the KomTech Institute for Communication and Technology Research in Germany. His work focuses on international and comparative media, and culture and technology policy. His recent publications include *Internet in Asia* (Singapore: AMIC 2001), *Internet in Malaysia*, (Bangi: University Kebangsaan Malaysia 2001), *Information und Gesellschaft* (Vienna: Springer 2002) and *Communication and Conflict* (New Delhi: Concept 2002 forthcoming).

Dr Jean-Claude Burgelman is principal scientist at the Institute for Prospective Technological Studies (IPTS), which forms part of the Joint Research Centre of the European Commission. Formerly, he was Professor and Director of the Studies on Media Information and Telecommunications (SMIT) research centre at the Free University of Brussels, where he obtained his PhD in 1986. He has worked as Professor in Communication Technology and International Communications, and as Visiting Professor at the University of South Africa. His research focuses on the socio-economic and regulatory aspects of information and communication technology policy in Europe.

Martin Cave is Professor and Director of the Centre for Management under Regulation at Warwick Business School, University of Warwick, where he specialises in competition law and policy, regulatory economics, and telecom. Previously, he was Professor and Vice Principal at Brunel University, West London. He is an advisor to the Office of Telecommunications and a member of the Competition Commission in the United Kingdom. He has undertaken a review of spectrum management policy for the UK government. He is editor of the *Handbook of Telecommunications Economics* (Elsevier Science BV, forthcoming) and has published numerous articles in the *Economic Journal, European Economic Review, Information Economics and Policy,* and the *Oxford Review of Economic Policy*.

Cho, Sung Woon is a senior research fellow at the KISDI (Korea Information Society Development Institute), Kwachun, South Korea. He received his BA and MA from the Department of Mass Communication at Yonsei University, Seoul and PhD from the Department of Communication at the Ohio State University. His current research interests include the metamorphosis of the media industry in the Internet age and the consequences of communication technologies from the perspectives of political economy. He is author of *The Dynamics of Institutional Reform in Telecommunications: Globalization, Liberalization and Regulatory Change* (Garland Publishing 1998) and *Understanding Webcasting* (Nanam Publishing 2001).

Dr Edward Comor is an Associate Professor in the School of International Service at the American University, Washington DC. He is the co-founder and former Chair of the International Communication Section of the International Studies Association. He is the author of *Communication, Commerce and Power* (Macmillan and St. Martin's Press 1998) and editor/contributor to *The Global Political Economy of Communication* (Macmillan and St. Martin's Press 1994). He has published papers in numerous academic journals, including *International Studies Quarterly, Global Governance,* and the *Journal of Economic Issues*. His research focuses on political, economic and sociological structures and processes related to capitalism and globalisation.

James Cornford is a Principal Research Associate at the University of Newcastle's Centre for Urban and Regional Development Studies (CURDS). His primary interests are in the regional development implications of technological and regulatory change and economic restructuring in the audio-visual and telecom industries and the application of communication technologies in large public organisations. He has carried out a wide range of academic and consultancy activities for a range of sponsors including the ESRC, the European Commission, the OECD, as well as local authorities, development agencies and private organisations. He is co-author of *Putting the University Online* (Open University Press, forthcoming).

Dr James A. Dewar is a senior mathematician and Director of Research Quality Assurance at RAND. He is also Director of the Frederick S. Pardee Center for Longer Range Global Policy and the Future Human Condition and Frederick S. Pardee Professor of Long-Term Policy Analysis at the RAND Graduate School. For the past 15 years, his main research interest has been strategic planning. He led the development and application of Assumption-Based Planning (ABP), a tool for reducing avoidable surprises in planning and has a forthcoming book on ABP (Cambridge University Press). His planning experiences range from projects for all four military services, higher education institutions, public corporations and Fortune 100 companies.

John D. H. Downing is the John T. Jones, Jr Centennial Professor of Communication in the Radio-Television-Film Department of the University of Texas, Austin. He is author of *Internationalizing Media Theory* (Sage 1996) and *Radical Media* (Sage, 2001). He is working with C. Husband on *Representing 'Race'*, a comparative study of media, racism and ethnicity, and is editor of the forthcoming Sage *Handbook of Media Studies* and the Sage *Encyclopaedia of Alternative Media*. He teaches courses including media theory, alternative media and social movements, and non-western cinemas.

Elizabeth Fox is Senior Advisor at the Global Health Bureau of USAID. She has published extensively on Latin American media and politics, including *Media and Politics in Latin America: The Struggle for Democracy* (Sage and G. Gili, Spanish edition 1988), where she brought together Latin American scholars to examine the relationship between media and the political turmoil that had engulfed the region. In 1997 she published a book on the relationship between Latin American broadcasting and the United States government and industry, weighing the relative importance of domestic and foreign influences, *Latin American Broadcasting: From Tango to Telenovela* (University of Luton Press 1997). She has co-edited a book with Silvio Waisbord, *Latin Politics: Global Media* (University of Texas Press 2002).

Christopher Freeman is Emeritus Professor at SPRU – Science and Technology Policy Research at the University of Sussex, which he founded, then directed from 1966 to 1981. He was Visiting Professor at the University of Maastricht in The Netherlands from 1986 to1996. His research interests focus on the relationship between technological and social change. He is the author of numerous books, including, with F. Louça, *As Time Goes By: From the Industrial Revolutions to the Information Revolution* (Oxford University Press 2001) and, with L. Soete, *The Economics of Industrial Innovation* (Pinter 1997).

David Gabel is a Professor of Economics at the City University of New York and a Visiting Scholar at the Massachusetts Institute of Technology Internet and Telecommunications Convergence Consortium. His area of specialisation is the telecom industry. He has focused on the evolution of telecom during the first competitive era of telephony (1894-1913) and on current developments in telephony. His recent studies focus on the pricing of interconnection in network industries, the cost structure of the telecom industry, retail pricing of network services under conditions of rivalry, and the deployment of advanced telecom services. His work has appeared in journals including the *Journal of Economic History*; *Harvard Journal of Law and Technology*; *Journal of Regulatory Economics, Law and Policy*; *Federal Communications Law Journal* and *Telecommunications Policy*. He is co-editor of *Opening Networks to Competition: the Regulation and Pricing of Access* (Kluwer 1998).

Oscar H. Gandy, Jr is the Herbert I. Schiller Information and Society Professor at the Annenberg School for Communication at the University of Pennsylvania. He is author of *The Panoptic Sort* (Westview Press 1993) and *Beyond Agenda Setting* (Ablex Publishing 1982), two books that explore issues of information and public policy. A recent book, *Communication and Race* (Edward Arnold and Oxford

University Press 1998), explores the structure of media and society, as well as the cognitive structures that reflect and are reproduced through media use. A book in progress, *If It Weren't for Bad Luck,* examines the ways in which probability and its representation affect the lives of different groups in society.

Nicholas Garnham is Professor of Media Studies at the University of Westminster. He has been an editor of *Media, Culture and Society* since its foundation in 1978. He is the author of *Capitalism and Communication* (Sage 1990) and *Emancipation, Modernity and the Media* (Oxford University Press, 2000). He directed the ESRC PICT Centre at Westminster from 1985 to 1995 and is a major contributor to debates in the fields of cultural and 'Information Society' policy.

Alison Gillwald serves on the South African Minister of Communications' African Advisors Group, chairs the Minister's Digital Broadcasting Advisory Body, and is a member of the Steering Committee of the International Telecommunication Union Task Force on Gender Issues. She is currently the director of the Learning Information Networking and Knowledge (LINK) Centre at the Graduate School of Public and Development Management at the University of the Witwatersrand, Johannesburg, South Africa. Prior to that she was appointed to the founding Council of the South African Telecommunications Regulatory Authority (SATRA). Before joining SATRA in 1997, Alison was responsible for establishing the Policy Department at the Independent Broadcasting Authority. She worked as a lecturer in journalism and politics for several years and as a journalist on some of South Africa's major newspapers.

John B. Goddard is Deputy Vice-Chancellor and Professor of Regional Development Studies at Newcastle University. He founded the Centre for Urban and Regional Development Studies (CURDS) in 1977 and led one of the research centres within the ESRC's PICT, which focussed on the geography of the information economy. He subsequently contributed to a project in the ESRC Virtual Society? programme on 'space place and the virtual university'. As Deputy Vice-Chancellor, he is responsible for the management of information systems and the university's regional policies. He has acted as adviser to the OECD's Institutional Management in Higher Education programme, the Finnish Higher Evaluation Council and the Higher Education Funding Council for England.

Dr Anders Henten is Associate Professor at the Center for Tele-Information (CTI), Technical University of Denmark. He is a graduate in communications and international development studies, Roskilde University, Denmark and holds a PhD from the Technical University of Denmark. His main areas of research are the socio-economic implications of information and communication technologies including e-commerce and business models, internationalisation of services, and communication regulation. He has participated in numerous research projects financed by the European Commission, Danish Research councils and ministries. He has published more than a hundred academic publications in international journals, books, anthologies and conference proceedings.

John W. Houghton has a PhD in Economics from the University of Queensland, Australia. He has held positions as Senior Research Fellow at the Centre for International Research on Communication and Information Technologies (CIRCIT); Principal Economist at the Bureau of Industry Economics (BIE); Adviser, Information Industries Policy at the Australian Commonwealth Department of Industry, Science and Tourism; Principal Adviser, State Development Policy with the Victoria Department of State Development; and Associate Director of the Australian Expert Group on Industry Studies, University of Western Sydney. He is currently Professorial Fellow at Victoria University's Centre for Strategic Economic Studies (CSES) and Director of the Centre's Information Technologies and the Information Economy Programme. He has had a number of years experience in information technology policy, science and technology policy, and more general industrial and policy-related economic research.

Heather E. Hudson is Professor and Director of the Telecommunications Management and Policy Program in the School of Business and Management, University of San Francisco. She was previously Director of the New Technologies Area in the College of Communication at the University of Texas at Austin and Director of Telecommunications Applications for the Academy for Educational Development in Washington, DC. Dr Hudson received her BA (Hons) in English from the University of British Columbia, MA and PhD in Communication Research from Stanford University, and JD from the University of Texas, Austin. She has consulted widely on telecom and development issues, and has planned and evaluated telecom projects in more than 30 countries. She is author of numerous articles and conference papers, as well as several books including *Global Connections: International Telecommunications Infrastructure and Policy* (Wiley 1997), *Communication Satellites: Their Development and Impact* (Free Press 1990) and *When Telephones Reach the Village* (Ablex 1984). She is co-author of *Rural America in the Information Age* (University Press of America 1989) and *Electronic Byways: State Policies for Rural Development through Telecommunications* (Aspen Institute 1995).

Contributors

Dr Meheroo Jussawalla is an Emeritus Senior Fellow/Economist at the East West Center in Honolulu Hawaii and Affiliate Faculty in the Department of Economics and of the School of Communications in the University of Hawaii. She is a leading scholar in the field of the Economics of Telecommunications and Development and her research focuses on the emerging economies of the Asia Pacific region. She is widely published with 13 books and many articles in accredited journals. She is on the Editorial Board of *Telecommunications Policy,* and the *Information Economics and Policy Journal.* She has served on the Board of Directors of the International Institute of Communication, London and is on the Board of Trustees of the Pacific Telecommunications Council. A festschrift was published in her honour, *Communications and Trade: Essays in Honor of Meheroo Jussawalla,* D. M. Lamberton (ed) (Hampton Press 1988).

Dr Tim Kelly is Head of the Strategy and Policy Unit of the International Telecommunication Union (ITU), where he has worked since 1993. Before joining ITU he spent five years as a Communication Policy Analyst with the OECD and three years with Logica Consultancy Ltd. He has an MA (Hons) in Geography and a PhD in industrial economics from Cambridge University. Over the last eighteen years, Dr Kelly has specialised in the economics of the telecom industry. He has written or co-authored more than 20 books and reports on the subject including the ITU's *World Telecommunication Development Report* (1998), *Direction of Traffic* (1999), *African Telecommunication Indicators* (2001) and *ITU Internet Reports: IP Telephony 2001.*

Dr Rolf W. Künneke is Associate Professor in the Faculty of Technology and Management, Delft University of Technology. He was a visiting Research Fellow at Auburn University in the United States and an Assistant Professor for over 10 years in the Faculty of Public Administration and Public Policy in the University of Twente, The Netherlands, where he completed his PhD in 1991. His research focuses on the privatisation of public utilities, particularly in the energy industry.

John Langdale is Senior Lecturer in Economic Geography at Macquarie University with research and teaching interests in economic restructuring and in the impact of telecom services on the economy. His research projects examine the growth of electronic trading in the foreign exchange market and the role of multinational companies in the Australian economy. He has published extensively in international academic and policy journals and has undertaken consultancies for Australian government departments, telecom carriers and private firms.

Contributors

Amy Mahan is a researcher in the Economics of Infrastructure Programme at Delft University of Technology (TU Delft) in The Netherlands. She has served as production editor and co-book review editor for the international journal *Telecommunications Policy*. She is co-author of *Global Media Governance: A Beginner's Guide* (Rowman and Littlefield 2002). During the past decade she has lived and worked in Canada – Centre for Policy Research on Science and Technology (CPROST), Simon Fraser University; Australia – Centre for International Research on Communication and Information Technology (CIRCIT); and Ecuador (private consultant). She has an MA from the School of Communication, Simon Fraser University; and a BA from McGill University, Canada.

Dr Carleen F. Maitland is Assistant Professor in the Information and Communication Technologies Group, Faculty of Technology, Policy and Management at Delft University of Technology (TU Delft). She received her PhD in the Economics of Infrastructure Section at TU Delft. Her dissertation explored the influences of institutions on firm behaviour, focusing on the issue of e-commerce in developing countries. Her research focuses on changing market structures in the mobile/wireless communication industry. Before coming to Delft, she was in the Mass Media PhD programme in the Department of Telecommunication at Michigan State University. She has also held positions in a variety of firms in the telecom industry and holds a BSc in Electrical Engineering and an MSc in Engineering Economics from Stanford University.

Robin Mansell holds the Dixons Chair in New Media and the Internet at the London School of Economics and Political Science where she works with Media@lse (Interdepartmental Programme in Media and Communications) and convenes and MSc in New Media, Information and Society. From 1988 to 2000, she was Professor of Information and Communication Technology Policy at SPRU – Science and Technology Policy Research, University of Sussex. She received a PhD (1984) and MA (1980) from Simon Fraser University, Canada where William Melody was her supervisor. She also has an MSc (1976) London School of Economics and a BA (Hons) (1974), University of Manitoba, Canada. She has held positions as research associate with W.H. Melody & Associates (1984-5) and the ESRC PICT (1985-6), and as Administrator OECD (1986-7). She has consulted with many governments, inter-governmental organisations, and firms. Her research focuses on the social and economic implications of information and communication technologies and the development of policy in the communication field. Author of many books and articles her most recent works are: *Inside the Communication Revolution: Evolving Patterns of Social and Technical Interaction* (Oxford University Press, editor/contributor 2002); *Mobilizing the Information*

Society: Strategies for Growth and Opportunity (Oxford University Press, with W. E. Steinmueller, 2000; 2002), and *Knowledge Societies: Information Technology for Sustainable Development* (Oxford University Press, editor/contributor with U. Wehn for the United Nations 1988).

Dr Werner A. Meier is a lecturer and senior researcher at the Department of Mass Communication at the University of Zurich, Switzerland, and has been working independently as Media Policy Adviser to public bodies since 1986. He is a member of the Euromedia Research Group and has published extensively on media policy and economic aspects of mass media.

Ian Miles is Professor of Technological Innovation and Social Change at the University of Manchester, and CoDirector of PREST (Policy Research on Engineering, Science and Technology) and of CRIC (Centre for Research on Innovation and Competition), both at the University of Manchester. Before moving to Manchester in 1990, he spent almost twenty years at SPRU – Science and Technology Policy Research, University of Sussex. His main research interests include innovation studies, especially with respect to services innovation; social aspects of information technology, especially with respect to working life and new consumer products; social indicators, and technology foresight, and futures studies more generally.

Bella Mody is Professor of Telecommunication in the College of Communication at Michigan State University. A former advertising writer, Mody also has worked at Stanford University, San Francisco State University and for the Government of India. Her research focuses on the political economy of the media, and the design and evaluation of development-oriented policies and programmes. She is author of *Designing Messages for Development Communication* (Sage 1991) and co-editor of *Telecommunication Politics* (Erlbaum 1995) and the *Handbook of International and Intercultural Communication* (Sage, 2001). She also edited the Policy and Regulation section in L. Lievrouw and S. Livingstone (eds) *The Handbook of New Media* (Sage 2002).

Vincent Mosco holds a PhD from Harvard University and is Professor of Communication with joint appointments in Sociology and Political Economy at Carleton University, Canada. He is the author of four books and editor or co-editor of eight books on the mass media, telecom, computers and information technology. His most recent books are *Continental Order? Integrating North America for Cybercapitalism* edited with Dan Schiller (Rowman and Littlefield 2001) and *The Political Economy of Communication: Rethinking and Renewal*

(Sage 1996 with Chinese, Korean and Spanish language editions). He has also published over one hundred journal articles, book chapters and reports. He is working on a project that addresses the social and cultural consequences of high tech development and is writing a book on *Myths of Cyberspace*.

Edwin B. Parker is President of Parker Telecommunications. He is a former Professor of Communication at Stanford University, where he specialised in the social and economic effects of information technology. The second edition of his latest book, *Electronic Byways: State Policies for Rural Development through Telecommunications*, was published by the Aspen Institute in 1995.

Aileen Amarandos Pisciotta is a telecom partner in the Washington, DC office of the law firm of Kelley Drye & Warren LLP. Prior to this, she was Chief of the Planning and Negotiations Division of the International Bureau of the Federal Communications Commission, where she directed analyses of world-wide developments in telecom privatisation, liberalisation, corporate alliances and new technology. She is chair of the Electronic Commerce Task Force of the American Bar Association Section of International Law and Practice, and past chair of that Section's Public International Law Division, Business Transactions and Disputes Division, and International Communications Committee. She graduated *cum laude* from Georgetown University Law Center in 1983. She received an MA in 1977 from the Annenberg School for Communications at the University of Pennsylvania,. She is listed in Law Business Research's *International Who's Who of Telecoms Lawyers 1999* and *2001*, as well as Strathmore's *Who's Who 1999* and *2000* and *Global Counsel 3000* (2000 and 2001 Editions).

Paschal Preston is Professor of Communication and Director of the Communication, Technology and Culture (COMTEC) research centre, Dublin City University. Following his PhD at the University of Reading, he was Research Associate with the ESRC PICT, London. His main research interests include political economy models and the regulation of communication services; the socio-cultural implications of new information and communication technologies; production, regulation and consumption aspects of digital media content and the cultural industries. He is author of *Reshaping Communications: Technology, Information and Social Change* (Sage 2001).

Marc Raboy is full Professor and Head of the Communication Policy Research Laboratory in the Department of Communication, University of Montréal, Québec. He has worked as a journalist in various Canadian print and broadcast media. He is the author or editor of thirteen books and more than one hundred journal articles and book chapters, as well as research reports for national and international, public and private sector organisations including UNESCO, the Japan Broadcasting Corporation, the Council of Europe, the Policy Research Secretariat of the Government of Canada and the Quebec Ministry for Culture and Communication. In 2002 he was expert advisor to a parliamentary committee studying the present and future state of the Canadian broadcasting system.

Rivka Ribak holds a PhD from the University of California, San Diego (1993) and is Lecturer at the Department of Communication at the University of Haifa, Israel. Her work concerns the ways in which communication technologies mediate individual and collective identity, and she is currently involved in a project focusing on the introduction of the Internet into the domestic sphere. Her research has been published in the *Journal of Communication, Communication Theory* and *New Media and Society*.

Liora Salter is a Fellow of the Royal Society of Canada and Professor at York University, where she teaches at Osgoode Hall Law School and in the Faculty of Environmental Studies. She has degrees in Sociology and Communication and is the author of a number of books and articles in the areas of communication, science and technology, law, public policy and interdisciplinary research, including such titles as 'The Housework of capitalism: Setting Standards for the New Communication and Information Technologies' (1994) and 'Standard Setting in Canada' (1995). Her books include *Mandated Science, Public Inquiries in Canada* (Kluwer, 1988) and *Outside the Lines: Issues in Interdisciplinary Research* (McGill-Queen's University Press, 1996), which she co-authored with Alison Hearn.

Rohan Samarajiva is Director of External Programs of LIRNE.NET (a learning initiative of the Technical University of Denmark and the Delft University of Technology), Visiting Professor of Economics of Infrastructure at TU Delft, and Senior International Specialist at the National Regulatory Research Institute in the United States. He is part of the management team of the World Dialogue on Regulation for Network Economies (www.regulateonline.org), headed by William Melody. He previously served in Sri Lanka as Director General of the Telecommunications Regulatory Commission and in the United States as Associate Professor of Communication and Public Policy at the Ohio State University. He chaired the International Telecommunication Union's expert workshop on fixed-mobile interconnection and is a member of the ITU's Expert Group on International Telecommunication Regulations. Samarajiva co-directed with Melody the LIRNE.NET regulatory training courses in Denmark (March 2001),

Morocco (September 2001), South Africa (November 2001), and Grenada (February 2002). He has provided expert assistance to government authorities, regulatory agencies and consumer and citizen groups in Australia, Bhutan, Canada, India, Mexico, Morocco, South Africa and several American states. He obtained a PhD from Simon Fraser University, Canada, where his supervisor was William Melody.

Roderick Sanatan is Manager, Research and Development, at the Centre for International Services, University of the West Indies, Barbados. He spent the last fifteen years working on telecom policy for the Caribbean region, in the regional trade and governmental body, CARICOM; the last five years of that tenure were spent as Secretary General of the Caribbean Telecommunications Union, the intergovernmental regional organisation for telecom policy in the Caribbean. He has undertaken research and studies in the Caribbean and Latin America, and has represented the Caribbean at major international forums in Europe and the Americas. He has published several articles in journals and conferences on telecom and information and communication technology policy and regulation.

B. P. Sanjay is Professor and has taught communication at the Sarojini Naidu School of Performing Arts, Fine Arts and Communication, Hyderabad Central University, Hyderabad, India since 1995, after teaching at the Universities of Madras and Tirunelveli. He completed his graduate studies at Bangalore University where he had the opportunity to conduct research on the Satellite Instructional Television Experiment (SITE), 1975-76. After teaching at the University of Madras he completed his PhD at Simon Fraser University, Canada. His research focused on institutional relations in the transfer of an advance communication technology, the Indian National Satellite System (INSAT).

Peter Sheehan is Professor and the Founding Director of the Centre for Strategic Economic Studies at Victoria University, Australia. He obtained his PhD from Oxford, and has held academic positions at the Australian National University and the University of Melbourne, including Principal Research Fellow at the Institute of Applied Economic and Social Research. He was Director General of the Department of Management and Budget from 1982 to 1990, and was the author of numerous government reports and statements. He has published eight books and some thirty papers. His most recent books include (with L. Xue and F. Sun) *China's Future and the Knowledge Economy* (Victoria University Press and Tsinghua University Beijing forthcoming) and *Work Rich, Work Poor: Inequality and Economic Change in Australia* (Victoria University 2001).

Dr Peter Shields is Associate Professor of Telecommunications at Bowling Green State University. He received his PhD in Communication from Ohio State University. His teaching and research focus on telecom policy and regulation, information technology and privacy, social theory and emerging media, and national security and telecom. His work has appeared in *Telecommunications Policy; Media, Culture and Society*; the *Gazette; The Information Society*; the *Policy Studies Journal; Communication Theory*, the *European Journal of Communication, Journal of Communication; Media Development* and *Media International Australia*. He is co-editor of *International Satellite Broadcasting in South Asia: Political, Economic and Cultural Implications* (University Press of America 1998).

Roger Silverstone is Professor of Media and Communications at the London School of Economics and Political Science, where he directs Media@lse (Interdepartmental Programme in Media and Communications) and Chairs the Department of Sociology. He has taught at Brunel University and the University of Sussex, where he was Professor of Media Studies. He has researched and written widely in the field, most recently, as author, *Television and Everyday Life* (1994) and *Why Study the Media?* (1999). His research focuses on empirical studies of diasporic media in Europe, issues of media and community, and globalisation and alternative media spaces. He also examines representational ethics and media, new media and morality. His book project, *Screen Deep: Media, Ethics and Everyday Life* will bring these two strands of work together.

Supriya Singh is Associate Professor and Senior Research Fellow at the Centre for International Research on Communication and Information Technologies (CIRCIT), Royal Melbourne Institute of Technology (RMIT University), Australia. She holds a PhD in Sociology and Anthropology from La Trobe University, Melbourne. Her work concentrates on the use and design of information and communication services from the users' perspective. She is Vice-Chair of the Conference Committee (2002) for the Pacific Telecommunications Conference and heads its socio-economic track. She is also a member of the international advisory board of *New Media and Society* and President-elect of the International Association for Qualitative Research (AQR). Her most recent books include *Marriage Money: The Social Shaping of Money in Marriage and Banking* (Allen & Unwin 1994) and *The Bankers* (Allen & Unwin 1991).

Knud Erik Skouby is Professor and Founding Director of the Center for Tele-Information (CTI) at the Technical University of Denmark. Since 1986, his research has focused on technological planning, development and assessment, particularly in the telecom industry. He has participated in and managed a number of national and international projects specifically related to the development and impact of new telecom services and infrastructures, and has been appointed to a number of government and professional committees, including the European Union's Economic and Social Committee (1994-98), serving on the sub-committee for EU legislation on information and communication technology-related matters. He has participated in the development of training programmes for developing countries and was a member of the Technical Programme Committee for International Telecommunication Union's Telecom '99 Forum. He is a member of the management teams of both LIRNE.NET and the World Dialogue on Regulation for Network Economies, each headed by William Melody.

Anthony Smith, CBE, has been President of Magdalen College, Oxford since 1988. During the 1960s, he worked as a television producer of current affairs programmes for the BBC, and was responsible for the key nightly news programme, *Twenty-four Hours*. In the early 1970s, he was Research Fellow at St Antony's College, Oxford, and worked for the Annan Committee on The Future of Broadcasting. He was deeply engaged in the national debate which led to the founding of Channel Four Television, and subsequently, was appointed a Board Director of Channel Four (1981-85). He carried out research for the McGregor Commission on the Press in 1976 and was Director of the British Film Institute from 1979 to 1988. He has written extensively on broadcasting and the Press, and on the modern information industries in general, including *The Oxford International History of Television* (Oxford University Press 1995; 1998) and *Software for the Self – Culture and Technology* (Faber & Faber 1996).

Ricardo Tavares is Research Associate at the Center for Economics of Telecommunications in Latin America (CELAET) and Senior Director of international operations at Wireless Facilities, Inc (WFI). He obtained his MA at the Rio de Janeiro University Research Institute and is currently pursuing a doctorate at the University of California, San Diego. After working for ten years as a journalist, he spent four years as editor and senior researcher at the Rio de Janeiro Federation of Organizations for Educational and Social Assistance. In 1993, he was a fellow at Brazil Network in Washington DC researching and writing on the North America Free Trade Agreement negotiations for the US Congress. He has published more than ten scholarly papers and articles on the political economy of Latin American telecom regulation.

Contributors

Harry M. Trebing is Professor Emeritus (Economics) at Michigan State University and Senior Fellow at the Institute of Public Utilities, of which he was both founder and a director (1966-1992). He served as Chief Economist at the US Postal Rate Commission and US Federal Communications Commission and has been a member of various advisory panels for Congressional offices and the National Research Council/National Academy of Sciences. He was President of the Association for Evolutionary Economics, and recipient of its Veblen-Commons Award, as well as Chairman of the Transportation and Public Utilities Group – American Economic Association, receiving the Distinguished Member Award. He also served as a board member of the National Regulatory Research Institute, the Ohio State University and is currently Vice Chair of the Michigan Utility Consumer Participation Board. He is author of numerous publications and holds a PhD from the University of Wisconsin.

Gaëtan Tremblay holds a PhD from the Université Louis Pasteur, Strasbourg, France and is full Professor at the Department of Communication, Université du Québec, Montréal, where he also co-chairs a research group on communication and cultural industries in the information society (GRICIS). Concentrating on audio-visual industries and communication networks, he employs a comparative analytical approach to assess the impact of new technologies on the cultural policies of communities in Québec, Belgium, Spain, France, Brazil and Mexico. His current research focuses on the complex inter-relationship between technological change, the effects of international trade agreements such as the North America Free Trade Agreement (NAFTA), MERCOSUR and the European Union, and national policies designed to protect and foster unique cultural attributes in a diversified world.

Joseph Turow is the Robert Lewis Shayon Professor of Communication at The University of Pennsylvania's Annenberg School for Communication. He is author of 60 articles and seven books on the mass media industry. The winner of a number of conference paper and book awards, he was a Chancellor's Distinguished Lecturer at Louisiana State University during Spring 2000. He serves on the editorial boards of the *Journal of Broadcasting and Electronic Media*, *Critical Studies in Mass Communication*, *The Encyclopaedia of Advertising*, the *Sage Annual Review of Communication Research*, and *New Media and Society*. William Melody was an esteemed member of his dissertation committee.

John Ure is Director of the Telecommunications Research Project at the University of Hong Kong. His many publications on the economic, policy and regulatory aspects of telecom include *Telecommunications in Asia: Policy, Planning and Development*

(Hong Kong University Press1995; 1997). He is section editor in L. Lievrouw and S. Livingstone (eds) *The Handbook of New Media* (Sage 2002) and joint author with P. Lovelock of the chapter 'The New Economy: Internet, Telecommunications and Electronic Commerce?' As a consultant to the International Telecommunication Union, the World Bank and telecom regulators around the region he has extensive knowledge of South East Asia. He serves on the editorial boards of the *info* and *Telecommunications Policy* journals. He also serves on the Hong Kong Government's Information Infrastructure Advisory Committee, and represents Hong Kong at international telecom forums.

Silvio Waisbord is Assistant Professor in the Department of Journalism and Mass Media at Rutgers University. He received his MA and PhD in Sociology from the University of California, San Diego. He was a fellow at the Kellogg Institute for International Studies at the University of Notre Dame, the Annenberg School for Communications at the University of Pennsylvania, the Media Studies Center at the Freedom Forum, and the Center for Critical Analysis of Contemporary Cultures at Rutgers University. His research interests are media and politics, audiovisual industries, nations and cultures, globalisation and Latin America. He is author of *Watchdog Journalism in South America: News, Accountability and Democracy* (Columbia University Press 2000) and editor, with E. Fox of *Local Politics, Global Media: Latin American Broadcasting and Policy* (University of Texas Press 2002).

Rudi Westerveld received his MSc in the Electrical Engineering Department at Delft University of Technology (TU Delft) in 1969. After graduation, he worked in the Department's particle accelerator laboratory and in 1971 joined the Teaching Laboratory Group, designing laboratory courses in measurement and electronics. From 1977 he lectured in Electronics, Instrumentation and Telecommunication at Eduardo Mondlane University in Mozambique, where he also consulted on telecom projects. In 1981, he returned to TU Delft, joining the Telecommunications and Traffic Control Systems Group in 1984 as an Assistant Professor. He supervised the TopTech MBT postgraduate telecom course and in 1994 joined the School of Systems Engineering, Policy Analysis and Management to lecture in Information and Communication Technology. His research interests are in the field of wireless communication systems.

Márcio Wohlers de Almeida is Professor of the Economics of Telecommunications at the Campinas State University, Brazil, where he completed his PhD in Economics in 1994. He has carried out several studies of telecom strategic planning analysis. In 1998-99, he joined the Advisory Board of the Brazilian

National Telecommunications Agency (ANATEL), and is currently a member of the Board of Trustees of the CPqD (the ex-Telebrás Telecom Research and Development Centre).

Dr Sally Wyatt is Associate Professor in the Department of Communication Studies at the University of Amsterdam. She is conducting research funded by the UK ESRC's Innovation Health Technologies Programme on the ways in which Internet users and non-users find and analyse information about specific health treatments and use that information in their discussions with health care professionals. She is editor, with F. Henwood, N. Miller and P. Senker, of *Technology and In/equality, Questioning the Information Society* (Routledge 2000). Between 1986-88, she worked on the ESRC PICT in London.

Author Index

Abramovitz, M., 154
Adams, H., 231
Agrawal, B., 276, 311-314, 383
Agre, P. E., 156
Alleman, J., 130
Anderson, P., 156, 157, 188-194, 383
Andreas, P., 199
Ang, P. H., 224, 249-253, 383
Arnbak, J. C., 78, 141-147, 384
Arthur, B. W., 175
Atkinson, D., 318

Babe, R., 224, 225, 254-259, 384
Bagdikian, B. H., 300, 301
Bakhtin, M. M., 321
Baldelli, P., 321
Bar F., 121
Barendse, A., 78
Baudrillard, J., 234, 235
Bauer, J. M., 77, 118-122, 384
Becker, J., 158-159, 216-219, 385
Bell, D., 174, 175, 230, 238
Beltran, S. L. R., 203
Beniger, J. R., 157
Benkler, Y., 121
Benneworth, P., 39
Bernier, I., 318
Bertram, E., 199
Bezanson, R., 302
Blachman, M., 199
Bocchicio, A. R., 201
Boltanski, L., 284
Bourdieu, P., 298, 344

Bovill, M., 329
Boxer, M. J., 60-61
Brin, D., 329
Buck, S., 121, 122
Buckingham, D., 328
Burgelman, J. C., 18, 21, 22, 47-53, 385

Cairnes, J. E., 234
Callon, M., 19
Calvin, W. H., 51-52
Cardilli, C., 119
Carey, J. W., 240
Carroll, J. B., 255
Castells, M., 176
Cave, M., 77, 120, 123-126, 128, 273, 292, 293, 296, 319, 385
Charles, D., 39
Chatterton, P., 39
Cho, S.W., 223, 225, 245-248, 385
Chubin, D. A. P., 60
Coady, C. A. J., 31
Coase, R. H., 119, 123
Cohen, J. E., 185
Cohen, S., 121
Colleran, E. K., 91
Collins, R., 280
Commons, J. R., 6, 7, 153, 224, 227, 234, 266
Comor, E. A., 223, 224, 239-244, 386
Compaine, B. M., 298, 299
Connolly, T., 60
Constantine, T. A., 200
Cornford, J., 21, 34-41, 386

Index

Costello, N., 48, 49
Cowhey, P., 121
Cranberg, G., 302
Cronin, F. J., 91
Cunningham, S., 309
Curran, J., 300

Dahlman, C., 22
David, P. A., 19
DeGraba, P., 132, 134
DeLong, B., 121
Denning, M., 264
Dervin, B., 158
Dewar, J., 224, 249-253, 386
Dewey, J., 24, 302
Dosi, G., 176
Downing, J. D. H., 277, 320-327, 386
Drotner, K., 330
Du Boff, R. B., 225, 245, 247-248
Duff, A. S., 175
Dunifer, S., 326
Dutton, W. H., 160

Ehrlich, W., 225
Eisenstein, E., 225, 253
Ellul, J., 47
Etzkowitz, H., 20

Falch, M., 174
Favero, R., 169
Foray, D., 19
Fox, E., 276, 303-310, 387, 399
Freeh, L., 198, 199
Freeman, C., xv-xvii, 12, 76, 153, 154, 160, 176, 229, 387
Friedman, S. S., 62

Gabel, D., 77, 78, 132-140, 245, 387
Gabel, R., 245
Gandy, O., 156, 157, 158, 184-187, 387-388

García Espinosa, J., 322
Garnham, N., xvi, 18, 20, 21, 24-27, 175, 176, 388
Geuna, A., 20
Gibbons, M., 19
Giddens, A., 298-299
Gieryn, T., 63
Gillett, S. E., 138
Gillwald, A., 75, 76, 109-114, 388
Girard, B., 274, 326
Glaeser, M. G., 6, 7
Goddard, J., 21, 34-41, 388
Gold, M. A., 91
Golding, P., 300, 318
Gomery, D., 298, 299, 300
Gruber, H., 120

Haas, E. B., 74
Habermas, J., 321
Hall, P., 223, 235
Hamilton, J., 323
Hamilton, W. H., 7, 9, 153
Hammond, P., 321
Hansen, P., 92
Hardy, A. P., 91
Hart, A., 231
Hayek, F. A., 255
Hearn, A., 60, 62, 394
Heidegger, M., 250
Henck, F., 72
Henten, A., 78, 174, 224, 226, 227, 265-267, 388-389
Henwood, F., 231, 400
Herbert, P. L., 91
Herman, E. S., 299, 300, 321
Herzel, L., 119, 123
Heyer, P., 223
Hirsch, E., 329
Hirschman, A. O., 226
Hoffmann-Riem, W., 319
Horkheimer, M., 217

Index

Horwitz, R. B., 76
Houghton, J. W., 44, 76, 154, 155, 166-173, 389
Hudson, H. E., 74, 75, 76, 77, 91, 96-102, 183, 389
Huws, U., 239

Innis, H. A., 10, 19, 20, 22, 23, 175, 203, 223, 224, 225, 232, 235-237, 240-244, 245-247, 248, 255, 256, 257, 258, 265

Jacka, E., 309
Juhasz, A., 324
Jussawalla, M., 158, 207-211, 390

Kang, S., 225, 251, 253
Kellerman, A., 331
Kelly, T., 73, 92-95, 390
Kleeman, M., 121
Klein, J. T., 60
Klemperer, P., 128
Knudtson, P., 256
Kogawa, T., 326
Künneke, R., 12, 335-342, 390

Langdale, J., 21, 42-46, 390
Lemish, D., 330
Lemley, M., 121
Lerner, D., 224
Lessig, L., 121, 263, 318
Lewitzky, S., 91
Leydesdorff, L., 20
Liebes, T., 330
Limoges, C., 19

Lindblom, C. E., xvii, 17, 23, 74, 223, 226-227
Littlechild, S., 226
Livingstone, S., 329, 330, 331, 392, 399

Louça, F., 76, 160, 387
Lundvall, B.-A., 155

Machiavelli, N., v
Machlup, F., 174, 254
MacKenzie, D. A., 155
MacPherson, C. B., 156, 327
Mahajan, V., 329
Mahan, A., 3-13, 17-23, 71-78, 151-159, 223-227, 271-278, 391
Maigret, E., 330
Maitland, C., 75, 76, 115-117, 391
Mansell, R., xvii, 3-13, 17-23, 47, 58, 71-78, 151-159, 205, 223-227, 271-278, 320, 323, 391-392
Marvin, C., 329
McChesney, R. W., 299, 300
McCourt, T., 320
McGee, M. C., 64-65
McLuhan, M., 175-176, 202, 225, 234-237, 255, 279
McQuail, D., 299
Meier, W., 275, 298-302, 392
Melody W. H. xv-xvii, 3-13, 17-23, 24, 28, 32, 33, 34, 42, 45, 46, 47, 53, 54, 60-63, 65, 67, 71-78, 79, 83, 85, 87, 90-91, 92-95, 96, 101, 103, 111, 118, 120, 123-126, 128, 129, 132, 141, 147, 151-159, 160, 165, 176-178, 184, 185, 186, 187, 195, 201, 203, 207, 208, 210, 211, 212-215, 223-227, 228-231, 234-237, 239, 240-244, 245, 254, 255, 260, 264, 265-267, 271-278, 279, 292-294, 296, 298, 315, 316, 318, 319, 335-342
Messer-Davidow, E., 60
Miles, I., 154, 160-165, 176, 228-229, 392
Mills, C. W., 237
Mitchell, W. C., 227

Index

Mkize, K. A., 112
Mody, A., 22
Mody, B., xvi, 22, 54-59, 392
Mosco, V., 224, 260-264, 392-393
Murdock, G., 300
Murroni, C., 280

Negroponte, N., 174
Nelson, R., 153, 155, 176
Neuman, R. W., 298
Noam, E. M., 120, 130
Nowotny, H., 19

Ó Siochrú, S., 274
Ostrom, E., 119
Oxman, J., 87

Parker, E. B., 72, 75, 90-91, 393
Perez, C., 12, 154, 229
Picard, R. G., 299
Pisciotta, A., 75, 86-89, 393
Pittman, T., 96
Pollock, N., 36
Porat, M., 254
Preston, P., 184, 186, 223, 224, 232-238, 393

Raboy, M., 276-277, 315-319, 393-394
Rappert, B., 157
Reed, C., 250
Ribak, R., 277-278, 328-333, 394
Robertson, R., 332
Robins, K., 161
Rocha, G., 322
Rodríguez, C., 324
Rossini, F., 60
Rotenberg, M., 156
Rothwell, R., 158

Sakolsky, R., 326
Salter, L., 18, 22, 23, 60-67, 223, 394
Samarajiva, R., 3-13, 17-23, 71-78, 151-159, 223-227, 271-278, 394-395
Sanatan, R., 155, 179-183, 395
Sanjay, B. P., 157, 202-206, 395
Sauvageau, F., 318
Sayer, A., 227
Schiller, D., 262, 392
Schlager, E., 119
Schumpeter, J. A., 51, 76, 103, 153
Schwartzman, S., 19
Scott, P., 19
Seaton, J., 300
Sen, A., 203
Senmoto, S., 208
Shapiro, C., 337
Sharpe, K., 199
Sheehan, P., 18, 20, 28-33, 395
Sherman, W., 251
Shields, P., 156, 157, 158, 195-201, 396
Shumway, D., 60
Shy, O., 134
Silverberg, G., 176
Silverstone, R., 12, 158, 274, 279-285, 329, 396
Sinclair, J., 304, 309
Singh, S., 158, 212-215, 396
Skocpol, T., 330
Skouby, K.-E., 155, 174-178, 396-397
Slack, J. S., 155
Smith, A., 274, 277, 286-291, 397
Smythe, D. W., 7, 8, 65, 203, 225, 245, 260, 272
Soete, L., 76, 153, 154, 176, 387
Soley, L. C., 326
Soloski, J., 302
Spiller, P. T., 119
Stald, G., 330

Index

Starr, J. M., 320
Stavrou, A., 112
Steinmueller, W. E., 19, 156, 392
Sterling, C. H., 298, 299, 301
Stevenson, G. G., 119
Stigler, G. J., 293
Strassburg, B., 72
Strinati, D., 300
Sunstein, C., 186, 262
Sutton, J., 120
Suzuki, D., 256, 257
Sylvan, D., 60

Tavares, R., 75, 76, 78, 103-108, 397
Thorburn, L., 44
Tillinghast, C. H., 301
Toffler, A., 174
Trebing, H. M., 6, 7, 12, 74, 75, 78, 79-85, 141, 266, 335, 398
Tremblay, G., 275, 292-297, 398
Trow, M. 19
Tunstall, J., 301
Turow, J., 277-278, 328-333, 398

Ungerer, H., 48, 49
Ure, J., 74, 77, 127-131, 398-399

Valetti, T. M., 120, 125, 128
Varian, H. R., 337
Veblen, T., 7, 73, 153, 227, 234
von Auw, A., 72-73
von Hippel, E., 158

Waisbord, S., 276, 303-310, 387, 399
Wajcman, J., 155
Wallerstein, I., 330
Watkins, M., 203
Webster, A., 157
Webster, F., 239
Wehn, U., xvii, 58, 205, 392

Westerveld, R., 75, 76, 115-117, 399
Whitley, R., 60
Whorf, B. L., 255
Williams, R. A., 155
Wilson, E. O., 258
Wind, J., 329
Winter, S., 153
Wohlers, M., 75, 76, 78, 103-108, 399-400
Wyatt, S., 223, 228-231, 400

Zysman, J., 121